THE COMPANION GUIDE TO

The Loire

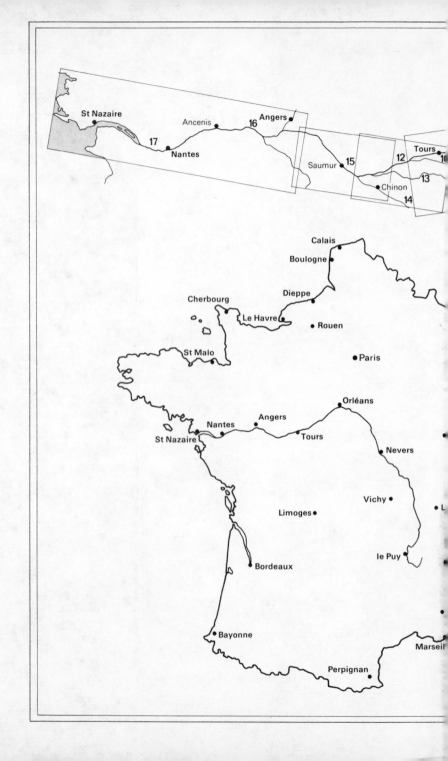

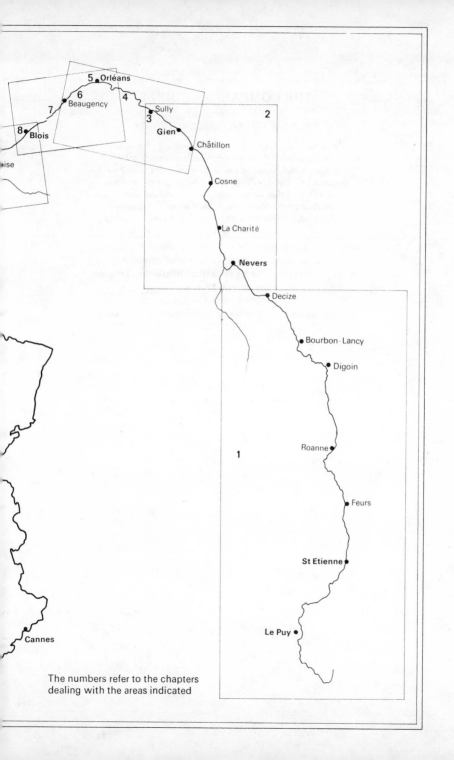

The numbers refer to the chapters dealing with the areas indicated

THE COMPANION GUIDES

GENERAL EDITOR: VINCENT CRONIN

*It is the aim of these guides to provide a Companion
in the person of the author, who knows intimately
the places and people of whom he writes, and is able to
communicate this knowledge and affection to his readers.
It is hoped that the text and pictures will aid them
in their preparations and in their travels, and will
help them remember on their return.*

LONDON · THE SHAKESPEARE COUNTRY · OUTER LONDON · EAST ANGLIA
NORTHUMBRIA · THE WEST HIGHLANDS OF SCOTLAND
THE SOUTH OF FRANCE · THE ILE DE FRANCE · NORMANDY · THE LOIRE
SOUTH WEST FRANCE
FLORENCE · VENICE · ROME
MAINLAND GREECE · THE GREEK ISLANDS · YUGOSLAVIA · TURKEY
NEW YORK

In Preparation

OXFORD AND CAMBRIDGE · PARIS

THE COMPANION GUIDE TO

The Loire

RICHARD WADE

A SPECTRUM BOOK

PRENTICE-HALL, INC.　　　　　COLLINS

Englewood Cliffs, N.J. 07632　　　St. James's Place, London

Library of Congress Cataloging in Publication Data
Wade, Richard, 1925-
  The companion guide to the Loire.

  "A Spectrum Book."
  Bibliography: p.
  1. Loire River Valley (France)—Description
and travel—Guide-books. I. Title.
DC611.L81W32   1983   914.4′504838   82-20469
ISBN 0-13-154526-4
ISBN 0-13-154518-3 (pbk.)

ISBN 0-13-154526-4

ISBN 0-13-154518-3 (PBK.)

Ce livre est dédié,
en témoignage de gratitude,
à Claude et Louisette Esther
qui en premier lieu m'ont appris à aimer
leur pays et ses habitants

First published 1979;
© Richard Wade 1979
ISBN 0 00 216141 9 hardback
Set in Monotype Times Roman
Maps by Brian and Constance Dear
Made and printed in Great Britain by
William Collins Sons & Co Ltd, Glasgow

U.S. Edition © 1983 by Prentice-Hall, Inc.,
Englewood Cliffs, N.J. 07632

A SPECTRUM BOOK

Printed in the United States of America
10 9 8 7 6 5 4 3 2 1

Prentice-Hall, International, Inc., *London*
Prentice-Hall of Australia Pty. Limited, *Sydney*
Prentice-Hall of Canada, Inc., *Toronto*
Prentice-Hall of India Private Limited, *New Delhi*
Prentice-Hall of Japan, Inc., *Tokyo*
Prentice-Hall of Southeast Asia Pte. Ltd., *Singapore*
Whitehall Books Limited, Wellington, *New Zealand*
Editora Prentice-Hall Do Brasil Ltda., *Rio de Janeiro*

Contents

✣

Acknowledgements

❧

Undoubtedly the most important help I have received in preparing this book has come from the local historians I have met in the course of my wanderings, who have so kindly spared the time to answer my questions and generously placed at my disposal the fruits of their own long years of research. Foremost among these has been Maître Jacques-Henri Bauchy whose field is the whole Val de Loire, but for invaluable help on their own particular locality or subject I am greatly indebted also to M. Soulier of Bas-en-Basset, M. Maurice Godon-Mallet of Saint-Satur-Saint-Thibault, Père Anselme of the Abbey of Saint-Benoît, M. Christian Loddé of Orléans, M. Ecosse of Meung, M. Daniel Vannier of Beaugency, the indefatigable M. Roger Lecotté of Tours, Mme Jeanne Fraysse of Le Thoureil, and Mr Hugh Williamson of Farnham, a passionate francophile who has immersed himself in the history of Saint-Florent-le-Vieil in Anjou.

On the subject of wine I have obtained most of my information from the *vignerons*, the jolly, but thoroughly practical, men who produce it and the only ones who really understand wine in spite of all the scientific hot air that is written about it. Among these I am specially thankful to M. and Mme Fouquet of Vouvray, M. Songy of Saumur and M. Joly of Savennières. Likewise, in relation to the old Loire mariners and their craft, I am particularly indebted to M. Besançon and M. Mercier of the Musée de la Marine at Châteauneuf and, in the matter of geology, to M. Jean-Jacques Châteauneuf of Orléans.

The encouragement and wise counsel I received at the outset from Vincent Cronin, editor of this series, will always be remembered with the greatest gratitude, and I am hardly less indebted to Philip Ziegler for similar blessings while the work has been in progress, and to Hilary Davies and Vera Brice for their cheerful competence in piecing the book together, an immensely complex task behind the scenes that the reading public seldom hears about. Another kind benefactor from Collins was Elizabeth Walter who, though in no way concerned with this book, spent part of a holiday in Touraine scouting in advance for me and making notes.

Nearer home, I have to thank my friend Philip Trower for access to both his extensive personal library and his equally well-stocked memory for the facts of history, also for reading the typescript and for keeping up my spirits whenever the desk-work began to pall. To my father I am indebted for checking the typescript with an eagle-eye for spelling and typing blunders, and – last but certainly not least – to my wife who has cheerfully assumed every rôle from office-girl to editor as circumstances required and been my tireless companion on all my journeys, her bright eyes – always eager for beautiful things and attentive to detail – discovering so much that mine would have missed.

List of Illustrations

❧

Maps and Plans

۶

KEY TO THE SYMBOLS USED IN THE MAPS

Megalithic
monument ••

Château ↑

Vineyards ◼

Church ☦

Introduction

'All other rivers in France, the Garonne, the Seine even, are regional. The Loire is not: it flows through the heart of France, a national frontier cutting it in two'. So said my friend Maurice Godon-Mallet of Saint-Thibault as we were chatting by the waterside one afternoon. He cultivates vines on the neighbouring hillsides of Sancerre and is a scion of that proud breed, the old Loire boatmen, so the river is in his blood and he could be accused of being partial in this remark; but a professor of geography or an historian could hardly have expressed the fact of the Loire's uniqueness more clearly. That it is the longest river in France at just over 600 miles from the mountains of the Cevennes to the coast of Brittany is incidental; but for involvement in the history of the country through which it flows, its effect on the geography, the economics and even the character of the people, few rivers in the world can equal it. To describe it all in detail would require a vast work in many volumes; but in this guide I have tried – while not forgetting to remind the reader of the many famous things he ought to see – to stray away from the trodden path as much as his time and the limitations of a book of manageable length will permit.

The immediate reaction of many people on hearing the name Loire is to think of châteaux. 'Châteaux of the Loire' has become a cliché bandied about for so many generations by tourist promoters that it has given rise to the gross error that this beautiful river – the very heart of France in so many senses of the word – has little else to offer. They are an essential feature of the picture as a whole and I have not failed to include them. But the picture is like a tapestry. The ancient Gauls, Romans, early Christians, Plantagenets, Renaissance, Revolution, Julius Caesar, Saint Martin, Joan of Arc, Louis XI, François I are just a few of the colourful threads of history which recur as we move across the canvas. With these are interwoven the patterns of topography and geology; forests, fields and waterways; agriculture, wines and river commerce; character and customs of the inhabitants, flora and fauna. The shining silver thread that runs through all, however, is the river itself, a physical, living entity.

I hope my book may give as much pleasure to the armchair traveller with only the vaguest dreams of seeing the Loire one day as it will be of real practical use to the tourist. I ask of both only that they will not be irritated at the detailed road and street directions which occur from time to time in the text. The armchair man must pass them over; the thoroughly independent holidaymaker will select and plan his own itinerary, which is preferable if you have time. I am not presuming to run a sort of guided tour over a compulsory route, but only to help the traveller who is not so well off for time, every moment of whose holiday is precious and who cannot afford to waste hours of it getting lost. Similarly my directions for finding places to park a car must not be taken to imply that this book is written exclusively for the motorist. Certainly motoring is the best way to see the Loire and get into its remoter corners unless you can get away long enough for cycling or walking. The point I have borne in mind for the motorist reader is that a car becomes an encumbrance as soon as you come to a busy town, and information about parking is not easy to get in advance, whereas the foot-traveller can obtain information about buses and trains by calling at the local *syndicat d'initiative* as soon as he arrives.

In the arrangement of the book I have followed the course of the river – from its source in south-east France to the Atlantic in the west. But few readers will perhaps have the leisure all in one visit to cover so much ground; there is too much of beauty and interest to be squeezed into three weeks or even a month. By keeping on the move and selecting what interests him most, the car-borne holidaymaker could cover the first two chapters in about five days each, the remaining fifteen chapters in one day each; but to enjoy everything and relax as you go these times should be doubled. Very practical starting-points are Gien and Orléans. There you may make your choice of turning westwards downstream or southwards through Bourges and Moulins, running fairly rapidly through the pleasant Bourbonnais (not within the province of this book) and by way of Ambert to Le Puy, thence to follow back down the river with me. Or those who have been to the fleshpots of the commercialized south will find it a refreshing change of scene, of atmosphere and of route to follow the Upper Loire on their way home, leaving it at Gien and postponing the pleasures of the rest for another occasion. In dealing with the section from Gien downwards I have gone into much greater detail as it is the part more easily accessible, where most travellers encounter the Loire at one time or another and which they are most likely to want to know more about.

The most useful maps for the journey are the well-known Michelin tourist series on the scale of two kilometres to the centimetre (which is, as near as not to matter, three miles to the inch) and the ones required, starting from the source and going downstream, are numbers 76, 73, 69, 65, 64 and 63. Every place and every road I have mentioned in the text is shown on the Michelin maps except in about three cases where I have said so and have explained how to find them without. I have endeavoured throughout to identify roads by their destination, because road numbers are not always shown on sign-posts and in any case are at present in the process of being altered. For street maps the *Plans-Guides Blay* series provide a good pocket plan of all big French towns and you can obtain a plan of most others free of charge by writing to or calling at its *hôtel de ville* or its *syndicat d'initiative*.

As to camp-sites, bearing in mind mainly the tourist who will be on the move, I have generally mentioned only municipal sites and usually because of an attractive situation. They are cheaper than private sites and do not require (in most cases will not accept) advance booking, but often their facilities are not of such a high standard. Readers who desire more luxury can easily find what they want from the booklet *Camping et Caravanning en France*, but had better book in advance if their trip will be in the busy season. The most up-to-date information for the hotel tourist is in the comprehensive hotel guides revised every year and supplied free by the French Government Tourist Office, 610 5th Avenue, N.Y., N.Y. or 178 Piccadilly, London, W1V 0AL. The titles to ask for are *Auvergne, Rhône-Loire, Val de Loire* and *Pays de Loire*.

As I am dealing with a river and angling is a favourite holiday occupation of many people, I have given information about the types of fish in different stretches of the river and the prospects of catching them. For the benefit of those unfamiliar with it, I should explain here the operation of the close season in France. In principle it applies to the particular stretch of water, not the fish. So generally you can fish for trout with a worm if you like, but you cannot do it out of season with the old schoolboy excuse that you were only after eels, because all other fish in that water will be out of season at the same time.

Waterways in which trout predominate are designated First Category and fishing in them is permitted for both trout and coarse fish from the third Saturday in February until the last Monday in September. The Loire from its source to the old bridge outside Solignac in its upper reaches is of this category, as also are most of its fast-running tributaries all the way down to Anjou. Waters of the Second Category – to which belong the rest of the Loire and all its slow-running tributaries – have their open season from the Saturday after 15 June until the Monday after 15 April the following year. These are the ones in which coarse fish predominate, but sometimes odd trout may be present and if you are lucky enough to find any you are free to try and catch them.

These provisions are really very sensible, but there is one great drawback: permits are issued purely on a departmental basis and for a whole year only. No exception is made for the holidaymaker on the move; he must buy a permit for each *département* within whose boundaries he chooses to fish although he may only be there for a few days. On the other hand the fishing is generally good in France, so it can be worth it if you like the sport and your holiday is long enough. There are some local exceptions of course: there are trout streams where the regulations are stricter, while some privately-owned moats and lakes are open all the year round on a modest day-ticket basis. Where the latter have come to my notice I have mentioned them. Salmon are a special case everywhere and not enough get past the licensed net-fishermen, who have a living to make, to justify the expense of angling for them. The place to seek detailed advice on any local aspect of fishing is always the tackle shop, which will often also be the agent for the sale of permits.

Another popular pastime is riding, and there are quite frequent opportunities for this along the Loire; those that have come to my notice I have mentioned in the text. Boating, although we have a river for our subject, is not so easy. Since the decline of its former use as a great commercial waterway the channels of the Loire have not been kept clear enough to facilitate pleasure-cruising, but on page 43 I have mentioned one place where cruisers can be hired on canals linking with it. Then in the few places where you can hire a punt, a rowing-boat or a sailing-dinghy I have tried to mention it in the text, but there will be others I have missed and it is always worthwhile to enquire. You can *carry* a canoe, and most of the Loire lends itself to canoeing if you are reasonably experienced and prudent; in backwaters behind the islands even the tyro can be safe. As to bathing, the Loire is generally clean enough but requires the greatest care: if in the slightest doubt about any particular spot, don't. The fast current is a hazard, except in backwaters, and increases rapidly as you move away from the shore. Then there are the *tourbillons*, miniature whirlpools (often near the piers of a bridge) which can pull the strongest swimmer helplessly under. Sometimes they make sinister little sucking noises which ought to be a warning. Lastly, there are the *sables mouvants* to keep a look out for: what has been a firm sandbank at the water's edge one day may be a sinister bog the next if the water has risen a little; test every forward step gingerly if this has happened. These warnings should not be taken as cause for alarm: there are plenty of places where it is safe to bathe on the shores of the Loire and its tributaries, many of them expressly made so by the local authorities. When I happen to know of such places, especially when they are safe for children, I have mentioned them.

This book is also a guide to the wines of the Loire, most of which are undeservedly too little known in this country and many of which are really superb. The need to keep the book to a practical length prevents my treating the subject in depth, but I have dealt with each area where the wine is worthy of attention and in every such case with the three most significant factors which determine the character of a wine. These, in order of importance, are the grape variety (the *cépage*); the nature of the soil (the *terroir*) and the degree of skill of the grower (the *vigneron*). Most English books on wine completely ignore the first two, which are not only paramount, but fascinating in themselves. As to the third, where a local procedure is especially interesting I have described it, but have considered it more important in every case to recommend a source (if possible an individual grower) which I personally know to be reliable. Diligently tasting the wines all the way down the river has been one of the pleasantest aspects of my work on the reader's behalf and I hope it will not have been in vain.

CHAPTER ONE

The Source to Decize

❧

The Loire rises among the peaks of the north-western end of the Cevennes in the Massif Central, less than a hundred miles from the Mediterranean coast. But it flows north instead of towards that sea, northwards for more than half its length before it turns westwards to make for the Atlantic, dividing France in two in the process. About a million years ago, towards the end of the Tertiary period, the region of its source was remoulded by a frightful cataclysm as pressure from the east pushed up the new mountains we now know as the Alps. The ancient Palaeozoic mountains of the Massif cracked and warped and in many places molten magma burst through the fissures to create an inferno of flame and smoke and torrents of liquid basalt which obliterated the landscape and all living things.

The bizarre peak of **Mont-Gerbier-de-Jonc** is a relic of those times. Viewed alone, a 500-foot cone of volcanic débris looming up above the plateau, it gives the impression that these calamities took place only yesterday. Its sides are of cinder-coloured rock, for the most part hideously bare, and its primitive shape seems to hold a latent threat. But the friendly mantle of life over the surrounding landscape, trees, grass and grazing cattle, is reassurance that the earth has long been healed. At the foot of the peak on the south side is an extensive mead of short grass pierced frequently by outcrops of rock and seeping everywhere with tiny runnels of water. All the way down for a quarter of a mile or so these little springs well up and congregate to form, near the lower loop of the road, a single stream about a foot wide and two inches deep. This is the beginning of the Loire, that wondrous beauty of a river, the longest in France, full of character and caprice, which crosses it for 620 miles to the Atlantic, strung with towns and castles which are at the core of the country's history and giving life to great forests, vine-covered hillsides and fertile plains.

Halfway down the meadow-slope, beside a large car-park, are two restaurants and the inevitable gaggle of souvenir shops. But the sense of space and grandeur is so powerful that there is no need to dwell on this aspect of the scene and spoil the magic; nor to be confused by the notices around proclaiming that this or the other of the springs is the '*source authentique*' of the Loire. The meadow itself is the source; and it is just below all this unseemly haggling that the stream acquires a recognizable unity.

An easy path skirts the western base of the peak, among rocks, heather and wild thyme, and a stroll leads to a crest with a view northward to Mont-Mézenc, at 5740 feet the highest peak of the group. If you have the time and energy you can climb Mont-Gerbier, which is itself 5084 feet above sea-level. Use the western side, follow the grass path where possible and beware of loose pebbles; it is then safe but laborious. The terrain at the summit is a surprise: fresh, even marshy, and studded with gorse-bushes. These give the mountain its name – the 'gorse-stack' – for in shape it resembles a typical French farmyard stack. In clear weather the views from the top are a good reward for the climb. To the west, in morning sunshine, you may see the extinct volcanoes of the Cantal some seventy miles away. Eastward, an occasional sparkle in the middle distance indicates the Rhône thirty miles off, and towards evening the sunlight may pick out the snow-caps of the Alps in the Dauphiné, anything from sixty to a hundred miles distant.

The road for Sainte-Eulalie follows the stripling river closely for a mile or so just after we cross its first tributary by a bridge near a white farmhouse. Already it is some ten feet wide and a foot deep. Mont-Gerbier looms at the head of the valley, in early spring still covered in snow while the river-bank is resplendent with wild daffodils. As the year advances they are replaced by a succession of many other wild flowers right through to sweet-scented pinks in autumn, for this remote but gentle countryside is a land of flowers. The livelihood of the Loire's first little town, **Sainte-Eulalie**, comes from the giant violets and aromatic herbs which grow naturally on the mountain slopes. In high spring they are gathered, to be carefully dried in the weeks that follow and sold at the annual *Foire-aux-Violettes* which is held on the Sunday following 12 July. Unusual farming this: without ploughing, sowing or hoeing; harvest in the spring of the year and the whole crop sold in one day. The eager buyers are the leading perfumers, pharmacists and confectioners of Europe, and the town becomes a lively international centre for the few days leading up to the fair. At other times it is simply pleasant and peaceful, an excellent base if you have time to linger and explore this little-known corner of the Auvergne. There are two hotels, and Monsieur Volle at the Hôtel du Nord can, in season (see Introduction), arrange trout-fishing in the Loire for his customers.

Beyond the Loire's first bridge outside the town, the road follows the river closely for four miles. The kingfisher is a common sight along here and among the wild flowers on the bank the rare marsh gentian grows with its spears of vivid violet-blue. The scenery is intimate and friendly by the waterside; lonely and awe-inspiring round about, not unlike the Highlands of Scotland. But the Auvergne has not the wildness of the Grampians: the contours are not so abrupt, and, lying 12° of latitude farther south, it enjoys a climate so much more temperate that even at an altitude equal to the summit of Ben Nevis there are deciduous trees, pastures and occasional arable fields. On approaching **Rieutord** we find the Suc de Bauzon raising its dark bulk ahead, and in the village at the very foot of the mountain, the Loire is halted abruptly in its southerly course and forced to make a U-turn and head back the way it has come before it finds a new path north-westwards a mile farther on. In the seven miles from its source it has now fallen 900 feet in altitude and has 3680 feet to drop in the remainder of its journey to the sea.

The road out of Rieutord climbs a mountain spur and opens up a fine vista along the valley all the way back to the peak of Gerbier. Just before **La Palisse** there is room to draw off for a moment and look down into a deep gorge where the young Loire is ferociously eating rock to force its way forward. But on the other side of the same village it meets a man-made obstacle it cannot eat: a dam checks its impetuosity and obliges it to spread into a wide lake. On the downstream side it is rather a shock to see our river shrunken to an infant trickle, obliged to start all over again. Our road runs up the side of another volcano and drops down into the crater which is filled with water to form the **Lac d'Issarlès**, almost perfectly circular in shape and 350 feet deep. Underground galleries through the mountain feed this lake with water from the Loire at La Palisse and another gallery eleven miles long leads it from the bottom of the lake to the eastern side of the Suc de Bauzon. There, after working an underground turbine, the deflected waters of the Loire run by way of the Ardèche river and the Rhône into the Mediterranean. There is a big village on the shore of the Lac d'Issarlès, popular in summer for swimming and canoeing holidays.

The next village of particular interest is **Arlempdes** (the *p* is not sounded), a cluster of houses around the base of the central core of a volcano which is topped by the ruins of a castle looking down 300 feet on to a loop of the river. Through the castle gateway (which was built in 1066) there is parking space in the outer bailey where the family-run Hôtel de la Tour has an excellent restaurant and café-bar.

To the right of it a twelfth-century church has a porch in the Moorish style which is not uncommon in this area. Beyond the castle is a tiny chapel perched on the pinnacle of one of a group of basalt needles surrounding a side-vent of the old volcano; its situation seems so precarious that it must tumble at any moment into the void, but in fact it has stood for nine centuries so far and should survive many more. The riverside below the castle is delightful for a stroll. Myrtle, wild strawberries and wild raspberries grow there and the trout-fishing is good. The river has now fallen another 925 feet in its sixteen miles of twisting and turning since Rieutord.

By **Ussel** and **Saint-Martin-de-Fugères** we can still follow the Loire more or less closely. This, in reverse, is the route taken by Robert Louis Stevenson and his donkey Modestine on the first day of their journey described in *Travels with a Donkey in the Cevennes*. Five miles to the east of Saint-Martin, at **Le Monastier**, he set out on an autumn Sunday morning in 1878 after a row with the local saddler in which they ended by throwing the pad of the pack-saddle at one another's heads. Though his comments on the inhabitants here are not flattering, he is still honoured as a local celebrity and there is a small exhibition devoted to him in the *mairie*. As most of the buildings in the centre of the little town are pre-1878, we still see it more or less as he saw it. In 732 a Saracen army sacked the great monastery from which the town derives its name. Saint Theofred (*Chaffre* in Auvergnat dialect) was bludgeoned to death while trying to protect his altar. Later the same year the same Saracen force was soundly defeated by Charles Martel at Poitiers and the pagan tide was turned back for ever. The present church has a beautiful twelfth-century front with different-coloured volcanic stones set in a pattern of (ironically) Moorish inspiration. In the time of Charlemagne there was quite extensive settlement here in the Velay by *Mozarabe* families – Christians from the Arab-dominated parts of Spain where they had absorbed Moorish influence. Their descendants are still numerous in the region, bearing such surnames as Maffre, Maurois, Espanhon, Cordouan and even Sarrazin.

Straight on the road leads to Le Puy; but to get back to the river turn left on to the road for **Chadron**, where a charming little tributary, the Gazeille, flows past the village and there is a strand by the bridge popular in summer as a safe place for children to play. Soon after this you re-cross the Loire by a bridge in the bottom of a gorge and can see the deep passage it has cut for itself through the rock. It is at this point that the Loire changes to Second Category for angling purposes (see Introduction). The road winds up the side of the gorge to **Solignac** on a mountain spur, then northwards by way of **Cussac** through dramatic scenery as we drop down from the last really big mountains on to the lava plain of the Le Puy basin at **Coubon**, now only some 1800 feet above sea-level.

Skirting the eastern foothills of the Velay bloc with the river for company we finally arrive at **Le Puy** itself – on the north side where the old quarter is, and where there is plenty of room to park in the Boulevard Carnot area. From here the Rue des Tables leads uphill past the famous lace shops to the steps of the **Cathédrale de Notre-Dame-du-Puy**, on whose fourteenth-century façade, even more distinctly than at Arlempdes and Monastier, we see Arab influence in the patterned setting of coloured stones and trefoiled arches. A flight of sixty steps leads to the great porch; and when you reach it you are really standing in a vault beneath the nave, for half the body of the church has been built out from the precipice on which the rest is based and its immense weight is supported on the porch columns – a daring feat of architecture which adds to the grandeur of this most unusual of cathedrals. Before going inside, be sure to look back at the colourful landscape framed in the main arch: the town of low-pitched, nearly flat, red roofs and the vividly contrasting green countryside beyond.

In the Romanesque nave the eye is led through a receding perspective of round arches and massive columns to the glitteringly decorated high altar, surmounted by the celebrated 'Black Virgin' of Le Puy. The present statue is a nineteenth-century version of the original which was ceremonially burnt in the street at the Revolution. It was said to have been brought back from the Crusades by Saint Louis, but the mystery of the black face has a disappointingly prosaic explanation. An eighteenth-century drawing of the original with the outer mantle removed shows the hands white. Black Virgins were not at all unusual in the Middle Ages and the cause was simply candle smoke. The mantle was washed from time to time, but not the wooden statue for fear of damage. The Church has never despised black faces and when Black Virgins became fashionable the practice of deliberately painting them began.

The sacristy contains the church treasures on permanent exhibition. They are numerous and exceptionally interesting, but the greatest among them is the eighth-century bible of Theodulf, Bishop of Orléans – 347 pages exquisitely written in the beautiful Caroline text employed in his school of calligraphy at Tours by Alcuin of Northumbria, the scholarly mentor of Charlemagne and his family. Through the north transept a door leads out to the cloisters: graceful arcades of Romanesque arches ornamented, like the west front, in Mauresque patterns of coloured stone.

Le Puy is a town of great individuality in almost every respect. But its most extraordinary feature is undoubtedly the two pinnacles soaring up from its very midst: bizarre and imposing natural freaks, whose phallic symbolism must have appealed greatly to earlier and more earthy religions. They are volcanic in origin, not of extrusive material like Mont Gerbier, but 'dykes' in geologists' parlance – intrusive upshots of liquid basalt which cooled beneath the surface and has since been laid bare by erosion of the earlier sedimentary rocks by the Loire and its local tributaries, the Borne and the Dolaizon; just the extreme tips of immense conic pillars whose roots are deep in the earth's crust. The **Rocher d'Aiguilhe** is the more imposing of the two. There is a small charge for the privilege of toiling up its 268 steps to the summit 270 feet above street-level, but if you can summon enough energy it is worthwhile. In Roman times there was a small temple at the top dedicated to Mercury, but in the tenth century the messenger of the old gods was ousted and an oratory built in honour of the Archangel of God; it was customary to place statues of Saint Michael in an elevated position. Two centuries later it was enlarged and embellished to take the graceful form in which we see it today. Morning is the best time to go up, so as to have the light fall on the beautiful mosaic patterns of red and white marble and the crisp sculpture over the trefoil arch of the doorway. Inside, the ingenuity of the twelfth-century architect in fitting a nave, sanctuary, ambulatory and apses on to an irregular groundspace the size of a small suburban building-plot arouses the greatest admiration.

The other peak is the **Rocher Corneille**, which is crowned with a cast-iron statue of the Virgin. Proudly the guidebooks reel off the vital statistics—weight 100 tons, height 52.49 feet, Child's head 15.75 feet round, Virgin's foot 6.23 feet, and so on. That these specifications have to be brandished in order to impress betrays the work's comparative insignificance. Cast in 1860 from cannon captured at Sebastopol, it is a notable feat of engineering; and the symbolic transmutation of instruments of death is a praiseworthy conception. But here beside the grace and grandeur of the Chapel of Saint Michael on the other peak so near, it is merely a distraction, like a garden gnome in the Louvre. If by now you have developed a real passion for steps in this city of steps, you can mount the rock and climb up inside the statue, peeping through portholes in Our Lady's robe on the way and eventually coming to an observation platform on top of her head.

Excellent liqueurs are distilled at Le Puy, several made from fruits grown on the ideal soil of the volcanic alluvium of the plain (raspberries, strawberries and cherries). But the one which is special to the region is Vervaine, a perfectly balanced blend of verbena, peppermint, thyme and other herbs from the mountainsides. It resembles Chartreuse slightly and is of equal strength, but more subtle. There are also local wines of the Auvergne, grown along the river valleys. The best are reds from the Gamay stock, but they are all inclined to be acid: a refreshing drink on a hot day, but lacking the character to warrant seeking them out.

Two miles out of Le Puy on the Vichy road is the square-towered fortress of **Polignac**. Scattered over the flat plain are more volcanic peaks of the dyke variety (*puys*), and the castle stands on one which has a flat table-top, formerly the site of a temple of Apollo. (It is open from 9.30 to 6.30 every day between 15 April and 30 September.) Here in these bizarre surroundings conducive to a sort of melancholy awe, the Polignac family lived for four centuries; and the castle served them well as a base in their constant wars with the Bishops of Velay, within sight at Le Puy. Our road, on the main Vorey road northwards out of Le Puy, squeezes for five miles between the river and the dark wall of rock it has cut in the side of the mountains. The *Peyredeyre*, deepest and narrowest of the Loire's gorges, brings us to **Lavoûte**, to which the Polignacs moved in the mid-thirteenth century. Alone on a slight eminence within a hairpin bend of the river, tall, clean and simple in style, their new château still stands, one of the most graceful of all the châteaux of the Loire. (Visits 15 June to 30 October: 9.30 to noon; 2.30 to 6; rest of the year Sundays and public holidays only.) Fastened to a tree by the gate is a letter-box for Jean-Héracle-Armand Polignac. After 700 years the family still lives here and he is the present Duke. Sometimes, if your visit is in the early afternoon, you can still enjoy the cosy smell of his lunch and cigars in the recently-vacated dining-room. The beautiful furniture throughout the rooms seems the more significant and impressive for being just part of someone else's home instead of a collection of cold unused exhibits artificially arranged.

Granted a respite now for a few miles, the Loire pursues a straighter and more leisurely course until it enters another gorge near **Vorey**. We drive above or beside it as it winds and wrestles through the hills, arriving six miles farther on at **Chamalières**, whose streets of old houses are squeezed in the narrow space of the valley bottom on the banks of the river. Half a mile downstream is a *village de vacances* of sixty-two delightful modern houses built of volcanic stone and of varying sizes. I mention it here because it is one of the best I have seen and in one of the most attractive settings. Information and bookings are handled by the *mairie*, Chamalières-sur-Loire, 43800 Vorey. Adjacent is a well-appointed camp-site for long or short stays. The river here is wide and calm because its bed for several miles is on a level stretch with little fall. There are even a few punts about. The fishing includes a small proportion of trout and weekly permits are available which make it a reasonable proposition. The village church, originally part of a Benedictine monastery, possesses an unusual curiosity in the twelfth-century hi-fi equipment in the vaulted roof of the choir – thirty sound-reflectors made of pottery and built into the masonry.

Four miles farther on, at **Retournac**, it may be said the Loire's infancy is over. At 1660 feet above sea-level it has dropped just over 2900 feet – nearly two-thirds of its fall in a little over one-tenth of its course. The gorge through which it has just passed was the end of the Le Puy basin and here it becomes *flottable*, which in former times meant it was fit for work, as it would float craft big enough for commerce. It was not navigable in the full sense, because they could not manoeuvre back again upstream; but even to be able to float a cargo in one direction meant a saving of time and energy: most of the roads were not good enough for carts, and a boat holds more than a pack-saddle. Retournac stands on a bluff, like Solignac, and has fine views down to the loop of the river, but it is pleasanter and more alive than Solignac and has good hotels and shops.

The Monistrol road is the one now to follow, and as far as Beauzac it runs along the side of the hills, high up. Across the valley the mountain bloc we have just left forms one of the most unforgettable panoramas of our whole journey – fold upon fold in graceful curves, fading from blue to diaphanous grey, with the Loire in the foreground. Stop at **Beauzac** if there is time, and walk through the big Gothic archway on the left of the main road. Here immediately is an intense feeling of the Middle Ages enhanced by the hustle and bustle of modern everyday life. You are standing in the tiny area which was the original fortified town, and another arch leads out at the opposite end. In between is a huddle of little streets and courtyards with busy shops and old houses decked with flowers and perhaps a songbird in a cage – the France of old times.

Next comes **Bas-en-Basset** where some maps still portray the Loire as dividing to form an island, but in fact the western arm has been dried up for many years and the former island is now an extensive common on the east of the town, a pleasant place to fish or picnic in comfort, sitting on the grass at convenient water level. The hills behind are clad in firs and pines, and on a spur jutting out into a deep cleft stands the château of **Rochebaron**. A small band of local enthusiasts, inspired by the infectious zeal of Monsieur Soulier in the town, has been digging out its impressive ruins. The building dates from the twelfth century and was well appointed in its heyday, boasting every ancient convenience including a sturdy stone lavatory seat on each floor of the main tower. From remotest times a stronghold has always stood on this site, for it guards the point where the Greek tin-merchants joined the Loire after crossing from the Rhône valley. They embarked their trade-goods on its *flottable* waters to be transported all the way down to Brittany and across the sea to Cornwall as barter for tin. The Phoenicians usually carried theirs all the way by sea, but the Greeks preferred the overland route – the 'Liger route' as the Romans later called it, Liger being the Latin name for the Loire.

Just above Bas-en-Basset, the Ance flows into the Loire. A good trout river, it is also one of the few in France (and one of the least known) where the handsome, sporting and most eatable grayling exists in quantity. The season is from mid-May to the third week in September only.

Cross the bridge at Bas-en-Basset for **Monistrol-sur-Loire**. It is not exactly *sur*, but about a mile from, the river. A nice spacious town, however, composed mostly of big eighteenth-century houses. Northwards out of the town the road leads across open moorland country for a while, then descends into another gorge almost as narrow as the *Peyredeyre* and follows the loops of the river. At the other end of the gorge stands the little industrial town of **Aurec**, where for the first time we see the remains of a commercial waterfront with long stretches of quay. Only a few plastic pleasure-cruisers lie alongside these days, but once it was alive with the Loire's first boat-building yards. From the pine trees so plentiful in the nearby forests light craft were constructed, called *sapines*, which drew less than a foot of water and were capable of carrying fifteen to twenty tons of Saint-Étienne coal over 400 miles down-river to Angers or Nantes. At their destination they were sold with their cargo and broken up for firewood. The crew walked home.

Our journey now brings us to the outer suburbs of **Saint-Étienne**, whose population numbers well over half a million throughout its total agglomeration. During the whole of our journey we shall not see any other town like it for size except Nantes, which is roughly equal. Details available from the year 1444 disclose that it was then

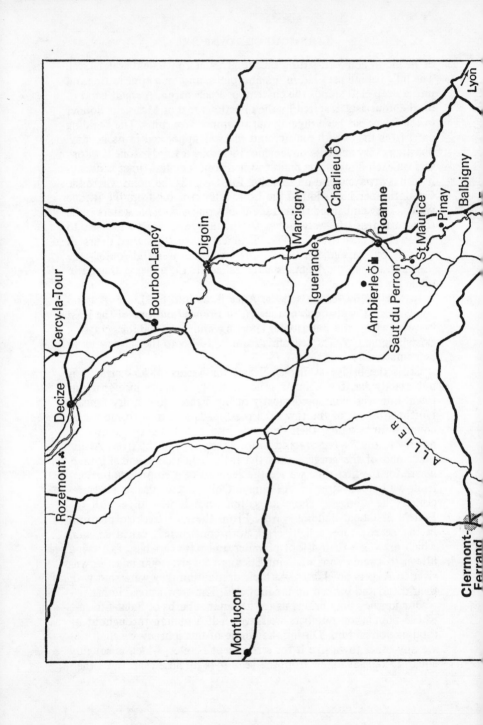

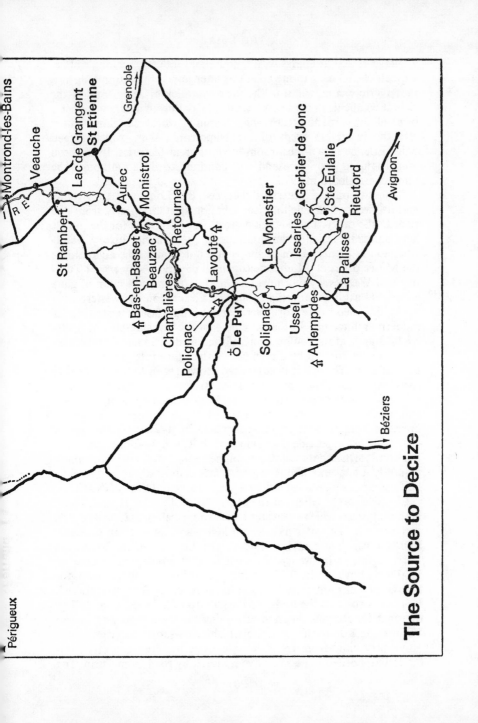

The Source to Decize

a village of 200 dwellings with a household industry making ribbon, a quiet, clean occupation which was later joined by coal-mining as a rather grimy companion in the near-by valley of Jarez, one of the richest coalfields in the Massif Central. Coal brought a new industry of small-arms manufacture which acquired worldwide fame. But it was the insatiable needs of the Napoleonic Wars which turned Saint-Étienne into a mushroom town of great factories. It has been mushrooming ever since and will continue to do so although the mines were closed in 1975.

It stands on the watershed between the Loire and the Rhône and its twenty-five-mile-long conurbation stretches nearly from one river to the other. There is not a great deal of interest for the tourist here unless he feels like an interlude of modern city luxury. Saint-Étienne has plenty of smart shops and hotels and nine night-clubs; the Musée d'Art et d'Industrie (open all day every day except Tuesday and Wednesday mornings) has an interesting collection of guns among its exhibits, and the suburb of **Firminy** on the western outskirts, designed by Le Corbusier, cannot fail to fascinate students of modern architecture. In the extreme west the pleasure-port of **Saint-Victor** stands at the southern end of the Lac de Grangent, an enormous reservoir formed by a dam across the Loire just over two miles downstream. Though it is advertised glowingly in tourist literature, the local boating fraternity keeps this urban play-centre very much to itself. There are no boats for hire, but the casual visitor can get a trip along the lake in Monsieur Michaud's *Amphitrite*, which operates from 15 June to 15 September. Saint-Victor has a certain charm, a sort of seaside atmosphere with its sailing-dinghies tacking back and forth and its restaurant on the shore, but there is something painfully unnatural about seeing boats sailing along a shoreline halfway up a mountainside like a scene from the time of Noah.

Chambles is the village at the other end of the lake. It stands on a high bluff from which the water seems so far below that boats on its surface look like water-flies. From here the road goes on to **Saint-Rambert** which lies at the head of the Loire's second basin, the Forez, a flat plain twenty-two miles long at an average altitude of 1100 feet above sea-level. There is no point in entering the town, for though of some antiquity it has been swamped by industrial sprawl. It is better to cross the bridge to the suburb of Saint-Just and follow the signs for Roanne. Soon after gaining the main road we come to **Veauche** on a loop of the Loire which is its most easterly point – only thirty miles from Lyon, less than one hundred and fifty from the Italian border and a mere two hundred by road from Turin. The left turn at the first traffic-lights leads to the river where there is a quiet spot (except when a frog orchestra strikes up after sundown) near the bridge in the shade of trees.

A run of six miles over the plain from Veauche leads to **Montrand-les-Bains** which has a spa, as its name implies. On a mound are the ruins of another of those massive old castles which protected the river traffic. Dating from the twelfth century, it is now in process of being restored. For the next ten miles the road is almost unwaveringly straight and the landscape is so fenny in appearance that one would never guess we are in excess of a thousand feet above sea-level. The poor soil yields little else than rough pasture. Locally called *chaninat*, it is clayey, practically non-absorbent and dries out on the least heat, but in the hollows accumulates water as in earthenware bowls. Along both sides the plain is strewn with *étangs*. These natural ponds are congregated in groups of up to fifty together and are used for rearing carp commercially. There is a fanciful tradition that the whole plain was a great lake until the Druids (always a handy embellishment for a tall tale) began to channel the Loire to drain it, but there is no evidence whatever to support this.

In the hills surrounding the plain the pasture is sweeter and richer and produces one of the finest cheeses in this country of cheese, the Fourme d'Ambert. Matured in caves, it resembles English Stilton a little and is made in the same cylindrical form. It has a pronounced scent of herbs. You can be sure to find it in the shops and in the market at **Feurs**, a quiet little town which knew greater days in Roman times, when all this area so close to Lyon was of more importance relatively than it is today. Chief market town of the Segusian tribe of Gauls, it was called *Forum Segusianorum*. Forez, the name of the region, derives from it and not from *forêt* as is often supposed – a mistake which gives a misleading picture of the terrain as it is in fact less forested than most other parts of the Massif. In the Rue Gambetta, just behind the church, there is a Roman wall almost intact.

Only eight miles to the west of Feurs on the Boën road, is the château of **Bastie d'Urfé** (visits at any reasonable time on application at the gatekeeper's lodge), an early-sixteenth-century residence in the Italian style and one of the prettiest châteaux along the Loire, too good to miss. Honoré d'Urfé grew up here, and the peaceful little river Lignon is the setting for his 5000-page pastoral novel, *L'Astrée*, which is one of the great landmarks in French literature. So artificial as to be almost unreadable now, it was a best-seller when it first appeared at the end of the Religious Wars, when a weary public was grateful for a chance to escape into romantic unreality.

At the northern end of the plain **Balbigny** has a large and very varied market on Mondays, most useful if you need to do shopping on that day when most shops are closed in France. Beyond the town, if you are not obliged to hurry along the main road, take the left fork and keep the Loire company. Now the river has to cut its way out of the Forez basin through volcanic rock again: not the recent Tertiary volcanic as at the start of its journey, but a far older Primary carboniferous rock, standing in a small local massif right across its path. The resulting gorge is seventeen miles long and the narrow road which follows it is described in one guidebook as '*sinueuse en diable*', which is true; but it is perfectly safe at a moderate speed, has a good surface and is negotiable right through – except for trailer caravans, which are forbidden.

The river here is awe-inspiring. The old-time Loire boatmen must have been strong and skilful men to come hurtling down it in their loaded *sapines* with nothing but poles to steer them, an example of what sheer muscle-power and brain can achieve with only the simplest tools. In fact for this sort of job there is no other means possible: no mechanical device could accomplish it. The traffic went on from remotest antiquity until the coming of the railways. The boats would stop first at Balbigny to take on more men from a permanent corps of 'extras' who waited in the quayside *auberges*. Their normal crew was two, but here in the gorge they needed five: three at the stern to steer and two for'ard to fend off. In the village of **Pinay** a massive stone mole, built at the instigation of Louis XIV to regulate the current, pinches the river in at the start of the narrowest part of the gorge. Shortly after, as we come round a bend, there is a dramatic surprise in the ivy-draped ruins of the fifteenth-century **Château de la Roche** built on to a rock jutting out into the river. Near by is a very good restaurant. At **Pont-de-Presle** the road crosses to the left bank and, just a mile beyond, on the left, is an excellent place to pull off in the mouth of a miniature glen where a stream runs in. The fine grass is spangled with mountain pinks and buzzards hover above the scarp. There is a great deal for the naturalist in the gorge, for it is an isolated world for plants and small creatures confined between its high sides. This applies particularly to insects. During one lazy late September day at this spot, without really searching, I saw swallowtail, peacock and brimstone butterflies and others I do not know; and a praying mantis, with a bright green body the size of a pea-pod, munching a cricket for his dinner, holding it up to his mouth like a gourmet with a chop-bone.

Saint-Maurice stands on top of the scarp, reached by a steep lane, and is all winding streets threading their way among houses built on or into crags of rock. Its castle dominates all, including the river below the so-called 'Roman bridge', which is neither Roman nor a bridge, but the remains of a small fortified outpost (probably for collecting tolls) of the early Middle Ages – so early in fact that it is referred to as an abandoned ruin in a document of 1340.

The next section of river consists of two loops and at the apex of the first a stone cross stands on the hillside. It was put there for the *mariniers* to say a quick prayer to before they descended the most dreaded rapids of all, the **Saut du Perron**, an apt name of which 'leap down the steps' is about the nearest translation. On a sudden steep gradient over a distance of less than a mile, seeming to fight itself as well as the rocks in its path, the water leaps and rushes like a stampede of wild horses. For the most part, unbelievable as it may seem, the *mariniers* brought their craft safely through. Over every yard of the course they knew just where to make for, just where to give a shove with the pole, just where to let her drift. And each of the rocks they knew by name: the Black Rock, the Wolf, the She-Wolf, the Stairway.

Just after this, the gorge ends abruptly at **Villerest**. Passing under its attractive railway-bridge, built in 1904 of local pink porphyry stone, we find the river broad and considerably steadier. It is below the 1000-foot contour-line now, all its major obstacles overcome and free all the way to the ocean 450 miles away.

We are through to another basin, that of the Roannais, and already on the outskirts of **Roanne**, an industrial town with about 55,000 inhabitants, prospering on steel, textiles and cotton, with little to show nowadays for its great antiquity. It arose in pre-Roman times because of its important position at the point where the Loire becomes truly navigable. A pleasant, clean place, its shops have a Parisian touch that is due to its prosperity and to its being a halfway stop on the main highway to the Midi. There are many hotels, and a riverside camp-site in the suburb of Coteau where a section of the river has been adapted for safe and easy sailing, rowing and water-skiing. The 'Central' restaurant opposite the station is world-famous, one of the top eight in France. The brothers Troisgros, who have cooked for the President at the Élysée, run it personally. If you like truffles with your scrambled eggs; juniper berries with your thrush pâté; lobster cooked in ways undreamed of; a huge range of champagnes to choose from, and if you have a long pocket, this is where you want to be.

The canal-basin in the town is the beginning of the lateral canal system which follows the Loire down to Briare, where there is a link through to the Seine and the whole continental waterway network. The future of this first section (the Roanne-Digoin Canal) is uncertain: there has been talk of closing it down, but in fact traffic has recently been increasing. Now that fuel economy has become so important, the Government may be less inclined to pay attention to the lobbying of powerful road transport interests. A big lorry will carry thirty tonnes, a standard *péniche* (canal barge) two hundred and fifty tonnes; so it requires eight lorries, eight drivers and vastly more fuel to move the same load as one *péniche* with its crew of two. So Roanne continues to maintain its canal port in the hope of better times to come.

Ten miles west of Roanne lies **Ambierle**, whose church contains one of the finest altarpieces in France, presented to the former Benedictine abbey there in 1466. The central panels represent in sculpted walnut, painted and gilded, within a canopy of intricately carved columns, arches and towers, the Passion of Our Lord from the kiss of Judas to the Resurrection. The sculpture is in full relief; the action, the attitude, even the facial expression, of every tiny figure is superb. The effect is like a Botticelli transformed into three dimensions with the figures about to move. It is well worth coming to see, as well as the five stained-glass windows of the same period in the apse, over fifty feet high and ablaze with colour. And on the hills here the first of the Loire's really drinkable wines is grown, the Côte Roannaise, a *vin délimité de qualité supérieur*. You can sample it at the premises of M. Tixier in the centre of the village. The red is light in body, strong in alcohol; the rosé is dry and only slightly acid. There is no white. It is claimed that these wines were greatly esteemed by important dignitaries staying at the monastery on their way to and from Cluny. But, wholesome as they are, I would not go so far as to put them before a discriminating abbot or cardinal when he comes to stay – particularly if he is just on his way back from Burgundy.

Charlieu, downstream of Roanne, has nothing to do with any of history's Charleses, meaning simply *cher lieu*, cherished place. It began as a settlement around a fortified monastery founded by one Ratbert in 872. Three centuries later Philippe-Auguste strengthened the fortifications because he regarded the town as an important gateway to Burgundy. The tower which he built still dominates the centre, seventy feet and five storeys high. Just below the top can still be seen the holes which took the beams of the *hourd* – the surrounding scaffolding from which boiling oil, hot cinders and other unpleasant items could be dropped on unwanted visitors below. In the Hundred Years' War the English were visitors of that sort on four occasions. The remains of the monastery are near the tower and may be visited any day except Monday all the year round from 9 to noon and 2 to 5 (7 in summer). The guardian's house is just beside the tower. Better preserved is the former convent of the Cordeliers just outside the parish boundary – as such establishments usually had to be, for the old regular orders looked askance at the shabby Franciscans and their revolutionary ways and would seldom tolerate them on their own territory. Open the same hours as the monastery, it has fine cloisters with humorously decorated capitals. The convent was sold in 1912 and was being dismantled for shipment to America to adorn a steel millionaire's park when the State hastily intervened and bought it back.

After **Iguerande**, interesting only for the canal and its old quays by the river, and **Marcigny**, which is spoilt by the deafening roar of main road traffic in its narrow high street, the road continues as straight as an arrow over the plain, through a landscape of rich pasture and little copses of acacia trees. Twenty miles away to the east are the hills of the Beaujolais in the valley of the Saône, and ahead is the Morvan, a small massif some forty miles by thirty in extent, composed of granite, very much eroded and mostly of moderate elevation. Its few high peaks are away near Autun, outside the province of this book. The river does not have to fight its way through this obstacle like the previous ones, but keeps to the plain by turning sharply left at **Digoin** and skirting the foothills. Digoin is an important water-junction. Not only does the Canal Roanne-Digoin end here and the Canal Latéral-à-la-Loire begin, but the last-named is joined by the Canal du Centre which by means of sixty-three locks comes over the watershed from Chalon-sur-Saône and links the Loire valley with the Rhône and the Mediterranean. It crosses the Loire in the town by a fine aqueduct of fifteen arches.

The main Bourbon-Lancy road along the hillside is the best one out of Digoin. The Loire winds its way below in a series of loops through rich meadows where millions of pounds' worth of beef cattle graze before our eyes. When the English agriculturalist Arthur Young passed this way on 6 August 1789, three weeks after the Revolution had begun, this rich soil was farmed as arable, but 'villainously' as he put it, with all the wrong crops. 'When I see such a country thus managed, I know not how to pity the seigneurs, great as their present sufferings are.' When one seigneur quoted the Abbé

Rozière, a fashionable farming authority at the time who had pronounced the land unfit for anything but rye, Young enquired dryly whether he or the Abbé 'knew the right end of a plough'. Fifty years later Touchard-Lafosse found things much the same, for violent revolutions do not improve agriculture, as more recent examples have shown. Most of the land was still farmed *en métairie*, a partnership system in which the landlord was of course the 'sleeping' partner (and he usually slept a long way off – most often in Paris) paying a proportion of the tenant's expenses (say on seed) and taking a half-share of the produce. It subsists even now, on rather fairer terms, as we shall find with some of the winegrowers farther downriver.

Bourbon-Lancy is another spa town, but more active and cheerful than most, with many pleasant-looking hotels, parks and gardens; a swimming-pool; tennis courts; a camp-site, and a casino which includes a theatre, an orchestra and a ballroom. The water is slightly radio-active and is used for treating rheumatism, arthritis and heart conditions. '*Le Grand Bain*', paved with marble, is a survivor of the original Roman baths. The old town on top of the hill was once fortified and the quiet little rue de l'Horloge there is almost unchanged from the Middle Ages with its fourteenth-century gate and its old half-timbered houses. At the bottom of the street, from the old fortress walls, there is a fine view across the valley of the Loire to the hills on its far side. Behind them, only twenty miles away, flows the Allier, closing now with its master, ready to render its enormous tribute of waters very soon.

The Loire is just out of sight on our left as we carry on northwards on the next stage of our journey which brings us to **Decize**, a small town standing on an island which is not flat like most islands in rivers, but a hill of lias shale sticking up fifty feet from the water. Being therefore easy to fortify, it has been a settlement from remotest times. To Julius Caesar it was of great importance as a border stronghold and the chief river port of his only Gallic allies, the Aedui, whose territory was roughly modern Burgundy. It remains important today as a junction of waterways and a centre of light industry and is one of the most pleasing of Loire towns into the bargain. To imbibe at once its true atmosphere as an island, turn right after crossing the bridge and walk round it, beginning with the lovely Promenade des Halles, a half-mile-long avenue of majestic trees whose branches meet overhead like the vaulting of an outsize Gothic cathedral. The middle section consists of plane trees some of which are over 180 feet high. Said to be the tallest planes in France, they are over 200 years old, still relatively young for that species which can easily live for 500 years and sometimes up to 2000. Emerging at the end of the avenue, we stand where the two branches of the Loire converge, the right branch now reinforced by its tributary the Aron. An immense barrage, adjustable like a giant sluice-gate, maintains a sufficient head of water at all times for barges to pass out of the Canal Nivernais (whose last lock is over on the right) and along the Loire to the Canal Latéral. The Nivernais, over a course of 108 miles, leads to the river Yonne at Auxerre and thus to the Seine. Migrating fish have to surmount the barrage and if you look carefully in late spring and early summer you may see the lampreys and shad doing so on their way upriver from the sea to spawn. Both (under the names of *lamproie* and *alose* respectively) are culinary delicacies of the Loire from mid-June onwards. Shad, like its much smaller cousin the herring, has a fine texture and flavour, and its hard roes are used to make a tasty omelette; but lampreys are exceedingly rich, as Henry I of England found to his great detriment when he ate a surfeit of them.

Outside the avenue a road runs right round the end of the island, so you can drive round it if there is not time to walk. On the right is the municipal park with a riverside bar, safe swimming enclosure, fishing punts and canoes for hire, and a four-star camp-site.

The main street of Decize, the Rue de la République, contains most of the shops – good shops too, mostly small family affairs anxious to please. The great *specialité de la région* to remember to ask for at the butcher's is Charolais steak. Its quality is incomparable here in the region where the famous breed originated, and where it thrives best of all on the rich natural pasture of the little hills to the west. At the end of the street the Place Saint-Just is so named to commemorate the town's most famous *enfant du pays* (albeit an *enfant terrible*), Louis-Antoine de Saint-Just, apostle of the guillotine and Robespierre's closest ally, eventually to perish on his own bloody altar when he was only twenty-seven years old. Where the Credit Lyonnais now has its offices stood once the home of the Robinot family, bakers and pastrycooks here for many generations until they climbed the social ladder as far as the *noblesse de robe*. Marie-Anne Robinot, at the age of thirty, climbed one step higher by marrying a cavalry officer of the old aristocracy twenty years her senior. Louis-Antoine was the offspring and his childhood in and near Decize was unhappy and devoid of any love from his selfish parents. As a result he grew up hard and loveless himself.

Another celebrity born and reared in Decize, and more in keeping with the cheerful spirit of the place, was Marguerite Monnot, composer of the music of *Irma la Douce* and many of Edith Piaf's greatest successes including *Milord*, whose lively strains have echoed their way around the world.

On top of the island-hill the Église Saint-Aré stands over an impressive seventh-century crypt with two naves and the remains of an exquisitely sculpted stone retable sadly mutilated by some of Saint-Just's Jacobin followers at the Revolution. The town also has the vestiges of a château (now a hospital) behind imposing ramparts on the south side and a fine medieval fortified gateway just below it in which the slots for the portcullis can still be seen. Its name, *Porte du Marquis d'Ancre*, is a good example of scholarly misconstruction. Just outside the gate the local boatmen used to lay up their boats in winter with anchors ashore in all directions to prevent their being carried away in a flood. So the spot was called *Maquis d'ancres* – tangle of anchors.

After Decize the main road is uninteresting and passes through the steel town of Imphy. The minor road on the other side is preferable, following the Canal Latéral most of the way, past bridges and locks, orchards and patches of woodland. Each lock has its cottage with a bright and carefully tended garden, traditional hobby of lock-keepers the world over. At intervals we pass a big *péniche*, the master smoking his pipe at the wheel and perhaps Madame beside him with her sewing.

A diversion left in Fleury leads, by way of a little road winding up the hillside with wonderful views across the valley of the Loire, to the lonely ruins of the castle of **Rozemont**, a completely unretouched stronghold of the Hundred Years' War.

CHAPTER TWO

Nevers to Gien

❧

As we cross the bridge into **Nevers,** its dual personality is plain: the old city ahead on the hill and, sprawling out of it to the right, the brave new world of skyscrapers and supermarkets. The chief pride of its municipal authorities is in the latter; they are zealous for change; aim to double its population to 115,000 in the eighties and are already busy with ambitious plans for AD 2010. However, the interest of the tourist will be rather in the old Nevers and the evidence of its history which remains.

In 1565 the duchy of Nevers passed by marriage into the Gonzaga family of Mantua and the elaborate style of the **Palais Ducal** in the town centre is a conspicuous example of the Italian influence they brought with them. The **Cathedral** near by is a veritable collation of architectural samples from Romanesque to Renaissance requiring time to appreciate and not particularly imposing as a whole. There is, however, an exhilarating feeling of space and light inside. The surviving Romanesque portion is the west apse in which an altar stands as well as at the east end: an unusual arrangement, but there has never been a west door.

When Ludovic de Gonzague arrived in 1565 he employed Italian workmen to found Nevers's famous pottery industry. It still survives and its high-quality products can be bought in the town. They are what we generally call majolica and the French call *faïence* after the Italian town of Faenza where the process originated. It is enamelled earthenware fired at around 1000°C to produce a hardness and fineness of texture next to porcelain in quality. Near the **Porte-du-Croux,** on the west side of the town (perhaps the finest fourteenth-century gateway anywhere along the Loire, and virtually complete) you will find the shop, Bout-du-Monde, and its **faïence factory,** founded in 1648 on this same site and the oldest surviving in the town. It has operated continuously since then and the proprietor, Monsieur Montagnon, is very proud that, apart from mechanical mixing of the clays, the whole manufacture is by hand just as it has been over three centuries. On attending at the shop at 2.30 sharp on

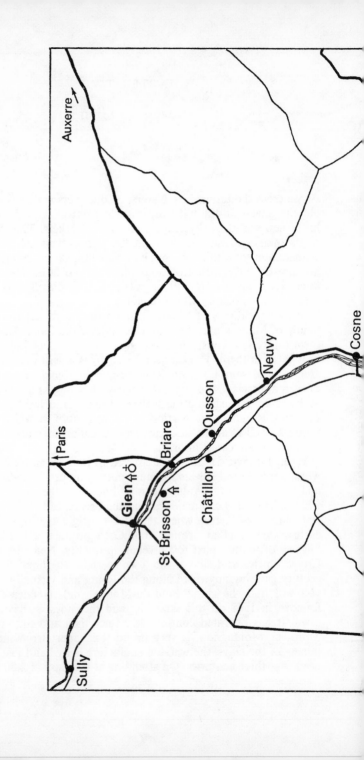

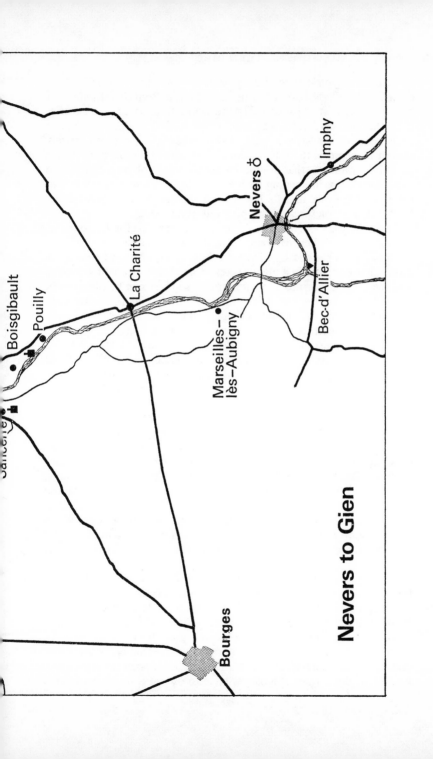

Nevers to Gien

a Wednesday you can be taken to see the craftsmen at work. Many of the original designs are still used at the Bout-du-Monde, but naturally the best place to study the whole trend over the centuries is at the **museum**, which has recently moved to better premises at 16 Rue Saint-Genest, just west of the cathedral. The style is purely Italian to begin with; then as local craftsmen take over there is a period (parallel to that found in architecture) of modification to something more in keeping with French taste. Of special interest to lovers of the Loire and its history are the designs intended for the boatmen, with pictures of shipping and river scenes.

At the **Couvent Saint-Gildard** in the Boulevard Victor-Hugo, Saint Bernadette, after her visions at Lourdes, took the veil in 1867 and remained until her death in 1879. In the chapel, which is open to the public, her body lies in a glass casket. It has been certified by doctors and the civil authorities as uncorrupted, so there can be little doubt this is true since any bias of the latter would incline the other way. The face and hands, having darkened on contact with the air, have been covered with a thin moulding of wax and the slightly false appearance occasioned by this must be discounted. The face has a serene and spiritual beauty. Outside the chapel is a replica of the grotto at Lourdes, but in the garden there is a statue of the Virgin which is of particular significance in understanding Bernadette. Called *Notre Dame des Eaux*, it was erected about 1856 in gratitude for the discovery of an underground water supply for the recently completed convent. It is well known that Saint Bernadette did not like the statue at Lourdes very much, as the sculptor paid little heed to what she told him and made it according to his own preconceptions. But when she first saw this one (made before her visions, but coincidentally involving discovery of a spring of water) she exclaimed 'This recalls to me most of all the Lady I saw at Massiabelle.' She would often pray before it here in the quiet garden. When a companion once remarked that she did not look at it as she did so, she answered 'No, I look higher.' The garden is open to the public.

The La Charité road northwards out of Nevers is one of the busiest in France, the one the Roman legions tramped on their way to conquer Northern Gaul and still the most frequented highway between Paris and the Mediterranean coast, so it is best to cross back over the Loire the way we came into Nevers and take the Bourges road to the west. After about five miles we cross the Allier and come to **Guétin**. Here the Canal Latéral crosses the Allier too, by an aqueduct where the barges have to mount a stairway of three locks and then descend a similar flight at the other end. Only a mile away is the **Bec d'Allier**, where after its own 200-mile journey from the Cevennes the Allier joins our river. Pushed by the force of it, the Loire loops round a great spur of high land on the other side, which is thickly wooded with oak and chestnut. Between them the two rivers have created on this side a wilderness of willow-crowned sandhills as vegetation has taken over their deposits of granitic sand. The variety of birds to delight the bird-watcher here is astonishing. Warblers, nightingales and long-tailed tits show themselves openly among the trees; the egret, that graceful little white cousin of the heron, flies low across the shoreline and terns dive for bleak in the river – 400 miles from the sea. Behind an island, in spring, you may see the nets extended on stakes which the local professional fishermen use in taking salmon and shad. I shall describe the procedure later when we get a closer look (p. 162). It is at this point that most of the salmon part company with the Loire, preferring the faster current of the Allier. Here too are born the sudden and terrible floods to which the Loire is subject, for this confluence is the outlet of its upper basin — 2000 square miles of primitive rock: basalt, granite and gneiss, for the most part impenetrable so that the rain which falls over that vast area is carried rapidly to the two rivers. There is no other sizable tributary until the Cher runs in just below Tours, so the quantity of water which passes this point determines the level of the Loire for the next 200 miles. Altogether, the Bec is a place to ponder many aspects of Nature and her forces.

Taking the minor road north from Cuffy, the near-by hamlet, we soon come to **Marseilles-lès-Aubigny**, with the Loire on one side and the canal running through it, a working canal-port with all the life and activity that that involves. Here you will see great *péniches* which may have come not merely from some distant part of France, but from Germany, the Low Countries, Switzerland or even Scandinavia. At the downstream end of the village is the yard of Loire Line beside the canal. Started by two Englishmen in 1974, this enterprise maintains a fleet of canal cruisers for hire. A fortnight's holiday from here gives time to follow the canals to Saint-Mammes, near Fontainebleau, and return through Auxerre and Decize. Bookings can be arranged through the company's English office at Wigborough, near Colchester (telephone 020-635-280).

Next comes **La Charité**, very old indeed and built in the form of an amphitheatre, with fortified walls along the ring of hills at the top. Its old name, Seyr, is probably of Phoenician derivation, signifying City of the Sun. The present name arose from the Benedictine monastery which stood here in the Middle Ages. On a pilgrim route to Compostella, it flourished to such an extent that the generous almsgiving the abbey was able to afford became famous for miles around - *'Allons à la charité des bons pères.'* The abbey church was consecrated in 1107 and was modelled on the mother church at Cluny. Unfortunately only vestiges of the original building and of the abbey itself remain. Both were ravaged in 1599 by a terrible fire which lasted three days.

In 1429 Joan of Arc laid siege to La Charité, but the redoubtable Perrinet-Gressard held on grimly for the Burgundians and she had to give up. This was her first setback, and at her trial the fact that no heavenly help had come to her weighed heavily against her. But the Devil looked after Gressard, who took a stiff ransom six years later from the weak Charles in return for changing sides. The town bridge was built in the sixteenth century and remains one of the handsomest on the Loire. It is in the *dos-d'âne* form and has ten arches with buttress piers.

There is no alternative but to take the main road now, and the next place is **Mesves**, a friendly little village on the Mazou, a trout river in which visitors are welcome to fish. And then comes **Pouilly-sur-Loire.**

There are many fine Loire wines, but only six really great ones. The four whites are the Pouilly-Fumé; the wine of Sancerre, only five miles away across the river; Coulée de Serrant (little-known), from a long way down in Anjou; and Vouvray, from nearly as far in Touraine, whence come the two reds, Chinon and Saint-Nicolas-de-Bourgueil. There is much misunderstanding about Pouilly-Fumé. Firstly it is often confused with Pouilly-Fuissé which is grown in Burgundy in a district happening to have the same name, but from a different grape and with a different character. Secondly, there is misapprehension concerning the term *fumé* and the famous *'pierre-de-fusil'* flavour. Smoke, gunflint! One might suppose it was called *fumé* because of its flavour and that the flavour must come from flint in the soil. But neither is correct. It is the Sauvignon grape which is locally called *'le fumé'* because towards maturity the little fruits, tightly clustered together and each smaller than a sparrow's egg, acquire a smoke-grey bloom. As for the flavour, the Sauvignon is noted for its spiciness (in some other regions it is known as *'l'épicier'*) and its facility for blending this with any special quality in the soil. In the Bordeaux region it produces the rich, full Sauternes; at Pouilly this dry wine with the unique 'gunflint' taste which it develops from the local soil of Kimmeridgian clay with its content of oölitic fossilized lime. It is a strong wine, usually around 13° alcohol, in good years more; a moderate keeper, but equally pleasant to drink young.

The district also produces a lighter, dryer and cheaper wine from the Chasselas grape, which is normally grown as a dessert grape: only here and at Chignin in Savoy is it used for wine.

Pouilly is a good place for an overnight stop. Its several small hotels have over a hundred rooms between them and there is a two-star camp-site by the river. There are also about a dozen restaurants, but none of them is very cheap as standards are high to tempt the Paris gourmets passing by.

Leave by the minor road along the right bank, through several little hamlets, each with its *caves* where the wine is cheaper than in Pouilly by the main road. Monsieur Roger Pabiot and his wife at **Boisgibault** are particularly kind and helpful. The wine is served with a *pipette* from the top of the cask (a rare sight these days); you can do your tasting in peace, chat with them about wine and come away with a bottle or two of the best Pouilly at a reasonable price. The next village is **Tracy** which has a château with a fantastically tall fifteenth-century keep. There is no visiting, but a rough lane opposite leads over the railway-crossing to a clearing in the trees by the river where there is a little sandy beach. Here is just the place, while contemplating the deceptively lazy-looking rips and swirls of the growing Loire, to open one of those bottles of wine. Looking downstream you can see Sancerre perched on its extraordinary hill, where we shall soon have to render further homage to the vine.

The minor road out of Tracy and a left turn at the next main crossroads brings us to the bridge over the Loire into **Saint-Thibault**. There is a large island just upstream where the local goats are grazed, for we are now entering *chèvre* cheese country. Each morning they are ferried across in a huge raft-like punt. From the left bank in the dry season you can walk across on to a nearer island of grass and willow trees and between the two islands is a slow-running arm of the Loire where bathing is safe – a most pleasant spot for a hot day.

The waterfront in the other direction is equally pleasing. First you come to a quiet hotel overlooking the river; then an old house in a garden with a judas-tree whose flowers hang over the wall in spring and, nearly opposite, a restaurant built on two *péniche* hulls moored in the river. Family-run, but only open at week-ends and so popular that you need to arrive early to get a table, it specializes in regional dishes such as *matelote* of eels in red wine (a favourite with the old Loire mariners) or bleak and other small fry of the river cooked like

whitebait, but with delicious sauces. It has a bar where local personalities often foregather; and there are many personalities in Saint-
Thibault, for it is a lively little place with a great community spirit
and sense of fun. Much merriment takes place at its annual water
carnival on 16 August, the feast-day of Saint Roch, patron saint of
the Saint-Thibault *mariniers*. The life and soul of all such junketings
is the energetic and cheerful Monsieur Godon, who comes from a
marinier family himself. There are many Godons living along the
Loire; by tradition they claim descent from English soldiers who
settled in Burgundian-held territory during the Hundred Years'
War, and who were dubbed '*godons*' from their constant oath
'Goddam!' which shocked Joan of Arc so much. M. Godon has a
big launch in which he runs river trips on week-end afternoons from
April to September, one of the few opportunities on the Loire for the
casual visitor to sail among its swirling currents, tortuous channels
and beautiful islands – a great experience. Next to his moorings is
an *école nautique* where you can hire small craft and take a lesson
in coping with the conditions yourself. Farther downstream is a
riverside camp-site among trees.

The mariners' chapel to Saint Roch in the centre of the village is
a charming little building which the villagers are trying hard to save
from falling into ruin. On the wall the banner of the former mariners'
guild depicts the saint with his staff and a dog, and an angel pointing
to a sore on his leg. He is usually invoked as a protector against
pestilence and not commonly encountered as a patron saint of
sailors. Almost everywhere else along the Loire their patron, as in
most of Christendom, was Saint Nicholas. But the *mariniers* of
Saint-Thibault were always a bit 'different', and in fact grudgingly
regarded by other watermen of the great Loire fraternity as something special. Saint Roch was born at Montpelier of a wealthy
family, but gave away his riches to the poor and made a pilgrimage
to Rome (hence the staff). On the way, in about 1348, he met the
Bubonic Plague ravaging Italy, devoted himself to succouring the
victims and afterwards went on to helping lepers, from whom he
eventually caught that disease (the sore on his leg). Withdrawing to a
remote hermitage, he was fed by the local seigneur's dog who stole
for him a piece of bread each day.

Saint-Thibault was a flourishing port up to about 1860. All the
wine of Sancerre was exported from here and most of the industrial
output of the region. The last cargo-carrying boats came here in
1903 and M. Godon's father can remember them. There is a little
junction-canal through to the Canal Latéral which has recently been

restored for use by pleasure craft, of which there will be more available here as time goes on.

Saint-Satur adjoins Saint-Thibault and is still a port on the Canal Latéral. An Augustinian convent was established here in the twelfth century and soon the monks planted many acres of vines on the surrounding hillsides (the beginning of the Sancerre vineyards) which produced a wine considered by its contemporaries the best in central France. They prospered greatly and spent their wealth in building the fine Gothic church which stands here now. It was nearly finished when in 1420 the English arrived and demanded a ransom of a thousand *écus d'or*. They would not believe the monks when they said they did not have this sum; so they first took all the valuables they could find, then locked up the senior monks in a tower and set fire to it. The younger ones they took away in chains and, when torture failed to reveal 'hidden treasure', tied them up in sacks and threw them into the river. The convent never recovered.

The style of the church of Saint-Satur was inspired by Bourges Cathedral, and the vaults of the nave and transepts have the audacious soaring lightness of the best of Gothic. But there is an odd feeling about the place: it seems too short – until you remember that the English rudely interrupted its completion and it ends where the tower would have been if the stricken convent could only have afforded one. Suspended from the ceiling before the altar is a votive ship, a fine model of a seventy-eight-gun ship-of-the-line. The work of a local *marinier* of the eighteenth century, it is named *Saint Roch* and has the saint as its figurehead. The Loire was a favourite recruiting-ground for the navy, its sailors being bred to the water, fresh and tidal, and exceptionally tough and skilled by reason of its special difficulties.

Under the railway viaduct and we are in **Fontenay**, which is the vineyard quarter of the town. Above us, **Sancerre** rises in solitary eminence out of the river plain, a sight at once bizarre and beautiful. The road begins to wind steeply round the side so that eventually we enter the town from almost the opposite direction, the west. At that point the road forks. Take the right fork for a preliminary excursion through the old quarter of winding streets and ancient houses. The streets are fairly clear, all parking being forbidden except in the squares. Eventually, on emerging by the Porte César on the north-east side, we come to the **Esplanade** and one of the most famous panoramas of the Loire Valley. There is usually room to park, but with more difficulty on a Sunday.

We are 440 feet above the valley, so that the horizon in clear weather is 24 miles away; and, since there are no obstructions, the eye is able to sweep through nearly 120 degrees of it. Immediately below lie Saint-Satur and Saint-Thibault with the viaduct crossing a little vale in a sweeping curve; strong and graceful, it remains to beautify the scene although the railway line it carried is now discontinued. Right across the middle distance are several miles of river in loops and bends, from La Charité to Villechaud downstream, where the ribbon of water becomes lost in misty-blue forest. Beyond the forest Cosne stands out clear and, beyond that, the hills above Auxerre. All along the horizon to the right are the hills of Burgundy.

On the left, a relief from the sweeping distances, stand the little hills beside the town, a colourful patchwork of small vineyards. The majority of *vignerons* in central France own less than two acres of vines, but here at Sancerre, as at Pouilly, very many have less than one acre. It is still worth their while with a wine of quality, as the yield from one hectare of well-kept vines spaced at 6000 plants to the hectare (which is not thick) can easily be 6000 litres or, say, 3500 bottles to the acre. Seeing the vines smiling in the sun on these slopes, one is reminded of Virgil's maxim: '*Apertos Bacchus amat colles*', for hillsides could hardly be more open than these. They produce red, rosé and white wines, and it is the latter which are the most famous. All are *appellation controlé*, except where they are grown on north-facing slopes. The white is produced from the Sauvignon which we encountered at Pouilly, but there is a difference: the Sancerre is fuller and rounder and has a different bouquet. Why this should be so is one of the mysteries of wine and the endless technical speculation that tries to explain it makes the head spin more than the wine itself. The explanation of a man who has spent a lifetime intimately with vines is probably as near the truth as any. One of the oldest *vignerons* at Fontenay tells me it is the greater preponderance of a different kind of clay, 'like brick-clay'. There are *tuileries* (tile-kilns) at Saint-Satur and near Sancerre, but none across the river.

Whatever the cause may be, I think I like the Sancerre just a little better than the Pouilly-Fumé, though the latter is admittedly more delicate. The Sancerre red too is a beauty: mellow, refreshing, deceptively light-seeming (but really very strong) and a good keeper. It is produced from the Pinot Noir grape, the same which is used for all the great Burgundies (and the great champagnes, since its juice is pure white if the skin is not crushed), one of the oldest and noblest French stocks. The rosé is strong, but thin-seeming and inclined to be a little sharp. It is uneconomical to buy your wine in the town

Le Puy: Chapel of St Michael on the Rocher d'Aiguilhe

Mont Gerbier de Jonc: the Loire
rises at its base on the right.

Le Puy: Cathédrale de Notre Dame

Lavoute Polignac

centre, and you can be unpleasantly 'stung' for just a *dégustation* in some of the fancy bars. Call instead on M. René Laporte at Fontenay or, in the town, on Pellay, Père et Fils, 12 Avenue Nationale (main road out to Bourges, west side of town). One last tip before leaving the subject: the Sancerre and Pouilly whites are at their best new – up to two years, no more.

Sancerre has an interesting history, but a couple of things must not be taken seriously: the Porte César, to begin with. France is full of 'Caesar's gates' and 'Caesar's towers' which had nothing to do with Caesar, but rather some minstrel's desire to flatter the local baron. Secondly if you read somewhere that the name Sancerre is a contraction of '*Sacrum Caesaris*', don't believe it. There is no evidence it was a Roman town, but the truth of the name's derivation tells a much more interesting story: it was Saxiacum, later Saxia, later Saxerre. After Charlemagne had subdued the Saxons in 804, he tried to split them up by forced emigration in small settlements to other parts of his domains. One colony was planted in this region and a fort was built on the hill to keep them in order and to bar their path should they attempt to fight their way home. This was the origin of Sancerre.

The fortifications were renewed in the thirteenth and fourteenth centuries, surrounding the town with a high wall having ten towers and four gates. It was then virtually impregnable and the English failed disastrously in an attempt to take it in 1420, after they had sacked Saint-Satur. No one seriously tried again until it became a Huguenot stronghold in the Wars of Religion, and then it had to be starved into submission by a siege lasting 220 days. The great fortifications were then systematically pulled down leaving only the Tour des Fiefs which still stands not far from the Porte César.

In 1745 a small colony of Scots who had followed Bonnie Prince Charlie back to France settled at Sancerre. Among them was a schoolmaster from South Uist, a Macdonald and cousin of the celebrated Flora. His house still stands at 3 Rue Macdonald in the town centre, so named in honour of his famous son, Étienne, who spent his boyhood there. In 1779, at the age of fourteen, Étienne was sent away to school to receive a military education which led to his career as one of Napoleon's most able generals, eventually to be entrusted by the Emperor with the unhappy and difficult negotiations which led to the abdication in 1814. Marshal Macdonald, Duke of Taranto, retained throughout his long life a sentimental affection for his country of origin and in his old age he came on a visit to see it.

One could go on writing volumes about Sancerre, but regretfully we must leave it for much still lies ahead of us, and we have not yet mentioned the famous *chèvre* cheese of this region – probably the best in France. If you would like to sample it in a happy atmosphere and make a cheap wholesome meal of it, go to the Coopérative d'Élevage de Garennes (Bourges road out of Sancerre; two miles out, *pass* the Vinon turn on your left and take the *next* turn left). Here, as you enter, you choose your *crottes* of cheese as you prefer, ranging from the new (sweet, soft and refreshing) to the fully mature (hard, rich and piquant); a crusty loaf in the size that suits you, and a bottle of Sancerre wine. These you consume at trestle tables amid happy French families all doing the same with gusto. Little known to foreign tourists, this remote spot has the genuine atmosphere of France on a day out. Outside, you can visit the dairies and the 300 sleek and handsome goats.

To continue the main journey, go back to Saint-Satur and take the left turn alongside the Canal Latéral. There is no means of following the river on the other bank, where you have only a railway line for company, but here there is the canal scenery and the good chance of seeing a *péniche* coming through a lock or steering with amazing precision through the arch of a bridge with only inches to spare.

Cosne began as a Stone Age settlement tucked in the angle of the confluence of the Nohain with the Loire, and has been inhabited ever since. The Gauls were there – they called it *Condate*, meaning 'angle' – and the Romans, whose baths with lead-pipe plumbing may still be seen. In the centuries that followed the barbarian invasions nothing much happened here until, in 1670, the Chaussade family set up iron foundries on the banks of the Nohain for the forging of cannon, muskets and ships' anchors, which could all be transported very cheaply down the Loire to the Atlantic coast. In 1781 Louis XVI compulsorily purchased the foundries by Order in Council and thereafter they became the '*Forges Royales*', but he forgot to pay for them and it is said that the Baron de la Chaussade died in poverty. They were closed in 1872 owing to the decline in river transport and the town suffered a long and miserable slump. It is just beginning to recover, striving to regain its importance with the manufacture of tools, furniture, confectionery and lingerie. There is every sign that things will go on improving, and one recent achievement is the provision of an extensive leisure area on the big island opposite the town; generous access has been provided and there are cool alleys among the trees, a wide sandy beach for children to play and bathe in safety, and a good camp-site behind it. The town also has several reasonable hotels.

Though there is hardly enough of interest to warrant a walk round Cosne it would be a pity to leave it without driving along its beautiful waterfront. Starting at the north end – Place de la Pêcherie, site of the original prehistoric village – we come to quays shaded by lime trees, planes and horse-chestnuts, and presently to the confluence with the Nohain where it comes tumbling over a weir and then beneath the road: a lusty stripling of a river which rises not many miles away in the forest to the east. A little farther, on the grass bank of the municipal gardens, lies a specimen of the manufactures of Cosne in the days of the forges – a ship's anchor weighing two and a half tons, cast here in 1861 and fished up out of the sea at Roche-fort exactly a hundred years later. Leave the quay at this point by turning left and we come to a remarkable set of wrought-iron gates to the Gardens, an example of early Cosne ironwork, made in the seventeenth century. A few more yards brings us to the twelfth-century church of Saint Aignan, formerly attached to a Cluniac priory. The doorway inside the north porch and the apse are the only interesting features; the interior is very plain. Just round the corner is the town centre. Cosne produces two good local wines from the Pinot Noir (p. 48), a red and a rosé, which resemble, but of course do not equal, those of Sancerre.

The busy Briare road northwards from Cosne leads past **Myennes, Neuvy** and **Bonny**, all little riverside ports in days gone by; **Ousson** likewise, but be sure to turn off the main road there as it has an interesting back road to Châtillon. Turn down the Rue des Pêcheurs, and on coming to the river you will be surprised at how it has broadened since last we saw it, when it was still restricted by the hills of Pouilly and Sancerre. Here is a tranquil stretch with fish leaping in the channels between tree-covered islands, and the cheerful little houses along the bank seem in an enviable situation. So they are; so long as the great floods never return! The house on the corner of the Rue de la Loire has records of some of them marked on its wall. 1856 and 1866 are on the lintel of the window and 1846 is not far below. The danger months for the *grandes crues* are November and December (the time of the autumn rains) and February to May (the wide period of possible melting snow and spring rain); but there are no set rules: notice that 1856, the highest flood on record, was in June!

By continuing straight along the riverside for another half-mile, we come to a run-up on to the Châtillon road on top of the *levée*, the flood-bank, the sole possible defence against the Loire's destructive floods. Charlemagne gave orders for the first of these, but they were flimsy affairs: earthworks reinforced with stakes and brushwood, and old boats filled with stones. In the seventeenth century they began to build more efficient *levées* of stone. But the constriction merely increased the power of the water, and when they broke in 1707 more than 50,000 people are said to have drowned. The unimaginative response of the authorities was simply to raise the height of the *levées* – a bigger bottle for a more powerful genie who, his strength thus nurtured, escaped more often: 1709, 1710 and 1711. Then at last someone thought of the obvious: the river must be allowed run-offs where it can spill its excess waters harmlessly. But it was not until the three terrible floods of the middle of the following century that these *déversoirs* were constructed systematically with a view to spilling the water in the right place at the right time. The *levées* are now, by regulation, five metres high and twenty-two metres wide at the base, and the ancient laws prohibiting building and tree-planting on them are still enforced. Allowing for one or two metres of natural bank, the river must rise six or seven metres above its *étiage* (normal summer level) to overtop the *levées*. But pressure can burst them before that. So could it all happen again – the ruin and the misery, the vast loss of life and property? Yes. The level of the water depends solely on the rainfall or the rate of thaw in the Auvergne. This century has been lucky so far, that is all. Only twice, in 1907 and 1924, has the rise been over five metres; and between 1957 and 1968 it was never more than three metres: a space of eleven years like that has never been known since records have been kept. If the fatal permutation of meteorological factors does turn up again, the effect will depend on how much better the *levées* and the modern *déversoirs* work; the latter have not yet been submitted to the supreme test.

Just before the suspension bridge leading into **Châtillon-sur-Loire** there is a camp-site between the river and a small disused canal, and beyond the first section of the bridge there is a sandy beach on an island where bathing is safe. In its vicinity a lot of fishing goes on for pike, perch and the lively *sandre* which is a cross between the two. The zander, a native of Eastern Europe, is a fairly recent introduction to France and is now one of the angling specialities of the Loire. Gleaming silver with the spiked dorsal fin of the perch, he is bigger – specimens of ten or twelve pounds not being at all unusual. He hunts in small shoals and, unlike the pike, feeds best in warm weather, so he is in good form for the summer holidays. He is good to eat too; if you can't catch one, you can buy one at most fishmongers along the Loire Valley.

Speaking of eating, it is appropriate to mention at this point that in the street leading from the bridge into Châtillon there is a small friendly restaurant and hotel, family-run, called the Hôtel des Trois Rois. The steep Rue Jeanne d'Arc, farther in and leading up to the church, is a wondrous survival of old times: nearly all ancient houses, and one of them even has a tower in half-timbering. The church at the top was built in the 1880s when the town had outgrown the former Benedictine chapel. For a piece of what we should call 'Victorian Gothic' it is of surprisingly elegant proportions. Down a pathway to the left on coming out of the door you can see the remains of the old castle walls. The castle itself has long since disappeared.

Although Briare, over on the other side, is next in order proceeding downriver, it can more conveniently be left until later so as to be able to make the best approach to Gien along the left bank. But at **Saint-Firmin** we do pass beneath Briare's mighty aqueduct (see p. 57) which carries the Canal Latéral across the Loire, and may have the pleasure of seeing a *péniche* passing sedately over our heads.

Shortly after, the road passes **Saint-Brisson** on the left. This sleepy little village, built on a hill around its castle and its church, merits a brief call. To get the full dramatic first impression of the castle, take the second turn leading into the village. On the left, halfway up the road, part of the moat remains. It is instructive to pause at this point and imagine you are one of Louis VI's soldiers just about to make an assault during his attack upon it in 1135. It would be a fearsome job to run up that hill and put a ladder against the wall – probably the last thing you would ever do.

This was a stronghold of one of the robber barons, the *seigneurs pillards*, who were so surprised and indignant when this king arose who presumed to interfere with the 'rights' they had enjoyed for centuries – to be a law unto themselves. The idea seemed preposterous to them, but Louis had determined to establish respect for a rule of law which embodied the rights of all; he declared himself the defender of the 'custom of the realm', a phrase which Henry II, the great English lawmaker, soon adopted. *Gourmandise* was the only weakness of this excellent and far-seeing monarch, and earned him his nickname 'the Fat'. He was always suffering internal upheavals and it was here that he contracted the dysentery which finally killed him two years later. This was his last campaign, but successful; he took the castle by storm and burnt it down. The present sturdy reconstruction, incorporating the original 'pepper-pot' towers, was effected by Pierre Séguier, a Paris magistrate who became Chancellor under Louis XIII. It is still occupied by the same family and is not open to the public; but at least this means the quiet rural character of the village remains to be enjoyed.

The view of **Gien**, approached from this side of the river, is one of rare beauty. As you come closer, all the component parts of the picture fall into a perfect composition. The old *dos-d'âne* bridge – now nearly five centuries old – leads the eye across the shining river to rest on an assemblage of ancient quays, trees and handsome waterfront buildings, and then to mount over the roofs of the town to the château and the church above.

Gien is the first town of that indefinite region loosely called '*Val de Loire*' and extending from hereabouts to Anjou. It stands approximately at the point where the Loire has completed its change of course from a generally northerly one to a definitely westerly one – where it begins to form a boundary-line, a physical barrier, right across the middle of France. To facilitate north-south communication it would be essential to have a crossing here, and in fact Gien's name is derived from the latinized Gaulish: *Divomagus* (*divo*: god, and *magus*: market) later contracted to *Giomus*. Charlemagne built a fortress here, and Anne de Beaujeu rebuilt it on his foundations between 1484 and 1500. This favourite child of Louis XI, of whom he made the famous remark '*C'est la moins folle des femmes; de sages il n'y en a point*', proved in fact to be at least his equal in statesmanship when she later acted as regent for her younger brother Charles VIII, and Brantôme described her afterwards as '*une des grands roys de France*'. She honoured Gien by making it her residence and was its greatest single benefactor ever; she gave it not only its château, but the beautiful bridge and a new church. The latter, except for the tower, was utterly destroyed in 1940 when, to cut off this important escape route for the French army, the Germans bombed the town for three days – 15, 16 and 17 June – setting it on fire. The conflagration burnt on for three days more, wiping out practically the whole of the old quarter, until a providential downpour of rain put it out just as the flames had reached the château roof. Four years later, this time to cut off German troops, Gien suffered a similar ordeal at the hands of the Allies. A fleet of fifty Flying Fortress heavy bombers pattern-bombed it to cut the railway bridge, missing the target and wrecking another huge slice of the town. An eye-witness has told me how grateful they all were on the other hand when the RAF, charged with cutting the road bridge, sent only one small bomber which flew in low along the river, dropped one bomb and neatly cut the second arch from the southern end – all that was necessary.

After all this devastation, it is the more remarkable, and a tribute to the patient courage and good taste of the French, that Gien is again so beautiful. The **church** is an example of what I mean: left only with Anne's tower, the people of Gien completely rebuilt the rest to a new design of considerable elegance on a framework of reinforced concrete with walls of attractive pink brick specially baked in wood-fired kilns. In the nave this brickwork glows ethereally in a soft, warm light from stained-glass windows designed by Max Ingrand. The capitals of the pillars are coloured Gien earthenware pottery illustrating episodes in the life of Joan of Arc (to whom the church is now dedicated), while round the walls the Stations of the Cross are depicted on plaques of coloured *faïence* from the town's own factory.

The Gien pottery industry was founded in the early nineteenth century, much later than at Nevers, but its best *faïence* is considered to be of equal quality. Its designs fall into two main categories: the blue (with or without other colours), resembling traditional Nevers; and the multi-coloured picture designs portraying birds, animals and field sports, which I find delightful and in which Gien excels. There is also the *vieux grès*, a brown glazed earthenware. The town is very proud of its pottery and displays it even on the name-plates of some of its streets, which are of handsome coloured *faïence*. If you want to go shopping in Gien it is a good idea to arrive early in the morning or during the *midi* break, when you will find space to park in the **Place du Pont** at the north end of the bridge. Here, and in the streets leading off it, are all the best shops. The château looms over the rooftops and a flight of steps from the corner of the square leads up to it, but there is a more comfortable approach to it of course by the ordinary streets.

There are fine old stone quays above and below the bridge, and a pleasant riverside walk in the **Jardins Publics** upstream of it at the end of the Quai Joffre. From the same quay, if you wish to see a few remnants of the medieval town which survived the war, drive up the Rue Victor-Hugo and at the top take the first fork right into the **Rue Lejardinier**. Some of the houses are original and on the right there are substantial vestiges of the old town walls. At the end of this street was once the 'Gate of the Golden Lion' where, on 1 March 1429 in the dusk of the late afternoon, seven riders approached from the sodden winter countryside. They were all tired and the guards felt particularly sorry for the youngest who appeared to be a page-boy. Next morning it was not long before the gossips were able to identify the 'boy' with certain exciting rumours they had been hearing. It was a peasant's daughter from Lorraine who had been sent by God to deliver France, and she was on her way to see the King. On 24 June, less than four months later, the peasant's daughter returned to Gien in glory with the King at her side. But behind the glory the timorous Charles was vacillating, listening to the advice of La Tremoïlle and the politicians of the Court, urging him to caution, inventing objections to Joan's plan for pressing on to Reims. With her common sense she knew the value of the *sacre* in the eyes of the people and, in a temper at all this exasperating hesitation, she left the town with her few faithful followers and camped several miles away in the countryside. Still in the heat of gratitude, Charles could not bear this, and on the 29th he rode out at the head of his troops to join the Maid and tell her he was ready to do her bidding. Seventeen days later he was anointed at Reims. Just before Christmas the people of Gien saw her again, praying in their church, disconsolate after her failure at La Charité (see p. 44); her worldly triumph was already in its decline.

There are so many châteaux in the Val de Loire that the tourist without unlimited time at his disposal is obliged to miss interior visits to some of them. In many cases this is no great loss as they have nothing original to offer. There are limits to one's appetite for faded tapestries, period furniture and 'royal' bedchambers. The main attributes of most of the castles are their architecture, their situation as a feature in the landscape, and often their history. But the **château** of Gien should on no account be missed out, for it contains one of the most fascinating specialized museums in France: the **Musée International de la Chasse**. Even if you don't approve of *la chasse* you cannot discount the works of art which have drawn their inspiration from this oldest of human pursuits, or the craftsmanship and inventive ingenuity which over the ages have by and large rendered it more humane. All are represented here in abundance. There is plenty of parking-space on the hilltop outside the château in the shade of big trees and with a view down to the town and the river. The architecture of the building is clean and well-proportioned; it was built just before elaborate Italian styles of embellishment had temporarily captured the French imagination and is plainly decorated in patterned brickwork. The museum is open every day from 9 to noon and 2.15 to 6.30 (5.30 1 November to Easter). Visits are not guided; you may admire at leisure or skip what does not appeal. Everything is well ticketed and the arrangement is roughly chronological. Besides weapons from prehistoric times to our own, there are fine bronzes by Florentin Brigaud, the twentieth-century animal sculptor; seventy masterpieces by Desportes, official painter of the hunt to Louis XIV; two by Oudry, his successor in the next reign, and splendid Aubusson tapestries by René Perrot, an artist of our own epoch with a profound feeling for nature, revelling in all its colour and variety. At least an hour and a half is necessary to enjoy everything in the museum.

There are several reasonably-priced hotels in Gien and, on the south side of the river, a camp-site with very good shops near by.

Briare, which we passed by on the other side, is six miles back upstream. Its ancient name, derived from Gaulish words for bridge and gate, indicates that it was a road crossing in some remote period, but it has had no road-bridge in recorded times and its importance was not regained until the early seventeenth century when Henri IV's minister, Sully, ordered the construction of the Canal de Briare and the Canal de Loing, a continuous waterway to link the Loire with the Seine. In doing so, he was repairing an accident of nature; for once the Loire flowed through the same valley to the Seine, forming one of the series of great north-flowing rivers in the European Plain, with the Vistula, Oder, Elbe, Weser and Rhine, until the disturbances of Tertiary times deflected it to the left. A glance at the map shows that it is now 'odd man out'.

The Briare-Loing Canal is sixty-five miles long and has fifty-two locks; it joins the Seine at Saint-Mammes, thus extending the Canal Latéral so as to make it a highway through to the Channel, the North Sea and the waterways of northern Europe. In 1890, to save barges the risky crossing beam-on to the currents of the Loire, it was joined to the Canal Latéral by the prodigious aqueduct, the **Pont-Canal**, which is Briare's proud showpiece. It was designed by Eiffel and is in every way as breathtaking as his famous tower in Paris; more functional and, some may think, more beautiful. Coming into Briare from Gien, you first cross the old canal. Carry straight on through the town centre, which is not very large, and soon you come to another canal bridge; cross this and immediately turn right. This brings you alongside the canal basin which is usually a scene of animation – *péniches* loading and unloading; perhaps a yacht or two on their way through the canals to the Midi. There is plenty of room for parking and beside the quay is a good bar-restaurant. Two handsome stone pillars decorated with wrought-ironwork flank the head of the Pont-Canal. For nearly seven hundred yards it stretches away, diminishing in perspective as it spans the river. On each side is a wide pavement flanked by a stone balustrade so that you can stroll across – enjoying the views up and down the Loire – to the woods and open country of **Saint-Firmin** on the other shore.

The district to the north of Gien and Briare is known as the Gâtinais and is worth a little excursion if you have time. The term *gâtine* (from the same root as *gâter*, to spoil) implies land marshy and sterile by reason of impermeable subsoil, but this purely technical description evokes a picture much too grim. It is a pleasant countryside of gentle elevations, woods, lakes, quiet little streams and small fields, unsuitable for large-scale cultivation, but lending itself to such pursuits as rose-growing and market-gardening. At **La Bussière**, six miles north of Briare, is another specialized museum beside a lake and surrounded by a moat. Angling is the theme, and its very extensive exhibition is the best I have ever seen on the subject. (Open every day all the year round, 9 to noon and 2 to 6.) Only six miles beyond that is the forestry school at **Les Barres**, with an arboretum 700 acres in extent, 150 years old in parts and containing every tree and shrub capable of growing in the temperate zones. Permits to wander round at leisure are obtainable for the asking at the Secretariat fifty yards up the drive.

Then, just to the west, lies the eastern bloc of the Forêt d'Orléans, the largest domanial forest in France, extending in a great arc some thirty-five miles across and one hundred and thirty square miles in area from north of Orléans almost to Gien. It grows on an ancient flood-plain of granitic sand from the Massif Central laid down over the clay by the Loire in prehistoric times as it changed its course westwards. Motor vehicles are allowed along all surfaced forest roads (tarred or gravelled) and there are plenty more minor paths for those seeking solitude on foot. There are some fine sequoia trees, hornbeams and oaks in this section. Of the forest trees of France 35% are oak; the Forêt d'Orléans once exceeded this national average, but now it is well below it owing to indiscriminate felling for firewood for Orléans in the Middle Ages, and later for the navy, without leaving 'tellers' to regenerate the forest. Ours is not the only wasteful epoch. As a result, much of it became waterlogged – hence the many lakes and ponds you will find here – and can only be reclaimed with resinous plantations, including many of Scots pine.

CHAPTER THREE

Saint-Gondon; Sully and Saint-Benoît

❧

Let us return to the river now, where we left it at Gien. By re-crossing the bridge to the south bank and turning immediately right we come on to the Sully road and, after four miles, to the village of **Saint-Gondon**. A little river, the Quaiaulne, runs through it, once the frontier between the Bitururges (the Celtic tribe which gave its name to the Berry) and the Carnutes, whose territory lay to the west on both sides of the Loire. In the early fifteenth century a fortified wall was built right round the village to keep the English out; vestiges of it and of some of its *tourelles* are still tucked away among the houses and gardens on the perimeter.

Two miles outside the village, on the left and close beside the road, is a magnificent dolmen called locally the '*pierre-à-crapaud*' because of its astounding resemblance to a huge toad. To keep a sense of proportion for later on, it is worth stopping here to reflect upon this venerable object. Along this historic river valley – especially from now on – there are many impressive architectural remains from remote times of which we shall be reminded that this one or that is 'the oldest in France' of its kind. He would be insensitive indeed who could gaze into a Merovingian crypt without a thrill of awe. But supposing an early Phoenician trader passed by here at the time Solomon's temple was being built – which is quite possible – this Neolithic monument was older to him then than a Merovingian crypt is to us now. It was erected about 5000 years ago – before the first of the Egyptian pyramids!

Lion-en-Sullias has nothing of particular interest to offer except a signal-mound half a mile to the east of it from which the Carnutes kept an eye on the Bitururges who were keeping an eye on them from the mound at Saint-Gondon; so just after entering the village fork right on to the minor road which leads to the top of the flood-bank two miles farther on where you are greeted by a notice-board warning that you continue at your own risk. There is no need to be alarmed, however, as the surface is good and the road would be dangerous only in fog. For four miles you can drive along the top of the *levée* with the Loire as your companion: a most delightful run, for by now, well out on to its flood-plain, the river has taken on the added grace of maturity: it is wider, steadier and more imposing. And the first building we come to in **Sully** is the **château** (visits, conducted, Easter to 30 September, 9 to 11.45 and 2 to 5.45; off-season by arrangement). A solid medieval fortress surrounded by a moat, its massive weight still rests on the very same piles the Romans drove into the river-bed when they put up the original to protect the stone bridge they built across the Loire. It was to this first castle of the Romans that Pépin le Bref came in 752 and established his court and royal mint shortly after he had been elected King of the Franks at Soissons. His queen, Berthe-au-Grand-Pied, and the young Prince Charles would join him here 'in the fine season'. The last of the Merovingian kings, Childeric III, whom he had used as a political tool to bring France under one sceptre, he packed off to a monastery. Ramistan, Duc d'Aquitaine, who had opposed him in the final struggle, he brought with him and kept in chains in the dungeons for several years before he finally brought him out and hanged him from the castle wall. It is unfortunate that the generally mistranslated sobriquet of this powerful monarch, coupled with that of his queen, should evoke a slightly ludicrous mental picture which is far from the truth. He was not 'Pepin the Short' to his contemporaries: *le bref* signified 'the Little' or 'the Younger', to distinguish him from his grandfather of the same name. Poor Berthe did have a deformed foot, but she deserves sooner to be remembered as the mother of Charlemagne.

Through the centuries many more kings came to Sully and most of its owners seem to have played a part in whatever of consequence was happening in their time. The whole of this book would be insufficient to tell its story, which if fully related would fall not far short of an unbroken commentary on the history of France. One brief involvement with our own was in the time of Henri, Comte de Sully. Friend and Keeper of the Keys to Philippe V, *Bouteiller de France* with jurisdiction over all inns and refreshment-houses throughout the kingdom, he was enjoying a very comfortable life when in 1320 Charles de Valois, the King's uncle, asked him as a favour to undertake a short mission to Edward II to try to arrange a marriage between one of Charles's daughters and the Prince Edward. The English king at that time was preoccupied with Scottish troubles and about to make an expedition across the border; so to ingratiate himself Sully, with his escort of two knights, offered to take part. In a skirmish Edward's ineffective generalship got the

English force into a tight corner and they fled the field, leaving the three bewildered Frenchmen behind. After a thoroughly unpleasant time as prisoners of Bruce's Highlanders they were eventually ransomed. But Sully found that his helpfulness and his hardships had earned him nothing with the effeminate king; Valois's offer was refused and Sully came home considerably disillusioned with English ways. Had he been successful, the future Edward III would have been brother-in-law to the future Philippe VI and his territorial claims in France might have been settled more amicably. But this is only one of the many missed chances which could have avoided the Hundred Years' War.

In about 1360, after something like a millenium of 'make-do-and-mend', the old Roman castle, together with the bridge, was swept away by an exceptional flood. The bridge was not replaced until the existing very fine suspension bridge slung from stone towers was put up in 1836. Until then Sully had to make do with a ferry. But they began rebuilding the castle right away, and already in 1363 the roof-frame of the keep had been installed. It is still there after 600 years: a masterpiece of mighty craftsmanship. Because sweet chestnut was used, a timber particularly unloved by insects, it is free from beetles, flies and cobwebs, as clean as if it had gone up last week. Like the framework of a great boat turned upside down, with massive ribs curving across to meet the roof-tree like a keel in the centre, the whole structure, which is of enormous proportions, rests of its own weight on the tops of the stone walls. There are no cross-beams or other support whatever, all the required strength being in the balanced counter-stresses of the Gothic arches formed by each pair of ribs. It was made by Tévenon Foucher, a simple master carpenter of the district, and he was paid 'five tuns of wine of the value of VIII *écus* and XXIV *écus* for his wages, not counting a *muid* [about sixty bushels] of corn'.

The château was captured by the Burgundians in 1428, but Georges de la Tremoïlle, the *comte* of that time, had it peacefully handed back to him in what some people considered rather suspicious circumstances. Even so, the following year, just after Joan of Arc had delivered Orléans, he succeeded in luring the Dauphin here where he could more effectively subject him to his baneful influence. By means of her womanly tantrums at Gien, as we have seen, Joan managed to get Charles away to be anointed at Reims; but he came back to Sully and when she herself returned in March 1430, La Tremoïlle persuaded him to keep her there virtually as a prisoner.

He was plotting an 'accidental' fall into the river for her when she quietly escaped one night with her page D'Aulon and a few other faithfuls. She never saw her King again, and a few weeks later fell into the hands of the enemy.

The most celebrated owner of Sully was not a Tremoïlle, but the man who bought it from the last of that family in 1602 – Maximilien de Béthune, chief minister to Henri IV and one of Europe's greatest statesmen of all time – better remembered as the duc de Sully, since the King soon raised the barony into a dukedom in his honour. To his new home he immediately applied the same creativeness and genius for organization that he had shown in affairs of state, and restored it from the condition of dilapidation into which it had fallen. It was he who moved the flood-bank northwards to bring the château ashore, so to speak – for until then it had stood in the river – and constructed the moat which not only surrounds it but carries on eastwards for a considerable distance to form a beautiful sheet of water called La Sange.

From the Allée des Tilleuls on the opposite bank you can fish at any time of the year (permits from any of the several shops in the town that sell fishing tackle); it is stocked with bream, roach and carp, and if you fail to catch anything the cause is likely to be that the splendid view of the château across the water has absorbed more attention than your float.

Beside the château is the park where Sully indulged his passion for planting trees. It is open to the public. No detail was ever too small for his attention: when he decided to have three rabbit-hutches in the park he designed them himself and the local odd-job man had to enter into a written contract wherein he undertook 'to construct the same according to the plans which Monseigneur has furnished to the contractor'. We still see Sully's office in the château, modest enough in size, but like every other room in his own quarters, sumptuously ornamented. He lived simply, was careful with his money, but he liked a bit of show. It was in this little room where he dictated his famous memoirs, and they were secretly printed on a press set up in one of the towers. When the book was published the title-page showed the name of an imaginary printer in Amsterdam. Why the subterfuge no one really knows, but it may have been another instance of his cheese-paring economy. He lived to be eighty-two (thirty-nine years after acquiring Sully) and towards the end of his life he developed many other oddities of character: he would often be seen wandering in the grounds in a parody of state splendour, followed by a guard of half a dozen elderly horsemen, himself dressed in outmoded finery taken from the back of his wardrobe where it had rested among the moths since his great days at the court of the Vert-Gallant. In the outer courtyard stands a fine statue of him, executed for his second wife by an unidentified Italian sculptor soon after his death. At the Revolution the Convention ordered that it be broken up, but it was saved by the Deputy Le Noir whom we have to thank for many similar rescues. A true likeness, as comparison with contemporary portraits confirms, it shows the real Sully as he was in the days of his greatness: the features and the attitude are those of a strong, dependable, thoughtful and honest man, fit indeed to be the well-loved companion and trusted minister of a great prince; indeed a friend whom anyone would be grateful to have in difficult times.

When Voltaire was exiled from the court in 1716 he was given shelter at Sully by the great-great-grandson of the first duke, and he repaid his host by putting his own special talents at the disposal of the household: he enlivened the conversation, wrote elegant verses and left them on people's plates before dinner; and he wrote *Oedipe*, his first play, for which the *salle d'honneur* on the first floor was converted into a theatre so it could be produced for the Duke's guests. Among these was an attractive young hussy of twenty-two, the same age as Voltaire: Suzanne de Livry from Henrichemont near Sancerre, whose ambition was to be an actress; and in him she saw her chance. She deliberately made herself his mistress and after he was allowed back in the capital, where the play was a tremendous success, she wheedled out of him the leading role of Jocaste. But alas! her ability was not up to her ambitions and was further hampered by the regional brogue of her native Berry. Her solecisms drew contemptuous laughter from the sophisticated audience at the Comédie Française, and when he gave her the lead in his next play, *Artémire* (also written at Sully on a second visit), she was whistled and hooted off the stage; whereupon Voltaire gallantly went on himself and addressed the audience in her defence. It was his first real love-affair and he was blinded to her defects by other attractions not known to his audience. He referred to these in a poem about her long after they parted company:

> *Deux tétons que le tendre Amour*
> *De ses mains arrondit un jour,*
> *Un coeur simple, un esprit volage,*
> *Un cul (j'y pense encore, Philis)*
> *Sur qui j'ai vu briller des lis*
> *Jaloux de ceux de ton visage.*

But she had to be replaced all the same; and having no further use for him she went to London to try her luck on the stage there – with the same unhappy results. The Marquis de Gouvernet, who was French Ambassador there at the time, found her destitute and fell in love with her. His initial courtship with flowers was repulsed by the proud young lady, but when he tried Indies lottery tickets and one came up, her heart gave way and she married him. Voltaire retained an affection for her all his life, and in fact they met in Paris at his request in 1778, both octogenarians, a few weeks before he died.

Of the original town of Sully not much remains. During the fighting in June 1940 the centre was virtually wiped out by German bombardment. Then four years later, when the storm-tide of war turned the other way, Sully was again caught in the current. The same fleet of fifty Flying Fortress bombers which had just visited Gien appeared high overhead in the peaceful summer evening sky and dropped a load of bombs to cut the bridgehead. All was over in about a minute and Saint-Germain, the old quarter of the town, lay in ruins to match the rest. Walking round the streets now, it is hard to believe all this happened as there is no monotonous uniformity to betray the fact that the town has been rebuilt; but the tall spire of Saint-Germain, which dominates the skyline to the west, gives the game away on close inspection for it stands in the ruins of the shattered and abandoned church. The other church, **Saint Ythier**, in the town centre close to the *mairie*, like the château escaped serious damage in the war. In fact it suffered worse four centuries ago when it was devastated by the Huguenot armies. It then stood in the grounds of the château and Maximilien got the ruins with his purchase. Being a Protestant he had no need of a Catholic church himself, but the town had, for it had grown eastwards away from Saint-Germain, its parish church. So he had the stones carefully numbered and re-erected the complete building on the spot where it now stands. On the façade is a statue of Maurice de Sully, to whom Paris owes its great cathedral. Born in the early twelfth century, he was not related at all to the nobility at the château, but came from a very poor family in the town. He entered the priesthood, where his exceptional ability soon attracted attention. He was still poor when his superiors offered him a sinecure on condition he should renounce all future right to a bishopric. Someone seems to have foreseen his possible destiny, but so had he and he refused. Instead he made his way to Paris where in 1160 he was elected Bishop. Only three years later he had put in hand the work

Blois: Spiral staircase in the
courtyard of the Château

Orléans Cathedral

Gien

Saint Benoît: West front of the Benedictine abbey

on Notre Dame, which was his own conception, and he devoted the rest of his life to the supervision of it. When he died in 1196 the chancel was roofed, and it fell to his successor, Eudes de Sully – who *was* one of the château family – to finish the work and take the glory.

A useful point to remember about Sully is that it has a very good market which is held on Monday, the day when in other towns most of the shops are closed and you can buy little more than a packet of Gauloises, a newspaper and a loaf of bread. At Sully you can stock up for a feast.

An ideal excursion from Sully is to take the Tigy road out of the town as far as the village of **Bouteille**. From here you can drive along the top of the *levée* for another four miles, following great loops of the river. It is all very peaceful and beautiful.

But our way on must be by crossing the river at Sully to the right bank so we do not miss **Saint-Benoît**, which is often disregarded by foreign visitors though discerning Frenchmen consider it the finest pearl on the whole string of the Val de Loire. Take the Orléans road and very soon the abbey looms on the horizon like a stately ship on a calm sea of open fields.

Immediately on entering **Fleury**, which is on the outskirts of Saint-Benoît and was the original village, by the roadside on the right you will see the Fontaine-Saint-Sebastien where a spring wells up at the base of a shrine containing a statue of the saint. It is one of many sacred springs in this area where a large number of Gaulish remains have been found – nothing spectacular enough to go and look at, but unusually concentrated within a radius of about seven miles. The preponderance of archaeological opinion now is that somewhere here was the 'umbilical centre' (*omphalos*) of Gaul to which Caesar refers in book VII of his *Gallic Wars*, the geographical middle point of the Gauls' territory and the chief *locus consecratus* of their Druids. When the monks came here in the early seventh century to recall the inhabitants from the paganism into which they had relapsed, they had powerful local traditions of the old gods to contend with. As soon as possible the springs were re-allocated to Christian saints: Saint Anthony, Saint James and Saint Aignan all have their holy wells near by. Nor did Léodobod, the founder of the Benedictine abbey, well endowed with the practical common sense of his Order, overlook the unusual fertility of the soil with which the ancient cults appear to have been connected. He was a wealthy man and he exchanged other lands belonging to him for Floriacum, 'the Golden Valley' as it was generally known in his time. Its fertility is still exceptional and the local peasant farmers – most of whom specialize in market-gardening – are a comfortably prosperous and happy people. Léodobod built his monastery downstream of the village, and in his Will of AD 651 he bequeathed the whole domain of the Val d'Or to the monks.

It was the second abbot, Mommole, who conceived the daring idea of removing by stealth the relics of Saint Benedict from the ruins of faraway Monte Cassino, laid waste by the Lombards over a century before. He sent a small party of monks there in 703 under the leadership of Aigulf. Research had been thorough so that, like any other competent burglar, Aigulf knew the lay-out of the place to be burgled and the exact spot to make for. The sepulchre was broken open and the bones of the saint, with those of his sister, Saint Scholastica, were wrapped in linen and placed on a horse. It was a dangerous journey of 700 miles back to Fleury; and in gratitude for the escort of a party of monks from Le Mans he fell in with, Aigulf gave them the remains of Saint Scholastica. There was great indignation when the Italian monks heard of this bold feat of pious larceny, and legal proceedings dragged on for many years until the Pope finally authorized the retention of the relics at Fleury on a small portion being returned to the claimants.

The **abbey** of Saint-Benoît, as it was henceforth called, did not waste the gifts and endowments which began to pour in from wealthy pilgrims. It soon became one of the most celebrated centres of learning in Europe, with dependent houses in many parts of France and one in England: at Minting near Horncastle in Lincolnshire. It was also during this period of its first flowering that Oswald, a monk of Saint-Benoît, became Bishop of Worcester and founded Pershore Abbey there before he eventually went on to occupy the see of York. But these days of glory were not free from tribulation. When periodically the Norsemen came pillaging up the Loire, the prosperous region around Orléans was where they generally stopped to disport themselves most. Whenever a raid was on its way, the relics were removed to safety within the walls of Orléans; but a tenth-century chronical relates that on occasion the indignant saint re-assembled himself and sallied forth on horseback to fight the heathen in person. In 1026 an accidental fire destroyed the abbey; but within a year or two a new church began to rise and it is the one we see today. Abbot Gauzlin, a natural son of Hugh Capet, first built the west belfry-tower and porch; his successors followed with the chancel, transept and crypt which were completed in 1108, and the nave followed about half a century later.

The result was the finest abbey church in the Loire Valley, and the new monastery buildings corresponded in magnificence. But this glorious phoenix arisen from the flames was not a very lively bird. 'Perfection of planned lay-out is achieved only by institutions on the point of collapse' is one of Professor Northcote Parkinson's maxims, a seeming paradox of which he cites several historical examples, including Versailles. Sad to say, he could have included Saint-Benoît. Soon after the new building was complete its glory in spiritual matters and in learning entered on a period of steady decline, the virtual culmination of which was symbolical: the indignity of being looted again, not by Norsemen, but by one of its own abbots. Odet de Coligny, brother of the Huguenot leader, was converted to the Protestant religion. Making use of his inside knowledge of the valuable objects which the abbey contained, he arranged for it to be sacked by Condé's troops and had the booty sold. Amongst it went the library, assembled over the previous 700 years; more than two thousand manuscripts were dispersed far and wide. Many are now untraceable; some are at Oxford, and some even in Moscow.

At the Revolution the almost defunct abbey was closed down, and in the nineteenth century the conventual buildings were demolished leaving only a dilapidated church. Small parties of caretaker monks came back from time to time and looked after the shrine, but it was not until 1944 that the present full community was established. The church was restored first and now the convent is being rebuilt to the south of it. The intellectual and spiritual life of the abbey is flourishing again and there seems no doubt that it has entered on a new era of great importance.

On coming into the centre of Saint-Benoît look out for signs on the left for '*La Basilique*', and they will bring you to a quiet square in front of the abbey where there is room to park under the lime trees. The great belfry of Gauzlin stands before you, supported on the fifty columns of its porch. The stone, mellowed to gold during 900 years and best seen in evening sunlight, was brought down the river from the Nivernais in boats. The only addition is the lantern-tower, put there in 1661 to replace the original top. In 1525 François I nominated his chancellor, Cardinal Duprat, as commendatory abbot. This practice of appointing favourites of the Crown (often laymen) as absentee abbots to provide sinecures had begun in the fourteenth century. It was a fraudulent imposition and a contributory factor in the corruption of monastic life. The community at Saint-Benoît did not want Duprat and refused to receive him; so to make his wishes clear the King came in person with a small army. When the monks took refuge in the tower he knocked the top off it, where-upon they took the hint and accepted the Cardinal after all. Walk into the porch and you see that each of the columns is topped with an elaborately carved capital. Some depict leaves and plants in the formal and truly Romanesque style. The rest are humans, devils, goblins and animals of disproportionate shapes and sizes: some comic, some hideous and unpleasant. A few still have eyeballs of lead which would have been polished originally to give an illusion of a strange, other-worldly life looking down on the world of mortals. To supply the right malevolent glint, little pieces of shiny coal would be used for the devils' eyes.

On entering the twelfth-century nave with its central vaulting of ogival arches we are in the age of the Gothic. In the chancel there is a Roman mosaic floor brought from Italy when it was built and, on its north side, the sarcophagus of Philippe I who was buried here at his own request in 1108. In the course of repairs to the tomb in 1830 the body was found to have been wrapped in herbs as the last stage of embalming and the leaves of wild mint, walnut, sage, balm and melissa were still identifiable. In the north transept, between two tiny chapels opening off, is a relic of Saint Benedict behind an iron grille, and on the wall facing it is an effigy of a Viking head (not a big one; you have to look carefully for it), a twelfth-century copy of a tenth-century original. The cheeks are pierced as an exorcism to prevent the spirit of the pagan from polluting the sanctuary. He was Reynaldus, a ferocious pirate chief who came from Rouen to sack the abbey, but he hurried home and died of fright after the saint appeared to him in a dream and clouted him over the head with his crozier. The effigy was put in the church to commemorate the miracle. Down the steps at the end of the north aisle is the very beautiful crypt where the relics of the saint are deposited in a little cell cut out of the central pillar which supports the high altar in the church above. A little door at its southern end leads to a small chapel which is a tenth-century portion of the original monastery, the only piece remaining.

Saint-Benoît is renowned for its Gregorian chant, although if you praise it to one of the monks he will remember his vow and tell you it is not as good as it should be, or even '*très mauvais*'. But I do have one criticism: the nave has been fitted up with loudspeakers which sometimes distort the sound rather badly. For this reason I advise those with a fastidious ear to attend one of the lesser-frequented services, such as Nones at 3 or Vespers at 6.15, when the microphones are turned lower, although Conventual Mass (11 Sundays; 12 weekdays) is grander and more impressive. Formal visits, conducted by one of the monks, take place every day, except in winter when they are only on Sundays. Times vary, so enquiry should be made at the monastery bookshop to the right of the porch – a very good shop, incidentally, well stocked and nothing tawdry. Visitors are welcome to look around on their own when services are not in progress, though it is unfair to interrogate at length any monk who happens to be about; in so doing one could be upsetting his whole day's programme. The great distinguishing feature of the Rule of Saint Benedict is *work*.

In the main street of the village, on the right of the Café de la Ville, is the house where Max Jacob lived. Son of a Jewish tailor in Brittany, he was born in 1876. As a young man he went to Paris where after several years of struggle he achieved recognition as a painter and a poet and shared the Bohemian life of Picasso, Braque and Cocteau, who became his intimate friends. In 1915 he embraced Christianity and Picasso was godfather at his baptism. Six years later he forsook the capital for Saint-Benoît, explaining to his friends: 'My life is one of unhappiness because I can no longer sin with pleasure.' Here he remained, apart from some breaks in the early thirties when the old life drew him back, and his new day-to-day friends were the village people. He is still remembered by the older generation not only for his sincere piety, but for his gaiety and informality; he loved practical jokes, everyone knew him as 'Max' and he preferred to be addressed with the familiar *tu*. When the Nazis came they made him wear the humiliating yellow star, but this made no difference to his attitude nor to that of anyone else. On 23 February 1944 the Gestapo came to his house and arrested him. On the train to the prison-camp at Drancy, he managed to get a note off to Cocteau; even his guards could not see the sense in taking away a man of sixty-eight in failing health so they connived and kindly posted it for him. Cocteau immediately compiled a petition to the German Embassy for his release and it was signed by all his old friends – except his distinguished godfather who did not wish to be compromised and when approached replied: 'It's not worth the trouble. Max is sharp enough; he doesn't need us to get him out of gaol.' The petition was nevertheless successful and an order was sent to Drancy for his release. But by the time his friends got there to collect him, he had died of pneumonia in the prison hospital – not without a touch of the comedy he always enjoyed when, with careful tact to cushion the shock, he asked the fellow Jewish prisoners at his bedside to send for a Catholic priest.

The poetry of Max Jacob, which is the most significant part of his work, has been neglected; but some consider him the greatest French poet of his time. Cocteau said of him: 'With Apollinaire, he has invented a language which dominates our language and gives voice to the depths.' Max was always ready to help and encourage young aspirants and his influence on the next generation has been considerable: even affecting song-writers like Charles Trenet who in the thirties rescued popular song lyrics from the banality into which they had sunk. The first essential in poetry, Max Jacob taught, is emotion: the second is clarity. He revolted against obscurity in any of the arts, and the best poetry in his view is such that even an uneducated peasant on hearing it would say 'Ah! how lovely!' and not 'What does it mean?'

To get to the riverside at Saint-Benoît, drive out of the centre along the Saint-Germigny road and take the left turn on the outskirts, signposted *'Le Port'*. No boats come there now to bring coal, timber and stone or to load corn, as they did for centuries until the last one; but some of the old *mariniers'* houses still remain. There is room to park on the grass and the little 'Auberge du Port' serves simple meals at reasonable prices – outside in its shaded courtyard, in fine weather. Near by on a wall, heights of three notable floods are marked. Saint-Benoît has been relatively fortunate in the great spates of the past. Even so, a glance at the marks before us, plus a little imagination, evokes a sad enough scene.

Saint-Benoît is a good place for an overnight stop. There is a small peaceful camp-site near the port, among trees and with provision for safe swimming; and back in the village there are two unpretentious, but well-run, hotels – La Madeleine (one-star, very good cuisine) and Le Saint (very much simpler, but the one used by passing *routiers*, which in France is invariably a guarantee of reasonableness and wholesomeness).

CHAPTER FOUR

Germigny-des-Prés to Combleux

❦

Immediately after leaving Saint-Benoît the road comes up on to the *levée* again, close alongside a particularly beautiful stretch of the river with several sandy islands where terns breed in the spring. It is generally supposed it was here that Caesar made his unexpected crossing of the Loire in 52 BC just after his defeat at Gergovia. It was still early spring and the snows of the Auvergne had begun to melt sufficiently to swell the river, but not enough to render the Cevennes passable so he could retreat on Provence and obtain food for his army. All villages and farms near the high-roads had been burnt down on the orders of the ruthlessly efficient Gallic leader Vercingétorix ('This is no time to cling to the sweets of private property,' he told the unfortunate peasants) so that Roman foraging parties had to venture far from their camp into open country where the Gallic cavalry could pick them off at leisure. It seemed Vercingétorix had Caesar trapped. Caesar's only hope was to join up with Labienus who was likewise cut off near Sens, fifty miles away to the north-east; but the river barred the way. All bridges had been destroyed, and it was never Caesar's policy to undertake the 'dangerous task of constructing bridges in the face of the enemy', to use his own words. So he sent patrols along the river bank to seek a ford, and along here they found a place where a man could cross with arms and shoulders clear of the water. By forced marches he quickly brought his army to the spot and got it safely across, the infantry wading through the freezing winter waters with their weapons held high while 'to break the force of the current, the horsemen made a living dam across the stream'. Looking at the river now, it is difficult to visualize such a proceeding in a time of semi-spate until one remembers that the Loire was not restricted between artificial banks in those days: it would be more widely spread across the plain and the current less concentrated. The manoeuvre would be one of those *just* possible things which most people think impossible – as the Gauls did – an opportunity for one of those military surprises that contributed so much to Caesar's success.

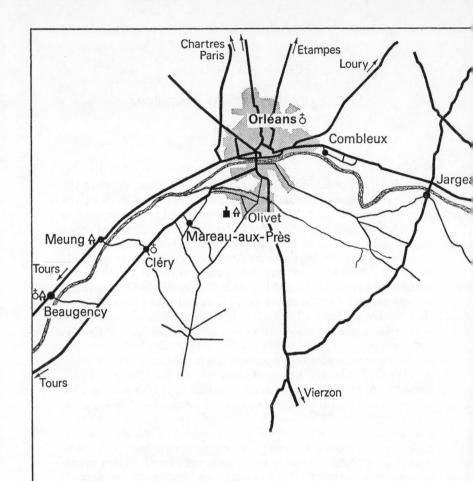

Sully to Orléans

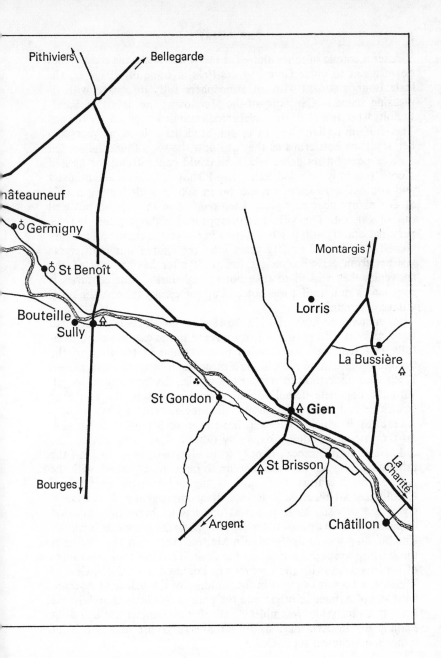

After a couple of miles along the top of the *levée*, the road comes down again to enter **Germigny-des-Prés**, a tranquil village by the little Bonnée stream with an atmosphere fully in accord with its pleasing name – Germigny-of-the-Meadows. The abbot of Saint-Benoît who founded the celebrated monastic school there was Theodulf, an Italian Goth by origin. Students a thousand years ago being just as boisterous as they are now, he soon found he needed a more peaceful residence where he could concentrate; for he had plenty to occupy his mind, being also Bishop of Orléans and minister and counsellor to Charlemagne. So in 806 he built himself a villa at Germigny: near enough to keep control of the school, but well out of earshot. The villa has disappeared without trace, but his personal oratory still partly survives in the **parish church** after many vicissitudes. Less than fifty years after the church was built, some visitors from Scandinavia set fire to it after having selected the souvenirs they wished to take home, and during four centuries it remained a ruin until it was botched up sufficiently to serve the small village community.

So matters continued until in the 1840s a mosaic ceiling which had been covered with plaster was discovered in the east apse and carefully restored. This reawakened interest; and in the time of the Second Empire there came along a rather ham-fisted amateur named Lisch who undertook to restore the whole. His 'restoration' began with the complete demolition of everything except the east apse (which he had to leave because of the precious mosaic) and an ugly square tower which could well have been dispensed with anyway. So the present building, frequently described as 'unique' and 'the oldest church in France', is only so in a certain sense. At least the rebuilding followed the original plan so far as possible and, with the genuine ninth-century east apse, is the only sizable example of Carolingian architecture in France. It is unmistakably Byzantine in style, and to visualize it as it was one has to forget the nave and replace it with an apse of the same pattern as the three existing ones. The building was in the form of a Maltese cross, and the outline of the missing west apse is clear on the floor. Theodulf took advantage of his friendship with the Emperor to borrow his architect, Odo of Messina, who was engaged in the building of the palace at Aachen. Odo was of Armenian origin and the plan of this little church in the French countryside resembles that of the famous cathedral at Echmiatzin in Armenia: as an architectural prototype it is of important technical significance.

No less important, from the artistic point of view, is the mosaic on the ceiling of the east apse. It was already at least 300 years old when Theodulf brought it from Ravenna – most likely from the ruins of the palace of Theodoric, King of the Goths, who had been an Arian heretic. Charlemagne was busy stripping it too, for decorations for his new palace at Aachen. Composed of 130,000 cubes of coloured glass, it depicts the Ark of the Covenant with the hand of God in the sky above and two angels beside it. The inscription round the edge, in silver letters on a field of blue, entreats us in Theodulf's own words to revere the ark of the Divine Testament, to serve the God of Thunder (of Sinai), and to mention the name of Theodulf in our prayers. Looking up into this cupola, we are gazing on what Charlemagne gazed upon without doubt, standing on the same spot nearly twelve hundred years ago, for he used to visit Theodulf here at Germigny. Shortly after the death of his old friend, Theodulf fell foul of his son, Louis le Débonnaire, and died in prison at Angers in 820.

Other items to notice are the alabaster windows in the end of the apse – another original feature – and the early-sixteenth-century carved wooden statue of Saint Anne teaching the infant Virgin to read. Saint Anne is portrayed as a peasant woman of the region, and Anatole France considered that the little scene contains 'all the wisdom of the Val de Loire'. If the caretaker is about – a most obliging lady who lives near by – she will unlock the vestry for you so you may see the beautiful little twelfth-century reliquary made of copper covered in Limoges enamel, and the fifteenth-century mirror hanging on the vestry cupboard, which the present priest still uses when he combs his hair before going into church.

In the garden outside the church, where in spring there is a mass of tamarisk in bloom, a sixteenth-century stone *lanterne des morts* stands beside the pathway. Such lanterns were placed in the cemetery the night before a burial was to take place. Also there is a seventeenth-century weathercock, most handsome and expressive, but it is a pity they had to stick it in the top of the lantern – on the same principle, presumably, as mixing the port with the sherry.

Just after Germigny we cross the Bonnée near an old watermill, its last before it runs into the Loire a mile away across the fields. The little meadow by the bridge is a traditional stopping-place for the ancient Gypsy families who ascend the valley during the spring and summer and sometimes their gaily-painted *roulottes* will be drawn up by the stream. Another colourful rarity I have seen in these meadows in the springtime is the swallowtail butterfly, but – as with the Gypsies – there is little use in searching for it: it is just a matter of luck.

In less than a couple of miles we are in the small market-town of **Châteauneuf-sur-Loire**, a favourite of mine and a place which is sadly undervalued (even sometimes derided) in many guidebooks. Its historical associations are quite fascinating and enough remains of its historic buildings to conjure up the past with a little imagination; its ambience is delightful; its shops are small, plentiful and good, and it has two reasonably-priced hotels (the Capitainerie and the Nouvel Hôtel du Loiret) and a camp-site by the river. Here is one of those places where a whole holiday could be spent in quiet contentment – especially by a nature-lover. For it has beautiful riverside walks where willow-warblers and reed-buntings can be seen, as well as waterfowl, terns, big carp and occasionally a leaping salmon. And its wild park, planted with rare trees and shrubs, is the haunt of red squirrels, woodpeckers, tree-creepers, and even kingfishers by the stream which flows from a waterfall gushing out of the hillside.

There are more Châteauneufs in France than there are Newcastles in England. The 'new' **castle** here was built in about the tenth century and was a royal domain until sold in the seventeenth century. Philippe I sometimes resided here and he enlarged it. The early Capetian kings spent a great deal of their time in their castles of the Loire; sometimes for safety when things became too precarious in Paris, sometimes to be nearer the centre of the country to exercise control in troubled times. Our old friend Louis le Gros was one of the latter; also Saint Louis, and his grandson Philippe le Bel, who was here often enough to deem it worthwhile to buy up twenty-six houses for demolition to enlarge the park. He spent Christmas here in 1308, whiling away the festive season in gambling. The royal accounts disclose that on Christmas Day *'le seigneur roy'* lost seventeen *livres*, and on the following Friday fifty-six *livres*, fifteen *sous*, four *deniers*, *'gagnés par P. de Varnes, le cadet'*. Obviously a bold young fellow, Monsieur de Varnes, daring to win so much from the fearsome *'Roi de Fer'*.

When insecurity returned at the end of the century under the Valois, Châteauneuf was occupied by the English several times, but fell again into the Dauphin's hands in 1428. On 24 June the following year the Dauphin came dithering into the town from Sully on his way downstream, held the council which decided on the consecration at Reims, and went trotting off back up the valley to Gien to dither again. In the Religious Wars the town was occupied so many times by the various contestants that the château became a useless ruin. In 1646 Mazarin procured its sale on behalf of the infant Louis XIV to Michel Particelli, Superintendent of Finance, one of his compatriots, who gave it to his son-in-law, Louis Phélypeaux de la Vrillière. It was this first private owner who built the magnificent new château, a miniature Versailles and in the same architectural style. He even got Le Nôtre to lay out the gardens, but these, like most of the château, disappeared in the years following the Revolution. In front of the terrace now one sees a landscape of fields and woods down to the river, which some may think more pleasing than a set of Euclidian problems solved in flower-beds.

Of the château itself there remain only the rotunda (now the town hall); a pavilion (called '*l'horloge*' although it no longer has a clock); some stables and an orangery, one of the largest and most elegantly proportioned in France, but without any orange-trees, the last of them having been borrowed at the Revolution for a 'Feast of Nature and Reason' in Orléans and never returned. Entry to the grounds is open to all and there is plenty of parking-space through the big iron gates. It is pleasant to walk round and admire the buildings, and beyond lies the park which I shall mention later.

The reign of the La Vrillières at Châteauneuf ended with the third generation, another Louis. He had a silver hand, to replace one blown off when his gun exploded while out shooting one day. Louis XV thought most highly of him and once said to him: 'Friend, you have only one arm, but remember I have two to serve you.' Some others took a different view. On his death Voltaire composed an epitaph referring to him as 'a rather common little man' who had 'born three names and left none'. Another wit bemoaned him with the words:

> Having only one arm,
> He stole by others' hands.

and the famous silver hand was itself stolen on the day of his funeral – a fact which gave rise to some disappointment when the *sans-culottes* eagerly opened the coffin in 1793.

Not long after La Vrillière's death the estate was bought by its most interesting and most tragic owner, Louis-Jean-Marie de Bourbon, duc de Penthièvre, grandson of Louis XIV and Madame de Montespan. In features he greatly resembled the Sun King, but with a pensive sadness about the eyes and an expression of the mouth that betrayed sympathy and kindness. This brave and competent soldier, son of the celebrated Toulouse, extremely wealthy man with estates at Rambouillet, Eu, Vernon and Dreux, was one of the few of his kind who showed active concern about the social inequalities and poverty of the time. Living the life almost of a monk, he devoted all his spare time to the relief of suffering and want on his estates. Donning an apron, he would go into the kitchen to supervise personally the meals being cooked for his pensioners; each of his estates had its *bureau de charité* to find out who needed help and to see that they got it (the one at Châteauneuf still survives as a local charity), and he even salaried the poachers so they would not need to poach. To improve the lot of the *mariniers* of the town he had the magnificent quays constructed to the east of the bridge which still bear his name. And to create employment for others he planted 5000 mulberry trees along the left bank; set up a silk factory, and publicized it by exhibiting the products in the gallery at the château.

When the Revolution came the Duke tried to go along with it, recognizing that much of the resentment and discontent was justifiable. His grandson, the duc de Chartres (destined to become the memorable Louis-Philippe, 'King of the French', and a red-hot Republican at the time) records in his diary a visit to Châteauneuf in November 1790: on the Sunday – 'I have been to Mass; there was no incense: my grandfather has insisted that the decrees of the National Assembly be observed to the letter.' In the same year the Duke gave his gold and silver plate to the Revolutionary funds, considering them a gift to the nation in time of need. But finally, while returning through the streets of Châteauneuf on 14 July 1791 after publicly swearing allegiance to the new Constitution, he was insulted by a local hothead and left the town for good, completely disillusioned. His sincerely well-intentioned actions had been too late, too exceptional and unsupported; unreasoning hatred was taking over and they alone could not stem *'le déluge'*. Penthièvre died at Vernon on 4 March 1793, only a month before the Convention ordered the arrest of all remaining Bourbons and the confiscation of their property, thereby just cheating the guillotine.

As soon as the decree was published his château was officially pillaged; the mulberry trees cut down to put an end to the manufacture of wasteful aristocratic silk, and the silks he had displayed in the gallery were burnt – together with his library and his collection of pictures which included works by Boucher, Veronese, Titian, Rubens, Holbein and Breughel, just to mention a few from the tantalizing list. The Commissaire Lambert in charge of these patriotic proceedings was a very thorough official who paid great attention to detail. In his dispatch he reports how, in addition to the *abominables personnages* portrayed in the pictures, there were two made of straw, twin dressed-dolls belonging to the Duchess of Orléans, 'one called Coxigru and the other Ritentum. Well, I had these characters stripped and their clothes sent to the municipality for the poor.'

The owner of the ill-fated Coxigru and Ritentum was Penthièvre's daughter Adelaide, who had made rather a wreck of her life by marrying the despicable Philippe Égalité. Of the Duke's six children only two had survived to get married and in both cases – in different ways – the results added to his cup of misery before he died. His son, Louis de Bourbon de Lamballe, married Marie-Thérèse de Carignon, a princess of Savoy, but he died within a year, at the age of only twenty, from the effects of dissipation. The princesse Lamballe became a close friend of Marie-Antoinette and on 3 September 1792, in the yard of the La Force prison in Paris, she was butchered in a most horrible way. Afterwards her head was cut off and paraded on a pike before the royal apartments at the Temple, where the King's valet noticed the poignant detail that her long fair hair was floating round the shaft. The news of his daughter-in-law's terrible end broke Penthièvre's heart, but he lived yet long enough to hear of the death of the King and to share Adelaide's shame at Égalité's part in it, and her concern for her own future.

Eventually Adelaide had to flee the country, and after many years of exile she returned to Dreux. In 1818 she came to look at Châteauneuf, to find only the few remains of the family château that we see now, and those in ruins. She returned to Dreux and died there three years later, too soon to see her son wielding his umbrella sceptre as the Citizen King.

The château had in fact been bought by Benoît Lebrun, an architect on the municipal staff at Orléans who specialized in picking up bargains in émigré and Church property. He had already bought the abbey at Saint-Benoît and begun demolishing it for building-stone. At Châteauneuf he knocked down what he could not afford to maintain and retained the rest as his home. It was his daughter, Eulalie Ladureau, who redeemed the situation to some extent when she succeeded him, by employing Huillard d'Hérou, Inspector of Libraries at Orléans, to restore the park. D'Hérou was not a professional landscape gardener, but a keen and very learned amateur botanist. He decided not to attempt to re-create Le Nôtre's design, but to make a new park in the English style. Leaving the stream and its cascade as a natural feature and the duc de Penthièvre's avenue of beautiful limes (still surviving and called the Allée Lamballe), he replanted all the rest in 1821 with four hundred and fifty different species of tree and shrub, among them thirty-four different kinds of oak, sixty-one of hawthorn, thirty-seven of rhododendron and twenty-six of azalea, as well as giant tulip-trees from Virginia and dainty-leafed cypresses from China.

The part of the park beside the château now belongs to the municipality and is open to the public. Nothing has been done to alter the informal character which D'Hérou intended, though many of his rarities have since perished one way or another, or (like many of the rhododendrons) reverted to more ordinary types. Others (like the tulip-trees) have grown to majestic proportions, and there are giant-flowered rhododendrons which provide a rare spectacle in May. There are some large and reverend carp in a section of the former moat which you may feed, but not of course catch. (The angler seeking carp stands his best chance along the wooded shore of the **Chastaing** upstream of the bridge, which is also another pleasant place just to wander in.)

The whole of Châteauneuf's two miles or more of riverside paths is in fact one delightful promenade. The fine suspension bridge which graces the river scene was built in 1936 by the local firm of Baudin. In the war it was broken by letting the cables go. The German authorities in the occupation forbade its repair, so Baudins secretly assembled all the necessary parts and restored it as soon as they had gone.

Not only the bridge, but a great part of the town, suffered in the war. The main street was reduced to ruins in the bombing of 1940, and the **church** with its wasp-waist bears testimony to those unhappy times; it caught fire and part of the nave collapsed. Instead of attempting the costly task of rebuilding, the Castelneuvians converted this section into a rather pleasant, and useful, arcade leading into the next street. The remainder of their restoration fund they spent on a really fine organ, built by Robert Boisseau, who is the expert in charge of maintenance of the organ at Notre Dame. Several recitals are held here each year by leading organists in France and from abroad. There is a very important work of sculpture inside the church, which was saved from Revolutionary wreckers by being hidden behind a pile of barrels. This is a statue of the elder Louis de la Vrillière by Domenico Guidi (1626–1701) who also sculpted the *Renommée* in the Bassin Neptune at Versailles. Guidi did the work in Italy and the whole massive affair of heavy marble was brought here by sea and up the Loire, just as the *Renommée* was transported to Versailles via the Seine. An arcade is supported by caryatids, macabre skeletons but wonderfully executed, and the statue beneath has La Vrillière down on one knee while an angel beside him points the way to Heaven. Everything about it is in the Italian style of the time, particularly the over-dramatic attitude of the man – hand on heart, head thrown back, like a Pharisee at prayer. The effect is a little too precious, to tell the truth, yet somehow moving; but the technique is superb.

Châteauneuf was the boyhood home of Maurice Genévoix, in France one of the most celebrated writers of this century and – rare for that country – a major author whose subject is nature and the countryside. If you wish for a really deep understanding of the Loire Valley and have sufficient French you must be sure to read his books, especially *La Boîte à Pêche*, which is about fishing; five minutes' conversation with a French angler and it is bound to crop up. Others I have listed in the Appendix of Further Reading.

There is one more place of considerable interest to visit in Châteauneuf and that is the **Musée de la Marine de la Loire**, situated down the steps at the side of the *mairie* in the rotunda: another of those specialized museums, a comparatively recent venture, not on so grand a scale as the one on *la chasse* at Gien, or even that on fishing at La Bussière, but of greater importance to our subject. It is open from 10 to noon and 2 to 6 on Saturdays, Sundays and public holidays from the beginning of April to the third week in May, and thereafter every day until mid-September – not long enough really, but the period may be extended in the future. The collection consists of original tools and tackle used by the old Loire boatmen, their clothes, their cabin furniture, anchors, sails, models of their boats, paintings, photographs, old documents and a host of other fascinating things. Here is a most worthy enterprise of a few local historians and enthusiasts, and so obviously relevant to the region that one is surprised that some larger town did not have the imagination to undertake it long ago. It deserves to prosper and merits the support of all who love the Loire and its history. Rather than describe its contents, the best way I can assist the reader's appreciation of them is to sketch in here a little background to the subject.

When organized navigation on the Loire began, no one can tell, for it goes back beyond recorded history. The first glimpse we get is of the Greek traders in the Bronze Age. When the Romans came, they found the Gauls with a regular system of river trade, in boats which had evolved to suit exactly the peculiarities of the Loire: much the same in fact as those still in use only a century ago. During the Roman occupation the rivermen remained a highly respected caste, governing their own affairs on a guild basis, headed by 'senators'. Later, an early-ninth-century decree of Louis le Débonnaire refers to this same body as the *Splendissimus Corpus Nautorum*. In the Middle Ages it was still flourishing as the *Communauté des Marchands fréquentant la Rivière de Loyre*, which dealt with wrecks, buoyage, dredging of channels and care of widows and orphans. Their expenses were met out of *droits de boîte*, a cargo levy deposited in a box on the quay before a boat departed. Then came Richelieu, and later Colbert, who gradually took control from them. The ruthless new bureaucracy wanted all the reins in its own hands and of course coveted the contents of those boxes. But the new *intendants* appointed to supervise the channels were mere jacks-in-office who neglected their job and by the end of the seventeenth century the river was beginning to silt up with sandbanks and its commerce likewise to be clogged with pettifogging regulations and increased levies. There were more than thirty toll-points between Roanne and Nantes and a merchant of the last-named, writing at that time, complains that the tolls were so high that a bale of cloth worth ten *écus* incurred forty *écus* in tax by the time it reached him, and his boatmen had to entertain the toll-keepers with drinks and bribes to avoid being deliberately kept waiting about. In 1787, the merchants, thoroughly discontented, but deriving hope from the wiser policies of Louis XVI, were preparing to petition the crown for the re-establishment of the old *Communauté*, but the Revolution supervened and such problems were forgotten for many years. After things had settled down the Government restored order for another half-century, until the railways came and the river was once more allowed to fall into disrepair and disuse. Several efforts were made to revive traffic with the steam *paquebots* for passengers; but by the end of the century all was over – France's greatest highway for 3000 years or more was a highway no longer.

As to the type of craft which frequented the river in its long Golden Age, I have already described the expendable, one-way *sapines*. Others were the *coches d'eau* for passengers: large, light craft, generally without sail and usually rowed both ways – even with the current. Most of the big towns had two departures a week, and the journey took about three days from Roanne to Nevers (longer when the water was low in summer) and about the same from Nevers to Orléans; from there to Nantes took eight days and at least a fortnight to get back. These were frequently used, even by kings and royal officials, in preference to roads; the water was safer and not a great deal slower. As late as the seventeenth century Madame de Sévigné reckoned on a week to get from Paris to Vichy in her coach and she always took to the roads with two carriages: the second one contained three or four strong men '*en cas de mauvaise rencontre ou d'accident*'.

But the typical Loire boat, and the mainstay of its commerce, was the *chaland*, traditional and unchanged in essentials from time immemorial, perfectly adapted to the unique conditions of this very individual river. It was flat-bottomed, shallow-draught and light, to come off easily if it went aground; it had no keel so it would be supple enough to be 'wriggled' off a shoal, and its bows were flat and raised so that obstructions would slide under instead of being rammed. Length varied from fifty to nearly one hundred feet; beam was about fifteen feet; draught less than a foot unladen, an inch or two under three feet with a full cargo. Capacity ranged from sixty tons for the big ones, sometimes called *gabares*, down to about twenty tons for the smaller *gabareaux*. Most had a single mast, square-rigged with main and topsail, sometimes simply with a long rectangular main, and the mast could be lowered for bridges by means of the *guinda*, a small winch, speedy in operation, but dangerous as it had no ratchet and its handles could take a man's arm off.

There is a fine model of a *chaland* in the museum, and there are several old contemporary pictures of them. Study of these reveals the most thought-provoking feature of all – they have no rudder! What looks like one at a superficial glance is a device which is encountered nowhere else in the world except on boats in use on the Nile around 2000 BC. Called the *piautre* on the Loire, it was really a sort of fixed oar pivoting on a tall post or cross-tree *vertically only*, to drop it deeper in the water to give stability in a side-gust of wind. It could not pivot horizontally to steer, but only impart a general direction to the boat when it was twisted by means of a long handle attached at right-angles to the loom. For finer steering a big pole was used (the *bâton*), by lodging its top end in one of the row of notches on the bow and quarter (the *dents d'arronçoir*) so that the boat pivoted on the axis formed by the pole and veered in the desired direction. Manipulating the *bâton* was a job requiring immense strength and nice judgement in selecting the right notch.

In this and in so many ways the men of the Loire had their own particular methods: in the nautical world they were a race apart. In order to tack, for example (which they would do only in going upstream as they need not bother to sail into a contrary wind going down with the current), they would sling the massive anchor overboard and pole the ship's head round until the sail filled on the other side, whereupon they hauled it back on board. And if they got stuck hard on a sandbank they used a V-shaped wooden plough (of which there is a specimen in the museum) to make a furrow round the hull so the current would wash the sand away. Running aground in summer was serious: they might be stuck for weeks. Sometimes for months, if no rain came until autumn; and if a merchant got several *chalands* aground he would go bankrupt. Shooting bridges was another risk, and a dangerous one, for a touch meant wreck; they had to fend off with their *bâtons* and sometimes towed a heavy chain to slow down the boat and keep its head straight. Pack-ice in severe winters was one more hazard; such conditions are called *embâcle*: big blocks of ice can form very quickly, surround a boat (or even a train of boats), then weld together, trap the craft and crush them.

If there was not enough wind for the upstream journey, the boatmen would usually drink and play cards in the waterside *auberges* while they waited for it, but sometimes they would row, or be towed from the towpath by oxen, horses, or even men. A north-west wind was their favourite for ascending because it was a fair one all the way. They called it the *galarne*, a word derived from the Breton Celtic *gwalarn*, meaning wind. Frequently the *chalands* proceeded in trains of three or four tied together in line ahead; the first was called the *mère*, the second the *tirot* and the rest *sous-tirots*. The *mère* would be under full canvas and each craft back along the line would be reefed down progressively so as not to steal the wind from those ahead. Cargoes were quite varied – going downstream: barrels of wine and vinegar, sacks of grain, timber, wool; items such as pottery, ironware, guns, bricks, slates, tiles, cattle and coal, to name just a few. Upstream from Nantes they brought salt, dried fish, fruit, cotton, sugar, rum, spices and, again, wine.

The men wore loose trousers and a short smock of blue serge or canvas, without buttons and held at the waist by a pin (often of silver). Round the neck they sported a brightly coloured scarf – called a '*tabac*' because they carried their tobacco in it – and on the head a felt hat with a wide brim, laced under the chin. Many had side-whiskers or a fan beard, but moustaches were not approved. On their feet they wore *sabots* of willow or poplar with a heel of acacia: never oak or walnut as they are too slippery on wet decks. For religious processions in honour of Saint Nicholas they donned '*redingotes*', top-hats and silver-buckled shoes. They were well-off: many owned their boats, or several boats, and although they spent most of their time on their voyages they all had their own little houses ashore. They were rough, tough and devout; had their own professional patois; were fond of drinking and whoring, and affected to despise folk who worked on shore. The peasants whom they observed at their daily toil as they sailed disdainfully past the fields, they referred to as '*vire-bouses*' (cowpat-turners) or '*culs-terreux*' (muddy-arses). In return the peasants, who had an equal opportunity from the fields of observing the customs of the watermen, called them '*chiers-dans-l'eau*'. But that was just one of the things that went with being a sailor, the very status on which they prided themselves – they were '*mariniers*', and very special ones at that:

> No, no, there are no
> Mariners in all the land
> Like those
> Of the Loire.

I feel this long digression needs no apology, because the Loire's waterborne commerce is really the most significant part of its history, after the fact of its being a geographical and strategic boundary. But certainly it is now time to continue our journey, and the pleasantest route for doing so lies across the bridge and along the south side of the river to **Jargeau,** thus keeping an island-studded stretch of the river in sight nearly all the way. Jargeau itself, a small town of about 3000 inhabitants, is however a rather dreary little place, though useful to the passing tourist in having three hotels and a very well-appointed camp-site among acacia trees by the river. It is noted for its artificial flowers, made locally, and its *andouilles*. The former are indeed very good, and the latter – a sort of sausage made from the shredded guts of pig or calf – are also pronounced good by connoisseurs of such things; not being so myself, I am told by French friends that I have '*le coeur fragile*'; it is not too fragile, however, to rejoice exceedingly in Jargeau's pastries, which are also renowned. There are four good pâtisserie shops in the town.

The last vestiges of the medieval château beside the river, the town's main link with its quite interesting past, were unfortunately demolished in 1853. The episode chiefly remembered is of course Joan of Arc's first victory after the delivery of Orléans. The English under the Earl of Suffolk still occupied the castle and Joan's faithful admirer, D'Alençon, after a day's fighting in which he only succeeded in taking the suburbs, considered it too strongly held and further attack inadvisable. 'Are you afraid, gentle Duke?' was Joan's reproach. 'Haven't I promised your wife to bring you home safe and sound?' So another assault was made with her in the lead. There is a very good bronze statue in the town, cast by Lanson in 1896, depicting the incident which followed. As Joan mounted a scaling-ladder, standard in hand, a stone struck her helmet and she fell back stunned. But before consternation could spread among her followers she was back on her feet shouting: '*Amis, amis, sus, sus!* Our Lord has condemned the English; they will be ours within the hour.' And so they were. Suffolk himself was captured by a mere squire from the Auvergne, and to observe the proper etiquette of chivalry the prisoner solemnly knighted his captor before handing over his sword. That was on 12 June 1429.

Though it has lost its château, Jargeau still retains its fine **church** with a vast and beautiful chancel, panelled all round, and an eighteenth-century wrought-iron pulpit of splendid workmanship. In the north transept is a chapel consecrated in 1624 to Saint Marcoul. The fairly modern frescoes round the wall show interesting episodes from his life, though they are rather naïve and garishly coloured. A noble of Bayeux in the sixth century, he gives all his wealth to the poor; is summoned to the court of Childebert I where he casts out a demon and is rewarded with land to found a monastery in the diocese of Coutances. From there he sails to Jersey, where he repulses a pirate raid; the picture shows him in a boat thrusting heathen freebooters into the sea with holy zeal; that part of the frieze I really like. It was from Saint Marcoul's relics that the Kings of France were supposed to derive their power to cure scrofula ('the King's Evil' there as here) and they made a pilgrimage to them straight away after consecration at Reims. But from Louis XIV onwards, for the royal convenience, the relics made the trip the other way!

The great annual event in Jargeau – when it does indeed become quite lively – is the *Foire aux Chats* in mid-October, a genuine and very ancient fair which has its origin in the legendary connection, persistent in many countries, of bridges with the Devil. In times long past, the story goes, Jargeau's first bridge was built by a young man whose reward was to be the hand of the daughter of the local seigneur, but in its final stages it was swept away by a flood. Desperately in love with the girl, he made a pact with the Devil to restore the bridge for him. The subcontractor's price seemed reasonable enough – the soul of the first living being to cross the bridge. However, who should be the first to run towards it in joyful surprise when it appeared, but the beloved herself? So to save her the young man picked up a poor old cat near by and threw it on to the bridge ahead of her. Her father was a little suspicious at these strange doings, but he allowed the marriage to take place and they lived happily ever after. How the cat fared the story does not relate. The present bridge is a modern suspension one with which the Devil had nothing to do so far as I know. It is not as graceful as the one at Châteauneuf.

Irishmen while here will doubtless consider it worthwhile to make the four-mile journey to **Sandillon**, south-west of Jargeau. There is nothing very special about the place itself, but its parish church has a relic (the pelvic bone) of Saint Patrick. Its presence here is explained by a local legend that long, long ago a local seigneur arrived late for Mass one Sunday morning and, in remonstrating angrily with the priest for having started without waiting for him, killed him. Rather drastic, but obviously there could not have been a very happy squire-parson relationship for some time! As a penance he made a pilgrimage to Ireland and brought back the relic for the church. There is nothing but this tradition to support its authenticity, but, as we shall see when we get to Tours, Saint Patrick had other associations with the Loire Valley during his lifetime.

Crossing to the north bank from Jargeau, we come to its twin town of **Saint-Denis-de-l'Hôtel**, which is not worth a pause. The only two things worth looking at are best seen from Jargeau itself – its church by the river, and the imaginative architecture of its water-tower: fluted and widening towards the top like a flower-vase, a distinctive landmark and a pleasing change from the dreariness of most water-towers. Turning now on to the main Orléans road, we come first to **Mardié** where we cross a small river, the Cens, and the old Canal d'Orléans by the Pont-aux-Moines. If you are the sort who carries golf-clubs in the car-boot, it is worth knowing that the turn right just before the bridge leads to the Orléans Golf Club a couple of miles up the Cens valley in a beautiful forest setting. If you are a loafer rather than a golfer, the next turn right is the one you want, leading past a set of locks and under a rather handsome old railway bridge along the tree-lined grassy bank of the canal – ideal setting for a picnic lunch.

The Canal d'Orléans, fifty miles long, was constructed at the end of the seventeenth century to provide a direct link between the city and the Briare Canal to Paris. It is now, alas, completely disused, but it is clean and picturesque and the very short diversion to follow its last two miles is far pleasanter than the main road. After leaving Mardié, take the first turn left for **Chécy** which overlooks the canal from a little hill. The church on its summit crowns it in a most pleasing manner, and in the Place du Cloître behind the church there is usually room to park in the quiet little square which has a good restaurant at one end. Across the main street from the church the shop of Marchand et Vasseneux specializes in cheeses, particularly the two celebrities of the region: the Foin d'Olivet and the Cendré. The former partakes of the fragrance of the hay in which it is matured, and the latter acquires an agreeable and appetizing sharpness from being ripened in ashes. Another local cheese is called Saint-Benoît, but don't be misled: it is regarded by local people as 'mousetrap' with a big name. Wine has been produced here too for centuries, but the wines of the Orléanais are an important subject and we shall have a better opportunity of going into it when we get to Olivet.

Farther along the road, after passing vineyards and orchards sloping steeply down to the canal, we come to **Combleux**. Turning left there down the narrow Rue de la Passerelle, we find ourselves in a quiet little waterside world, remote and peaceful despite its proximity to Orléans. The lock downstream was where the canal entered the river in the great days (an extension for cement barges was built in 1917) and in those times it was a busy port. A letter of 1806 from the Prefect of Orléans to the lock-keeper mentions the fact that *on one evening* 300 boats were waiting to enter the canal. On the island between the canal and the river, the Hôtel de la Marine, which served all those watermen of days gone by, remains in business and is still very popular, serving excellent meals at reasonable prices. To get to it you have to cross the lock-bridge on foot. It closes on Fridays.

A short lane leads from Combleux back to the main road, and then we are on the outskirts of Orléans.

CHAPTER FIVE

Orléans

✦

As we enter Orléans by its eastern suburb of **Saint-Loup**, it is a sobering thought that in 1814 the Russians got as far as here – on horseback. In mid-February, as the Allies were beginning to close their net around Napoleon, a forward detachment of 1500 Cossacks turned up unexpectedly. The mayor of Châteauneuf died of a heart attack the day before when they descended on his little town, but they paused there only long enough to steal a few provisions and hurried on up the road. Orléans was the plum these notorious plunderers were anxious to have to themselves, and the city came within an ace of being sacked, for it had no garrison to defend it. But a certain Major Lagneau happened to be there on leave: one of those minor men of destiny who sometimes emerge briefly from obscurity to meet a crisis. He quickly assembled what few soldiers he could find about the place, with a handful of civilian volunteers, then carefully disposed his tiny force as snipers in the houses along here. As they rode in the Cossacks got such a peppering that they lost 200 men, and they very quickly galloped out again. Next day, on hearing of Napoleon's temporary victory over the Austrians at Montereau, they fell back to join the main Allied armies and the city was saved.

Orléans was lucky to get away with only a minor fright on that occasion, for in other wars – from earliest times to our own – it has been much more drastically involved. Being on the most northerly point of the great river which makes a natural barrier across France, halfway along its navigable section and at the top of a loop, it is both the central bridgehead and a bastion against attack from any northerly direction. As such it was the chief town of the powerful Carnutes tribe in ancient Gaul. *Genabum* was their name for it, and as allies of Vercingétorix they volunteered to open the revolt against Rome by murdering the whole Italian colony of merchants in their town. This they accomplished while the victims were in their beds, and the news of the deed – the signal to set Gaul ablaze – was telegraphed across the land by the Gaulish practice of shouting messages from one stentorian herald to another. 'Thus on the present oc-

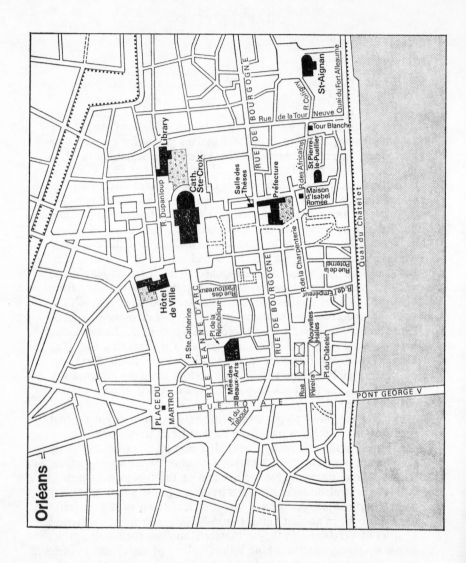

Orléans

casion,' reports Caesar himself, 'an incident which happened at Genabum at sunrise was made known before the close of the first watch of the evening [i.e. 3 or 4 p.m.] to the Averni 150 miles away.' The Gauls planned to garrison the town long before the Romans could mount a spring campaign and come to seek revenge; but as we have already seen (p. 71) Caesar crossed the Loire at Germigny in the season when he should not have done so according to the rules. After joining up with his subordinate at Sens, he came south immediately to Genabum; slaughtered the inhabitants as they tried to do a moonlight flit across the bridge; plundered the town and then burnt it.

Once Roman power was established Orléans, like most of the rest of Gaul, enjoyed peace for nearly five centuries. When it began to break down, the first to come was Attila with his Huns, followed only twenty-seven years later by Childeric and his Franks, squabbling with Odoacre and his Saxons for possession of the town. Soon the mighty Clovis established his court here after he had accepted Christianity. Later Hugues Capet, founder of the Capetian dynasty, made it his headquarters: in fact he hardly ever dared to leave it for Paris because of the powerful rivals who stood in his path; but as Maurois points out, summing up the very essence of Orléans's importance, 'he stood at the country's centre and his rivals were geographically divided.' Many of Hugues's successors, right down to the last of the Valois in the sixteenth century, continued to use it as a second capital. The English chose it as a principal objective in the Hundred Years' War; both sides in the Religious Wars; the Prussians in 1870, and finally (one hopes finally) the Germans and the English in the last war. The place has seen much and suffered much and a great deal of its stirring history is still recorded in its streets and monuments.

The handiest and most interesting way into the city centre is by turning left in Saint-Loup (Rue Jousselin) to come along the quays. They lead under the railway bridge which spans the river. Here there is a large island and, after passing its downstream end, the third turn right (Rue de la Poterne, but if you miss it the next turn right will do) leads to a spacious, free and central car-park less than a hundred yards after turning, in the **Rue de la Charpenterie**. From here the whole centre, and the old city, can be walked comfortably, but a street-map would help. Orléans is not immense, considering its importance (its population is now only approaching 100,000), but its streets are complicated and it is a pity to waste precious time in getting lost.

Walking first up the **Rue de la Poterne**, which was the north-south axial road (the *cardo*) of the old Roman city, we turn right into the **Rue de Bourgogne**, which was the east-west axial, or *decumanus*. In other words, we now stand at what was the hub of the Roman city, although you would never guess that to look at it today. The Rue de Bourgogne, however, is a fascinating street where the best small shops are situated. A little way along to the right, opposite the *Préfecture*, is the **Salle des Thèses**, the sole surviving building of the old university, which lay in this area south of the cathedral. The *salle* was built in the mid-sixteenth century as the law section of the library and the examination room. One may visit on application (and a *pourboire* of course) to the concierge at the *Préfecture*. It has a high vaulted ceiling and large Gothic windows giving a profusion of light, and is claimed to be the only medieval university building still extant in France. Orléans was a centre of learning as early as the sixth century, when Guntram, the Merovingian king, was welcomed to his capital, according to Gregory of Tours, with formal speeches in Syriac, Hebrew, Aramaic and Latin, which must have been rather boring for him. Later it became renowned for Canon and Civil Law and among its many famous pupils were Clement V, Erasmus, Calvin and Molière. But it had already become decadent by the time this handsome *salle* was built, and Charles Perrault relates in his *Contes* how he and two young friends knocked up the learned doctors here on the night of their arrival as students in the city, and asked for their degrees. With their academic gowns hastily slung over their nightshirts the doctors asked a few questions, to which 'the rattle of money being counted in a corner was the only answer', and the three aspirants went home to bed holding their diplomas. The university was formally suppressed in 1793, not for any political reason, but because there was only one student on the register. It was not re-established until after the last war and is now across the river at Olivet. Emphasis is on scientific subjects, but it is intended to revive Civil Law eventually.

Turning back now along the Rue de Bourgogne, it is interesting to take the fourth turn right, **Rue des Pastoureaux**, in our progress towards the centre, for here is a typical street of old Orléans: narrow and still bordered with its medieval houses, their fronts only superficially changed. Its name goes back to an ill-fated day in June 1251 when the mysterious 'Master of Hungary' came to town with a large troop of his raggle-taggle following. The *Pastoureaux* were wandering aimlessly over the land, not knowing quite what they wanted, but feeling a profound unease. They, the common people, somehow felt let down, it seems, by the failure of the Seventh Crusade. This was still the age of faith, but after 150 years of crusading fervour priests and barons alike had become suddenly lukewarm. In a vague way they, the poor, were making for Palestine themselves, but without proper leaders they did not know how to get there. Other countries were having their 'Shepherds' Crusade' too; it was Europe's sick headache after five generations of spiritual intoxication. As the 'Master' began to preach in this street, tightly packed with on-lookers and his own supporters armed with cudgels, plough coulters and sundry makeshift weapons, a young cleric unwisely heckled him and had his skull split by an axe immediately. A riot ensued and twenty-five other priests and students unable to escape from the crush were killed. It was largely this incident which persuaded Blanche of Castille, the Regent, who had hitherto tolerated the *Pastoureaux*, to take measures to have them dispersed.

Far from a riot, nowadays one can sometimes walk the length of the street without meeting anyone at all, and therefore the surprise is all the greater on emerging at the top into the wide and imposing **Rue Jeanne d'Arc** with its fine shops and its glorious vista up to the front of the **Cathédrale Sainte-Croix**, dramatic, inspiring and beauti-ful, despite the stock jokes about its supposed resemblance to a wedding-cake. The foundation-stone of the present edifice was laid in 1287 and the finishing touches were put to the nave and central spire in 1829, so it is certainly polyglot; nevertheless there is a harmony in the different parts, while the whole is refreshingly individual, resembling no other cathedral church anywhere. The oldest part is the apse, with the ambulatory, being of the thirteenth and fourteenth centuries; the nave and transepts are of the seven-teenth, when Louis XIV ordered that construction should continue in the Gothic style for the sake of harmony (most commendable, as it was the fashion in his time to despise Gothic), and the front and towers were added in the following century just before the Revo-lution. The original tower, an enormous affair some 320 feet high, was a victim of the Wars of Religion when Orléans became the centre of especially intense violence and hatred on both sides. The Calvinists were too hot even for Condé, who had in mind to preserve the Cathedral for *'un beau temple calviniste plutôt qu'une ruine papiste'*. He had its doors and windows boarded up so the wreckers couldn't get in, and when he later saw some zealot up on the roof chipping away the gilded sheathing as he sang 'So shall Babylon be destroyed', he had a culverin trained on him to compel him to come down. But in this French Belfast of four centuries ago fanaticism had explosives at its command just as in our own time and got its way in the end: a party of Huguenot activists got in through a window at night and laid fused powder-kegs round the four pillars that supported the tower. When this immense mass came crashing down it brought most of the nave with it, and that is one of the reasons why Sainte-Croix has been so long in reaching completion.

The interior of the Cathedral is majestic, and not much smaller than Notre Dame in size. The fine rose windows in the transepts are suns, it will be noticed, in honour of Louis XIV. The unbelievably beautiful high-backed choir-stalls in the chancel were designed by Lebrun and Gabriel and subsequently carved by Degoullon, who decorated the Trianon at Versailles. The medallions portray scenes from the life of Christ, and the perpendicular plaques between them various objects of ritual in Christian and Hebrew worship. Above the stalls hang splendid chandeliers, borrowed from Châteauneuf (like its orange-trees already mentioned) for the 'Feast of Nature and Reason' and never returned. Such benefits, left by the Jacobins in a church, must be extremely rare, but it was the duchesse d'Orléans, their rightful owner by inheritance, who gave permission, after the Restoration, for them to remain. From the chancel (at lower level anyway) to the eastern apse, we are in the building which existed when Joan of Arc came here to give thanks after her first victory, and in the north ambulatory just past the transept is a chapel dedicated to her; at the foot of its altar is the tomb of Cardinal Touchet, Bishop of Orléans, his statue kneeling in prayer before the saint. He wished to be buried here, for he devoted a great part of his life in striving to secure the official recognition so long delayed in her case. By sheer persistence with the Vatican he procured her beatification in 1909 and her canonization in 1920. The statue of Joan triumphant by Vermare is symbolically supported by two heraldic English leopards; but although all the blame for her martyrdom is so often heaped on the English, it is touching to find, on the column on the left, a plaque which reads: 'To the glory of God and to the memory of one million of the British Empire who fell in the Great War 1914–1918 and of whom the greater part rest in France.'

The first cathedral on this site was built towards the end of the fourth century by Saint Euverte, the first Bishop of Orléans, who enlisted the financial support of the Roman Emperor – most likely Gratian, although the name of Constantine is often incorrectly mentioned in this connection. At all events he dedicated it to the

Holy Cross which had been discovered by Constantine's mother at Golgotha earlier in the same century.

A short walk along the north side of the Cathedral (where, incidentally, there is room to park in the shade all day if you arrive early in the morning) brings us to the gardens and rear entrance of the **Bibliothèque Municipale,** which seventeenth-century building was formerly the Bishop's Palace. The gardens are a peaceful place to sit down and contemplate the side and apse of the cathedral, which from this viewpoint has all the qualities of the richest period of the Gothic with its gallery, buttresses and flying-buttresses, although so much of it was not built until nearly 300 years after that period. In the south-eastern corner of the gardens a small section of the ninth-century city walls remains.

The library is of course open to the public in normal working-hours; it has a fine wide stone staircase and a beautiful gallery which is near the reading-room. Here, in a not very dignified fashion, the Empress Marie-Louise spent four of her last few days in France in April 1814. Her stay began inauspiciously with a visit from an envoy of Louis XVIII who confiscated all the jewellery she had determined to escape with. He even took her gold plate and table-ware so that she had to borrow the Bishop's crockery for the evening meal. The rest of her time was mostly spent sulking in her room with a host of whining complaints – no warm baths available; her hairdresser having shamefully deserted her in Paris so that her coiffure was 'like a mad dog's'. Every day, affectionate and sympathetic letters came from Fontainebleau signed '*Tout à toi, Nap*', asking her to come back, but her replies lacked the same warmth, and her excuse for not returning was that she must first have her father's permission! On the fourth evening, when she was about to set out on the first stage of the journey to Austria, a local lady stooped to kiss the hand of the three-year-old, forlorn little Prince of Rome; as she did so he burst out, amid tears, '*Je veux aller voir mon papa!*' – a wish that was never granted, for Napoleon never saw his wife or his son again.

Leaving the library by its front entrance we come out into the Rue Dupanloup, from where a few paces back towards the town centre will lead us to the **Hôtel de Ville,** just out of the right-hand corner of the square. The central section of this graceful Renaissance *hôtel* was built in the early 1550s for Jacques Groslot, a wealthy merchant who was also *Bailli* of the city. The two wings which match it so well were added in the last century. The statue of a pensive Saint Joan, standing among flowers at the foot of the steps, is a bronze replica of an original in marble at Versailles by the princesse Marie d'Orléans, presented to the town by her father, King Louis-Philippe. Marie was an artist of great susceptibility and this statue is fraught with deep, feminine tenderness – so different from the theatrical, sword-waving hoydens so many other sculptors have imagined.

The interior of the building may be visited between 9 and noon and 2 and 6 every day save Sundays, on application to the concierge. The lay-out of the rooms was extensively changed in the nineteenth-century alterations, but it would be somewhere in the central portion (not the *Salle de Mariages* in one of the new wings as one is sometimes told) that the sickly François II died on 6 December 1560 at the age of seventeen of some sort of growth in the ear which reached his brain, despite the attentions of his eighteen physicians and fourteen surgeons. Three months earlier he had made his formal entry into Orléans accompanied by the court and his radiant girl-bride, Mary, one day to be better known as Queen of Scots. Attired in a dress of gold brocade trimmed with diamonds and pearls, as beautiful as he was puny and ugly, she won all hearts in the town. A local poet wrote:

> Be content my eyes!
> A sight so lovely you will never see again.

The purpose of the visit was to hold an Estates General and – secondly and secretly – to get rid of the two Huguenot leaders, Condé and Antoine de Bourbon, King of Navarre. They were both summoned to appear here under promises of safe-conduct. Condé fell into the trap, was arrested on his arrival, tried in this building on charges of treason and condemned. The King's death in fact saved him just in time: his execution had been fixed for 10 December. Navarre was a more ticklish proposition for he was, after all, a king and there were no charges to make against him; so it was arranged he should be goaded into anger with François who would stab him with his dagger 'in self-defence' and others would fall upon him as defenders of the royal person; but Catherine de Médicis, the Queen Mother, heard of the plot and warned him. Several years later he recounted the experience himself: as he entered the room the hard-faced Guises and their trusty supporters were strategically posted among the courtiers, and he noticed the Cardinal de Lorraine carefully closing the door behind him. When the King approached him, wearing his dagger and shouting reproaches, he replied so quietly and humbly that he scarce gave excuse for wrath, let alone the planned attack, and they had to let him go in peace. After all these

Fishing for salmon and shad in Anjou

Early nineteenth-century engraving showing
commercial river traffic at Orléans

Statue of Joan of Arc by Marie, daughter of Louis-Philippe,
at the Town Hall, Orléans. The holes were made by
machine gun bullets during the last war.

nice people had departed from his house, Jerome Groslot – son of the first owner and himself a Protestant – soon showed that he was no better, though inspired by a different cause. As chief magistrate of the city, when Condé came back with an army and occupied it, he instituted a local Reign of Terror for the Catholics, plundering their houses, arresting as many as he could on trumped-up charges and hanging them. His own end eventually came with an invitation to that fateful royal wedding in Paris in August 1572 which put him conveniently on the Guises' list for the Saint Bartholomew Massacre.

Turning back westwards now down the Rue Jeanne d'Arc, take the second turn left beyond the Rue Pastoureaux to the **Place de la République** where there is a cheerful little flower market. It is useful to remember also that the 'Supermarché Francis' on the corner is open on Mondays when other shops are closed. On the other side of this little square is the **Hôtel des Crénaux**, whose handsome belfry was built in 1448. It contains the city's art museum (open 10 to noon and 2 to 5 except Tuesdays) wherein are works by Velasquez, Van der Velde, Ruysdael, Gaugin, Boucher, Fragonard, Delacroix and several others of international fame. I am particularly fascinated by Claude Lefèvre's fine portrait in the seventeenth-century room, of Le Nôtre as an old man, looking every inch a gardener with his lean, weather-beaten face, observant, reflective and rather austere. Two local masters must not be overlooked: Desfriches, who painted little country sketches in the style of Rowlandson and modestly signed them '*Desfriches, négociant à Orléans*', and Michel Gobin, whose best is of a boy reading by candle-light. And those of us who have been to Saint-Benoît should reserve time for the Max Jacob room which is last. Mainly watercolours in a fresh and easy style, of Breton country scenes, of the Seine in Paris, and religious subjects, his works reveal his profound joy in life.

In the next street westwards, Rue Sainte-Catherine, we find the Louis XIII façade of the building we have just left and, facing it, the **Hôtel Cabu**, a fine Renaissance building (burnt down in 1940, but restored with discretion) which houses the history museum, open the same hours as the art museum. It contains a rare and priceless temple treasure found in a sandpit a few miles from Saint-Benoît in 1861, chiefly bronze statues of animals and human dancers full of ease, grace and vitality. They had been hastily concealed in some emergency in the fourth century: probably the severe measures being taken against paganism at that time on the orders of Saint Martin of Tours. The most precious item, and quite unique, is a handsome high-stepping stallion over three feet high, his beauty all the more amazing when one realizes that he was made around AD 100–150 of *beaten* bronze, only his detachable mane and tail having been cast. The base has rings for slipping poles for carrying in procession, and a Latin inscription reveals that he was dedicated to a god called Rudiobus, probably derived from Celtic *reuddha*: 'red and strong', a sort of Gallic Mars therefore. The words *CUR/CASSICIATE/ D.S.P.D.* (*Curia Cassiciate de sua pecunia dedit*) further indicate that the statue was subscribed by the people of Cassicius, which still survives as Chessy, the name of a field close to where it was found at Neuvy-en-Sullias.

The Rue Sainte-Catherine crosses the Rue Jeanne d'Arc and a left fork leads to the **Place du Martroi**. '*Martroi*', by the way, has nothing to do with martyrs, but is a word from Low Latin signifying merely a cemetery. In the centre stands Foyatier's statue of Joan of Arc, executed in 1855: the most widely known, but undeservedly, for it is rather lumpish and the horse is too small for the rider. The frieze round the plinth, carved a few years later by Vital Dubray, deserves close study however. In a delicate and detailed sculpture, almost neo-Renaissance in style, it illustrates the main events in the life of the saint.

There are several restaurants and cafés in this area, inevitably of course including Joan's own: she has a school, a bookshop and many other enterprises in the town; you see her name at almost every turn. But Orléans can be excused for overdoing her a bit, for after all it not only cherished her at the time of her brief heroic career, but remembered her after her death when everyone else conveniently forgot her, and has continued to honour her ever since. Without interruption (even during the Revolution) on 8 May each year it has held the great *fête* of thanksgiving which she herself instituted in 1430, and you cannot be in the city on that day of joy and splendour without being caught up in its enthusiasm for her.

Running straight down from the Place du Martroi to the river is the imposing Rue Royale with its arcaded pavements and Parisian-style shops. In the second right off it, Rue du Tabour (where the *tambour*, the town drum, was kept), there is a so-called **Maison Jeanne d'Arc**. True it is that in May 1429 Joan lodged here in the house of Jacques Boucher, the Royal Treasurer, but in the following century a well-meaning owner, in the course of tarting it up, demolished the very part in which her room had been. Then in 1940 the rest was bombed flat. So the apparently fifteenth-century house which stands there now is completely false, though not with intention to deceive (no secret is made about it); even so, as a sentimental exercise it seems rather pointless. The Rue Royale was laid out in the time of Louis XV by demolishing a huddle of medieval streets. At the same time the old bridge of Joan's day, whose nineteen arches were an obstacle to navigation, was replaced by the Pont Royal. As it was being built many people questioned its safety, as it was flat and the idea still persisted that a bridge must be humped in the middle for strength; but after Madame de Pompadour formally opened it in July 1760 a local wag published a poem reassuring the doubters on the ground that it had just borne 'the heaviest weight in France'. The bridge was renamed 'George V' after the First World War in honour of the alliance between England and France.

William Wordsworth lodged in the lower Rue Royale in 1791 in a house where now stands the shop 'Aux Coin Maugars'. He was only twenty-one, and fell in love with Annette Vallon, a fellow lodger four years his senior. He was an ardent admirer of the Revolution and delighted in attending all the Republican junketings that were going on in the town at the time. Annette, on the other hand, was a Royalist, a secret agent of the *'Chouannerie'*, counter-revolutionaries of the west. But these ideological differences did not stand in their way and a year later a daughter was born to 'Monsieur et Madame Williams' and christened Caroline at the cathedral. When war broke out between France and England, Annette persuaded her lover to flee. They continued to correspond afterwards; met at Calais in 1802 and again at the Louvre in 1820 when the grown-up Caroline and Wordsworth's wife and sister were also present.

A short street left off the lower Rue Royale (Rue Péreira) leads through to the **Nouvelles Halles**, the new covered market which is an excellent place for food shopping, especially good for a wide choice of cheese, fish, vegetables and *pâtisseries*. It is open on Sunday mornings, but closed on Mondays. Leaving the market by the side entrance, we look down on to the **Place du Châtelet**, where stood the rear of the old palace residence of early kings from Clovis onwards, then of the Dukes of Orléans until 1460. For the last three centuries of its life it served as the law courts until its demolition in 1803. There is nothing to see, so it is a good idea to turn left into the Rue de la Charpenterie and our circle is complete; shopping can be unloaded, and if it is lunchtime and suitable weather for a picnic one can move the car across to the **Quai du Fort Alleaume**, a massive cobbled quay many centuries old. There is a grassy bank below where bright-green lizards come out to sunbathe, and you can drive down to the water's edge. Huge iron mooring-rings in the quay wall are a reminder of the great days of navigation when the river here was an ever-changing pageant of boats. La Fontaine has left an account of what he saw here in 1663 – boats sailing up and down whichever way he looked, their big sails giving them the majesty of deep-sea ships; the whole scene reminded him of 'the port of Constantinople in miniature'. And Madame de Sévigné, coming here on the morning of 11 September 1675 to take a boat to Tours – 'Hardly had we arrived here than behold twenty boatmen round us, each boasting of the quality of the persons he had carried before and the excellence of his boat.' But in characteristic feminine fashion, the lively Marquise resolved the problem on neither of these grounds: she chose 'a big well-made lad, whose moustache and civil manner decided us'. Obviously he was a bit of a dandy to be sporting a moustache in defiance of the *mariniers*' general custom; but her choice turned out to be a fortunate one, for during the voyage the boat ran aground several times on the summer shallows and she had to ride on his muscular back to get ashore for the night. Nowadays such a journey could only be made in summer in a canoe, for the shoals have been allowed to grow and often only trickles of water (called *luisettes*) run between them. The seasonal variation of flow here past Orléans is staggering; around twenty-five cubic metres (5500 gallons) per second at summer level, and between a million and a million and a half gallons per second in winter. Incidentally we are now just about 200 miles from the ocean and the height of the river-bed above sea-level is 300 feet.

Our next walk in the old part of the city begins by ascending the **Rue de la Tour Neuve** which is the fourth opening off the quay eastwards of the Rue de la Poterne (see p. 92). The *tour* from which it takes its name was *neuve* in the time of Philippe-Auguste, having since grown old and disappeared; it was the south-eastern corner-bastion of the city wall. Second right along the street is the **Rue Coligny**, named after the Huguenot admiral because his Orléans residence stood at the far end of it, overlooking the cloisters (now a pleasant little square) on the north side of the **Church of Saint Aignan**. From the windows his wife used to have great sport shouting insults at the canons on their way to say the office. The original church was built in 1029, but had to be demolished exactly 400 years later as it was outside the walls and would have served the English as a ready-made siege-tower. It was rebuilt at the end of the Hundred Years' War; but in 1567, a year or two after Madame de Coligny's verbal assaults, her husband and Condé came back and made a physical attack, wrecking the nave and bringing down the tower.

We are left with the remains, which are entered by the door of the north transept. In the south-east of the ambulatory is a model (partly guesswork) of the imposing edifice it was before the Huguenots performed their amputations. One of the earliest kings, probably Clovis, was responsible for the first little chapel on the site to house the relics of Saint Aignan, immediate successor to Saint Euverte as Bishop. An arm-bone, rescued from the routine pillaging at the Revolution, still reposes in a double reliquary of fine wrought-iron work on the outside and a golden casket within; you will find it in the side-chapel opposite the architectural model. On the north wall of the chancel is a painting of the saint on the city ramparts, calling up the legendary storm which frightened Attila away. Orléans has been extremely fortunate in finding a saviour when under attack: Major Lagneau against the Cossacks, Joan of Arc against the English and Saint Aignan against the Huns. On hearing of Attila's approach in 451, although a very old man, he undertook the difficult journey to Nîmes to make a personal appeal for help to Aëtius, the Roman general there. Having taken this practical step he hurried back to his flock, soon to see the huge barbarian army approaching from the north.

The situation was desperate: the Roman legions had not arrived and Sangisban, commander of the garrison and a secret accomplice of the attackers, was advising surrender. Attila came to the gates formally to demand it. To gain time the old Bishop mounted the ramparts in full regalia and solemnly spat in the pagan chief's direction. He may have noticed some portent in a distant cloud; more likely he simply relied on faith that Providence would intervene; at all events a terrific storm came up with thunder and lightning and lowering clouds that turned the day into twilight. The prestige of the Church was high then, even amongst the heathen, and Attila was impressed. He camped to think it over. But by the time he had done so, the trusty and capable Aëtius, 'the last of the Romans', was on the scene and the Huns had to pack their tents in haste and retreat the way they had come. It was as far west as they got: not only Orléans, but Gaul itself was saved.

Returning by the Rue Coligny and looking across the Rue de la Tour Neuve, we see the **Tour Blanche** close to the opposite corner. The base of it is Gallo-Roman and it was a fair age on that far-off day when Saint Aignan spat at Attila. The walls were commenced in the reign of Aurelius (270–275) or soon after; medals bearing his name and head have been found in their foundations, and it could have been then (though there is no proof) that Genabum became

101

Aurelianum. We are now in the **Rue des Africains**, on the other side of which is the vinegar factory – you can smell it! In the days when the West Indies trade was thriving it was a sugar refinery, the raw cane being brought upriver from Nantes, but Orléans has always been famous for vinegar and it was changed over to that product in 1795 by the firm of Dessoux who still run it.

Behind the factory walls, invisible from the street, unmentioned in any of the guidebooks and virtually forgotten by the authorities who have been at such pains to build a spurious 'Maison Jeanne D'Arc' in the city centre, is one of the most precious and most touching historical relics in the whole of the Val de Loire. Fortunately the proprietors of the factory are kind and courteous people who are proud of their property and willing to show it to anyone sincerely interested. Call at any time in working hours and as soon as convenient they will take you to it. There is no charge. If Monsieur Sautereau, the foreman, is available so much the better: mention my name and this Guide; if he is not, apply at the office, 2 Cloître Saint-Pierre, a little higher up the street.

In a courtyard which has gradually become surrounded by additions to the factory is a medieval house with beautiful half-timbering, and lovely old windows – the **Maison d'Isabel Romée**, partly demolished and rebuilt in the early seventeenth century, but still the house where Isabel d'Arc (née Romée), mother of Saint Joan, came to live in her widowhood, from about 1440 until her death in 1458. Her two sons were with her; they had been ennobled with empty titles, but not a *sous* did the family receive from the King. Charles, duc d'Orléans, the King's cousin, after his ransom from captivity in England, made them a little annuity, but it was mainly on the kindly charity of the city fathers that Isabel subsisted, and they provided this home for her. Wandering through the dusty and deserted rooms, one can feel the ghost of a great sadness of long ago: Joan's mother and brothers alone with their heart-rending memories and their sense of injustice. Isabel's greatest grief was that her daughter had been condemned as a heretic, and it was from here that she petitioned for her rehabilitation. It was some comfort therefore when, two years before she died, the enquiry set up by the aged Calixtus III (the *good* Borgia pope of whom we seldom hear) reversed the dishonourable verdict of the ecclesiastical tribunal at Rouen – pushing the blame on to the English, of course, as the French often still do. But, ardent Francophile that I am, I cannot swallow that, and always remind them it was Joan's companions-in-arms who shut the gates of Compiègne and left her outside to be captured; fellow Frenchmen of Burgundy who sold her to the English; the French king and his advisers who made no move to ransom her, and a court of seventy-five Frenchmen – bishops, inquisitors, priests, lawyers and university dons from Paris – which tried and condemned her. Isabel's house was just inside the city walls, part of which still survives inside the factory: complete with arrowslits, and a dark passageway descending to a fanwork of vaulted tunnels (now blocked up) beneath the walls. After this fascinating visit a short walk straight up the street leads past the twelfth-century **Église Saint-Pierre-le-Puellier** (the old parish church of the university quarter and the one used by Isabel; now deconsecrated and destined perhaps to be a university museum) to the Rue de la Charpenterie. So our second circle is complete, and it is time to cross the river by the wide and graceful Pont Georges V.

At the south end of the bridge, turn on to the **Quai du Fort des Tourelles**, only a few yards along to the left, where there is room to park for a few minutes. There is a plaque on the quay wall recording the position of the Tourelles, a miniature fortress on the end of the bridge of which the English made a bastion for their siege in 1428. They in fact had Orléans ringed round on the south, the west and the north-west by some nine other bastions, but the main part of their 10,000-strong force was encamped around Olivet on this side. The footings of the old bridge still show above the water except in times of spate. Three of the nineteen arches were cut when the defenders fell back from the Tourelles at the commencement of the campaign in October. Sir William Glasdale was put in command of the fort, and it was felt that this key position assured eventual success. 'There's your city, my Lord,' was the phrase which had just fallen from Glasdale's lips in talking to the Earl of Salisbury, his superior, as they stood on this very spot a few days later, when on the other side of the river a mischievous boy noticed a cannon loaded and put a light to the priming. So runs a contemporary account which may or may not be true; anyhow a cannon-ball certainly came whistling across and took off Salisbury's head before he could reply. On 30 April the following year, the second day after her arrival in the city, Joan came across the bridge to the broken arches and shouted across to Glasdale in the name of God to surrender and so save lives. In reply she received only insults, calling her 'strumpet' and 'cowherd'. On 7 May the French attacked the Tourelles, after having driven the besiegers out of their strongpoints south of it. The Bastard was in command; Joan and her standard inspired his men to superhuman efforts. Launching their assaults from the street on this side, they fought all day, and Joan was wounded by an arrow. By evening they had crossed the broken bridge on a flimsy wooden tightrope of old guttering and planks and had the English in a pincer grip from both sides. In panic they rushed out to make a last desperate sally across the drawbridge, Glasdale and his knights at their head. But a big old boat had been placed beneath it and set alight and, knowing this, Joan called out to him: 'Clasda! Clasda! Render yourself to God. You called me harlot, but I have pity for your soul.' Under the weight of the armoured knights the charred timbers of the draw-bridge collapsed and they were all drowned. There, amid the tumult and in the moment of victory, the little 'cowherd' burst into tears for them.

There is yet another statue of Saint Joan across the road, sculpted by Gois in 1804. The likeness to a masterful suffragette is extra-ordinary considering he never saw one.

Just downstream of the bridge, on the **Quai de Pragues**, there is plenty of room to park with a good view of the city, the bridge and the waders and terns that haunt the sandy islands. Close by is the pleasant **Jardin Botanique** with over 500 varieties of rose, among other interesting flowers, and some fine carp and red gurnet in its pond. Only a short distance downstream is the riverside racecourse where horse races are held in the spring.

CHAPTER SIX

Olivet to Beaugency

❧

Although now a suburb of Orléans and growing fast, **Olivet** remains, and probably always will remain, a country town with a character and a charm all its own, something more than a mere commuters' dormitory. On the banks of the Loiret, the 'Little Loire', a tiny tributary of the great one which has given its name to the whole *département*, it is primarily an agricultural settlement of vineyards, orchards and fields. Of no great antiquity, the place first appears in written records in 1022 under the name of Saint-Martin. One hundred and thirty years later, Louis VII gave some land there, with a water-mill, to the canons of Mount Sion of Jerusalem whom he had brought back with him from Palestine after the failure of the Second Crusade, and it was they who nostalgically renamed it after the Mount of Olives. Under these and the Benedictines who were feudal lords of most of the other land, the peasants who cultivated the little valley were enfranchised very early and became absolute owners of the small farms they had wrested from the heath and marsh. The land is still held in small units and some of the proprietors are of families which have been here continuously for more than eight centuries. They are a placid people. The Revolution passed them by despite all the ferment across the river, and of all the events of the nineteenth century the ones most remembered up to quite recent times were the glorious vintage of 1811 – 'the year of the comet' – and the phylloxera plague. Some still recall a local ditty which expresses well their attitude to life:

> They speak of murderers,
> Of thieves and rogues;
> But the greatest scoundrel of all
> Is the phylloxéra.

Although only eight miles long, the Loiret is an attractive and most unusual river, and as it rises only two miles east of the town we can begin there and follow it down. After crossing the Pont Georges V out of Orléans, therefore, take the first main fork left which leads to the Olivet by-pass. At the first junction on the by-pass the left turn is signposted '*La Source*'; this is the road we want and it brings us to the **Parc Floral** (open 9 to 7, April to October; the rest of the year 9 to noon and 2 to 5; there is an entrance fee for over-fourteens, but it is worth it). The park is laid out mainly in the English style which became fashionable under the Second Empire as a result of the affection Napoleon III developed for Hyde Park during his exile in England. In a setting of beautiful trees, arranged in copses as well as avenues, the alleyways lead past open lawns, hedges, rhododendron thickets, and flower-beds where a feast of colour is maintained from the daffodils, narcissi, tulips and irises of spring to the asters and chrysanthemums of autumn. There is a restaurant on the little hill and, just below it, in the shade of the trees near the south entrance, a small *parc zoologique* where you can get a close look at wild boar and white deer. On Wednesdays, Saturdays, Sundays and public holidays a miniature railway will take you round in a lazy fashion, but of course it is more interesting to walk.

The source of the Loiret is in the middle of the park. Beneath the overhanging boughs of a horse-chestnut tree, in a pool where big trout glide drowsily in the shade, a mysterious turbulence wells up from below, expanding and contracting in a regular pulsation but never ceasing – though it did nearly dry up in the exceptional drought of 1976. The effect of this strange issue from the depths is surprising in its suddenness, for immediately before your eyes is an adult river some sixty feet wide. From a chasm about three feet in diameter in the limestone rock at the bottom of the pool, the '*Bouillon*', as it is named, pours forth between 100 and 150 gallons a second to feed it. You would travel far in the world to witness anything else of the kind, for this is the rare phenomenon of resurgence. For a long time it was realized that the origin of the Loiret was not of a usual kind and many fantastic theories were advanced to explain it; but it was not until 1865 that Sainjon, a waterways inspector, established that the Loire progressively lost about twenty cubic metres of flow per second between Sully and Orléans and surprisingly made up that loss after the confluence of the Loiret. This was too much of a coincidence and he postulated an *effondrement* of the Loire, even calculating its vicinity correctly as Bouteille just upstream of Saint-Benoît. His theory has since been confirmed by the injection of dyes into the river-bed in that area and their reappearance here at *La Source* a few days later. The workings of this prodigy involve a combination of hydraulic causes too complex to concern us here, but in simple terms the permeable sand of the Loire's bed permits water to filter through to fissures in the underlying limestone where it is siphoned down into a fault. How deep into the earth's crust it is led before it forces its way up again no one yet knows, but obviously far enough to be influenced by heat, for on re-emergence it has acquired a constant temperature within the narrow limits of 12–15°C. It never freezes, hence another surprise – a flock of pink flamingoes (imported but at liberty) living here all the year round, with black swans for company.

On the slope overlooking the first stretch of the river, in formal gardens of the school of Le Nôtre, stands the seventeenth-century **Château de La Source**: of the Classical style, elegant but a little severe. It now houses the university offices and cannot be visited. The university quarter is across the road from the Parc Floral and is destined to become a satellite new town of Orléans.

For a brief period two and a half centuries ago the château was an intellectual centre, known as '*L'Académie de la Source*'. Between 1720 and 1725 it was leased by that enigmatic figure, Henry St John, Viscount Bolingbroke, Member of Parliament for Wootten Basset, who attached himself to the Tory party; became Minister of War under Queen Anne, negotiated the Treaty of Utrecht which ended the War of the Spanish Succession at the expense of England's allies; and eventually, as a secret Jacobite, fled to France on the accession of George I. His 'little circle' here (as he called it in a letter to Swift) was a bizarre collection of French *philosophes* and revolutionary politicians from various parts of Europe and the Middle East. Voltaire came once, while still in his twenties and on the threshold of his career. He stayed only two days and a night, during which he read the manuscript of the *Henriade* to his host, but it was the beginning of a lifelong friendship. In 1726, when it was Voltaire's turn to be an exile, Bolingbroke, by then repatriated, took him under his wing, initiated him into Freemasonry and introduced him to Swift, Pope and all the literary world of London. His influence on the development of the younger man's ideas was considerable. This ostensibly conservative English statesman rejoiced in 'the great name of Theist', made light of 'the Jew they call Christ' and wrote about that time 'I conclude that every sensible man, every good man, should hold the Christian sect in horror'. Such phrases may have made even Voltaire blush just a little in those early days, but later he emulated them – almost word for word – in the *Dictionnaire Philosophique*.

Returning by the same route to the by-pass and crossing straight over into the Avenue de Verdun, we come to the traffic-lights where there is a big flower-bed clock. Straight across again and we are in the **Rue Albert-Barbier**, where rowing-punts may be hired at the 'Manderly' – boats made of good solid wood. If these are all out, the 'Pavillon Bleu' near by has less prepossessing plastic tubs, but steady enough and a means of enjoying the beauty of the wide, gently-flowing river. Upstream is the stone bridge, built in 1872 to replace the earlier one erected by the Benedictines of Micy in the thirteenth century at the height of their prosperity. All along the banks here are picturesque little houses, quite Venetian in aspect, right at the water's edge and almost at water-level; but they are safe from serious flooding because there is a limit to the quantity of water which can filter through the underground channels to the Loiret, however wildly its giant parent may be behaving. Most of these houses are week-end retreats, much more common in France than with us and by no means a modern idea. As early as the twelfth century the small bankside plots were in great demand from middle-aged Orléans merchants for building *maisons de plaisance* where they could snooze their leisure hours away behind a fishing-rod or potter round a diminutive vineyard, while their bored youngsters enlivened their Sunday strolls with acts of petty vandalism. The monks complained to the King that 'the townspeople who frequent this river cause great damage in breaking the lock-gates of our mills and throwing tree-branches, pieces of wood and great stones in the water'. A royal decree resulted, but decrees do not alter human nature and the present-day owners of the mills have the same complaints to make. These watermills, not far downstream of the bridge, are well worth a few pulls on the oars for a look. At one time there were about a score of them; now five remain, all close to one another, seventeenth- and eighteenth-century successors of older ones on the original sites: the Moulin de Samson (the one given to the Canons of Mount Sion), de la Motte and du Bac on the left bank; the Saint-Julien and the Bechets on the other. Fishing on this upper section of the Loiret is private and, trout being plentiful, it is First Category (see Introduction). Day-tickets are obtainable at most of the restaurants in the town.

There is a very good modern hotel not far from the 'Pavillon Bleu', opened in 1976 and called 'La Reine Blanche': a bit expensive, but not unreasonably so for the luxury it offers. If simple comfort and cleanliness suffice, 'Les Canotiers' near the north end of the bridge is extraordinarily reasonable. 'Le Beauvoir' at the other end of the bridge is more renowned for its excellent restaurant. For anyone visiting Orléans and having his own transport, Olivet is really better for small hotels than the city itself, and most of them are in this area near the bridge. Across the bridge, the first turn right leads to the centre of the old town, the *mairie*, post office and shops. The street with a church on the corner (appropriately named Rue du Pressoir Tonneau) is where we find the **Cave Coopérative**; look out for its trade name 'Covi-fruit' at number 613 on the left. It is open Tuesday–Friday, 8 to noon, 2 to 6; Monday afternoon only; Saturday morning only to 11.30. Here is the best place for a complete choice of the wide range of wines of the Orléanais, a V.D.Q.S. area extending from Chécy to Beaugency.

The wines are light, pleasant, underrated and inexpensive. The Gris Meunier is the most ancient *cépage* of the region and the one it considers specially its own. A variety of the Fromenté, it owes its name to the white down on its leaves which comes off on your clothes, like flour on the miller. Poets may like to know that Jean de Meung is said to have taken it copiously while finishing the *Roman de la Rose*. Certainly it is a heady wine, though only just over 11°, and its flavour is quite distinctive. Best of the reds because so perfectly suited to the soil, it should nevertheless be drunk young. For a keeper (four or five years from a good vintage) the Cabernet red is best. A rosé is produced from the same grape, quite different from the Cabernet of Anjou, combining dryness with fruitiness. Two other reds are the Pinot Noir, which does not fare so well here as on the hillsides of Sancerre, and the Gamay, the grape of Beaujolais and the lighter Burgundies, which succeeds well here in the soil of alluvial sand and clay over limestone and should be drunk new like Beaujolais itself. As to the whites, the Sauvignon does not succeed here really; the Auvernat on the other hand is a luscious, fruity, medium dry white; the name is the local sobriquet for none other than the noble Chardonnay, from which all the great white Burgundies are produced. A point worth remembering by caravanners about to return home, and with a couple of empty water-containers, is that this is one of the places where wine can be bought in bulk. Lighter wines do not travel happily in this way, but something robust like the Cabernet is not troubled at all.

The *cave* also sells Eau-de-vie de Poire William, an excellent local speciality, but only for those who enjoy an intense flavour of pears. The largest bottles have a full-grown pear inside; don't be puzzled – the bottle is hung against the tree and the set fruit-bud inserted to finish its growth inside. There is also an Eau-de-vie de Cerise, a dry cherry liqueur resembling Kirsch. Free tasting of these, as well as of the wines, is readily given on request.

Travelling westwards out of the centre of Olivet we pass the church of Saint-Martin on our right, with its handsome tower built in 1132; and the Rue du Bac (fourth turn right past the church), an opportunity to see three of the watermills if you haven't already done so from the river. Then we begin to enter the orchard district (which positively sparkles with the joyous blossom of cherry and pear at the beginning of April), soon coming to a crossroads where, turning right down a lane called Chemin des Valins, we find the *'Pierre du Duc'*, only a simple block of stone beside a little copse, but a monument to a dark deed which brought incalculable misery upon France. In 1563 François, duc de Guise, was lodging near here while he besieged Orléans, then in the hands of the Huguenots. In the darkness of the evening on 18 February he was riding home alone and unarmed, having just dismissed his escort at the bridge at the bottom of the lane, when he was shot full in the face by one Poltrot de Méré who had waited concealed in the bushes. Intolerant bigot that he was, and not averse to political assassination himself, Guise had nobility of a sort; he was a popular man and a fine soldier, the one indeed who had seized Calais from us and caused it to be written on Mary Tudor's heart. He was on duty as a soldier at the time of his death, but this was not war: it was a cowardly and foolish murder. Coligny was blamed (most probably unjustly) for having plotted the deed, and it rankled in the hearts of Guise's son (only thirteen at the time) and the leaders of the Catholic party until they exacted retribution for it nine years later. Vengeance for the murder committed in this lonely lane was not the sole motive for the Massacre of Saint Bartholomew, but it was an important one, particularly so far as young Henri de Guise was concerned.

If you follow the road round eastwards after crossing the bridge, it leads along the *levée* of the Loire back to Orléans; if you turn left *before* crossing it, the rough track (not too rough) takes you to the confluence where the Loiret returns its borrowed waters to the Loire. Our way on, however, is by returning to the main Cléry road and heading south-westwards inside the curve of the Loire, which lies to the right just over the fields. Orchards and vineyards become more frequent, and in the latter it is no uncommon sight to see plough or harrow being drawn between the rows by a sturdy horse. There is another *Cave Coopérative* at **Mareau-aux-Prés**, open only on Monday, Thursday and Saturday mornings. Though smaller than the one at Olivet, and with a range more limited, it is more informal and has a merry, friendly staff who insist on your tasting almost everything, no matter what you are going to buy, and would soon have you singing drunk. They sell a white wine made by the proper champagne method, nothing great, but one of the best bargains you could find anywhere for a cheap sparkling wine – better than the over-sweet Astis and the Rhenish guts-gripers (into which the gas is *pumped*) which people so often use as substitutes for champagne.

At **Cléry-Saint-André**, two miles down the road, the **church** of rather hefty Gothic, with its tower standing out of true, is such an ancient place of pilgrimage as to have been accorded the status of basilica. In 1280 a local peasant found a statue of a woman in his fields and brought it to the priest. It was rather a fortunate find, as the village was right on the main road from Paris to Bordeaux – one of the few metalled roads in the country – used by large numbers of pilgrims to Compostella. The discovery was immediately proclaimed 'miraculous' and the statue put in the church as 'Notre Dame de Cléry'. But the circumstantial evidence connected with the find points to its being genuine: the plough had first brought up old weapons, broken pottery and human bones, so the statue may originally have been a pagan goddess. We shall never know now because the Huguenots burnt it and the replacement in solid oak over the high altar was made from memory afterwards. The parish prospered greatly from the cult until Salisbury came by in 1428 on his way to Orléans and paused here to allow his men the fun of knocking the church down. All they left was the square tower already mentioned and now on the north side of the building. When he got his head knocked off by a cannon-ball soon after, there were some who said that the Virgin personally guided the missile to its target as a punishment for desecrating her shrine.

After the war, Dunois and the King, his uncle, provided funds for the church to be rebuilt, and these were increased soon after by the Dauphin Louis, who had vowed his own weight in silver in return for his victory in driving the English out of Dieppe. Later, as King Louis XI, he became very attached to Cléry and often used to come here. The house where he used to stay still survives on the right of the church and is now a school. His small secret oratory, with its opening above the sacristy door, is also still in the church. This arrangement, similar to the one he had in the *Sainte Chapelle* in Paris, enabled him to hear Mass without being seen by the rest of the congregation. Such was his veneration for Notre Dame de Cléry that, at his own request, his remains were laid to rest here in 1483. The vault was dug out in his lifetime and occasionally he used to go and lie in it. The bronze monument which surmounted it was taken away by the Huguenots and melted down; the beautiful marble statue which replaces it was executed by the Orléans sculptor Michel Bourdin in 1622.

Bourdin's statue has captured perfectly the hardness and cunning of Louis's features which contemporary portraits confirm. It is a face fraught with covert menace, and somehow he looks incongruous on his knees, as Arthur Young obviously felt when he wrote in his journal for 12 September 1787: 'Dine at Clarey and view the monument of that able, but bloody tyrant, Louis XI . . . he is represented in a kneeling posture, praying forgiveness I suppose . . . for his baseness and his murders.' Cruel, ruthless, perfidious, nicknamed *'le Renard'* by his own father, he repudiated all the tenets of chivalry which had tempered the conduct of affairs in the early Middle Ages. *'Qui a le succès a l'honneur'* was his cynical pronouncement on that score. None the less, his reverence for Our Lady seems to have been genuine and without it he would doubtless have been more fearsome still.

Sometimes, instead of in his secret oratory, Louis would pray in the **Dunois Chapel** through the door in the south aisle, at the tomb of his cousin, to whom he had shown little friendliness while he lived. Jean, comte de Dunois et de Longueville, better known as the Bastard of Orléans, whose remains still lie undisturbed beneath the chapel floor, was quite a different sort of man: generous, sensitive, kindly, Joan of Arc's *'gentil Bâtard'*, her staunch friend from the moment of their first meeting. Aristocrat and brilliant commander though he was, he always sought her advice and took her seriously, submitting to her scolding with good humour. After her death, he was the leader who completed her work, finally achieving it twenty-five years later when he drove the English out of their last stronghold in Guienne. His long lifetime of hard work ended, he was buried here in the beautiful little side-chapel he had founded. While in the south aisle, notice also, behind a locked grille, the **Chapelle Saint-Jacques**, set up in Renaissance times for pilgrims on their way to Compostella; its ceiling is decorated with delicate carvings of various trappings of the pilgrim's garb – girdles, wallets and staves. To gain entry, as well as to the vaults of Dunois and Louis XI, one must apply at the presbytery behind the church between 10 and noon or 2 and 7. There is no charge, but something for the offertory is an expected courtesy.

The heart of Louis's son, Charles VIII, who completed the rebuilding of the church, is buried near the royal tomb; there is an

Meung: The Château where François Villon was imprisoned

The swift-running Loire: Beaugency

The quiet Cher: Chenonceau

inscription on the pillar near by. Half a century after Charles, yet another king, Henri II, interested himself in Cléry; he presented the south door of studded oak, which is well worth stepping outside to see, and the stalls whose ends are carved with human faces. Both door and stalls bear the initials of Henri and – inevitably – his concubine, Diane de Poitiers.

A journey of three miles along the road west out of the village brings us back to the Loire at the suspension bridge which leads into the town of **Meung** – pronounced *mahng* with a suspicion of the *g* sounded. At the town end of the bridge there is a camp-site in a meadow on the right, and a nice swimming-pool on the left. Beyond the latter, just after the avenue of trees called the Mail, the **Quai du Mail** on the left leads into the town centre. On the way, Meung proudly greets us with a statue of its most famous son, Jehan de Meung, who in the fourteenth century, some forty years after the death of Guillaume de Lorris, its original author, rounded off the *Roman de la Rose* by adding another 14,000 stanzas to Guillaume's original 4000-odd. Nothing is known of Jehan's parentage, and little of any certainty about himself. He was born at Meung about 1260; studied at Orléans University (where he produced his first literary works, poems of a mere few hundred lines relating his adventures with certain ladies there), and eventually became a prosperous lawyer in Paris with chambers in the Rue Saint-Jacques. A considerable scholar, producing philosophical commentaries and translations from Latin texts, in his reading he was much influenced by Aristotle and Roger Bacon. Among his patrons he numbered the King himself, Philippe le Bel.

The romantic style of Guillaume was not for Jehan: an original thinker and a questioner, he introduces all sorts of new characters into the *Roman*, with a prophetic ring of Rousseau and Voltaire about them – Reason, Nature, Genius and the like – and makes them speak in terms most revolutionary for those times. All men are born the same physically, he points out, and true nobility can come only from the heart. He who has not this nobility is only a *'vilain'*, whatever his inherited social position; and this applies even to a king, who is only a *'grand vilain'* elected to defend the country. (Did the *Roi de Fer* read *that*?) He subscribes to none of Guillaume's romantic notions about love: it is simply a natural need, and you might as well praise a man for eating his dinner as for loving his wife or his mistress. Such was the originality of this new contribution to the *Roman de la Rose* that it became a best-seller; copies spread all over Europe, and when printing was invented a century and a half later, it was one of the first works in France to go to the press – in three successive editions. For his effect on the thought and history of Europe Jehan has never been given sufficient credit. Nor does his statue in the Mail do him credit. Inevitably guesswork, it is an unlikely bit of guesswork – an effeminate-looking oaf in a contrived, unnatural stance.

Meung is a quiet little place, built round the river Mauve which forms a complex pattern of channels dividing, merging and re-dividing as it meanders among the streets, after having risen only seven miles away in the Bois de Bucy. The part of the town inter-laced by this delta is called *Les Marais*, while the portion to the west – on the strength of being a few feet higher – is proudly entitled *Les Monts*. The former affords the most delightful walks, not only along the avenue of the Mail, but westwards along the **Route de Boulette** which follows the river (after it has gathered itself into one again) out of the town on its way to the Loire. Northwards also is pleasant strolling, by the Mauve's several channels, straddled at intervals by old watermills to way beyond the main Orléans-Blois road which roars through the top of the town. Before the Revolution there were twenty-nine mills in Meung, mostly grinding corn from the Beauce, some pulping paper. Now nine of them remain in use, hidden away in alleys and side-streets – still grinding corn, but wastefully powered by electric motors in order to produce the un-sustaining fine-ground white flour in vogue today.

Strolling eastwards now, from the Quai du Mail along the Quai Jeanne d'Arc, we pass on the corner of the **Rue Ingres** on the left the house where the painter after whom the street is named dwelt for several years. An elegant eighteenth-century building looking out on the sparkle of the Loire through the trees of the avenue, it belonged to Maître Guille, a notary, Ingres's brother-in-law, and is still occupied by a *notaire*, whose business is probably a continuation of the old firm, for the past has a habit of lingering quietly on in Meung. Farther on, facing us on the next left corner, is a big rambling medieval building called the **Stables of Louis XI**. That king certainly used them for his relay mounts, but they are older than his time, for it is on record that Joan of Arc, Dunois and the duc d'Alençon lodged their troops and horses here on 15 June 1429 before going on to take Beaugency from the English next day. The building would then have been a fortress at the head of the medieval bridge; a little turret of the period, sticking out of the side wall of a modern house on the opposite corner, testifies to this, and a line of rapids across the river betrays the foundations of the old bridge which was built in about 1216.

That was a long time ago; but the other end of the town, *Les Monts*, is the really ancient part. Built on the slight rise of ground in the angle of the Mauve's delta, it was an important market town to the Gauls. *Magdunum* (notice why the *g* sound still survives in the modern pronunciation) is Celtic meaning 'fortified market', and if legend means anything – as it usually does – it was a main stop for Greek traders on the tin route from Marseilles to Cornwall. For although they still call themselves *Magdunois*, the inhabitants have an ancient nickname, *'les ânes de Meung'*. The legend goes that Silenus, the jovial, portly, generally tipsy preceptor and attendant of Bacchus, came riding into town one day on his donkey and, being ill-received, invoked Jupiter to turn his insulters into asses. The Greek trade in wine and other goods of course lasted well beyond the end of the Bronze Age, as did the trade in tin itself; and the Gauls, who came to France in the early Iron Age, became expert metal-workers and miners. It was indeed the Bitururges of this very region who first discovered the process of tin-plating. It would therefore be less surprising to learn that the Greeks were frequently here than that they were not; but neither is demonstrable at the present time. What is certain is that the facile and naïve explanation usually given for the ancient *âne* sobriquet – Meung sent a convoy of asses bearing flour to Orléans during a famine and the Orléanais cried out *'Voici les ânes de Meung!'* – is rubbish.

The **Place du Martroi** is in the centre of the old town and, except on the busiest days, there is parking-space to be found there. The church of Saint Liphard in the corner is a very fine example of Romanesque with its eleventh-century tower and handsome doorway surrounded by a simple dog-tooth pattern on the arch. Like so many country churches in France, this one began with a primitive chapel built over the relics of the hermit saint to whom it is dedicated. Son of Rigomer, King of Le Mans, Saint Liphard was born at Orléans in the first decade of the sixth century, studied law there and eventually became its governor. But at the age of forty he was ordained, and set out with one disciple, Urbice, to reconvert the people around Magdunum which had been left in ruins by barbarians, deserted and overgrown. They made their cell among the tumbled walls of the old Roman castle and began by slaying the customary monster: in this case a serpent-dragon down by the Mauve. This episode occurs frequently in the legends of the early missionary saints, and its significance seems to be deeper and more mysterious than appears on the surface. Obviously in one sense the dragon is a symbol of paganism, but nearly always it dwells near water and in more primitive imagery is the guardian of the source. Not only Saint George and Saint Liphard had such monsters to overcome, but Krishna, Apollo and Perseus. In the south transept of the church a very ancient wall-painting depicts Saint Urbice standing by the river just after he has killed the dragon with his staff; there is something about it which is uncannily stirring. However these early hermit missionaries were practical men, and the important thing is that they went on to preach, to civilize, to cultivate the land and rebuild the town so that it became once again a prosperous little river port.

Through the iron gates beside the church is the **Château**, which has been open to the public only since 1976. The hours are 10.30 to noon and 2.30 to 5 every day, but the present season is only from Easter to 15 September, to be extended if it becomes popular – as indeed it should, for although the entrance fee at Meung is one of the highest for any château along the Loire you get considerably more for your money here than at most. The newer part was erected in the seventeenth and eighteenth centuries. In 1770 Jarente de la Bruyère, friend of Louis XV's minister Choiseul, shared the latter's disgrace and was banished here. The great ones of Paris seldom knew what to do with themselves out on their country estates in such circumstances except spend money. Choiseul built a folly which we shall see when we get to Amboise; but La Bruyère spent his on putting the finishing touches, expensively but tastefully, to his house. This eighteenth-century portion is occupied by the present owner, a native of the Channel Isles and a most amusing and well-informed man who sometimes acts incognito as guide when the mood takes him. The visitor is shown many remarkable pieces of furniture from French fourteenth-century to English Chippendale. However it is in the eleventh- and twelfth-century part of the house that the greatest fascination lies, with its two old brooding towers, underground passages, prisons and vaulted subterranean chapel where the population took shelter, and often lived for weeks, in time of raids or war.

For 500 years the castle of Meung was the second residence of the Bishops of Orléans, who dispensed justice as local temporal lords and had their prisons here. Nowhere else, except perhaps when we get to Loches in the Touraine, shall we receive such a vivid impression of what it was like to be a prisoner in those tough times, of the hopelessness, the isolation and the dark, cold fear. In one gloomy passage is the euphemistically named *cachot d'accueil* (with a skull let into the wall) where new prisoners were temporarily confined. No doubt the skull was meant as an aid to thought before being taken over to the *salle de question* opposite, really the torture chamber. Once condemned, you were lodged outside in the *oubliette*, a well into which prisoners were lowered to spend their days living on an unfenced ledge halfway down. If anyone lost his head and dived in, there would be no changing his mind at the last moment, for the well is shaped like an inverted cone so that no man could ever climb out of it. Of the countless criminals who suffered in such appalling places we know little, but many had behaved with equal brutality to innocent fellow-citizens in the world outside.

One of these, assuredly the most famous prisoner the bishops ever had there, was the poet François Villon in 1459, then about twenty-eight years old. Scruffy, disreputable and of no fixed abode, he hardly looked like a Master of Arts of the University of Paris or a future celebrity in the world of letters, and had in fact been picked up with a gang of thieves in the neighbourhood. This was not his first spell 'inside': he had been convicted of murder in the capital four years before, but eventually released with a pardon. Not long after that he was on the run in the provinces following a burglary. An accomplice, under torture before being hanged, had implicated him, and here at Meung the Bishop's hangman employed the best of his arts to help Villon make a clean breast of it. He submitted him to the *question par l'eau* (enforced water drinking until the victim is ready to burst) and the *éstrapade* (repeated hauling to the ceiling on a block-and-tackle to be dropped with a jerk just short of the floor). Whether or not Villon betrayed himself and was condemned is unsure; but in 1461, when Louis XI passed through Meung during his coronation celebrations, he was released under an amnesty. He was lucky: in view of his fondness for Cléry the King might well have passed by on the other side of the river. While in despair during his long confinement at Meung, Villon had written his famous *Epître à mes Amis* in which each verse ends '*Le laisserez là, le pauvre Villon?*' It is a very moving poem. But when his plaintive question received its favourable answer our '*pauvre Villon*' returned to Paris, committed another burglary and became accessory to another murder.

The village where Villon was arrested is **Huisseau**, five miles north of Meung. The road to it lies in the pretty little valley of the Mauve, and the **Château de Montpipeau** near the village, now a private farmhouse, has a fine medieval gateway flanked by towers, which are topped by ancient wind-vanes in the shape of crowned dolphins, the symbol of the Dauphin. Beyond is the **Bois de Bucy**, where the Mauve rises, geographically part of the Forest of Orléans, but private with grim notices nailed to trees – *Chasse gardée*; *Poison*; even *Pièges*, but surely not man-traps! In these woods in spring the Star-of-Bethlehem grows wild, and cowslips and little wild daffodils, so those nasty menaces would not deter me from a stroll, any more than they appear to frighten the local children who come out here to picnic and gather flowers.

Leave Meung, not by the main road, but by the Chemin de la Fontaine out of the south end of the town, and go through **Baule**, a quiet hamlet beside the Mauve, with vineyards on the steep hillside to the right and meadows on our left where butterflies and dragon-flies abound. This is the western limit of the Orléanais V.D.Q.S. Exposed at a better angle to the sun, the reds here should in theory be a little fuller, but I have not found them so particularly. On the other hand Baule specializes in the Gris-Meunier rosé with great success. The *Cave Coopérative* is open only on Wednesday and Saturday mornings and the individual *vignerons* hardly at all, to the public, but this wine can be bought reasonably enough in the shops at Beaugency, which is our next stop after turning left on to the main N152.

Just after entering **Beaugency**, turn left and make for the quays. The best starting-point for an exploration is the bridge and there is extensive parking-space both above and below it. You can also drive on to the wide meadows at the south end of it on the downstream side, whence there is a splendid view of the town through the plane trees lining the quayside on the opposite bank. At the same end of the bridge on the upstream side is one of the most spacious and pleasantly situated camp-sites along the Loire – eighteen acres between the river and a quiet backwater. For campers who prefer a base rather than taking daily chances on where to rest as they move along to visit the crop of châteaux we shall be coming to in the next two chapters, Beaugency is ideal – quieter and more rural in character than Blois which is the alternative (see p. 158). In fact a radius of thirty miles from here covers an area as far forward as Chaumont and as far back as Châteauneuf. Such a point is worth considering now that we are in a more frequented region, especially in the height of the season. For those relying on hotels the town has seven with about eighty rooms between them. The Hôtel du Mail in the Place du Martroi is in the lower price bracket, but considered locally as exceptionally good, clean and comfortable.

In the Middle Ages Beaugency had a better bridge than its neigh-bour, Meung. This made it a desirable military objective in every war, and sometimes the inhabitants must have wished they didn't have a bridge at all. Like the one at Jargeau, it was supposed to have been built by the Devil in exchange for the first soul to cross it. On Opening Day, as the crowds stood well back for fear as to who might be chosen, the mayor turned up with a bucket of water and the inevitable poor cat, set the animal down on the bridge and sloshed the water after it to send it scurrying across. Taken in by the same old trick (less worldly-wise perhaps in those days), Satan thought it such a hellish good joke, and the mayor such a fine fellow after his own heart, that he burst into roars of laughter which shook the top off the Tour de César, the mighty square keep across the river in the town. Its top is still missing, as you can see – *voilà la preuve!* But in truth I think we may assume the Devil had as little to do with the tower as Caesar; for it was built in the eleventh century at the same time as the bridge in question, and to protect it. The bridge we see now, most handsome and impressive with its twenty-three arches, is a sixteenth-century rebuilding of the original. The French army blew up the south end in 1940 to delay the pursuing Germans and you can see that the repaired arches there are wider.

With a population of just under 5000, Beaugency is slightly larger than Meung, but its centre of interest is more compact and can be seen on a comfortable walk. Before ascending the Rue du Pont, straight up from the bridge, notice the former abbey of Notre Dame and the **Tour du Diable** to the left of it, not to be confused with the one damaged by diabolic laughter; Old Nick liked Beaugency so much that he took up residence in this smaller tower, which must have been embarrassing for the Augustine canons next door. One is told that he is still there. The abbey, now an hotel, was built in the eighteenth century to replace the twelfth-century original, but the archway on the left just up the street leads through to the front of the **abbey church** which still survives from the first period, though in a maimed condition. When the Huguenots took Beaugency in 1567 their zeal, as so frequently, got out of hand; La Noue, one of their own captains, felt obliged to report afterwards that 'the soldiers conducted themselves as if a prize had been offered for the one who behaved the worst'. They set fire to this majestic building and brought the whole roof down. The unfortunate sequel was that in the repairs the original Romanesque vaulting was replaced by a cheap bit of bodging-up – an imitation Gothic ceiling in wood, painted to look like stone! Apart from this jarring false note, it is too low and smothers all the *élan* which the nave once had. But if you don't raise your eyes too far the rest of the solid construction of Beauce stone is impressive enough. In 1940, enemy bombardment shattered all the windows, but the new ones, made in Orléans, are very beautiful, even if the colours do lack a little subtlety. There is a war memorial in the church which includes the civilian victims of the Allied bombing of 14 June four years later. There were sixty-seven of them and the names tell a distressing tale – Marie, Denise, Monique, and so on: mostly women.

In 1152 a Great Council of three archbishops, forty bishops and numerous barons packed into this church to consider the suit of Louis VII for the annulment of his marriage with Eleanor of Aquitaine. After fifteen years he had found the green-eyed beauty too vivacious, too cultivated, too warm-hearted for his dull, morose disposition. For ten days the proceedings droned on with a great deal of canonical argument and rather too much mud-slinging against the Queen, considering that so far as the parties were concerned it was a 'by consent' affair and she was not defending. The agreed pretext was consanguinity – nine degrees apart however, which made the case a bit thin; and it was the legal acrobatics required to make it look like five degrees that took up most of the time. The decree of nullity was pronounced on 18 March – Palm Sunday. Eleanor was not present; she had not once appeared, but waited in her manor of Tavers just outside the town, dreaming perhaps of the handsome youth from Anjou she was going to marry.

Young Henry Plantagenet – unlike Louis – shared her culture and refinement; was fluent in the Latin tongue and several others; could turn troubadour when he wanted. This intellectual sympathy drew them together despite the eleven years' difference in their ages. He was eighteen, she was twenty-nine; but she was at the height of her physical beauty. Only eight weeks after the decree they were married, and Eleanor's returned dowry, nearly half of France, went to her new spouse. With his own estates he now owned more of that country than the French monarchy itself and, succeeding two years later to the English crown, he became virtual master of everything between the Cheviots and the Pyrenees, the King of France being simply his feudal overlord for some of it. The English ambitions which arose from this were a major cause of the Hundred Years' War that was to bring misery to generations yet unborn. Vaguely this could have been foreseen here at Beaugency and was no more irrelevant than consanguinity in the ninth degree, but it didn't stop a selfish king wishing to be rid of an irksome wife and an obsequious tribunal bending principles to oblige him, while the Devil laughed in his tower near by.

Almost facing the church across the little square, the **Tour de César** looms up to a height of 110 feet, even in its shortened form, a perfect example of military architecture in the eleventh century before it was generally appreciated that scaling-ladders are more easily dislodged from round towers than square ones. Massiveness was the quality most esteemed then and its walls are twelve feet thick. When Dunois and Joan of Arc attacked it on 16 June 1429 the garrison Talbot had left behind was only a small one, but it took the French all day and half into the night to overcome it. Even then the defenders were in a strong enough position to obtain terms, marching out next morning with their weapons on the promise only that they should not fight for another ten days. Up the narrow lane beyond the keep stands a more elegant tower of about the same height with its little spire, all that remains of the vast sixteenth-century **Church of Saint Firmin**, destroyed at the Revolution. Patron saint of Beaugency as well as Amiens, where he was beheaded in the persecutions of Diocletian, Firmin is also the subject of a festival of international renown at Pamplona in Northern Spain, but otherwise not often met with south of Picardy. His cult was very likely brought by Flemish pilgrims on their way to Compostella, Beaugency being on a secondary route from the north; but it has also been suggested that its old name *Balgentiacus* may indicate colonization of the town at some time by Belgians. Etymological theories founded on the mere resemblance of words are risky, but at least Saint Firmin provides a speck of circumstantial evidence. The people of Beaugency still call themselves *Balgentiens*.

In the corner of the square which we recently left the **Château Dunois** now merits our attention. The Bastard had it built in 1440 after he had been given the fief of Beaugency in recognition of his services in the war, and this is where he generally lived when not away on campaigns. Now it contains a regional museum of real interest, thanks to the zeal of Monsieur Vannier, its curator, and the imaginative lay-out he has devised. Each room is furnished according to a different period, and one of the most interesting is an eighteenth-century peasant's parlour – not the mud-hut of popular imagination, but surprisingly comfortable. Another room is devoted to nineteenth-century toys, dolls, puppets and games. Off the guard-room at the top (which has a fine timber roof) is a tiny watchtower with views over the town and the Loire. The château is open all the year round, every day except Tuesday, 9 to 11 and 2 to 6 (4 in winter) and again in the evenings for *son et lumière* from Whitsun to the end of August.

Continue up the Rue du Pont after leaving the château and either of the next two left turns will lead to the **Hôtel de Ville**, a perfectly proportioned little masterpiece of Renaissance architecture. On application to the conciérge and the payment of a very modest fee (plus a tip, for she is a most obliging lady, even if her historical information is not entirely accurate) you can visit the Council Chamber which contains the town's proudest art treasure: two enormous early-eighteenth-century embroideries in a vertical stitch which is *point surmonté*, not *point de Hongrie* as you may be told. On the left, four dramatic pieces illustrate the theme of pagan sacrifice, three being Druidic and the other a fancied Peruvian sacrifice to the Sun-God. On the right four others have the continents as their theme. Europe is badly faded because of the cleaning necessitated to remove a coat of black paint put over it by a keen 'patriot' at the Revolution who spotted Anne of Austria among the figures. Of unknown origin, but believed to be Flemish, they were presented to the abbey about 1784 by the Marquis de Lucker, an officer in the Royal Guard, descendant of Jacobite exiles from Ireland, the 'Wild Geese' who eventually had to abandon hope of flying home when the Stuart Spring failed to return. Many, like the Luckers, restored their fortunes at Nantes in the West Indies trade as well as through royal favours. The Marquis de Lucker was commendatory abbot of Beaugency.

Carry on northwards from the Hôtel de Ville, up the Rue du Change, under the **Tour de l'Horloge** (the old medieval north-west gate) and turn left into the Rue Porte Vendômoise where, at number 15 on the left, is a lovely old sixteenth-century house with a wide arched doorway, formerly a coach entrance. Here in 1746 Jacques Alexandre César Charles was born. He grew up to have a wide range of scientific interests and eventually became Professor of Physics at the Sorbonne, where he worked on the expansion of gases. By the application of these studies he fathered practical aviation, for which the Montgolfier brothers are usually given the credit because they were the first to put men into the air – on 21 November 1783: for twenty-five minutes at three hundred feet over a distance of five miles in a clumsy hot-air balloon forty-eight feet in diameter. But only ten days later, Charles, with a companion, made his own ascent from the Tuileries Gardens with a hydrogen balloon only twenty-six feet in diameter. He landed twenty-seven miles from Paris two hours later and, elated with this success, went up again alone to attain a height of 9000 feet. This time the awesome experience of looking down on the cosy world from nearly two miles up completely overwhelmed him and he never made another ascent. The danger of stoking a fire in the neck of a 'Montgolfière' soon put it out of the running for practical work, and when Blandford and Jeffries crossed the Channel two years afterwards it was in a 'Charlière'.

A few paces along the main road from the top of this street brings us to the upper end of the beautiful **Grand Mail**, a wide and shaded pedestrian avenue with views over the Sologne beyond the river, leading down past the Porte Tavers, another old fortified gate, to the **Petit Mail** and, by a flight of steps from there, to the quay. Nearly always a few local people will be playing the popular game of *boules* on the Petit Mail. In an earlier age it would have been a sort of croquet called *jeu de mail* (from Latin *malleus*, a hammer) for which these shaded avenues, a feature of so many French towns, were set aside – as was the Mall in London.

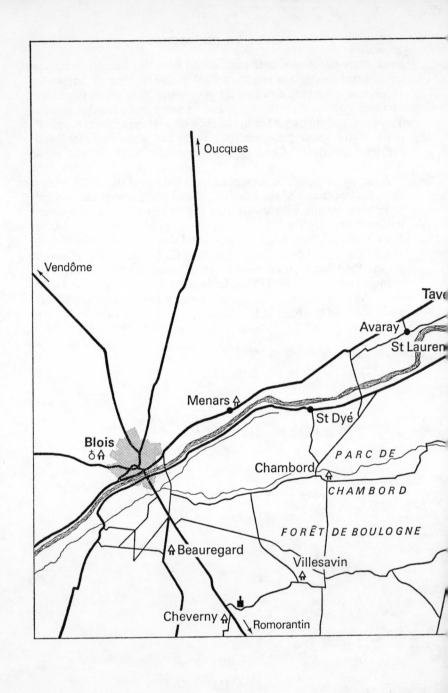

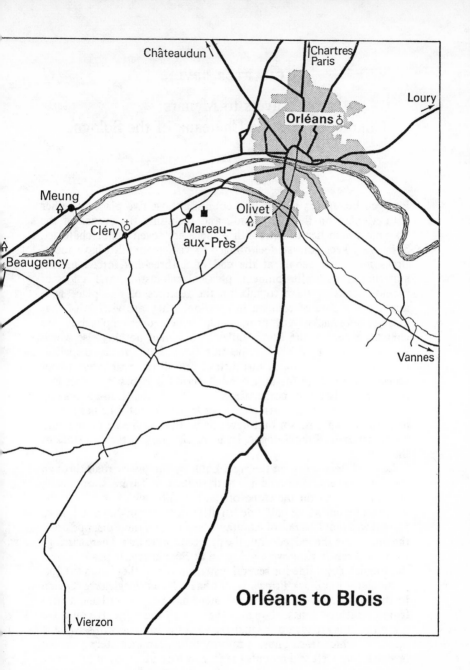

Châteaudun

Chartres
Paris

Loury

Orléans

Meung

Olivet

Cléry

Beaugency

Mareau-
aux-Près

Vannes

Vierzon

Orléans to Blois

CHAPTER SEVEN

Tavers to Menars;
Chambord and the Châteaux of the Sologne

✦

Between Beaugency and Blois – counting those two places together with Menars on the right bank, and including the corner of the Sologne which lies to the south – there are seven major châteaux. Some very keen tourists feel obliged to visit them all. I have some-times met such people at the end of a three-day forced march, suffering from disillusionment, physical exhaustion, and a loss of memory causing them to mix up the features of one place with another – a sort of château indigestion. They are victims of that glossy, but hackneyed, propaganda which over-emphasizes the château aspect of the Loire Valley as if it had nothing else worth seeing, an error which I hope this book has already dispelled. Certainly the châteaux in this district are all of great interest, but unless you are here for an extended period it is best to select and leave one or two for another time. I shall describe them all, leaving the reader to make his own choice, or tackle the lot if he has legs of iron and an enthusiasm that never flags. But before we plunge into the forest area of the Sologne, let us briefly look at the two sides of the river.

Leaving Beaugency on the right bank by the minor road through the Porte Tavers, we soon come to the village of **Tavers**, sleepy, very, very old, spread on the slope of the low hills which overlook the Loire and from which half a dozen little streams run down to join it. Here it was that Eleanor of Aquitaine had a castle (now disappeared), the one where she lodged while the proceedings to annul her marriage with the French King were going on at Beaugency. It passed down the English royal line for several generations and they often used it, particularly the Black Prince. It still has a Rue d'Angleterre. Owing to the many clear-water streams, there has been a settlement here from prehistoric times, though higher up on the ridge. If you drive up to the cross-roads on the main road at the top you will see a lane opposite, which leads under a railway bridge. Immediately after the bridge it forks left and mounts the scarp where outcrops of limestone stick out of the turf on the left, and even out of the wide cornfields on the right. In this small valley, at the beginning of October 1870, General Chanzy won the first of the astounding victories of the hastily assembled 'Army of the Loire'. With a couple of brigades he drove back the main mass of the Prussian army trying to advance down the valley to Blois, and there is a monument on the left of the road commemorating this. Had he and Gambetta had their way against the more cautious generals, he might have slipped past them and relieved Paris. But the opportunity was missed; two months later, at Origny only two miles north of here, he was defeated and the *'retraite infernale'* of the remnants of his force closed this heroic chapter.

About a mile beyond the monument the road ends. The spot is called **Feularde**, a hamlet of Tavers, comprising now only a couple of farms. Walk to the right, along the rough track to the little wood on top of the rise and, in a clearing among acacias and blackthorn, you will find the dolmen locally called *'La Pierre Tournante'*, a flat stone about thirteen feet wide resting on five pillars, a mysterious, lonely relic of Tavers's antiquity and of a remote age beyond our ken. What the purpose of these things was, and who put them there, it is useless to guess. They are far, far older than the Druids. Local legend usually contains a clue to such mysteries because, although distorted, it is transmitted from a time when the truth was known. There is a legend here that a great treasure lies beneath the monument, richer and richer the deeper you go, and that the stone makes one complete turn at midnight every Christmas Eve, revealing the entrance to the secret chamber. But woe betide anyone who enters, for it turns so rapidly he will be trapped – to starve alone with the object of his cupidity. Diggings made beneath it in 1882 revealed a Roman coin, an iron dagger and – farther down – some human bones.

From Tavers we can now either proceed straight along the main road, or continue to hug the Loire for a little while longer by passing through the villages of **Lestiou** and **Avaray**. They contain nothing of note. Their waterfronts are pleasant; they are spoilt only by the science-fiction view across the river, to the nuclear power-station of Saint-Laurent. Between Avaray and Blois, either by the main road or the minor ones, there is nothing special until you come to **Menars**, and that *is* special; as an example of graceful, well-proportioned domestic architecture of the age of elegance it is unequalled any-where in the Val de Loire. Owned by the Saint-Gobain glass company since 1939, it is open to the public every day (except Tuesdays and the whole of November) from 8.30 to 11.30 and from 2 to 6 (4.30 in winter). The central part is the original except for the gallery and a few other embellishments by later owners; it was erected in 1645 by Guillaume Charron, grandson of the *maître de poste* (man in charge of the post-horses) at Saint-Dyé across the river. From his relatively humble origins he 'made good' in the army, eventually becoming its Treasurer-General. For the interior decoration in his new home he employed the remarkable local artist, Jean Mosnier of Blois, whose work we shall meet again in this chapter.

In 1760 the little château was bought by Madame de Pompadour and she employed Gabriel, who had designed the École Militaire for her in Paris, to add the two wings which now give the whole its beautiful proportions. She intended the place to be a quiet haven from the court in her old age. With this in mind she applied to it not only her lavish extravagance, but her good taste and her practical knowledge of housekeeping, botany and gardening. For all her faults, she had those accomplishments among others, and one cannot help feeling sorry for her in that she had little time to enjoy Menars; less than four years later she died at Versailles, having come to stay here only twice. The wags of Orléans made their jokes about 'the heaviest burden in France' when she crossed their bridge, but she did leave behind one great benefit to the whole district: she had the road built from Orléans to the château, which her brother, the marquis de Marigny, completed as far as Blois. Before that there was no road of any consequence on the right bank and Menars had to be approached by boat from the other side. Marigny carried out a few more improvements, mostly exterior, employing Soufflot – who constructed the Panthéon in Paris – to add the lovely gallery; the double exterior stairway leading down to the terrace; the orangery and a grotto by the little lake. Inside one is shown the gallery and four of the rooms, and the kitchens with their underground passage to the house. The rooms are furnished mainly in eighteenth-century style, but of course none of the Pompadour's treasures remains.

After the visit you are released by the guide to wander where you like, and as long as you like, in the lovely gardens. This is the part I like best, for you can stand back and admire the architecture of the house from every angle; lounge on one of the terraces by the Loire; visit the orangery where oranges are still grown; even have a chat with the gardeners about the flowers. And then there are curiosities such as the lake and grotto; the two sphinxes with human faces – one Pompadour, the other her rival du Barry – and the fine sundial on the Allée du Méridien (not *the* meridian, just plain south; we are a degree and a half east of Greenwich) which tells the date as well as the time. Altogether Menars is something not to miss, and it is an easy excursion from Beaugency or from Blois.

Let us turn our attention now to the left bank. The road out of Beaugency to the south joins up with the main road from Olivet to Blois, and soon comes to **Saint-Laurent-des-Eaux**, where the nuclear power-station is certainly worth a call if you are scientifically minded. It has an observation-tower open to the public with a little exhibition-room beneath it containing fascinating models, diagrams and explanations which are not hard to follow. There are no formalities, no charge, not even an attendant; just follow the signs, park outside and walk in. Electricité de France is proud of its achievements in atomic power and anxious that the public should understand them.

Built on an artificial island in the bed of the Loire in the late 1960s, Saint-Laurent is original in having complete integration of the heat-exchangers with the reactor in the same container of pre-stressed concrete, which the authority contends is safer for the whole. Its functioning is entirely automatic, conducted from a control-room at the side of the massive paraphernalia of machinery. But it does strange things to the river, which local anglers, among others, are none too happy about. Its coolers discharge a current of warm water which in summer soon evens out by convection with the temperature of the river; but in winter this miniature Gulf Stream thirty to forty yards wide maintains its boundaries for a considerable distance just like the warm currents of the oceans, discernible by the steam that rises from it for twelve miles or more downstream. Fishing on the left bank where it passes closest is good at such times as it stimulates the fish into activity, but its temperature can reach 30°C or more which is above the tolerance limit of many species – trout for example – and in the long run it means a decline in the fish population. There also seem to be problems of oxygen impoverishment, the proliferation of plankton, and the growth of toxic algae and certain strange micro-organisms not yet clearly identified. So, after barrages, embankments, theft of its waters and chemical pollution, our poor old river now has to suffer a new form of interference from technological man.

The road carries on to **Muides**, which is of no special interest except that it has a bridge across the Loire at a convenient halfway point between the two main towns, and then brings us to **Saint-Dyé** whose quays, more than a mile long, are lined with majestic plane trees and provide a most pleasant walk or drive, according to the time at one's disposal. The river here is wide and the current consequently slower, giving an impression almost of tranquillity – though the Loire is never really tranquil, a point for the venturesome always to bear in mind.

Here at Saint-Dyé we have another dragon legend, but this dragon was not aggressive like others; it just killed everything that went too near by its stink. Living in a deep cave where the villagers left offerings of carrion to keep it happy, it grew so fat that it found its apartments too cramped and set out waddling round the neighbourhood in search of new ones. Gregory of Tours relates that it spoilt all the fields, caused the inhabitants to flee and 'infected the air to such an extent that birds flying above fell dead on the spot'. Something had to be done and the right man came along in the person of Saint Dyé who succeeded in strangling the loathsome creature with his stole.

The church stands over the spot where he had his cell; it is in bad repair, but the west tower retains vestiges of Romanesque, and (proof that Saint Dyé existed if not his dragon) his sarcophagus is beneath the floor where you may view it through a sheet of plate-glass. Note the rough-hewn sandstone of the little crypt, for this is part of the original Merovingian chapel, thirteen hundred years old.

Two miles beyond Saint-Dyé, on the right through a copse of poplar trees, are some riding-stables where you can hire a horse to ride in the park of Chambord, the open portion of which is close by on the south-east. From this point the road stays close to the river the rest of the way to Blois, and one of the particularly fine prospects to be enjoyed is that of the château of Menars shining white across the water, with its terraces sweeping gently down to the river's edge.

And now for the châteaux of the Sologne, which I include in this chapter as geographically belonging to it, but which are equally within reach from Blois. The principal one is of course **Chambord**, standing in its enormous park surrounded by a wall twenty miles long. Public roads have made gaps in this 'longest wall in France' so from whichever way you enter you will be greeted by a big notice-board: '*Vous êtes dans le parc de Chambord, circulation réglementée*'. Now this is a bad start, because a lot of reglementing is apt to dispel the magic of a place and this one is very reglemented indeed – to such an extent that the only fairy people of these woods are the gendarmes and one has a feeling they are behind every tree. Stop a minute by the roadside and more than likely they will appear from nowhere to tell you gravely that it is an offence to stop *anywhere* except on the authorized car-parks, and hand you a leaflet with a rather indistinct map of those sparsely scattered places and a list of other dos and don'ts. Anyway you will get one on arriving at the château, where you are charged for parking as well as for admission, an unusual unkindness in France. Near by are souvenir shops selling a rather limited range of goods and the wine of Cours-Cheverny among whose vineyards we shall soon be, so they can be disregarded and we can give attention to the château before us: a huge, expensive architectural folly, not entirely unpleasing, but overbearing in its vastness. It is open 9 to 11.45 and 2 to 6.30 from 1 April to 30 September; the same hours, except that it closes at 5, during October; 10 to 11.45 and 2 to 4 during the rest of the year. Closed Tuesdays except only 20 June–30 August. *Son et lumière* in high season; times variable; enquire on the spot or at any *syndicat d'initiative* in the district.

Originally a comparatively small medieval castle stood here, the property of the Counts of Blois, which François I acquired and demolished in order to replace it with something in the new vogue and more suitable to his extraordinary needs. He preferred the Loire to Paris and had other establishments along the river of course, the chief being Blois. But he had a passion for hunting (the Venetian ambassador reported of him: 'He is forever chasing now stags, now women') and the hunting, of stags at any rate, was especially good in this thickly wooded part of the Sologne. He decided to have a hunting-lodge here, but it had to be rather bigger than anybody else's hunting-lodge for wherever he went the whole court went with him. A cavalcade of 12,000 horses carried family, officials, nobility and their attendants, together with everyone's servants, furniture, crockery and baggage, and all had to be housed. Then there were the artists, writers and scientists who gathered round him in considerable numbers. 'Anyone who came was received,' records Brantôme, 'but he'd better not be an ass nor dither.' For the King was something of an expert on almost any subject.

But the new building had to be imposing for another reason. This was the epoch of the Field of the Cloth-of-Gold and other such ostentatious frolics of those outsize, bombastic monarchs who jostled for the leading role on the stage of Europe. François must have something grander than Henry VIII or the Holy Roman Emperor, to dazzle and intimidate. In this respect Chambord certainly achieved what he desired: when Charles V was brought here in the course of his state visit in 1538 it took his breath away, and despite his usual taciturnity he was obliged to say so. For its more basic purpose it was never a great success: comfort and the ordinary needs of housekeeping in a large establishment seem hardly to have been considered at all in this extravagant complex of 'architectural megalomania', as one French writer has called it. No Pompadour, as at Menars, no sensible home-loving woman ever had a say in this. How can a host entertain guests scattered throughout more than 400 rooms, separated by some eighty staircases and literally miles of passages, with a heating system devised to fit in with the whim of having 365 chimneys? Chateaubriand romantically compared the skyline to 'a girl with her hair tossing in the wind'; presumably his own hair had never tossed in the draughts that blow within. Nobody ever took the place seriously as a residence. In eighteen years, after it was ready for occupation, François I stayed there a total of about forty days; several of the monarchs who followed him never came near it; Louis XIII dumped his tiresome brother Gaston d'Orléans there for a time; Louis XIV paid it about nine short visits; Louis XV gave it to the maréchal de Saxe who lived here for a few months all told, and he was the last resident owner.

The construction of Chambord commenced in 1519 and was still not really complete when François died in 1557. It had no single architect and followed no definite plan. Several Italians, including Domenico Cortone and Leonardo da Vinci, seem to have had a hand in mere sketches from which local masons and a team of 1800 workmen improvised as they went along. There is no ground for ascribing the result to Leonardo, as is sometimes done, for he died the year before the work started. Posterity is chiefly indebted to him in the matter for his part in persuading His Majesty that it would not be practicable to divert the Loire for a moat!

The principal feature was always intended to be the central staircase, the main building serving only to house it, and the rest is a series of afterthoughts added on. The staircase, built of stone in a double spiral so that people can pass without meeting one another, and ending right on the roof eighty feet above, certainly remains the most staggering showpiece, but only as a curiosity, 'an extraordinary work, but of far greater expense than use or beauty', as John Evelyn expressed it. Once out on the flat roof you find yourself in a maze of elaborately sculpted chimneys, turrets and minarets like the miniature spires and towers of a town in Fairyland. A promenade all the way round serves as a vast belvedere from which the ladies of the court could watch the hunt for miles across the forest spread out below, and undeniably it is an impressive view. The maréchal de Saxe watched the manoeuvres of his troops from up here. The hero of Fontenay could not long bear to be parted from a martial atmosphere and brought his own personal regiment with him, about 1000 strong, mostly cavalry: a veritable Foreign Legion comprising Germans, Poles, Flemings, Hungarians, Alsatians, Turks, Tartars and Negroes – the latter all mounted on white horses. For the entertainment of his guests he staged parades or mock battles almost daily. The great stable-block he put up for his mounts to the south of the château is still there and you can hire horses from Monsieur Poisson who lives in the middle of it through the first opening in the wall. Hiring is unaccompanied by the hour; or by arrangement in advance (telephone 463438) you can join one of the twice-monthly *'promenades organisées'* in the parts of the forest generally closed to the public.

Inside, the hollow discomfort of the château is emphasized by its mainly unfurnished condition. The *Chambre royale*, occupied during a spell of residence here by Stanislas Leczinski, exiled King of Poland and father-in-law of Louis XV, is furnished with a few of his own things; but the coaches, throne, toys and other souvenirs of the equally unfortunate comte de Chambord (titular Henri V whom Louis-Philippe usurped) have a more tenuous connection with the place for he never lived here. In the small room which François I used as a study, a window is pointed out where he scratched on the pane with his diamond ring: 'Woman is often fickle; great fool he who trusts her.' The tale is told (in slightly varying versions, but it could be true) that Louis XIV came across it during a visit here as a young man. Marie Mancini stood beside him, Mazarin's enchanting niece whom he deeply loved but was not allowed to marry for reasons of state. Piqued by such cynicism which he was far from sharing at the time, he smashed his cane through it. Another, much later, incident is related of him, on the authority of Madame de Maintenon. In 1669 Molière and the composer Lully collaborated in staging a comic ballet, *Monsieur de Pourceaugnac*, for which the guardroom was adapted downstairs. It was one of those evenings when the King was not easily to be amused and unresponsive gloom prevailed as the piece proceeded; so in desperation Lully jumped from the stage into the orchestra, landing on the harpsichord which shattered in pieces. This at last appealed to the King's sense of fun, though he showed no sign at the time and reserved his praise until the repeat performance next evening, complaining only that Lully had not jumped into the orchestra again. The following year a greater masterpiece of Molière's, *Le Bourgeois Gentilhomme*, was given its first performance here.

At the Revolution Chambord presented the new régime with some problems. First, the usual orders that all royal emblems be erased from the stonework could not be carried out: there are hundreds of them – on doorways and windows, fireplaces and the outside chimneys – and there just were not sufficient *sansculottes* keen and agile enough for the task. Then they found they couldn't even sell it, the only bidder being the Society of Friends in England, who had the idea of using it for a Quaker orphanage, and that deal of course fell through when war broke out. In 1829 a national subscription was raised to buy it for the comte de Chambord and it was eventually from one of his heirs, Elie de Bourbon, that the state confiscated it in 1915 because he was serving with the Austrian army. In 1947 the present Commission was set up to manage the property 'on behalf of the nation', which it does by excluding its citizens from the greater part of the forest and severely restricting what they may do in the rest – about 3000 acres opened to the public during a period of enlightened administration by Monsieur Belorgy, the present Prefect. The Commission claims to be proceeding on 'scientific' lines to 'provide a convenient sylvo-cynegenetic balance'. In fact the woodlands here are as poor as anywhere else in the Sologne – even poorer, for the wild animals (about 450 red deer, 50 roe deer and 350 wild boar) have to be artificially fed to prevent them eating up the forest, and the food put out for them has to be dosed with medicaments to prevent disease. The reason for this overcrowding is that Chambord is a *Réserve Nationale de Chasse*. Reserved, that is, for members of the government and their guests. Humbler folk may watch the game from authorized 'watching-posts' indicated on the map on the leaflet. We may also photograph them if we apply not less than four days in advance to the *Commissariat du Domaine de Chambord, Service Photographique, Maison Forestière des Réfractaires*, 41250, Bracieux, for a permit and are lucky enough to get any response. I was not, when I wrote several times for information, and it was the Prefect himself who kindly supplied it for me in the end. All this bureaucratic fuss for so little result in terms of anything truly wild and natural makes one wonder whether Arthur Young's suggestion when he saw Chambord would not be better. Noting the great tracts of wasteland he 'could not help thinking that if the king of France ever formed the idea of establishing one compleat and perfect farm under the turnip culture of England, here is the place for it'.

A run of five miles southward from Chambord through the Forêt de Boulogne (which is an extension of the park and equally *réglementée*) brings us to our next château: **Villesavin**, just west of the village of Bracieux. It is open all the year round save 20 December –

20 January; every day 9 to noon and 2 to sunset. Despite its sorrowful state of disrepair, which the owner is now rectifying with the help of grants from the Beaux Arts, Villesavin is refreshing to the eye after the ostentatiousness of Chambord. With just a ground floor topped by an attic with the same sculpted dormer windows, it is in a sense a miniature of its royal neighbour and was completed only a few years afterwards. But there is a difference of architectural interest: whereas Chambord is of the First Renaissance style, built upon the Gothic plan of a square round a central keep, Villesavin is Second Renaissance, built on the 'horseshoe' plan round an open courtyard; the exuberance of embellishment is toned down and there is already that tendency towards the Classical style to come – a feature also of Fontainebleau, with which it is almost exactly contemporary. This trend will be noticeable again when we come to Villandry, near Tours, which was built at the same time and for the same man, Jean le Breton, Financial Secretary to François I. He intended Villandry as his main residence, but he had so efficiently supervised the bills-of-quantities at Chambord that the King wished him to continue as its Administrator and gave him the use of his masons to build Villesavin as a second residence at hand for his duties. Indeed, such was the King's faith in the whole family that when Jean died in 1543, only a few years after Villesavin was completed, he appointed Anne, his widow, to succeed him as Administrator of Chambord with the additional title of Governor; and after her death their daughter took over these offices. In a sense then, this little château at the other end of the forest was the *conciergerie* to the greater one.

The guided visit is not extensive, but reveals a few other items of interest besides the architecture. These include a beautiful sixteenth-century Italian marble fountain in the courtyard; the chapel with frescoes attributed to Niccolo dell'Abate, now in a rather poor state as it was used for many years as kennels, and a collection of old vehicles among which is a sixteen-seater horse-drawn omnibus. But the most intriguing feature of all is the big round stone dovecote; there can be few anywhere so fine and so complete. The wall inside is pierced all the way round from top to bottom with 1500 nesting-holes, and a great ladder from the ground to the summit, perpendicular and pivoting on a central column enabled every nest to be reached on one climb. It is still sound and in working order, and only lacks its 3000 doves.

Villesavin is on the southern boundary of the forest overlooking the valley of the charming little river Beuvron. At the bridge there is some open waste land where you can get down beside it for a picnic, in solitude on ordinary days, on high days and holidays in the merry company of French families with a van in attendance selling *frites* piping hot. One May Day as I passed by, the *frites* man was selling pork chops cut from two whole pigs spit-roasted in the open, a scene reminiscent of Obélix and his friends feasting on wild boar in the Astérix cartoons – and not inappropriately so, for this little road and the village on the other side, **Ponts d'Arian**, date back to ancient Gaul. At the cross-roads outside the village is a very popular *café-bar* where day-tickets are obtainable all the year round for fishing in the mere near by.

The real Sologne now stretches away to the south and east of us, geologically a wide expanse of soft deposits of the Miocene Tertiary, giving a countryside so different in character from that on the slightly earlier Oligocene which is harder and forms the plateau of the Beauce on the other side of the Loire. The *'triste Sologne'* it has often been called: a flat plain extending as far as the Berry, a lonely land of meres, ponds, heaths, poor woodlands and notices on trees. At some places where you cross its boundaries a big roadside board announces that *'La Sologne vous souhaite la bienvenue'*, but those smaller notices on trees and gateposts make it clear how welcome you really are – *Défense d'entrer*; *Chasse gardée*; even *Champignon interdit* from some absentee owner who seems unlikely to come down from Paris every morning to pick his mushrooms for himself. I concede his right to be so mean with his own if he wishes, but I do reprehend the brochures and guidebooks which burble so prettily about the *'Pays de la Chasse'* and imply that the tourist may spend a happy holiday down here shooting those handsome pheasants illustrated on the local postcards. Apart from a few exceptions about which it is wise to enquire of the French Tourist Board in advance he has little hope. There are a few local poachers, but they need to be highly skilled to survive, and even then seem to require a patron saint – Saint Viatre, whose shrine used to be at the village of that name just north of Romorantin.

Once this was all fine oak forest, but indiscriminate deforestation in the Middle Ages in the hope of providing arable land reduced it to a sour wilderness. Big trees are water-pumps, and an acre of adult broad-leafed trees will pump 3000 gallons or more of water a day out of the soil. Remove them without draining or leaving a proportion of trees to drain for you, and the soil becomes water-logged, especially where, as here, there is surface clay. Once this happens, it is too late to reclaim with hardwood forestry; but in the last 150 years widespread attempts have been made to do so with pine and generally they have succeeded. The Scots and Corsican varieties are chiefly used because they are hardiest; the usually equable climate of the Val de Loire can spring surprises and the winter of 1878–9 practically wiped out all the young Maritime pines, a species so successful in reclaiming the Garonne district in the south. The plantations are cultivated commercially on a sixty-year rotation. Economically this is a good thing for the people who live here, but aesthetically, of course, the plantations do not improve the scenery. Nevertheless the Sologne is not all monotonous; the map gives the clue to the old neglected parts (the areas dotted bluest with meres – *étangs*) where by now a certain natural balance has been reached, and these have an appeal of their own and the wistful charm of open-air solitude. Here the keepers cannot do much about a harmless passer-by strolling quietly among the beautiful silver birches of the heathlands to enjoy the colours of the broom, the heather and the ling, or beside an *étang* to watch the duck and the elegant crested grebe. To avoid trouble though, take nothing away – not even that humble forbidden mushroom.

The villages and towns of the Sologne are generally small, quiet and not particularly interesting. Life in them is unhurried and, outside the shooting season, the small hotels and restaurants are not too busy and often very reasonable. **Romorantin** is the chief town and even its population is under ten thousand.

Our next château, **Cheverny**, lies four miles south-west of Ponts d'Arian. It is open to the public all the year from 8.30 to 11.45 and 2 to 7 (sunset when earlier) every day. It is the home of the marquis de Vibraye, scion of a collateral branch of the original family who built it in 1634; so understandably, but regrettably, we are not free to wander round the beautiful gardens which surround it. However we can pause to feast our eyes upon them as we walk up to the house. Lawns, grass paddocks and wide alleys give a spacious setting to fine, well-shaped, uncrowded trees – horse-chestnuts, limes, cedars, wellingtonias and many others. The atmosphere is that of the parks surrounding so many of our own great country houses, except that in this more favourable climate the trees are bigger. On turning into the main pathway leading up to the main entrance (although occupied, this is one of the few châteaux where the tourist enters by the front door) we are greeted by the façade of the house gleaming white across the lawns. It is built of the white tufa stone of which we shall be seeing more and more as we move farther into the Touraine, and has the appearance of having just been expensively cleaned, but it has never been cleaned at all in 300 years: tufa is a soft limestone that hardens on contact with the air and stays white.

The proportions of the façade have an unusual aspect, a certain heaviness, because the central pavilion is small in comparison with the two wings, which are taller with domed roofs and seem to crush it a little. But the result is not ugly: the heaviness gives an air of solid dignity at the expense of elegance, that is all. Moreover its architectural interest is all the greater for the fact that it remains unaltered in any way; it is pure Louis XIII. The same applies inside where there is a beautifully proportioned staircase in white stone. No stunt staircase this one, but designed for comfort in use and repose of mind, the latter afforded both by its proportions and by the delightful sculpture which adorns it. Not only are the conventional themes there in flowing grace – the garlands, fruit, cupids and laurels – but on the pillars and pilasters of the first floor, themes of war and the arts are illustrated by minutely detailed weapons and armour; a lyre; an artist's palette with a sheaf of brushes and so on. All are cut with delicacy and precision by a hand that was quick and sure – a hand unknown as is so often the case with sculpture. Whoever this master was, he modestly cut 'F.L. 1634' on the ground-floor balustrade when he finished and went his way.

Painters on the other hand have much more chance of being remembered, and so it was with Jean Mosnier whom we have already encountered at Menars. Here is the widest range of his work to be seen anywhere, for he was engaged here for eighteen years. His ceilings are astounding in their grandeur of conception, the movement and perspective of the figures and in their colours all set off by rich gilding; and in the dining-room his humorous little scenes from *Don Quixote* deserve the closest attention even if this means falling behind in the flow of the guided tour for a few minutes. Born at Blois in 1600, of a family of glass-blowers, when only sixteen years old Mosnier attracted the attention of Marie de Médicis with a Virgin he had copied, and she paid for him to go to her native Florence where he worked under Passignano and Allori for several years before going on to Rome. On his return to France after an absence of nine years, he worked for the Queen Mother at the Luxembourg in Paris where two of his ceilings are still to be seen in the *Salle du Livre d'Or*. But her influence had declined by then and she was unable to push him through the barriers of the art 'establishment' in the capital. Disappointed at obtaining no further advancement there, he returned to Blois and undertook these local commissions, with the result that his best work is here in the countryside of his boyhood. There would have been more of it if he had not over-indulged and died of gout in 1656.

Outside, although the gardens are out of bounds, there is a **Museum of Hunting** where connoisseurs of stags' antlers will find 2000 pairs of them to study; and you can visit the kennels where a pack of about eighty hounds is maintained, cross-bred – English for sturdiness and Poitevin for 'nose'. From November to Easter hunts are organized on Tuesdays and Saturdays and processions are held when the big coiled horns, the celebrated *'Trompes de Cheverny'*, are played. The kennels, stables and other *communs* stand on the site of an earlier château which was built in about 1519 by Raoul Hurault who belonged to another of those bourgeois families who attained fortune in the royal service. But during the reign of Henri IV one of his successors, Henri Hurault, deserted the *robe* for the *épée* and followed the royal army, a vocation which involved his absence from home for long periods so that his young wife, Françoise, became bored alone in the country. This led to a tragedy, the awful story of which is borne out by the parish register as well as contemporary records at Blois.

At the court in Paris on 25 January 1602, a Friday, Henri was about to leave a room in which several people were talking to the King when he heard laughter behind him and, glancing in a mirror, he saw the King holding two fingers to his head signifying horns while the other courtiers tittered and glanced in his direction. Pretending not to have noticed, he walked on, and once outside sent immediately for his horse. Riding through the night he arrived home at five o'clock in the morning. The sound of the gates being opened gave a little warning to those inside, but only enough for the page who had been snug in bed with the comtesse to jump from the window. He broke his leg in doing so, and was quickly despatched by the angry husband's own hand. Sending for the village curé as witness, Henri soon after entered his wife's chamber with a cup of poison in one hand and his bloody sword in the other, giving her one hour to choose which of the two she preferred. She chose the cup which he had left behind, and an autopsy after her death disclosed another victim – a five-months infant in her womb. What happened to the curé as a result is not recorded; but as far as Henri was concerned the King, feeling himself partly responsible, merely banished him for three years – to Cheverny! Not an excessive penalty for a triple homicide. But during those years of gloom and remorse on the scene of his crime he attracted the sympathy of Marguerite Gaillard, the pretty daughter of his bailiff, and married her. They lived happily ever after and had seven children, and in due course the comte was readmitted to the royal service and to court. To wipe out sad memories he had the new château built and the old one demolished. Marguerite supervised the work and what we see today is said to be, for the greater part, her choice.

The neighborhood of Cheverny is a V.D.Q.S. area.* The soil is principally clay and gravel, so that the wine tends to be of good strength and dry. Several *cépages* are used, including the ubiquitous Gamay of Beaujolais fame which we have already met: here also it produces a light, smooth, fruity red, but rather better than at Olivet. Others are the Chardonnay, the grape of the best white Burgundies though it cannot attain the same excellence here, and the Sauvignon which we have already tasted at its best at Sancerre and Pouilly. The two regional *cépages* are the Menu Pineau, grown quite extensively in the eastern Touraine and producing a light dry white, and the Romorantin (here the name of the grape, not of the town) which is *the* local wine, almost exclusive to the district. It produces a dry white, less acid than the others; is distinctive in flavour, though with some resemblance to Sancerre; keeps well for a year or two and will travel if allowed a rest on getting home. These can all be sampled in the friendly kitchen of Monsieur Michel Repinçay, the youngest of the vignerons in the local *Confrérie*. His premises are on the Blois road just outside the town and he sells retail. Cheverny is one of the lesser-known and most under-valued wine districts of the Loire.

Four miles to the north-west of Cours-Cheverny is the last of our Sologne châteaux, **Beauregard**, on the southern edge of the Forêt de Russy, overlooking the valley of the Beuvron (open daily all the year except 15 January to 5 February; 9 to noon and 2 to 7; 5.30 in winter). It is said to have been built not long before 1520 for François I as a hunting lodge. If so it is an example of his undoubted good taste when unmixed with motives for ostentation. It is small and elegant, of the Renaissance style, though its proportions have been just a little unbalanced by the high, steep roof which was substituted in the last century. In about 1545 Beauregard was acquired by Jean du Thier who eventually became a Secretary of State to Henri II. He was a bibliophile, a scholar and friend of artists and poets. His beautiful little study, panelled throughout, walls and ceiling, remains

*Vins Délimités de Qualité Supérieure — covers more than 50 better-than-average wines; a secondary designation.

as he left it. On the top panels of the walls is a series of superb paintings, each with a theme – sports, hunting, the table and so on – executed for him by an Italian, Francesco Scibec di Carpi.

In the next century the property was acquired by the Ardier family and Paul Ardier, one of Louis XIII's ministers, added the long gallery which is the showpiece of the house. In three rows around three of its walls are 363 portraits of fifteen sovereigns of France and the notabilities of their times. The majority are of course seventeenth-century copies of larger paintings elsewhere, but what a fascinating work of reference to have on one's wall! A complete illustrated catalogue, even at a fairly high price, would sell well I am sure, but no one seems to have thought of it. The caretaker does her best to point out particular individuals when asked, but she can hardly be expected to remember them all. The lower panels are painted by Jean Mosnier with allegorical motifs; he also painted every beam, cross-beam and panel of the fantastic ceiling. And as if this were not enough for one room, the floor is a whole army on the march, on Delft tiles each of which bears a soldier in the somewhat ludicrous military costume of Louis XIII's time. In other rooms a selection of seventeenth- and eighteenth-century furniture is displayed, and the visit includes an unusually light and salubrious kitchen for the period. For sheer detailed interest Beauregard has perhaps the most to offer of all the châteaux of this area.

I have suggested no particular itinerary in this chapter. Some may be coming out on day trips from Blois, others may be hurrying towards it, worn out after attempting to see everything between here and Beaugency at one swoop. But those who have time should not miss the valley of the Beuvron which flows on seven more miles after **Cellettes**, the village just down the hill from Beauregard, before it joins the Loire. We have already paused beside this small, gentle river at Ponts d'Arian, so appealing in a quiet, intimate way, flowing by wide cornfields (for we are now just out of the badlands of the Sologne) and fringed with woods. On the left, as you follow it along, are several watermills and at **Seur**, by the bridge, it widens into a big pool where the village children swim, and even have a proper diving-board, and the women still use the old *lavoir* to do their laundry. You could hardly imagine a more tranquil village scene than this, but Seur becomes the centre of much clamour and stir for a few days in early September each year when the devout of the avant-garde descend upon it in large numbers for a '*Fête de l'Humanité*'. At **Les Montils** there is a pleasant camp-site by the side of the river, and at **Candé** a nice clean little country *auberge* on the corner by the bridge. Shortly after this the Beuvron is joined by the Cosson, a sister tributary which has also come across the Sologne a little farther to the north, through the park of Chambord, and they flow into the Loire hand-in-hand. A minor road from Candé leads along the left bank of the Loire, with good views across it, to Blois just upstream.

CHAPTER EIGHT

Blois

✤

The skyline of **Blois** as you approach along the left bank and see it
across the river is one of the prettiest of the Loire; only Gien perhaps
is its equal. And the long, elegant eighteenth-century bridge, with
its little pinnacle in the middle surmounted by a cross, is in complete
harmony with the scene. The whole arouses a feeling of expectancy –
which indeed will not be disappointed. Like La Charité it is very old
indeed and was built on a site with the shape of an amphitheatre,
which is still apparent. Its name is from an old Breton dialect word
bleitz meaning wolf, and that animal was the emblem on its shield
in the Middle Ages. Its chief economic function for centuries was
that of a central market for the agricultural region of the Beauce
at its back; it has never really figured largely as a strategic point, so
its story holds nothing sensational from the annals of war – until
1940 when it was bombarded, set on fire, assaulted, desperately de-
fended and finally occupied. But that was a time when every town
with a bridge over the Loire acquired strategic significance.

Nevertheless the name of Blois is renowned in history by reason
of the extraordinary personages who have been associated with it.
The first of these to come to English minds is most likely to be
Stephen of Blois, second son of the comte de Blois and Adèle,
daughter of the Conqueror, who usurped the throne of England on
the death of Henry I. He lived here only in infancy however, being
brought up afterwards at the English court. The limelight did not
really begin to fall on Blois until nearly two centuries later, at the
end of a new line of counts, the celebrated Chatillon family. The last
of these, Guy de Chatillon, was a hostage at the Savoy in London
with Jean II in his second captivity. On coming home he settled to
the quiet life of a bibliophile and in 1383 appointed Froissart as his
chaplain, settled him at the château and commissioned him to write
the second (and more chatty) part of his famous *Chronicles*.

When Guy was an old man, without heirs and in debt, Louis
d'Orléans approached him to buy the estate. Aided by a little royal
pressure from his brother, Charles VI, and bribes to the old Count's

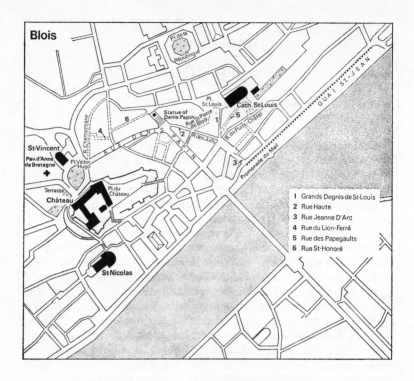

young wife as well as to his most trusted servant, he got it at a bargain price – a rather shady deal altogether, but the beginning of the town's long era of fame and prosperity. Louis lived ten more years to enjoy what he had coveted, then in the struggle for the regency after the King lost his reason, he was murdered in Paris by Jean sans Peur. They were an odious crew, the 'establishment' of that time; Louis had married his cousin Valentine Visconti of Milan, but was having an affair with the Queen, Isabelle of Bavaria, so that 'he had his cousin for a wife and his sister-in-law for a mistress', as the marquis de Sade put it; and later when Isabelle tried to bastardize her own son, the Dauphin Charles, she named him as the father. He could well have been; but the list of other candidates is long and does just include the King himself. To complete the pattern, Valentine was at the same time an occasional mistress to the King. She was deeply grieved however by her husband's violent death, and shut herself up in the castle here for the rest of her life, in a chamber draped with black, its wall engraved *'Plus ne m'est rien; rien ne m'est plus.'*

Her son Charles – destined to be the most appealing, and perhaps the greatest, figure in the history of Blois – was then fourteen. He loved the conversation of his mother's literary friends and the books of old Guy de Chatillon's library. His ambition was not for political power, but simply to be a poet; none the less he eventually found himself the unwilling substitute for his father at the centre of the conflict with the Burgundian-English party. The outcome was his capture at Agincourt and imprisonment in the Tower of London for twenty-five years until his ransom could be paid. There he whiled away the time playing his lute and writing songs and poems which expressed the revulsion of a sensitive mind against the brutality of his times. He returned to Blois in 1440, his estates in the meantime having been faithfully managed for him by his half-brother, Dunois the Bastard, and for another twenty-five years until he died he was able to lead the sort of life he had always wished for. He took as his motto *Nonchaloir*, perhaps best translated 'Keep cool'. His days were filled with quiet and gentle pursuits: walks in the forest in preference to hunting; a book by the fireside; the conversation of others who shared his tastes. For this last he kept open house for all who cared to call, and one day in about 1457 a raggedy young man came to the château announcing that he was a poet. The Duke replied that this was most fortunate as he had just organized a competition: to compose a ballad containing contradictory propositions in each line, and here was the first:

I die from thirst beside the fountain

Borrowing the Duke's pen, the vagabond immediately added:

. . . Not as fire, with chattering teeth,
I am at home in a faraway land;
Beside a brazier, I shiver flame.

Overwhelmed with admiration the Duke feasted him and asked him to stay, but he declined. On being pressed for his name before he departed the guest replied that it was of no importance, but that he generally called himself François Villon. The two greatest French poets of their time, the prince and the beggar, never met again.

There was a sensibility and refinement about Charles d'Orléans that made him a forerunner of all that was best in the Renaissance,

and in his verse a serene tenderness which reaches even further
forward to the Romantics of the nineteenth century. Keats might
have written the piece in celebration of spring which he joyously
composed soon after his homecoming from captivity and of which
this is the first verse:

> The season has dropped its mantel
> Of Wind, cold and rain,
> To dress itself in
> Sparkling sun, clear and beautiful.
> There are no beasts or birds
> That in their language don't sing or cry.
> The season has dropped its mantel.

At the age of seventy-one he had the happiness of an heir being
born to his third wife, Marie de Clèves (though some said, on the
thinnest of evidence, that a valet named Rabadage had the happiness
of producing it), and this child's reign as Louis XII was indeed to be
a bridge to the Renaissance. Louis grew up at Blois and remained
fond of it all his life. After he became King at the end of the century
he extended and improved the château, aided by Anne of Brittany,
his new Queen, who had done the same for her previous spouse,
Charles VIII, at Amboise. Here now was the court, and Blois became
for all practical purposes the capital of France.

The first effect on the town was a housing crisis, and a fever of
building supervened, the signs of which are plainly noticeable all
over the town today. The King had scores of houses put up for his
servants and one even, it is said, to store the cheeses which he
collected in the course of his tours about the country. Perhaps they
smelt too strong to have them near him at the château. Meanwhile
ministers, courtiers, ambassadors all vied with one another to
acquire a plot of land and build a residence worthy of their status,
and the merchants and artisans necessary to serve all these exalted
folk flocked to the town and squeezed in where they could.

In 1514 Louis gave his daughter Claude in marriage to his cousin
François who would be the next king, and as part of her dowry the
comté of Blois. In the same year he himself, by then a widower,
hastened François's inheritance by marrying the young, gay and
flighty Mary of York, sister of Henry VIII. It was an anxious time
for François and his creditors, who had lent vast sums on his
prospects; an heir would have ruined him. But Mary's lively Tudor
temperament was too much for the King and she wore him out with
fêtes, balls and late nights. The following New Year's Day he died.

Poor Claude was then seventeen and survived only nine more years, during which she bore the new King seven children. Tiny, narrow-shouldered, congenitally lame like her mother, pale and rather plain, with a timid smile always on her thin lips, she has left little for posterity to remember her by except the French word for greengage, a new fruit brought to Blois from the Middle East by one of François's gardeners. But when speaking of *reine-claudes* few people actually think of the frail little Queen who took refuge from her contemptuous, masterful mother-in-law, Louise of Savoy, by working tapestries, reading good books and saying prayers in her own little circle of respectable ladies-in-waiting. Among these exemplary females was the daughter of a squire from Blickling in Norfolk who was English Ambassador to France for a time. Anne was her name, and it was soon after she went back to England from Blois, her country manners french-polished and her Norfolk surname Bullen frenchified to Boleyn, that she caught the roving eye of Mary of York's wicked brother.

François continued to use Blois as his court for a time, until he became almost completely nomadic as we have seen in the last chapter, and he added yet more to the château. He also took over the late King's fool, nicknamed Triboulet, of a peasant family in the suburb of Foix, just outside the city wall on the west. Not to be confused with Renée d'Anjou's dwarf of the same name, he was of normal stature but of a remarkably magnificent ugliness which is what had attracted Louis's attention. Delighted to find a brilliant wit joined to this attribute, the King gave him the usual fool's licence to talk scandal about anyone at the Court. This he once did to such effect in François's time that an outraged Admiral Bonnivet privately threatened to have him flogged to death. Seeking the King's protection he was assured: 'Have no fear. If anyone dares to do such a thing, he shall hang within a quarter of an hour after your death.' Thanking the King for this, Triboulet asked: 'But could you possibly arrange to have the Admiral hanged a quarter of an hour *before* I die?' Present, another time, at a discussion of the projected Italian expedition which was to end in François's capture and imprisonment, Triboulet cut in with the remark: 'You talk such a lot about how to get *into* Italy, but that isn't what really matters.' 'Oh! what does then?' someone sneered, annoyed at the interruption. 'The essential is,' replied the King's fool, 'to come out again, and no one mentions that.' Le Férial was Triboulet's real name; through Victor Hugo's *Le Roi s'amuse*, where he was used as a character model, he eventually became immortalized as Verdi's *Rigoletto*.

Royalty continued to use the château during succeeding reigns until the death of Henri III in 1589. The Loire Valley had come into favour with the early Valois kings, and with the end of their line the centre of government shifted back to Paris. Blois was the last of the châteaux of the Loire to fill that rôle and the final act played out there, the murder of the duc de Guise, was one of high drama: a circumstance which perhaps accounts for its receiving the greatest number of visitors of any in France, next to Versailles. Visits are guided and it is open every day from 9 to noon and 2 to 6.30 (5.30 October–March); *son et lumière* is held there every evening; the **Place du Château** has a large car-park.

Architecturally the château is far from being completely genuine. For a century and a half up to Napoleon's time it was allowed to fall into ruin and then brought back into service as a barracks. The additional dilapidation and ramshackle alterations effected by the army rendered it almost unrecognizable, and the common mistake of over-restoration followed in the mid-nineteenth century when it was practically rebuilt. But at least the rebuilding was more or less faithful to the original in form and even in detail. What has to be remembered is that the whole affair was much more extensive than now, with an enormous acreage of gardens stretching northwards as well as westwards as far as the site of the present railway station, from where tree-lined alleys led directly into the forest for hunting. Several fine pavilions stood in these gardens, but only one, which we shall come to later among the streets of the town, still survives.

Facing us as we walk to the château from the square is the wing added by Louis XII when he made Blois his headquarters. It is in the late Gothic style, and pleasing to the eye in its softly contrasting colours of brick and stone. The equestrian statue of Louis over the archway is a copy (more or less) of the original destroyed at the Revolution. Through in the courtyard and on our left is the chapel of Saint Calais of the same period with its beautiful little outside gallery, but minus its nave which Mansard demolished to make room for the Gaston d'Orléans wing which extends along the rest of the left-hand side and the bottom, save for a gap leading to the *Terrasse du Foix*, one of the only two relics of the old thirteenth-century castle. From the terrace one has a wonderful view over the town: eastwards the cathedral and southwards, just below, the three-steepled church of Saint Nicolas and the roofs of many houses; then come the river, the Forest of Russy and the wooded plain of the Sologne fading away into the haze.

On the right-hand side of the courtyard stands the flamboyant

Renaissance pavilion put up for François I, with another of those spiral staircases he liked so much, but this time on the outside where it served as a sort of grandstand for watching displays in the yard. The statues adorning it are not original, but very well executed twentieth-century copies. The eastern end of this wing, linking it with the Louis XII front, is the *Salle des États*, the other surviving vestige of the medieval castle. In the ensemble of three styles so interestingly juxtaposed around the courtyard there can be no mistake which is 'odd man out'. The Gothic and the Renaissance have something in common, a sort of cosy naturalness touched with very human fantasy, but the Classical grandeur of the Gaston wing belongs to a new way of thought altogether. Eschewing all decoration it relies on pure line and geometrical symmetry for its appeal to the senses. Here is the real dividing-line (rather than the Renaissance, which merely prepared the ground) between the medieval world and our own: the mathematical philosophy of cold unsentimental reason as personified in Mansard's contemporary, Descartes.

Mansard had no intention that his work here should remain as an oddity in a setting of days gone by; he intended to knock all the rest of the old down and the new would have been bigger, complete and alone. Fortunately he was unable to carry out his scheme to the end, because as soon as Gaston's political nuisance value faded Richelieu cut off his money supply. He had been given Blois, and encouraged to play at building, to keep his silly mischievous mind occupied after many hopeless intrigues against his brother Louis XIII, in which he betrayed his friends without compunction whenever he was cornered. He took after his mother, Marie de Médicis, with his lumpish, rather stupid features, his selfish and contrary ways, and was her favourite. Earlier in the reign she too had been sent here out of the way, imprisoned in the old building which her son's new wing now replaces. D'Épernon, duc d'Angoulême, organized her escape. He was no knight-errant and she was by no means the traditional beautiful princess locked in a tower, but he was moved to this gallantry by hatred for De Luynes, the King's new minister. Ladders were brought at great risk by night for Marie to climb down to the ground outside the walls. There is a painting by Rubens in the Louvre depicting, on her own description, an heroic scene, but it was not at all like that. On the night of the rescue the huge fat queen lost her nerve after the first ladder and had to be lowered the rest of the way with ropes, like a circus elephant into a ship's hold.

Inside the Gaston wing, on the first floor, is the **municipal library**, one of the finest along the Loire, especially for history. Admission is free for anyone going there to read, and it is a soothing retreat for scholars and bookworms in its quiet atmosphere of a past age, among its 80,000 books, many of them extremely rare. The staircase leading to it was built in 1932 from Mansard's plans.

Much of the rest of the interior of the château is a disappointment: so many of the rooms are bare and empty, devoid of any feeling of life either past or present. But the apartments of Catherine de Médicis are an exception. Here is the chamber where she died on 5 January 1589 after her son, Henri III, came down triumphantly from the floor above to announce the assassination of Guise. In final despair after all her years of effort to end the rancour and violence which was tearing her adopted country apart, she told him: 'I can stand no more; I must go to bed.' This she did and, rising again only once to go to Mass in the chapel, just willed herself to die. It took her a fortnight. Adjoining is her study with its 237 carved panels, four of which on pressing a hidden pedal in the skirting-board swing open to disclose secret cupboards where most likely she kept her jewellery and private papers; but people seem to prefer the unsupported story that they were poison-cupboards.

Then we are shown the King's apartments above (somewhat altered in lay-out since the event) where the murder of the duc de Guise by twenty royally-hired assassins took place. This is the chief spine-chiller of the visit and will be described in loving detail by the guide, as it has been in a thousand books, so there is no need for me to recount it here. Arthur Young was regaled with it on a visit 200 years ago and his reaction, which I am sometimes inclined to share, was: 'Bigotry and ambition, equally dark, insidious and bloody, allow no feelings of regret. The parties could hardly be better employed than in cutting one another's throats.' Henri de Guise, like his father who was murdered at Olivet sixteen years before, was a fine big, courageous man, a good soldier and generally popular. But he was also bigoted and ruthless, as he had shown by his leading part in the Massacre of Saint Bartholomew. His ambition was the throne itself, and with this in view some genealogists had been paid to trump up a supposed descent from Charlemagne. To further his plans he had become a secret agent of Spain, in the pay of Philip II. His bold entry into Paris on 12 May 1588 (the day the Armada was due to sail), in defiance of Henri III's orders and with 2000 Leaguer troops infiltrating secretly, was to prevent France from striking at the Low Countries while Parma and his armies would be absent subduing England. But the Armada failed; Philip's hope of conquering the heretic island was abandoned, and Guise was dropped.

Seeing his influence dwindling without Spanish money to support it, Henri III decided he could now be safely removed. As much as any of those poor Spaniards who drowned in the stormy seas round the British coast, he was a casualty of the Armada, and Pope Sixtus is said to have exclaimed on being told the news of the murder at Blois: 'So the King of Spain has lost another of his captains!'

Simultaneously with the murder, Louis de Lorraine, Cardinal de Guise, the Duke's younger brother, was arrested and the next day (24 December 1588) was taken to a dark cell beneath the château and pole-axed with a halberd by soldiers of the royal guard. So there should be no possibility of veneration of the two brothers' remains, their bodies were burnt and their ashes thrown into the Loire. That Christmas can hardly have been a very merry one at Blois, despite the King's unconcealed joy at his cleverness. 'I don't know whether you have clearly foreseen the consequences,' his mother had remarked to him in that little bedroom talk. Within a year one consequence was his own assassination in Paris.

There is a **museum** in the Louis XII wing, to which entry is free and unconnected with the guided visit. Gradually, owing to the devoted work of Madame Tissier de Mallerais, the young resident curator, more and more objects are being brought out of attic hiding-places and put on show: furniture; tapestries, including a pair of Gobelins depicting the life of Louis XIV; and paintings by Mignard, Philippe de Champaigne, David and Ingres.

On the north side of the Place du Château (left on coming out) is the **Musée Robert-Houdin** (open every day from 10 to 11.30 except Sunday mornings, and 2 to 6). Jean-Eugène Robert (better known to us as Houdini, but not to be confused with the American 'escapol-ogist' who purloined the name much later) was born in 1805, the son of a watchmaker in Blois. He grew up with a most original and questing mind, and in his father's workshop revealed a great flair for mechanics. After a varied early career as a lawyer's clerk, apprentice watchmaker and fairground juggler, he went to Paris, where he married Céline Houdin, whose surname he hyphenated to his own. Her father was a clockmaker and for a time he settled down in partnership with him, but with the older man's encouragement he continued his 'magical' practices and by combining the new and little understood science of electricity with them he eventually had fashionable Paris agog with wonder at his tricks and mechanical devices. Among the latter were several useful inventions such as the periscope and an electric clock; he also constructed the very first electric motor.

After his fame spread abroad, Queen Victoria became one of his keenest fans, sending for him twice more after his first appearance at Buckingham Palace. The French government even employed him to assist in the pacification of Algeria by demonstrating the superiority of European magic over the native *marabouts*. There is not a lot to see in this little museum, but all these activities are illustrated in some way with relics, models and old photographs. These last, of Napoleon III's court and the celebrities of his time, are of great interest in themselves. By inspiration or heredity, originality seems to have descended in the family, for Houdini's grandson Paul Robert-Houdin, an architect, was *Conservateur* of the château at Blois for many years after the last war and the initiator – one might almost say the inventor – of *son et lumière*.

Leaving the neighbourhood of the château now, it is time to consider the rest of the city. The best place for long-term parking is the **Promenade du Mail** along the riverside upstream of the bridge. The old quarter is close by and is reached by walking up the Rue Jeanne d'Arc. On the right in that street you come to a half-timbered fifteenth-century house and, fanning out from this point, the **Rue du Puits Châtel**, the Rue des Papegaults and the Grands Degrés de Saint-Louis. The first of these – 'Street of the Castle Well' – was originally mostly military lodgings and prisons, and the lower parts of some of the buildings still have ancient bars over the windows. But in the housing boom of Louis XII's time much of it was bought for smart residential development and they were either completely rebuilt or had new tops put on them. One example is no. 5 on the right, the 'Cours Pigier', a handsome balconied stone house through an archway; another is no. 7 with Louis's emblem, the porcupine, over the doorway. About two-thirds of the way up we come to the Petits Degrés de Saint-Louis, with a night-club on the corner in an old house with a Renaissance window.

From here the street becomes less interesting and one might as well return and mount the **Rue des Papegaults**. Steep and narrow as it is, this was one of the principal streets of Blois in the Middle Ages. The *papegaults* were unfortunate parrots, kept in the vicinity for use as practice targets for the crossbowmen. No. 4 has a beautiful carved-oak doorway, and through the iron gate of no. 10, beyond the courtyard, you can espy a squared spiral staircase. When you reach the top of the street, and the south side of the cathedral, turn and admire the stirring medieval scene behind you. Near by – most intriguing of all – is a fifteenth-century half-timbered house which completely bridges the **Rue Saint-Pierre de Blois**.

We now arrive in the Place Saint-Louis, face-to-face with the **Cathédrale Saint-Louis**. It is not very imposing to look at. In the ninth century a church stood here which was dedicated to Saint Solenne, a Frankish priest, friend of Clovis, who was buried here. Alternatively pronounced Soulaine, his name became associated with *souler* (to get drunk) and his relics eventually acquired a popular reputation for curing alcoholics. Many a purple-faced, red-nosed pilgrim in days gone by must have puffed up the way we have come. Part of the large crypt of this early building survives, but is kept locked; to see it you must apply at the Presbytery, 4 Rue Porte Clos-Haut, on the north side of the square. A larger edifice grew up by stages in the centuries that followed, but could not have been very stout in the end, because in 1678 it was demolished by a whirlwind. Luckily however, it was the church in which Colbert had got married to a young lady of the Charron family of Menars (see p. 128). Even a hard case like Colbert can be sentimental sometimes, and for old times' sake he used his influence to persuade Louis XIV to hand out the money for its rebuilding in the Gothic style. The bishopric was then created and the church was rededicated to Saint Louis – a *double-entendre* of course. The interior of the cathedral is graceful, light and imposing, and it is really only the ill-fitting tower, survivor of the older work, that makes its outer aspect so odd.

We can now return by the **Grands Degrés de Saint Louis** – easier to walk down than up – and turn right into the **Rue des Juifs**. About fifty yards along, at no. 3, is a fine old medieval front with an archway, a little reminiscent of the Jew's house at Lincoln, but its rear space was sold in Louis XII's reign and a sixteenth-century *hôtel* stands in the courtyard. At the top of the short **Rue Haute**, which continues from the Rue des Juifs, a little restaurant called 'Aux Caves', in arched vaults in the hillside and open to the street, serves inexpensive single dishes which make an excellent light lunch. This is the beginning of the shopping centre of Blois, and from the top of the wide, steep and graceful flight of steps in front of us the statue of yet another of her clever sons looks down.

This chief place of honour in the town has been accorded not to any of the gilded great ones whose deeds or misdeeds have brought drama to its history, but to an inventive genius whose achievements all took place in exile abroad. Denis Papin was born in 1647 of an old Huguenot family in Blois and qualified as both a doctor of medicine and an engineer. A portrait of him by Lemaître in the Bibliothèque Nationale in Paris shows a young man with level, piercing eyes, a large hook nose and a square, determined jaw.

Proud and extremely intelligent, he was not prepared to put up with the obloquy Louis XIV was heaping afresh on his Calvinist subjects, so he came to England where he worked with Boyle and became a member of the Royal Society. On hearing of the revocation of the Edict of Nantes in 1685 he decided never to go back: a typical example of the 'brain-drain' caused by the King's unwise policy. Two years later he developed a piston machine operated by steam which James Watt was to perfect a century afterwards. He is chiefly remembered though for his '*marmite de Papin*' which he originally intended simply as a means for extracting nourishment from bones by cooking them at temperatures above boiling-point, but which turned out to be the versatile pressure-cooker. In 1707, at Kessel in Germany, he constructed the first steamboat in the world and tried it out on the Weser; but the local watermen feared its eventual consequences for themselves and smashed it up. Papin came back to London, but his resources had run out and he was unable to achieve anything more before he died in poverty in 1714.

The **Rue Denis-Papin**, running southwards towards the river and westwards to our left, is the principal shopping street of Blois – smart, wide and imposing. Among the many excellent small shops are several pâtisseries, and I mention this because the *pâtissiers* of Blois are outstanding in their art; some of their quite everyday products are so elaborate that they can really only be described as creations, and if they were not so delicious it would be a shame to eat them. The ones made of leaf chocolate look as if they had been fashioned on a potter's wheel. On the south side of the street notice a particularly fine medieval half-timbered house, now a bookshop, and observe that many of its neighbours are the same beneath the eighteenth- and nineteenth-century stucco. This is in fact the case in many old French towns though not apparent at a cursory glance. Two doors from the bookshop is a handsome Renaissance house with François I's salamander over the arch. At the far end the **Place Victor-Hugo** slumbers in the shadow of the château, a cool oasis on a hot day, with its gardens, fountains, enormous old cedar and benches to sit on. It also deserves commendation for the cleanest public lavatories to be found in provincial France – or anywhere for that matter.

Facing on to the square the **Église Saint-Vincent-de-Paul** is a good example of Classical church architecture, built in the mid-seventeenth century and therefore contemporary with the Gaston wing of the château. The proportions of the front are very satisfying and, being relieved by a moderate amount of embellishment, the note of severity is absent. It is even more absent from the interior – a rococo riot of statuary, marble columns, gilding and bright colours. The paint on the walls is flaking, but the ceiling of gold scrollwork on a blue ground is still more or less intact. Close by, the **Pavillon Anne de Bretagne** (no visiting) is the only survival from the many ancillary buildings which stood in the grounds of the château in its greatest days. Louis XII had it built for his queen and in the little oratory beside it they frequently prayed together for a dauphin which Heaven, in its wisdom, saw fit not to grant – to the relief of Louise of Savoy, who had marked her François for the throne and suffered years of suspense over the matter.

The street which leads out of the north-east corner of Place Victor-Hugo, the **Rue Chemontant**, contains several more Renaissance *hôtels* from the Louis XII boom. No. 18, with a frieze of heads of the Caesars in the courtyard, was that of the Guise family. The street is very steep (its name is a corruption of *chemin montant*) as it climbs up the north wall of the amphitheatre in which the city lay. The **Rue du Lion-Ferré** (Street of the Chained Lion), a right turn off it, consists mainly of Louis XII buildings, most of them unfortunately stuccoed over; but no. 7 with a medieval turret is a beauty. Turning left at the end of the Lion Ferré and first right afterwards, we come to the **Rue Saint-Honoré** in which the best preserved of the *hôtels* is to be found: the Hôtel d'Alluye built of stone and brick like the front of the château contemporary with it. The Baron d'Alluye was the national Treasurer under Charles VIII, Louis XII and François I so he could afford something a bit special. To keep up with the Guises down the neighbouring street he had to have the heads of the Caesars round his courtyard too. We are now at the top of the steps by Papin's statue: they bring us down to the other leg of the street named after him, and that in turn leads back to the river where we started. On the corner by the bridge are several bars and cafés with outside terraces where again a light meal can be obtained at small expense and in a cheerful, lively atmosphere.

In the new quarter on the eastern outskirts of the city **Notre-Dame de la Trinité**, a modern church of architectural merit, is worth a visit. True, the plain silhouette of its 200-foot belfry is of a different order from the spires of Saint-Nicolas, but so different that it is invidious to make comparisons. Where it certainly excels is in being heard, as I shall never forget hearing it one Easter morning from across the wide river; for it contains a *carillon* of forty-eight beautiful bells, the biggest of which is a five-tonner. Every Sunday from Easter to end of October a concert of bells is given at 4.45 p.m. The church was completed just before the last war, in the first few days of which Rouvière, the young architect who had designed it for the Franciscans, was killed on active service.

Needless to say anyone who takes the trouble to mount the 240 steps leading to the top of the tower – and anyone may – is rewarded with a prodigious view, for the building itself stands on a hill. But bells and views apart, the sculpture on the façade, the huge mosaic of the Coronation of Our Lady inside, the tapestries and the statue of the Virgin in the side-chapel are worthy of attention as examples of modern art at its best. The last-named is one of the best I have seen – a wistful, gentle maiden, perfectly human and devoid of pious sentimentality.

The **Church of Saint-Nicolas** on the other (west) side of the town is clearly identifiable by its three spires; it is far and away more beautiful than the cathedral. Originally constructed as a Benedictine abbey church, it has that unity of form and style which comes of rapid construction before fashions can cause haphazard changes of mind. The choir, transept and eastern end of the nave were built between 1138 and 1186, and the rest (apart from a fourteenth-century chapel in the apse and the seventeenth-century lantern-tower) followed quickly after an interval of only twenty years. There is indeed a subtle difference as a result of that short pause: the first part is late Romanesque, distinguished by that simplicity which the Benedictines favoured, while the lovely high three-storeyed nave is early Gothic inspired by Chartres Cathedral, its contemporary. But the difference does not affect the harmony: the feeling of height in the nave complements the spaciousness of the transept and choir. The most appealing feature perhaps is the row of narrow arches supported on Corinthian columns behind the altar, through which the apse appears with a certain allure of dreamlike mystery. The abbey was destroyed by the Huguenots, but completely replaced in the seventeenth and eighteenth centuries, and still survives as the main part of the city hospital which faces on to the quay and the river.

Farther west beyond the church the famous Poulain chocolate factory still flourishes, having been at Blois since the days when its raw materials were brought upriver in boats from Nantes. It was this firm which made the last gallant attempt to revive the shipping of the Loire as late as 1898 when it was already virtually dead, for only two battered old *chalands* were still using the port, one selling pottery from Gien and the other bringing apples from Anjou. At its own expense Poulain had a 130-foot (40-metre) steam tug built at

Nantes, the celebrated 'Fram', which will never be forgotten. Specially adapted for the river – flat-bottomed, shallow-draught, twin-screwed – it was in regular service for ten years, bringing cocoa and sugar for the factory, seven tons in its own hold and seventy more in the barge it towed, and thereby proved that the proposition was feasible. But such ventures seldom succeed alone and no one else had the courage to follow Poulain, so that in the end they were obliged to go back to the superficially cheaper rail transport. It had been an heroic effort, and it was most fitting that in Papin's birthplace a brave smoky little steamboat should sing the swansong of '*la marine de la Loire*'.

By crossing the railway near the chocolate factory and driving northwards a short way until opposite the railway station, then turning left into the **Avenue Médicis**, you suddenly pick up the great alleyway which once led out from the château to the forest. In John Evelyn's time it was called Pall Mall and in 1644 he recorded that 'On Sunday, being May-day, we walked up into Pall Mall, very long, and so noble shaded with tall trees, being in the midst of a great wood. . . .' He was on his way to the forest 'to see if we could meet with any wolves, which are here in such numbers that they often come and take children out of the very streets, yet will not the Duke, who is sovereign here, permit them to be destroyed.' The Duke of course was the detestable Gaston, but perhaps the locals had been exaggerating a little to enlist his sympathy. He did not see any wolves, but met a man who said his horse had been set upon half an hour before. Be reassured: there are no wolves now in central France. The **Forest of Blois**, the only vestige left in the Val de Loire of the intermittent oak forest that spread right across the Beauce in ancient times, is still about four miles by six in extent and in considerably better condition than the forests of the Sologne. Its long straight rides are fine for a stroll, especially in spring and autumn, but on the whole it lacks variety of scenery and can therefore be monotonous.

A couple of miles along the south bank of the river, going upstream towards Saint-Dyé, a vast establishment calling itself the 'Lac du Loire' provides four-star camping on an extensive area, and sports and leisure facilities which are open to non-campers on payment of a small entry fee. Behind a barrage right across the river it has calm water with a mile or so in one direction for sailing and another mile in the other for water-skiing. Skiers must of course bring their own boats, but sailing-dinghies can be hired from the sailing club, or beginners can take a lesson with the sailing school. Tennis, bowls, a children's play-centre, a swimming-pool and a restaurant are also available. An ideal break for the holiday-maker with a young family, this is run by the *département*. As the municipality runs another camp-site across the river at La Boire, the camper is well provided for; likewise the hotel tourist, for there are twenty-eight hotels in Blois at the time of writing, with five hundred and fifty rooms between them. Altogether therefore, it is a good base: Orléans is only forty miles away and the subject-matter of the next three chapters is all within a forty-mile radius.

CHAPTER NINE

Onzain to Vouvray

✴

On leaving Blois the question is which route to take. At the end of Chapter 7 I have mentioned (in reverse direction) the road between the town and Candé on the left bank. That on the right bank is much busier but a better road and with views of the Loire which are closer and more impressive. There are also several ramps leading down to old gravel workings where you can get to the waterside; but do remember in stopping and turning for them that traffic on this main road to Tours is fast and heavy.

About nine miles out of Blois on the right, nearly opposite Chaumont, is the turn for **Onzain**. Just before entering the village we cross the Cisse, one of the many friendly little streams which skip along close beside the Loire for miles and miles in its middle and lower reaches, like children holding Grandfather's hand. Not that Grandpa Loire is always genial company. One summer evening, 4 June 1856, after pretending for a few hours to subside from flood level, he suddenly gathered strength and broke a 400-yard gap in the *levée* at the point where we turned off the main road, the hamlet of Escures. Twenty houses and the gendarmerie were swept away without trace. The inhabitants fled in time to save their lives, but next day the whole valley as far as Amboise was a tumultuous sea covered with a melancholy flotsam of household furniture and uprooted trees.

Onzain is a fairly big village with very good shops, and the people seem exceptionally kind and friendly. At the butchers', buy local lamb, for fine sheep are reared in the Cisse valley.

There was once a great castle at Onzain which Louis XI used as a special prison for some of his iron-cage cases. The site is a little way north of the church, but only a few tumbled stones remain as it was pulled down in the 1820s. We shall hear more of Louis's iron cages when we get to Loches. Meanwhile it is something much more cheerful which has brought us here. Turning down a narrow street first left after the Post Office, we come to the *Cave Coopérative*, one of the best such establishments I know, selling most of the wines of the Touraine, but particularly those grown at Mesland on the hills above.

We have already come across our first Touraine wine at Cheverny, which is the only V.D.Q.S. of the region. But the labelling of the different *appellation controlé* wines which go to make up the rest can be confusing because the wine-growing areas of the Touraine are so widespread and so varied. Some explanation is required. First there are those districts producing a wine of such excellence that their own name stands alone – Vouvray, Chinon and so on, which we shall come to as our journey proceeds. Then there are three whose product is considered distinctive enough to couple their name with the region in the appellation – Touraine Mesland, Touraine Amboise and Touraine Azay-le-Rideau. Lastly all the rest, from widely separated districts, of A.C.* quality but less individual in character, are dubbed simply 'Touraine'. In total Touraine produces an annual average of about forty-four million gallons of good wine.

Here at Mesland then, we have one of the distinctive growths. This is not because the soil is basically different: it is alluvial granitic sand and clay overlying the characteristic soft tufa limestone of the Touraine which not only nourishes the roots of its vines, but builds its churches, châteaux, houses and garden-walls. The advantage of the soil at Mesland is that it is very pebbly, and the vine likes pebbles because they inhibit evaporation, regulate soil temperature and reflect sunlight back on to the grapes. Also here the hillsides are exposed just nicely to the south and south-east. The local red wine is the Gamay, not so light as in the Orléanais, but more robust and with a fuller flavour. The rosé, generally from the same *cépage*, is excellent with good bouquet, dry but not acid (two different attributes often confused in discussing wine). I prefer Touraine rosés to all others and this is one of the best of them. The white is the Pinot de la Loire, the same as the Vouvray grape. It resembles a light Vouvray and is available demi-sec if you prefer it that way. Mesland wines are inexpensive, not long keepers, but good travellers; and the caves at Onzain export a large quantity to England. The caves are open for retail sales – even single bottles – from Monday to Friday from 8.30 to noon and 1.30 to 5.30.

North-westward out of Onzain the minor road leads along the ridge of the hills, flanked by vineyards on either side, to the village of **Mesland** itself, which is interesting for the archaeological mystery of the 'Porche des Barbus' on its little-known church. Many a

Appellation Contrôlée — designates a set of laws controlling wine quality. Covers the top 20% of French wines.

Christian church stands on the site of a pagan temple, for the early missionaries were practical men and saw no point in wasting a sound building; a tnorough exorcizing and a good dowsing with holy water after the idols had been thrown out, and it was made to serve until they had time to replace it with something new. Even then they frequently incorporated bits of masonry salvaged from the old or allowed the masons to copy apparently harmless aspects of its decoration. The church now standing here dates back to 1060 and its porch bears traces of such usages not only in certain longitudinal tool-marks of early origin on the stone pillars, but in the twenty-six bearded heads round the beautifully proportioned Romanesque arch which seem to owe their inspiration to a barbaric Gallic custom. Very stylized, they all wear a warrior's helmet and have a look of horror in their protruding eyes, but each beard is different. The Gauls were head-hunters; they made a practice of decapitating a gallant foe in honour of their horned god Cernumnus (later Romanized as Hermes), and preserved their trophies pickled in cedarwood boxes or as skulls fixed in niches in stone columns. The strength of the conquered warrior was then at the owner's service and a collection of heads was a reserve of vital force for the tribe. Several archaeologists have postulated a connection between this old custom and the *barbus* over Mesland's porch, pointing to Ammon of Thebes (who was horned like Cernumnus) on one of the capitals of the central doorway and two rather suspicious-sounding saints on either side of the altar – Hermes and Sylvain. True, Christian tradition speaks of an early martyr at Rome called Hermes, but if this be he what is he doing in company with the old god of the woods? Moreover I prefer the derivation of the village name as a contraction of *Hermèslande* (Hermes's heath) to the fanciful theories which try to link it with Merlin. A tradition of sorcery attaches to the place though, and its inhabitants were feared in the neighbourhood as the '*sorciers de Mesland*' because they had the supposed power of diverting storms by ringing their church bells. A writer of the 1890s refers to this as happening in his time. The prettiest young women in the parish were employed to do the job and on a storm approaching even in the night would run barefooted, nightshirted to the church to fling themselves furiously on the ropes, chanting: 'Clear off wicked storm! Go and burst over Seillac; go and drown Onzain.'

I shall have more to say of the delightful valley of the Cisse later on, but at this stage we must go back to the Loire and cross the bridge to **Chaumont**, a little town strung along the left bank with a handsome fortress on a wooded hill above. Victor Hugo considered the whole picture had about it an aspect of a village on the Rhine.

The settlement began in 980 on a spot hitherto called '*la Vacherie de la Comtesse*' when Thibault II, comte de Blois, was obliged to take over his wife's cowhouses and pastures to build a stronghold to protect his territories against his terrible brother-in-law, Foulque-Nerra of Anjou. The town still only has one street which leads from the bridge along past its houses and shops to the quays at its western end. Here by the tree-shaded mall (and virtually here only) is there room to park in safety.

The boats are interesting as quite a few of the local men still fish commercially, netting or line-fishing from small punts for gudgeon, bleak and roach for *friture*, or larger fish under licence from the bigger flat-bottomed boats (called *toues*) with a cabin at the stern where the fisherman lives alone for two or three weeks when working, the boat moored up against the line of nets staked from the bank outwards for one-third of the width of the river. A long spar looking like a bowsprit and called the *balancier* is pivoted over the bow and a square dip-net rather like an upside-down umbrella, the *carrelet*, hangs from it so it is submerged against the wall of net. A salmon or a shad ascending the river to spawn runs against the obstruction, swims along it trying to find a way through and eventually passes over the *carrelet*. Everything that touches the taut strings supporting that instrument with its framework of flexible rods is felt as a vibration by the fishermen in the boat with the end of the line round his finger, and by experience he knows whether it is flotsam, small fry or a big fish. If the latter, he quickly trips the *balancier* so that it whisks the *carrelet* out of the water with the fish in the bottom of it.

Salmon of course is the most desired prey, but not more than about a thousand of these are caught each year in the whole Val de Loire nowadays. Of the tasty, but bony, shad on the other hand, the river yields some forty tonnes or more annually. Even the ordinary angler may have the luck very occasionally to take him on a spinner, but Chaumont should appeal to him anyway as there are plenty of pike and zander along this stretch. For the camper too it has one of the nicest camp-sites to be found, among trees beside the Loire, with all facilities and a beach. It is at the east end of the town down the lane which leads beneath the bridge.

The château, acquired by the state in 1938 and run on rather bureaucratic lines, is almost not worth a visit so far as the interior is concerned, so few of the rooms are open to the public (and most of those unfurnished), and so off-handed and impersonal are the guides. But I would advise paying the fee anyway, if only to see the exterior; it is most impressive in its almost storybook medievalness and in the solidity of its towers; moreover it commands fine views of the valley. Opening times are from 9 to 11.45 and 2 to 6.30 every day, April to September inclusive; the rest of the year it opens an hour later in the morning and closes at 4 as well as all day on Tuesdays. You pay at the gate just off the street and have to walk up the steep hill from there, but in the shade of a magnificent cedar halfway up is a seat – provided by the Touring Club de France, not the inconsiderate bureaucracy that runs the place. At the top we come to several more of these beautiful trees as we approach the gate which is preceded by a drawbridge and flanked by two stout towers with machicolation and pepper-pot tops, exuding the very spirit of the fifteenth century when the castle was built. Thibault's original fort, which was of wood, has of course left no trace.

No really stirring history attaches to Chaumont, but the inter-laced Ds and emblems of hunting between the machicoulis are a reminder that it once belonged to Diane de Poitiers. Not that she really wanted it, but after the death of Henry II from a jab in the eye jousting in the lists in 1559 his widow, Catherine de Médicis, bought it for her as an exchange for Chenonceau which she con-fiscated. Hence Chaumont is often described by Catherine's de-tractors as an 'instrument of revenge', but this is most unjust. Chenonceau was Crown property although allotted by the late King to his strumpet for her use, and the Queen was entitled to take it back without any recompense at all. Chaumont therefore was gratuitous compensation. If you look along the machicoulis (aided by binoculars if possible) you will notice that on the tower on the north-east corner, overlooking the Loire, the emblems between them suddenly change to triangles in three interlaced circles. These are assumed to have a cabbalistic significance, although just possibly they could have been symbols of the Trinity. At all events, on very thin evidence, this tower has been dubbed 'the Astrologer's tower' where Catherine's astrologer, Ruggieri, was provided with lodgings and an observatory and where she is supposed to have been shown the future of her sons in a mirror. It is true that, like many other political figures of her time, and even of our own, she believed in astrology. Indeed she was brought up so to believe. Luc Gauric, a Neapolitan, cast her horoscope when she was a child, and her con-temporary Brantôme tells us that the same man later sent a letter to Henri II warning him to avoid 'combat in an enclosed place . . . which might result in blindness or even death'. Nostrodamus, in one of his burbling couplets, had also uttered what could be taken as a prediction of the King's death, and he was sent for to cast the horoscopes of all her children. They were not very cheerful, and when she turned to Cosmo Ruggieri his mirror visions were just as melancholy. Poor woman! After thirty years' unfolding of such dark prophecies no wonder she finally lay down and deliberately died at Blois as we have seen. The '*affaire du miroir*' may have occurred at Chaumont, but I do not believe Ruggieri had the tower for an observatory – for two reasons. Firstly, although inside we are shown another of those 'Catherine de Médicis' bedrooms', almost as widespread in France as Queen Elizabeth's in England, there is no evidence that she ever set up residence here in the short time between buying the place and handing it over to Diane. Secondly the tower is on the north side, so that the roofs of the rest of the castle rise between it and the southern hemisphere where the main constellations and the zodiac are to be found. No astrologer would say as much as thank you for such an observatory. What I like about the 'Astrologer's tower' is its reassuring, earthy view of the village, the river and the Touraine from just at the foot of it – one of the best vantage-points. To enjoy the same view from the courtyard, an eighteenth-century owner had the whole of the north block, except the end towers, demolished, and I don't blame him. Before that the castle was on the traditional enclosed-square plan.

Apart from the view and the lovely wooded park, Chaumont would not be everyone's idea of an ideal home. Diane did not think it so and soon deserted it for the royal château of Anet near Dreux, which Catherine had allowed her to keep. And Madame de Staël, who hired it for a time when banished from the capital by Napoleon, remarked that the view of the Loire was well enough, but that she longed for the muddy ditch by her house in the Rue du Bac. Nevertheless one owner made much of Chaumont and spent a fortune on it. In 1875 a millionaire sugar-refiner named Say happened to be passing by in company with his sixteen-year-old daughter Marie, who fell in love with it on sight and announced that she *must* have it. What can a rich daddy do in such circumstances? He bought it for her immediately. Eventually she married a prince, Amadée de Broglie, and the young couple set to work with enthusiasm to transform the place. The Palermo tiles now in the *grande salle* for example were bought by them from a palace at Salerno, but that is nothing. They completely restored the whole building; installed heating, lighting and piped water; bought and razed two hamlets near by to enlarge the park to 2500 hectares (over 6000 acres); demolished the church halfway down the hill and built a new one; finally they rebuilt the village almost entirely and connected it to electricity so it had street-lamps and not long after became one of the first villages in France to have a cinema. For entertainment up at the castle, the de Broglies thought nothing of hiring the Paris Opera or the Comédie Française and bringing them to Chaumont by special train. They entertained lavishly and one distinguished guest, a maharajah, gratefully presented them with an elephant, which was housed in a purpose-built stable among the horses. Then suddenly one day news came that the refinery had gone bankrupt and the managing director had committed suicide. At a hastily-summoned family conference it proved difficult to persuade Marie to see the need for economies. To be parted from her darling elephant would be heartbreaking; without her yacht and her ponies life would be unbearable, without the army of servants the house unmanageable. But finally she did agree to give up her afternoon snacks of rolls and foie gras.

Let us proceed on our way towards Amboise, ten miles farther on, by keeping to the left bank. I shall deal with the other side of the river later. The road on this side is quieter and allows frequent inspiring views of the wide island-studded river, where in spring and summer wheeling terns flash white in the sun and their wild cries send your thoughts racing down the remaining 150-odd miles of the great waterway to the sea. If you stop a little while in a quiet spot near the bank you will notice that other seabirds too are becoming more numerous, especially waders, who love the sandy shores and islands of the Loire. You are likely to hear the redshank's desolate call and almost sure to see little flocks of ringed plover flitting along the water's edge.

On the left a wall of limestone cliff rises close beside the road. At the top, though you cannot see them, are many of the vineyards of the appellation Touraine Amboise. All you can see are the *caves* of the *vignerons* cut into the rock: some closed with big ancient wooden doors, battered and patched; others open for direct retail sale to the passing public. If you want to buy a bottle or two it is cheaper to do so here than in the town. The third open cave after the village of **Mosnes** is that of Monsieur René Vigneau, a cheerful friendly fellow unstinting in allowing *dégustation* and delighted to explain everything to anyone interested. A little farther on, at **Chargé**, Monsieur André Poupault and his wines are equally to be recommended. He and his direct ancestors have grown vines here since the sixteenth century. On this side of the river the production is mostly red (from the Gamay grape again, like the Mesland which it resembles) and rosé from the Cabernet (as in Anjou, but drier) and from the Cot which is just a local name for the well-known Malbec *cépage* of the

Bordeaux region. A white is also produced, but rather illogically it is mostly grown in vineyards across the river in the Cisse valley, using the Vouvray grape, and was once called Vouvray until under the appellation system Vouvray was separated because of its supreme excellence and its neighbours were designated Amboise.

Coming along the quay on the outskirts of **Amboise**, notice a big island in midstream, most of which is now given over to the municipal camp-site, a very good one. In AD 503 Clovis, King of the Franks, and Alaric II, King of the Visigoths, chose this Ile d'Or as safe neutral territory for a peace conference, for they didn't trust each other at all and their soldiers could be kept out of reach on the banks. The Loire was the frontier between Aquitaine (which Alaric ruled together with Spain and Portugal) and the northern territories by then almost completely conquered by Clovis – much to Alaric's alarm. He had asked for the conference in an attempt to gain time; the easy-going Arian-heretic south was in no shape to fight the vigorous newly-converted barbarians of the north backed by the Church still in the prime of its vitality. The two kings drank and feasted, slapped each other's backs and swore eternal friendship. It was rather like Chamberlain at Munich except that the Goths failed to rearm in the respite gained. Four years later Clovis attacked and the armies met near Poitiers. 'The Goths fled as they were prone to do,' Gregory contemptuously reports, 'and Clovis was the victor for God was on his side.' Having killed Alaric in personal combat, Clovis marched on and wintered at Bordeaux. Gothic power in future was virtually confined behind the Pyrenees.

The centre of the long bridge rests on the western tip of the island amid a little conglomeration of houses. The island's rocky base providing this convenience in bridge-building attracted the Romans: the more so as the town is protected on the north by the Loire and on the south by a small tributary, the Amasse. After this latter they named it Ambacia, and Caesar's lieutenant, Crassus, chose it as his base for the attack on Tours. The oldest of the great caves dug in the plateau on which it stands are traditionally (and this time perhaps correctly) called 'Caesar's granaries'.

Parking in the town centre is all regulated by meter and the streets are narrow and subject to tedious traffic-jams. There is plenty of free parking not far out on the Quai du Mail at the western end. Near by on the Promenade du Mail is a fountain presented to the town in 1968 by Max Ernst, the Surrealist, sculpted by himself and apparently meant to represent a squashed teddy-bear on a pile of potatoes.

The street beside the post office opposite the parking of the Quai du Mail leads through to the **Church of Saint-Denis**, early Roman-esque with fifteenth-century additions, on the site where the Romans had a colossal statue of Mars, which Saint Martin found still standing, though rather decrepit, in the fourth century. His usual policy was to knock down idols, but this was too big; so he prayed for it to fall down and it did – in a storm. After consecrating the spot he built the first church on it. The present one has some very interest-ing treasures, including a fine statue of Saint Mary Magdalen re-clining and reading a book, and the unusual *Femme noyée* attributed without complete certainty to the great Primaticcio. Primaticcio came over from Italy in 1531 to decorate Fontainebleau for François I and introduced Mannerism to French art, which he came almost to dominate in the remaining thirty-nine years of his life. His wife is supposed to have been drowned in the Loire; but whoever the poor lady was, and whoever the sculptor, this naked recumbent figure of a middle-aged women portrays with astonishing realism all the ghastly tragedy of a drowning.

At the bottom of the south aisle there is another splendid sculpture with a sad theme: the Entombment, coloured, life-size, artist un-identified as usual, but in the Italian manner of the sixteenth century. Here again is wonderful realism in the atmosphere of silent reverence conveyed – except for one of the women at the back who has a rather flippant look, which may be due to the fact that the models were the donor, Philibert Babou, one of François I's treasurers, and his family. Some of the Babou womenfolk had a flighty reputation, including Philibert's wife Marie, '*la Belle Babou*', who had a weakness for really great folk, sometimes slept with the King and granted the Emperor Charles the comfort of her bed during his visit to France. Her granddaughter Gabrielle d'Estrée achieved more public renown as mistress to Henri IV.

Next, on the fresco in the Lady chapel, we find poor Jeanne de France founding the religious Order of the Annunciation in 1500. Her marriage with Louis XII was annulled in this church in December 1498 on several grounds which seemed rather specious considering they had been married for twenty-two years. One allegation was constraint on the young bridegroom by Jeanne's father, the fearsome Louis XI, which could have been true; but the time to act on that would have been on his death fifteen years before: he could hardly have exercised any constraint afterwards. Another was non-con-summation owing to physical incapacity of the bride. Apart from her pure-formed face which radiated spirituality, she was indeed ugly and malformed with a shoulder out of line, a short body and a twisted hip which caused her to limp; and to go with all this (perhaps because of it) she had a bad temper which she could not always control. But she denied incapacity and alleged complete coitus on several occasions. To avoid further humiliating questioning she offered to accept her husband's evidence on oath, trusting in his truthfulness and chivalry. He let her down badly, not only denying a complete sexual act, but adding gratuitous insults of a gross kind. When the decree was announced her temper flared and she shouted curses at her ecclesiastical judges and had to be removed. When the judges came out of the church themselves they were cursed in even rounder terms by the crowd, for Jeanne was popular. With the help of Saint Francis de Paul she eventually overcame her bitterness and her rages, though the first nuns of the Annunciation suffered from them sometimes in the early stages of the Order. She was canonized as Sainte Jeanne de Valois in 1950.

Lastly, in the fine Second Empire chandelier hanging in the choir, Saint-Denis has what few other Christian churches can possess – a handsome gift from a devout Mahometan. Abd-el-Kader was chosen by the Algerian Arabs as their Emir soon after the French invasion in 1830 and opposed them in battle and diplomacy with great skill and courage for seventeen years until the unequal struggle ended inevitably in his surrender. Brought here and confined honourably at the château as a state prisoner until Napoleon III released him in 1852, he became a friend and admirer of France and popular supporter of charities in the town. He was quick of intellect, erudite, and though a staunch upholder of his own religion a liberal-minded man. On his release he went to live at Damascus, and in the turmoils of 1860 when all the Christians of Syria were threatened with massacre, he protected them 'with sleepless vigilance' and saved many thousand Christian lives at the peril of his own.

Walking eastwards now along the narrow streets of the little town, we soon come to the **Tour de l'Horloge** which Charles VIII had built in the last years of the fifteenth century as the main gateway of the town; now it is squeezed tightly amongst the shops. Close by, and mostly belonging to the same period, the massive bastions and curtain-walls of the château loom intimidatingly over the streets, particularly the Rue Victor-Hugo dominated by the Tour Heurtault with its unusual castellated doorway, called a *bretèche*. Nearly opposite is a *charcuterie* which I have found exceptional for its wide range of delicious salads.

The way in to the **château** is near the *mairie*. It is open every day from 9 to noon and 2 to 7 (5 in winter). *Son et lumière* is given every evening from March to October. We enter by the vaulted ramp, a survival from the older castle which preceded the fifteenth-century reconstruction. Here Louis XI housed his wife and children, partly for security and partly so as not to have them under his own feet, and here his only son, Charles VIII, was born. Charles spent his boyhood at Amboise and became inseparably attached to the place. He came to the throne when he was thirteen, with his twenty-two-year-old sister Anne de Beaujeu as Regent. We have already met her briefly at Gien. Charles had not inherited his father's nature but she was a real 'chip off the old block', cunning, resourceful and ruthless.

When the Duke of Brittany died leaving a daughter (also called Anne) as his heiress, Maximilien of Austria was the chief suitor, and if he had succeeded in thus acquiring Brittany he would have had Northern France nearly encircled. So the young Regent sent an army 40,000 strong to propose on her brother's behalf. Charles was not handsome with his huge beak of a nose, his round staring eyes and fat lips forever hanging open; but the little duchess found this form of courtship irresistible and accepted. She herself was no dazzler, and skinny and lame into the bargain, but highly educated and a patron of the arts. The young couple became very fond of one another and extremely house-proud. Together they supervised the reconstruction of the château of Amboise, which Charles still considered as his home.

In 1494 he set off across the Alps and invaded Italy, largely to impress his wife but against the advice of his wiser sister who told him 'those who govern should renounce adventures in distant lands'. Savonarola from his pulpit announced 'a cohort of angels' coming from France to deliver Italy from Papal extortion (Alexander VI was Pope at the time), but Charles's campaign merely united the hitherto divided Italian states against him and he eventually had to withdraw. While there, however, he was captivated not only by the women of the country, but by its architecture; and he brought Italian craftsmen back to Amboise. Their influence is clear in the left-hand pavilion (as you face the château from the courtyard) which bears his name, as also in the little *Chapelle Saint-Hubert* on the wall, which he built for Anne. On the strength of one or two items like this it is sometimes claimed that Charles 'brought the Renaissance to France', but this is an exaggeration. He brought only a few samples and it was his successors some years later who transported it in bulk. What he did bring back – a more dismal thing equally new to France and destined to have an effect as far-reaching as the Renaissance itself – was syphilis, carried home by his 'cohort of angels' from Naples. But like the Renaissance it would have come anyway.

Charles and Anne had been married in 1491 and only seven years later a wholly unexpected event put an end to their happiness. The King had been inspecting work on the château and was on his way to watch a game of tennis in the moat. On the way he struck his forehead on the lintel of a rather low doorway which is still there and which the guide will point out. Replacing his cap he assured everyone he was all right and carried on, but soon after he collapsed and fainted. At midnight he died. Not long before the incident he had eaten an orange brought to him by a Neapolitan of his court and inevitably the gossip went round – and still goes round – that he was poisoned; but officially death was attributed to the blow, although it had left no bruise or other mark. Although he had become addicted to whoring since the Italian expedition, Anne seems to have been genuinely grieved and surprised (incidentally she was the first royal lady to wear black instead of white for mourning). But she nevertheless became Queen of France a second time, for Louis XII gained not only the throne by his cousin's sudden death but the lady too, marrying her after he obtained his release from Jeanne de France. During his rebellion at the beginning of the reign he had taken refuge at the Duke of Brittany's court and had there become secretly affianced to Anne. Politics had taken her out of his hands, but he had loved her ever since. He had recently been plotting another possible rebellion and a couple of days before the tragedy the rumour was abroad that the King was going to have him arrested. But we should not jump to conclusions about Charles's death; the affair remains a mystery.

The first two storeys of the right-hand pavilion were built by Louis, but were not good enough for François I, who added the other two on top, and there at last is the full Renaissance style. Louis, as we have seen, spent most of his time at Blois; but François the nomad stayed often at Amboise where he kept lions, tigers, leopards and bears in the dry moat on the east side of the château. Sometimes, as an occasional guest, one of these animals would be allowed to sleep at the foot of his bed, and some of the leopards were trained for hare-coursing in the open countryside. He once had a bull put into the lions' enclosure so the Court could watch the bloody combat from the ramparts above. On another occasion he livened up a wedding-feast by having a wild boar brought on to one of the galleries; it broke loose and stampeded the guests, which enabled him to play the hero by confronting it personally and killing it with his sword.

It is a pity that one is obliged so often to proceed from one tale of horror to another when dealing with these beautiful châteaux, so peaceful now beside the river with only the tread of tourist feet to disturb their tranquillity; but life was full of horror in the days when they were inhabited. An account of Amboise would be incomplete without mentioning one of the most frightful of such episodes, usually referred to as the 'Tumult of Amboise'. In 1560 the Protestants planned an uprising in large numbers to seize the fifteen-year-old François II, with Mary Stuart his girl-queen, and remove them from the baneful influence of the Guises whose rule from behind the throne boded ill for religious toleration. The coup was to take place at Blois, but the Guises got wind of it through careless talk of some supporters in England and hastily moved the Court to Amboise, a walled stronghold whereas Blois was open. This put the plotters off their stroke and when they burst out of the woods on the appointed day, Saturday 15 March, poorly armed, ill-prepared and without proper leaders, they were easily defeated. The woods were hunted and the fugitives rounded up. The hanging of them took a month. There were not enough gibbets for the 1200 summarily condemned, so they strung them from the town walls from the 300 iron hooks on the front of the castle where flags and tapestries were draped on feast-days, from every tree on the terrace, and from the balcony of the King's Lodging – called *Balcon des Conjurés* to this day. The whole town was eventually decked with a macabre bunting of corpses, and the leaders were beheaded in the courtyard watched by the whole Court; for to stay away on any excuse would have aroused suspicion. Even Condé, who was involved in the plot, had to watch his colleagues die; but some under torture had implicated him and three months later he was arrested at Orléans. Of the other spectators, Mary was sick and had to leave; even the duchesse de Guise was moved to remark to Catherine de Médicis: 'This will bring great misfortune; blood calls to blood'; and the Chancellor Olivier, who had conducted the prosecutions, died of shame and sorrow a few days later, saying on his death-bed to the Cardinal de Guise: 'Cursed Cardinal! You've damned yourself and us too.' The Court soon had to quit the town because of the smell of corpses.

Nobody cared much to live at the château for a long time after that, but in 1816 it was given to the duchesse d'Orléans. From her it passed to Louis-Philippe, the 'Citizen King', who patched it up and used it sometimes. His room, furnished to the period and with a good full-length portrait of him, is included in the visit. Through him it devolved on the comte de Paris, who gave it to the nation in 1975.

After the guided visit one is free to wander the battlements and gardens and inspect at leisure the lovely little **Chapel of Saint Hubert** perched on the edge of the battlements. In the arch of the façade the kneeling figures of Charles VIII and Anne pray to the Virgin while, just above the doorway, a fine piece of sculpture depicts the legend of Saint Hubert, France's popular patron saint of hunting. A dissolute young Frankish nobleman, he was hunting in the woods one day when the stag turned to reveal a cross shining between its antlers and spoke to him, warning that he must mend his ways or soon go to Hell. Recognizing Christ himself in this dramatic manifestation, Hubert fell on his knees and swore to devote the rest of his life to His service; which he did by entering the deep forests of Flanders and converting the pagan inhabitants, an undertaking quite as dangerous then as the nineteenth-century missions in Equatorial Africa. From 705 to 727 he was Bishop of Liège. The interior of the chapel is very small, but even so the royal couple required a little warmth during their devotions and there are small fireplaces in the corners. Buried beneath a flat stone in the floor on the left are some old bones which may or may not be the remains of Leonardo da Vinci. Anyhow there is little profit in contemplating flat stones and doubtful issues when you can raise your eyes to the friezes round the wall: there some other master whose bones lie Heaven knows where, whose name has been forgotten, has turned stone into lace.

Leonardo came to Amboise in December 1515 at the invitation of the young François I. The King's reign had just begun in glory with his victory at Marignano, and he was lodged at the **Château Clos-Lucé** at the other end of the town by way of the Rue Victor-Hugo, which it is as important to visit as the main château when you are in Amboise. In this delightful little fifteenth-century manor-house Leonardo contentedly spent the last few years of his life and died peacefully in May 1519. The King's generosity and his recognition of Leonardo's genius are examples of the finer side of his complex nature; and the admiration was mutual, for the artist recognized in François a fellow giant of the Renaissance. The château, with its terraced gardens going down to the Amasse, is open every day of the year, except in February, from 9 to noon and 2 to 7; and has a resident chief guide who is one of the best I have ever met. He is so knowledgeable and so obviously proud of his charge – quite rightly so for it is fascinating. Every room is completely furnished and many of the items are rare and delightful: an original Dührer of Maximilien I in the upstairs reception room for example, a fragment of fourteenth-century Arras tapestry depicting the Song of Roland in the *grande salle*, and two big Renaissance chests in the kitchen which were designed to serve the double purpose of a bread-bin beneath and a servant's bed on top. In Charles VIII's time this was Anne of Brittany's private house and it still contains a splendid little oratory chapel the King had built for her. Poor Anne's two husbands were always presenting her with chapels in which to pray for heirs. In this one Commynes tells us 'she shed the most piteous tears that woman could weep' for the Dauphin Charles-Orland who died of smallpox in this house at the age of three.

Unfortunately there are none of Leonardo's pictures here, but the view from his bedroom window across the town to the castle is interesting because the fine sketch he made as he stood there is now in the royal collection at Windsor. He undertook no great paintings in these last years of his life as his right hand had become partially paralysed. The masterpieces he brought with him, including *The Virgin of the Rocks* and the *Mona Lisa*, François bought after his death. Perhaps the most absorbing feature of all at Clos-Lucé is the museum in the basement, a collection of models of Leonardo's inventions made up from his own detailed plans. Certainly here is the place for parents with bored youngsters; it is something children will never forget. Among the many inventions on show are a swing-bridge; an air-conditioning plant; a clock-work driven motor car for two (could this yet be the solution when oil has run out?); a flying-machine, a turbine, a projector and a parachute. To see this extraordinary man's ideas in solid shape is staggering. How could he be so far ahead of his time – three centuries at least? All his inventions are feasible; and if his contemporaries had possessed the technology of the late nineteenth century they would have been perfected and produced. François I would have enjoyed showing off his aeroplane to Henry VIII.

Just over a mile south of Amboise on the Bléré road, on a hill nearly 200 feet above the river level and one of the highest of the cliff system which encloses the valley for most of the Touraine, stands Chanteloup. In 1761 the domaine was purchased by the duc de Choiseul. He was then at the height of his career as Louis XV's chief minister, a position he had attained through the patronage of la Pompadour. Through the displeasure of her successor the du Barry he fell from grace ten years later and was banished here. To overcome the tedium of an alien existence far from Versailles he proceeded to dissipate his fortune in rebuilding the château, lavish entertaining and expensively organized hunts in the surrounding forest. To these activities he added a few dilettante experiments in farming which failed to impress Arthur Young when he came by in 1787, two years after the Duke's death. The place had 'all the mischievous animation of a vast hunt, supported so liberally as to ruin the master of it'. Such great lords, he opined, would do better by 'marking their residence to the accompanyment of neat and well-cultivated farms, clean cottages and happy peasants . . . [whereupon] their harvest, instead of the flesh of boars would be the voice of chearful gratitude.' He did however commend 'a noble cow-house' and the best-built sheep-house he had seen in France, and he noticed some good ploughing.

Under Napoleon I the property passed into the hands of Jean-Antoine Chaptal, comte de Chanteloup, one of his ministers and an industrial chemist who got him out of one of the difficulties caused by our blockade of the West Indies trade. Here at Chanteloup he experimented with sugar-beet and invented the process of extracting an artificial sugar from it, an inferior substitute the beleagured French had to put up with and the rest of us have had to suffer ever since. He also introduced *chaptalisation*, the addition of sugar to the must before fermentation to strengthen wine, a dubious practice generally and, in the case of A.C. and V.D.Q.S. wines, permitted only in a bad year under strict supervision. Young would have been interested to meet Chaptal, though he might not have approved.

Nothing remains now of Choiseul's costly château. Even the 'noble cow-house' has gone, and the marble stables where he kept his hunters. Everything was demolished in the nineteenth century except the famous pagoda, a rather depressing folly in the *chinoiserie* style standing beside a reedy mere: sad and lonely monument to a frivolous age. Admission is obtained on applying at the caretaker's house at the end of the avenue between 8 and 7 from Easter to end of October, and 9 to 5 the rest of the year. For a most modest charge you can walk in the grounds and in the woods, which are very pleasant, for the Forest of Amboise is mixed wood with a good showing of oak. For a little more you can look round the pagoda and climb its 142 steps to its summit 144 feet above the ground to enjoy the view. For a little more still you can get an angler's day-ticket and try your skill at tempting experienced and wily tench and carp from the ooze and reeds of the lake.

Our next objective being Vouvray, we can attain it by crossing the bridge at Amboise and turning westwards along the N152. Alternatively, we can turn eastwards and enjoy fresh views of the island-studded river close on our nearside until we come back to the turn for Onzain, whence a minor road leads all the way down the vale of the Cisse to Vouvray. This means extra time and mileage but it is well worth it, for here is a smiling, intimate, warm and fertile valley, sheltered from the north by the proximity of the ridge of tufa hills so that it derives the full benefit of the moderate climate of the middle and lower Loire Valley which is dominated by the prevailing mild maritime air-streams that are funnelled into it. Giant orchis grow on the sun-exposed road verges to our left as early as the last week in April, by which time the lilac, laburnum and horse-chestnut are in full bloom and the apple blossom is beginning to fall. Everywhere are orchards and little farms where sheep (not a common sight in other parts of the Val de Loire) graze the meadows, and thousands of ducks are reared in true 'free-range' conditions by the banks of the streams. Where the scarp of the hillside is steep there are many troglodyte houses, their fronts looking perfectly normal and often recently built, but their chimneys sticking out of the top of the hill. A cave with a few mod. cons. can make a very cosy residence, especially when facing south as these do.

The greater part of the white wine of Amboise is grown on the slopes above, as we remarked when we were there. **Cangey, Limeray, Pocé** and **Nazelles** are the communes within this appellation. **Noizay** has no less than three of the many delightful small private châteaux along this prosperous valley, and it is in that village that we enter the boundaries of the Vouvray appellation area as well as that part of the Touraine known as 'the Balzac country'. Soon we come to the village of **Vouvray** itself, built in terraces at varying levels on the hillside near the point where the Cisse abruptly turns a right-angle to pass almost unnoticed beneath the busy highway to Tours and lose itself at last in the Loire on the other side. There is nothing extraordinary about Vouvray except its wine and its situation among the group of steep little valleys which here suddenly slice into the hillside, the most renowned of them bearing the suitable name of *la Vallée Coquette*. Balzac loved Vouvray and gives a lyrical description of it, much too long to quote here, in the first chapter of *La Femme de Trente Ans* – a description which still largely holds good. He chose it as the setting in that romance for the tenderest episodes in the love-affair between Julie and Lord Grenville. Also in *L'Illustre Gaudissart* it is at Vouvray that the rascally commercial traveller finally meets his match among the wily inhabitants, and in the Rue Victor-Hugo there is a most expressive bust of him, put up in 1934, and the only public statue of a character from the *Comédie Humaine*.

When we were far away upriver at Pouilly I mentioned that there were six truly great wines of the Loire. Apart from a rare and little-known one in Anjou (which we shall come to) Vouvray is the greatest of these. Some may not believe me, but we seldom see the best of it here on the English market; generally we get the blended wines from many vineyards. Fortunately, as well as producing the best, Vouvray has the highest production of any Touraine appellation, an average of 46,000 hectolitres (over a million gallons) annually; Borgueil comes next with only half that quantity. The finest growths can only be bought on the spot, produced from a single vineyard on the right soil. For the topsoil which overlies the tufa base here to a depth of from three to five feet is of two kinds. The *aubuis*, composed of clay and sedimentary limestone in just the right proportions, produces a wine of great body and unique fruity flavour with astonishing keeping qualities. The other soil, the *perruches*, is a silicious clay, and flint will always produce a wine delicate but light. When the two are blended they tend to cancel out each other's qualities. Monsieur André Fouquet and his wife, of 47 Rue Gambetta (which starts near the post office), are very old friends and will do their best to help anyone who calls and mentions my name. M. Fouquet is not only a *vigneron* but a vine nurseryman who replants many of the vineyards in Vouvray so he knows just which of them are on the best soil and the best cared for. If he happens to have sold out what you are seeking he will tell you where else to look for it; for in a good year the smaller *vignerons* (eighty per cent of the 3000 of them have holdings of less than two hectares) can quickly sell out. All from the same grape, the wines are produced in a range to suit all palates: *sec* (which is never acid), *demi-sec*, and *moëlleux* which is sweet like a Sauternes. Moreover, with its natural inclination to 'pearl' Vouvray is obtainable *pétillant* and as *champenoise* manufactured by the full process of closed fermentation and having the champagne pressure in bottle of about four atmospheres. This last, at a far more modest price, is very near to a good champagne and infinitely superior to an ordinary one. From a good vintage year Vouvray will keep for fifty years or more. Some people have a few bottles of 1921 tucked away and it is still luscious: 1947 likewise. Of more recent vintages, '71, '73, '75 and '76 are already fine and will be good keepers.

At the other end of the Rue Gambetta, the turn up the hill just past M. Fouquet's premises leads to the vineyards on the windy hill-tops – miles and miles of vines, a sight worth seeing. The Vouvray grape is the famous Pinot (or Pineau) de la Loire, local nickname 'Chenin'. Centuries ago the river commerce of the Loire introduced the noble Pinot grape from Burgundy. Whether it was the Noir or the Blanc (alias Chardonnay) the authorities seem uncertain, but by selective breeding over many years (complete well before Rabelais's time) the present local variety was established, a white grape with a sky-blue bloom, ideally suited to the soil, but since widely used up and down the valley. The vines are short in the wood, requiring close pruning: in winter they look like stunted bushes blasted black as if by some catastrophe. They ripen late and are therefore exposed to the 'noble rot'. This is climatically favoured along a narrow strip about six miles either side of the Loire in this part of the valley, the influence of the water moderating the temperature and moistening the air. So the Vouvray harvest has to await this great blessing, and this means several selective pickings over the same vines which may last right into November. It is a very worrying time for the *vignerons*, for only the benign microbe *Botritys cinerea* produces the *pourriture noble*. Once it has taken, north winds and dry weather – appropriate to that season in any case – are prayed for; if much rain falls a different rot, the *pourriture grise*, takes over and the grapes are ruined.

The château, west of the village, dating from the thirteenth century and used by Balzac as part of the setting for *La Femme de Trente Ans*, sells wine from its own vineyards and provides *dégustation*. It is a fine sight on the hillside and worth a visit, but is open only to prospective customers. The *Cave Coopérative* halfway up the Vallée Coquette is another fascinating place with its miles of galleries and millions of bottles; but its wines, though a little cheaper, are of course blended.

Farther west beyond the Vallée Coquette, in **Rochecorbon**, a stark square tower, built in 1095 and sole remnant of a great fortress, stands solitary on the hilltop, a landmark for miles around. In the valley, in a little garden of grass and trees in the middle of the village, the parish church is very pleasing with its sturdy aspect, big transepts and square belfry. It is of the eleventh and twelfth centuries and the west door has a Romanesque arch with the 'dog-tooth' pattern so much less common in France than in England. Inside the north transept Saint Roch stands with his faithful dog, and opposite him, holding a bunch of grapes, Saint Vincent, the patron saint of vine growers, for Rochecorbon too has many vineyards. The saint's feast is 22 January and here in the Touraine there is an ancient saying that '*à la Saint Vincent l'hiver perd sa dent*', which more often than not turns out to be true owing to its moderate Atlantic climate.

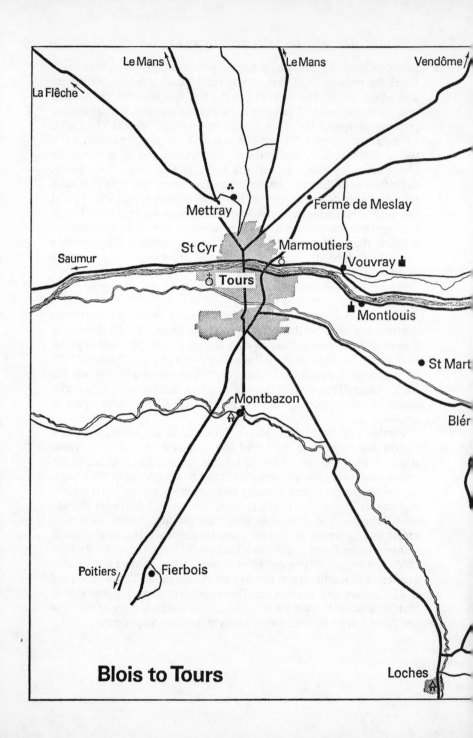

Blois to Tours

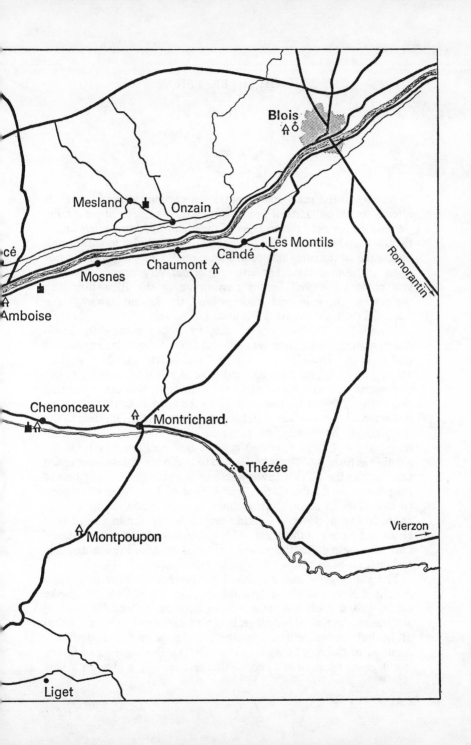

CHAPTER TEN

Tours

❧

Returning to the main road from Rochecorbon, we find ourselves already on the outskirts of Tours; but on the way, after about a mile, we pass on the right the remains of the abbey of **Marmoutiers** and if the time happens to be after 2 o'clock it is a good idea to make one's visit while on the same side of this busy road. Unfortunately it is not open in the mornings. The entrance is not very conspicuous, but you come to it well before passing under the Paris–Bordeaux motorway. Drive in and park beyond the second gateway, the beautiful thirteenth-century Porte de la Crosse.

Founded in 372 by Saint Martin, the abbey became the head-quarters from which Gaul was recalled from its lapse into paganism and anarchy. The Hungarian-born Saint Martin, while a Roman soldier, took pity on a beggar and gave him half his cloak. Shortly afterwards he had a vision of Christ wearing it; was converted and eventually obtained his discharge from the army in order to become a missionary. Driven out of Italy by Arian heretics for holding to the doctrine of the Trinity, he came to Gaul and founded a small monastery at Ligugé near Poitiers, the first on French soil. On his election as Bishop of Tours he decided to found his *majus monasterium* here among the hillside caves where in the previous century one of his predecessors, Saint Gatien, first Bishop of Tours, had often gone to say Mass in secret during times of persecution. Saint Martin chose to live in poverty, looking very unbishoplike in an old torn cloak in memory of the cause of his conversion, and devoted himself and his disciples to the reconversion of central France and the reclamation of its towns and agriculture.

The abbey grew and flourished for several centuries and when Alcuin of Northumbria became abbot in the time of Charlemagne he established a great monastic school here as well as his famous *scriptorium*, one of whose magnificent bibles we saw in the cathedral at Le Puy. It was pillaged by the Northmen in 853, and over a hundred of the monks were murdered. The Benedictines of Cluny got it going again at the end of the next century and soon a vast complex of buildings went up. The great refectory built with the aid of donations from William the Conqueror no longer stands, but the bell tower of that period consecrated by Urban II in 1096 still does. A cross stands on the spot where he stood to preach the First Crusade, the object of his visit. Marmoutiers enjoyed a second flourishing which lasted 500 years until it was pillaged again: by the Huguenots. Finally it was suppressed at the Revolution and sold to a speculator from whose demolition very little of it escaped. In 1847 the Congregation of the Sacred Heart bought it and today it is occupied by a community of nuns of that Order.

Reception is in the office on the left just inside the La Crosse Gate: the secretary rings a coded call on an ancient bell which re-echoes through the stone corridors to summon one of the older nuns who act as guides. I was taken round by a gentle old Sister who skimped nothing although the flights of worn steps and uneven floors of caves must have been a great trial to her. At the end when I complimented her in tackling them all she replied it was nothing, Saint Martin kept her fit so she could do the job in his honour. One may give the guide some money (for herself or her Order as she pleases, I understand) and this is a necessary courtesy as there is no official entrance fee.

The visit is something not to be missed, and there is a particular thrill of awe in looking out from the caves in the hillside where the early hermit saints dwelt, cutting out and enlarging their solitary little homes with their own hands. Besides the *Repos de Saint Martin* with the vestiges of a Romanesque chapel later built on to it, we are shown the cave-cells of Saint Gatien, Saint Patrick and Saint Brice. That of Saint Gatien is the oldest, for he died in 301; he was one of the Seven Bishops sent from Rome at great risk to themselves to reconvert Gaul. Saint Denis, who went to Paris at the same time, was another. As to Saint Patrick, there is a very ancient tradition that he was a relative (probably a great-nephew) of Saint Martin, and that he received part of his training here. Certainly when he went to Ireland he was filled with that special missionary zeal which was the stamp of Marmoutiers at the time. In front of his cave there are some remnants of a medieval stained-glass window showing the shamrock as a symbol of the Trinity. Saint Brice was a different sort of man. While a young deacon he copied the attitude of the high-born prelates who despised Saint Martin for his failure to keep up appearances. Once when a sick man came enquiring for the saint, Brice pointed and said: 'If you're looking for that idiot, behold him over there: gazing at the sky as usual like a fool.' Martin came over

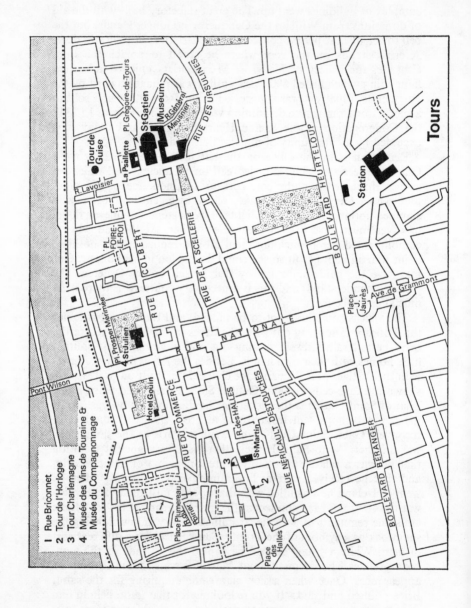

Tours

1 Rue Briçonnet
2 Tour de l'Horloge
3 Tour Charlemagne
4 Musée des Vins de Touraine &
  Musée du Compagnonnage

Station

Pont Wilson

Place des Halles

Place Plumereau

Rue Plumereau

Rue Poirier

RUE DU COMMERCE

RUE NATIONALE

RUE NÉRICAULT DESTOUCHES

St-Martin

R. des HALLES

Hôtel Gouin

4 St-Julien

Pl. Prosper Mérimée

RUE DE LA SCELLERIE

RUE COLBERT

PL. FOIRE-LE-ROI

R. Lavoisier

La Psallette

Tour de Guise

St-Gatien

Museum

R. Général Meusnier

Pl. Grégoire-de-Tours

RUE DES URSULINES

BOULEVARD HEURTELOUP

Place J. Jaurès

Ave. de Grammont

BOULEVARD BÉRANGER

BOULEVARD

and reproved him, telling him that God had chosen him for his successor. 'Am I not right?' the other remarked to the bystanders; 'just hear the nonsense he talks!' But he did become the next Bishop; had a rough time of it; suffered exile and returned at the end of his life to found many churches in Touraine.

Four miles north of Marmoutiers, at the height of its prosperity under the Benedictines, the abbey had one of its farms just beyond the village of Parçay-Meslay, marked on modern maps as the **Ferme de Meslay**. Among the remains of the thirteenth-century buildings it has what is perhaps the finest surviving medieval tithe-barn in Europe, but because it is tucked away off the conventional tourist route most people hurry past without even knowing about it. Personally, if pressed for time, I would rather miss out one of the châteaux than this glorious and unusual monument. It can be reached by the minor roads from Rochecorbon or reserved as a short excursion from Tours by taking the main road out through Saint-Cyr. When you arrive you will probably find no one about. There is no charge and you may wander in at any time of the day. Park outside the handsome gatehouse which has a little chapel over it.

You can see the barn beyond, framed in the great arch, but before setting off towards it notice the ancient, solid surrounding walls: the farm was strongly fortified. Observe also the weather-vane on the north-east corner with the papal insignia, a sheaf of corn, and symbols of sun, rain, wind and cloud, all delicately fashioned in wrought iron. Below the wall is an old stewpond, and there is another in the courtyard. The barn itself is bigger than many a church: about 180 feet long, with a high roof of massive chestnut beams and rafters, supported on two central rows of timber columns thirty feet high with two rows of shorter columns in the aisles. Because of the excellent acoustics the building is used for concerts and recitals in early summer, and the stage and sounding-board in one corner detract somewhat from the beauty of the interior. Aircraft noise from a near-by aerodrome is another distraction; but when all is silent and you hear the farmyard cock crowing in the yard outside everything seems much as it was at the beginning and you half expect a lay-brother to emerge from the cool shadows with dust and chaff on his gown. For the whole building, including the timber roof, is original. It was put up just over 750 years ago.

Capital of a rich and fertile region, standing at the crossing of the main Bordeaux highway and the Loire, **Tours** has always been one of the most important cities in France. In recent years it has taken on new growth as an industrial centre, filling the two-mile gap between the Loire and the Cher and measuring nearly four miles from east to west. Its population now touches the 135,000 mark. As one approaches from the outskirts it seems an untidy sprawl of factories and skyscrapers; but the old and interesting part is still there, and within quite a small compass, so don't be put off. Cross by the temporary bridge alongside the Pont Wilson, a wide and graceful stone bridge built in 1779, three arches of which unfortunately collapsed in April 1978. Take the second turn left (Rue Colbert). Drive down a ramp on the left into a car-park under the trees in the **Square Prosper Mérimée.**

The old city is best explored in two halves anyway – east and west – and we are now east of the Rue Nationale, the main Poitiers road, which is the boundary between them; so we can take the **Rue Colbert** down towards the cathedral. Across the street on coming out of the car-park is an old gabled house, now a hairdresser's, which bears an iron sign depicting a girl in armour – *La Pucelle Armée*. About 21 April 1429, after weeks of questioning to determine that she was not an impostor, Joan of Arc was brought to Tours to be fitted out for her self-imposed mission. Hamish Power, a Scottish sign-painter who lived somewhere in the city, painted her standard, and here on this spot stood the armourer's shop where her suit of armour was made. The present building is not the original, but belongs to the century after Joan. In fact during that period of renewal and prosperity which eventually followed the end of the Hundred Years' War, it seems that practically the whole street was rebuilt to look sparkling new, for most of the buildings have the high gable-ends of the late fifteenth and early sixteenth centuries. You can only appreciate their antiquity, however, on standing back, as the majority have been stuccoed over and look nondescript at close quarters.

Nowadays the Rue Colbert is in my opinion the best shopping street in what is an exceptional town for shopping anyway, because here is the greatest concentration of small establishments. Tours is particularly well endowed with shoeshops and bookshops and there are several of each here; also there are antique and bric-à-brac shops, a marvellous *charcuterie* near the top of the street ('Au Cochon Fin') and a *fromagerie* near by ('La Calendos') which illustrates De Gaulle's famous remark about the difficulty of governing a country which has 246 cheeses: it stocks no less than 200 of them. There are several cafés, bars and small restaurants, of which latter La Renaissance, though dowdy in appearance and in the lowest price bracket, is clean and good and much patronized by local people.

All the side-streets on the left lead quickly through to the water-front, rather uncongenial in itself because the busy N152 runs along it. The fourth of these, the **Place Foire-le-Roi**, offers repose in its little public gardens where once stood the booths of the medieval provision fair (on the lines of Stourbridge Fair at Cambridge), conveniently near the quays whence all merchandise would come. It has two fine half-timbered houses and one in Renaissance style (no. 8) which was the Tours residence of the Babou family whom we met masquerading as saints in the church at Amboise. The **Rue Lavoisier**, crossing the Rue Colbert at its end, leads down past the barracks on the site of the old city gates and castle built by Henry II of England in the days when Tours was Plantagenet property. Only two twelfth-century towers remain now, sticking up among the modern barrack buildings. The most conspicuous, the north-east one, is called the **Tour de Guise**. After the murder of the duc de Guise at Blois his fifteen-year-old son was imprisoned there on the top floor but one. Since he was the rising hope of the Catholic League, Henri IV after his accession ordered such close surveillance that escape should be impossible; the young Duke only ever came down from the tower to go to Mass in the chapel, and then surrounded by guards. But after he had been a prisoner nearly three years a laundress smuggled a rope in to him, and next time coming out of chapel he challenged his guards to a race up the stairs hopping on one leg. Young and supple, he got well ahead round the first spiral, then broke the rules and hurried to the top on both legs, bolted himself in his room and slid down to the ground outside on the rope while the guards wasted time banging on the door. Pursued by cries of '*Alerte! le Guisard se sauve!*' he ran along the quay, stole a baker's horse and rode away to join the Leaguers.

The other arm of the Rue Lavoisier leads along to the **Cathédrale de Saint Gatien**, the most striking part of which is its west front soaring up before us as we enter the tiny square. Unfortunately the tufa limestone has begun to crumble and no satisfactory remedy has been found for this so that it has a slightly shabby look, but its aspiring proportions and graceful embellishments are very beautiful and it is a good illustration 'at a glance' of development from Flamboyant to Renaissance. The façade went up between 1427 and 1484, the north tower (representing the Father) was finished in 1507 and the south tower (representing the Son and six feet lower than the other's 229 feet) just forty years later, thus completing an entire reconstruction from scratch which had begun in 1239. As nearly always the work began at the eastern end, so that the apse is in purest thirteenth-century style; this is best observed from the Place Grégoire de Tours behind the cathedral, named incidentally after the celebrated historian of the Franks who was Bishop of Tours in the fifth century.

Following the same order of progress inside, we find that the three middle chapels of the five opening off from the chancel still have their original thirteenth-century windows and the chancel itself has fifteen beautiful clerestory windows whose stained-glass panels were put in place there just over 700 years ago. They depict the Passion, the Stem of Jesse and legends of various saints, while the capitals on the pillars are carved with common flora and fauna of the Touraine – oak, vine, watercress, hare, rabbit, squirrel and so on. The transepts of the same period have magnificent rose windows. The one on the south is a pattern of concentric circles in varying tones of blue; that on the north resembles the rose windows of Notre Dame somewhat and is a gallery of angels, patriarchs, prophets, apostles and bishops. The nave follows chronologically, its vaults having been finally set up in the 1460s; the great rose window above the west door is of the same period. In harmony with the rest of the building the nave is modest in height for a cathedral, only eighty-five feet to the apex, so that the interior lacks the grand sense of space to be found in most others. Saint Gatien's unique treasure is of course its large number of early stained-glass windows, which happily survived the bombing of the last war when in most other great churches of the Loire they fell in fragments on the flagstones.

An exit off the north aisle leads through to the *Cloître de la Psalette*, completed in the sixteenth century. *Psalette* means choir-school, which was its function before it was altered into an apartment-house after the Revolution. Balzac has Mlle Gamard reside there in the *Curé de Tours* and the curé himself at 8 Rue de la Psalette. The cloisters have now been restored to their original form.

On the other side of the cathedral the **Musée des Beaux Arts** stands on a corner of the square (open 9 to noon every morning; 2 to 6 afternoons April to September, 2 to 4 the rest of the year). Once the bishop's palace, it was rebuilt in the reign of Louis XV. I am sorry to say the art gallery is badly managed, but it contains treasures most visitors will not want to miss. Some of the exhibits are labelled, some are not; and many of the best items are hung in silly places hard to find. They include a fine portrait of Balzac in a monk's habit (by Bertall I believe) which is on the top floor; a good Louis XIV by Rigaud on the ground floor on the way out when you are frustrated and weary and liable not to notice it; an exquisite tiny

Rembrandt of the Flight into Egypt tucked away in a small room of Dutch paintings near by, and an interesting portrait of William Cecil, Lord Burghley, in the basement! Then, finally to baffle the visitor, the works they hold in greatest pride – two by Andrea Mantegna: *Garden of Olives* and *Resurrection* – are down a separate staircase at the back of the building. The only thing is to ask for what interests you and not waste time on a random search, for there are also works by Rubens, Dégas, Houdon, Claude Vignon, Philippe de Champaigne and Jean Fouquet. The last-named was born at Tours, the offspring of a servant-girl and a monk, and established a school of painting here which obstinately resisted early Renaissance influences and persisted in a purely French style for long after his death in about 1480, although he had spent several years working in Italy.

The area behind the cathedral and the art gallery is the site of the old Roman town. It was the capital of the Turones tribe of Gauls when Caesar came, and he renamed it Caesarodunum. The **Rue Général Meusnier**, now a quiet alley between high walls, is almost perfectly semi-circular in shape because it was built on the lip of the old amphitheatre, every stone of which disappeared long ago; but its outline has been traced among the houses so that we know that it was big enough to seat twelve thousand spectators. If you take the only right turn halfway along the curve and walk through to the Rue des Ursulines, turning right again there, you will soon come to a conspicuous rotunda of modern apartment houses, beneath which is a passage leading through to a public garden. Along the bottom of this garden is a big surviving section of the Roman city wall built about AD 275 after the barbarians ravaged the town. It is an impressive and venerable sweep of mighty masonry with the characteristic courses of brick among the stone. Part of the ramparts and a round tower in the south-east corner are still intact. We are standing on the outside of the *southern* wall and the river is not very far away to the north, so the old Roman city was not very big. The western quarter which we shall be visiting later on did not come into being until the fifth century and was a separate town called Châteauneuf. It was not until the Hundred Years' War that the fortifications were extended to surround them both, in order to prevent the English from executing a forcible entry into what they still regarded as their own property.

To make our way westwards now, the **Rue de la Scellerie**, starting opposite the art gallery, is convenient. Not quite as interesting as the Rue Colbert, it has nevertheless two good bookshops (one secondhand). At no. 71 Honoré de Balzac received the first rudiments of his education as a day-boy, from the age of five until he was eight. He describes his experiences there – none too happy – through the mouth of Félix in *Le Lys dans la Vallée*.

At the end of the street we come to the wide and busy **Rue Nationale** where all the big shops are to be found and where on 20 May 1799, when it was known as the Rue Napoléon, Balzac was born. The house stood on the west side, just south of the corner of the Rue Néricault Destouches, on the site now occupied by the Pharmacie Principale. Balzac's father, Bernard-François (real surname Balssa), a commissary of the army who became Deputy Mayor of Tours, was then fifty-three and had married a Parisian girl thirty-two years his junior. Bernard was a disciple of Rousseau, much concerned with social problems, and himself wrote several small works of more practical than literary merit on subjects such as prostitution and rehabilitation of criminals, and on *A History of Rabies, with the Means to Save Human Lives and Put an End to Other Evils by a Tax on the Canine Population* – which might now be worth considering.

Balzac had great affection for the street where he was born and wrote of it later as 'the queen of streets . . . a street so wide that no one ever cries "Make way!" a street which doesn't wear out, well paved, well built, well cleaned.' That description largely applies today, for Tours – in the centre at least – is a clean and spacious city and must long have been so, since John Evelyn remarked in his diary: 'The streets are very long, straight, spacious, well-built and exceeding clean' – exactly the same testimony two centuries earlier. Evelyn was here with the object of perfecting his French; Tours has always been famous for purity too in its grammar, syntax and especially accent. It is better-sounding French than the Parisian and it is still noticeable that in the countryside of the Touraine there is virtually no local patois. The reason is not clear; by some the state of affairs is attributed to a decree of a ninth-century bishop that clerics in his diocese should always use the vernacular in addressing even the educated laity.

A few steps northwards along the street and we come back to the Rue Colbert and the car-park. Hard by is the **Church of Saint Julien** with a most unusual tree in the churchyard; it has enormous rounded leaves and sprouts from its branches in May what seems to be a profusion of foxgloves. It is in fact a fine and rare paulonia. The lovely church is kept locked all the week and here in the city centre no one can be found to hold a key for visitors, but it is open on Sundays. An abbey founded by Clovis was once here, and this its church was rebuilt in the thirteenth century. In the course of clearance after the 1940 bombing the long-forgotten cellars of the abbey were discovered and since 1975 they have housed the **Musée des Vins de Touraine** whose entrance is just past the west door of the church (open 9 to noon and 2 to 6 every day except Tuesday or a day following a public holiday). Another of those museums really fascinating because it has a theme, this was the brainchild of a local historian and ethnologist, the learned, lively and imaginative Monsieur Roger Lecotté. There is no other museum like it anywhere because its theme is not simply wine as such – the growing of it, the varieties of grape, the tools of the *viticulteur* and related craftsmen like the cask-maker and bottle-maker, the care and drinking of wine – but has a special emphasis on its relationship with archaeology, ethnology, legend, religion and social customs. Its wonderful range of exhibits and documentation is to be increased as the years go on, and for anyone interested in any aspect of wine it should on no account be missed.

Before leaving be sure to look in the old cloisters outside where there are a Gallo-Roman wine-press and a medieval one. The former is of big hollowed stones in which a wooden crusher was operated by a lever. The medieval model is all of wood and was hand-operated by a capstan: this type lingered on up to fairly recent times before the steel screw entirely displaced it.

Out on to the Rue Nationale now, and a few yards along in the direction of the bridge we come to yet another of Monsieur Lecotté's splendidly original ideas, the **Musée du Compagnonnage** (same opening times as the wine museum) where are exhibited examples of the finest work from every craft and the tools used. *Compagnon* and its popular derivative *copain* denote one with whom bread is metaphorically shared (Latin *cum panis*); *compagnonnage* came into being in the 1480s when craftsmen began to organize themselves against the medieval guilds and corporations which had degenerated into fixed monopolies where the status of *maître-ouvrier* descended from father to son and the humble workman no longer had a chance to rise in his trade by his own skill and effort. Through the nation-wide organization of the *compagnonnage* with its lodges called *cayennes* in every big town, the postulant – chosen for his good workmanship, honesty and devotion to his comrades – made his *'tour de France'*, perfecting his skill as he went. This process was for the man of promise, to enable him to escape from mediocrity; but for the workers generally the *compagnons* strove for better conditions and pay. Naturally they were disliked, often proscribed, so their organization was obliged to be clandestine and had a secret ritual from which Freemasonry may have borrowed later. However this was not Freemasonry or anything really like it, but a working-class movement, a forerunner of the trades-unions, though with a more responsible attitude in stressing '*l'amour du travail bien fait*' as a main principle. The whole affair is a fascinating piece of social history and I think M. Lecotté is right in claiming this museum as 'unique in the world'. But if anyone should think the subject dull for a holidaymaker he would be mistaken, for most of the exhibits consist of the *chefs-d'oeuvre* which a workman had to submit as a prelude to full initiation. Every craft is there: wheelwright, black-smith, tyler, stone-cutter, cabinet-maker, cask-maker, basket-weaver, ropemaker and many others, the work of every one exemplified at its very best and most beautiful; even a child could not be bored here.

Crossing the Rue Nationale now into the **Rue du Commerce** almost opposite, we are in the western half of old Tours, the erstwhile Châteauneuf. On the left in this street is a well-stocked English–French bookshop, and nearly opposite that the **Hôtel Goüin**, a most beautifully proportioned and elegantly ornamented Renaissance building which houses a local history museum, open 10 to noon and 2 to 6 every day except Tuesday (Wednesday, Saturday and Sunday only from November to February). Its exhibits are bygones of the Touraine from prehistory to the eighteenth century.

The Rue du Commerce eventually leads to the **Place Plumereau**, which is visually quite stunning for it is nearly all half-timbered, gable-ended buildings. Unfortunately in the last war, when Tours suffered over nine thousand killed and a total of twelve hectares (nearly thirty acres) of buildings destroyed or seriously damaged, this quarter suffered exceptionally and what we now see is largely restoration – but it is well enough done to invoke strongly the feel of the Middle Ages.

Turning into the **Rue Briçonnet** out of the north-west corner of the square we penetrate even deeper into the Middle Ages. Almost at once, on the corner of the Rue du Poirier on the right, we find a *twelfth*-century house with Romanesque window-arches facing on to the side-street. No. 31 just past it has a Gothic façade of the late thirteenth century. No. 29 has a fifteenth-century gable-end, which is unusual in being entirely constructed of stone, and the additional charm of a tall half-timbered turret. Farther down, no. 16, the Hôtel de Tristan, is a grander residence of the end of the same century built of brick and stone. Retracing our steps, we turn left opposite no. 29 into a tiny pedestrian square where the bombed ruins have only recently been most cleverly restored to make small residential apartments in an atmosphere of cloistered peace. On the left is another thirteenth-century house with a magnificent Gothic balcony and several more houses have tall half-timbered turrets. A passage-way leads back into the Place Plumereau, in whose vicinity are several restaurants, a *crêperie* and, for the real John Bull who must have his English beer wherever he goes, a Whitbread's pub on the corner. But the price of a pint is enough to buy at least two litres of sound wine.

The little streets just to the south of the square are all medieval and some retain their colourful ancient names – de la Rôtisserie, de la Monnaie, du Petit Soleil and so on. In the **Place de la Victoire** just a little farther to the west an open-air flea-market is held on Wednes-day mornings; an amusing atmosphere, but the goods offered are mostly horrible junk and the prices outrageous. On the well-stocked old-postcard stall, for example, don't be beguiled by the pencilled '25' on a dog-eared seaside postcard of the 1930s: it doesn't mean centimes, it means francs! If you want a market for real shopping, a short way southwards down the Rue de la Victoire there is a splendid and extensive covered *Halles* in daily session with a big car-park near by.

Eastward from this point the **Rue des Halles** is a main shopping street secondary to the Rue Nationale, leading through to it and thence to our starting-point. A third of the way down we pass the **Basilique Saint-Martin** signalized by two dominating old Roman-esque towers, the one on the left called the Tour Charlemagne, after a predecessor on the same site, and the other, on the opposite side of the street, the Tour de l'Horloge. The vast complex of buildings which stood between them was completely razed at the Revolution, and after more than a century deprived of the support of the transept of the church the Tour Charlemagne collapsed in 1928 and had to be rebuilt. The architect in charge refused to fake the details of the former construction, considering the proportions of more importance, and merely restored the volume with a blank façade. The new basilica, in contrast, is a massive pile of nineteenth-century pretentiousness with a dome that seems to indicate the architect had illusions of being another Wren. But it is not lacking in grandeur and the high altar inside is impressive when regarded from the marble-columned nave. The crypt is otherwise, looking like an oversized Victorian waiting-room with an inglenook fireplace added. It contains a fragment of the skull of Saint Martin, all that was retrieved from a

Huguenot bonfire in 1562. The crypt is on the site of the original where his remains were entombed at the end of the fourth century. Queen Clothilde came to pray here daily (and often all night) after she moved to Tours following the death of Clovis in 511. She forsook Paris, where her husband had spent his last days in purple robes imitating the Caesars, and occupied the remaining thirty-three years of her life in works of charity and prayers for peace in the kingdom which was torn by civil war between her murderous sons squabbling over their portions.

If we turn right on reaching the Rue Nationale we come to the spacious and busy **Place Jean-Jaurès**, which is the centre of the city as a whole, and at the railway station a short way eastwards along the wide Boulevard Heurteloup there is a big car-park handy for this quarter.

Southwards from the Place Jean-Jaurès the **Avenue de Grammont** (which is the main through road to Poitiers) runs absolutely straight for about a mile and a half. A left turn at the Carrefour de Verdun, just before the bridge, brings us into the **Boulevard Richard-Wagner** where there are two car-parks a short way along on the right; a sailing centre close by; safe bathing in the quiet waters of the Cher; a bridge across to a park on an island and a long pedestrian promenade westwards along the river-bank. We shall be seeing more of the Cher in our next chapter.

There are of course plenty of hotels in all price ranges in this big city. The camper is not so well catered for: there is nothing near the centre, nor on the banks of the river as is usually the case, but there is a two-star camp-site nearly three miles south at **Joué-lès-Tours,** a suburb just beyond the Cher, and another at Montlouis (see next page).

Henri, Duc de Guise, assassinated
at Blois in 1588: portrait in the
Château of Beauregard

Mme Dupin, last *châtelaine* of
Chenonceau; portrait by Nattier

Château of Angers: portion of the Apocalypse tapestry—the
angel emptying his vial

Château of Angers: deer in the
dry moat

Sully: its moat filled with water
and stocked with fish

Villandry with its formal gardens *à la française*

CHAPTER ELEVEN

Montlouis;
Chenonceaux; Montrichard and Loches

✦

So far we have been able to follow the valley of the river in a more or less logical way, but here in the Touraine where three big tributaries – the Cher, Indre and Vienne – close in from the left to meet it the field of relevant interest widens to include the Cher and the district lying south-east of Tours. One relevant interest which expands in Touraine is wine; and this beckons us to Montlouis to begin with. Take the right turn out of Tours (towards Amboise) just before the Pont Wilson. The road closely follows the Loire with views across to Marmoutiers and Rochecorbon and past **Ville-aux-Dames**, opposite which is a rough but negotiable track through the trees to the shore. Being so near a big town it is not very tidy, but the view across to Vouvray with the château of Montcontour among its vineyards up on the hillside is quite inspiring, and the bird population is considerable in spring and summer, with waders and terns out along the sands and nightingales singing one against the other in the copse behind. I have also seen anglers catch some fine zander on spinners in the clear fast-running water where the river is nipped in by the headland on which we stand and the cliffs of Vouvray on the other side. Two miles farther along the road on the right, on the outskirts of Montlouis, there is a neat clean camp-site among trees, the handiest for the holidaymaker who wants to be near Tours. It is not beside the river of course, but it has a nice swimming-pool.

For the centre of **Montlouis** fork right just past the camp-site. The village is on top of a scarp with views right over the valley. In John Evelyn's time all the houses were caves with merely their chimneys above ground, and many still are. There are a few little shops and, as so often where people come to seek a well-known wine, quite a few good restaurants. Near the entrance to the village is a rather touristy-looking *Cave Coopérative*; I have not been in because there are plenty of private *caves* retailing single-vineyard wines of their own growing. Those of Martin-Serrault at the other end of the village, in the quarter called La Barre, are a good place to call because Monsieur Martin, a jolly young fellow with a great sense of humour, who likes English people and enjoys airing his knowledge of our language, will insist on taking you round his fascinating galleries cut out of the substratum of tufa rock. Whenever he needs more space he just digs out a new one and in these sections you can see just how soft and yet how strong the tufa is. It is easily workable and yet there is no fear of collapse. No wonder people have resorted to it for a quickly-made and practical home since time immemorial. In the office at the entrance to his *cave* M. Martin has saved all the interesting fossils he has found in the course of his burrowings.

The vineyards of Montlouis stand on the southern slopes of the cliffs nearly opposite Vouvray and have the same basic soil structure. Like Vouvray it has the distinction of its own appellation, produces only white wines from the wonderful Chenin grape, and awaits the noble rot before harvesting. Yet its wines are not quite the same. They are not so *corsé* (nearest translation: robust) and do not keep for long periods. The reason for the difference is that there is less clay even in its best soil – known here also as *aubuis* (see p. 176). On the other hand sand and flint occurring in greater proportion make this lighter wine more *parfumé* and remarkably good to drink for its own sake. That it cannot stand up to Vouvray is no condemnation, for Vouvray is a giant among wines. It is a little cheaper and it travels well.

By taking the minor road (close to M. Martin's premises) southwards out of Montlouis we pass among the vineyards on the gentle reverse slope of the hills and eventually come to **Saint-Martin-le-Beau** where we are greeted by an enormous bottle beside the road, higher than a house and bearing the label '*Saint-Martin-le-Beau, Cité des Grands Vins*'. The great wines are of course Montlouis, for we are still in the appellation area; but the place is hardly a city – a quite modest-sized village in fact. To the right of the Romanesque church stands an outdoor pulpit with a canopy roof.

Leaving Saint-Martin by the Athée road we soon find ourselves crossing the Cher, calm, deep and steady, entirely different in character from the Loire as its fall throughout is less pronounced. Two hundred miles long, it rises in the north-west foothills of the Massif Central, not far from Aubusson the famous tapestry town, about sixty miles west of the Allier, and runs parallel with it for a while, cutting itself a deep funnel-shaped valley in order to reach the plain at Montluçon. Meandering through the Berry and the city of Bourges, it soon meets the southern scarp of the Tertiary deposits near Vierzon where it is deflected westwards, gradually closing with the Loire as it ambles along the edge of the Sologne and finally joining it a few miles below Tours, the first important tributary since the Allier came in way back at Nevers.

Soon after crossing the bridge (which has a camp-site near it, incidentally) turn left on to the Vierzon road, which diverges from the river for a short while, but rejoins it just before **Bléré** which has a twin town, **Sainte-Croix**, on the other side. We are still in former English territory and Henry II had the first bridge built to connect the two towns. They have good shops but are otherwise rather plain. Nor is the river specially attractive, though it has a barrage near the bridge creating a good expanse of calm water upstream for boating, fishing or swimming. Once Bléré had a château where Jean-Lambert Tallien, Deputy to the Revolutionary Convention for Indre et Loire, was brought up. Offspring of a retainer in the household of the Seigneur de Bercy, he showed promising intelligence and was educated together with the seigneur's own son by the Abbé Morrelet, a witty writer of the period. Though he became a prominent Jacobin, Tallien was one of the most moderate among them, 'doing a lot of good because he did the least possible harm', as a contemporary remarked of him – and that is about the highest possible praise for a member of the Convention in those hysterical times. When he was put in charge of the Terror at Bordeaux at the age of twenty-four, he fell in love with a pretty and rather flighty nineteen-year-old aristocrat, Thérèse de Cabarrus, one of his prisoners, recently divorced from her husband, the marquis de Fontenay. The debate in the Convention on the subject of her proposed execution was the one in which Robespierre came unstuck: in defence of his mistress Tallien led the tyrant's overthrow and earned Thérèse a place in history as 'Notre Dame de Thermidor'. He married her soon afterwards.

Proceeding still eastwards out of Bléré, we pass through a countryside of water-meadows, peaceful as an idyll when the river is behaving – as it usually is. But the Cher is deceptive, for when it floods and spreads out across these fields it can be more sudden, more deadly than the Loire. After three miles we begin to catch glimpses through the willows of a château right in the midst of the meadows. The first impression is one of surprise at finding so large an object in such a setting, but more profound impressions await us; for this is **Chenonceau**, unquestionably the most delightful of all the châteaux in the Loire Valley. To reach it, cross the bridge a little farther on and turn left into the village of Chenonceaux (the settlement as a whole is spelt with an *x*, the château alone in the singular).

Chenonceau is not only the most delightful château of them all, but the best administered. Visits are without a guide unless you want one; you can take your time; it is fully furnished and there are many lovely things to see for your money. You are *given* a substantial and informative explanatory leaflet (in English if you wish) at the gate; each room has a plaque against the door to tell you where you are and each painting is labelled as to artist and subject. In the former coach-houses of the courtyard is a restaurant with a reasonably priced menu and the estate retails quite good appellation wines from its own vineyards – again at a reasonable price. The shop has a wide selection of cards, books and pictures, and a visit to the little waxwork museum is included in the entry charge. Chenonceau belongs to the Meunier chocolate family and the state bureaucracy which runs so many other historic establishments with such paucity of imagination would do well to take a lesson from them.

Having parked and paid at the outer gate, we approach the château by a pleasant walk (or a ride on a miniature train, if you prefer, in the summer season) along an avenue of majestic plane trees. At the end we come to an open space and then a courtyard on which once stood a small medieval castle protected by a moat which still subsists; for in those days Chenonceau was just a fortified mill, the working part of which stood on the river-bank behind the fortifications.

For generations the mill belonged to the de Marques family of the *petite noblesse*. In 1420 Jean de Marques threw in his lot with the Burgundian party and accepted an English garrison, which proved to be his family's undoing when the fortunes of war turned the other way. By the end of the century the de Marques were in reduced circumstances and their little riverside property attracted the envy of Thomas Bohier, Baron de Saint Cyergue, Mayor of Tours, one of the 'new men' of that epoch, a tax-farmer and soldier who ended by having been Chamberlain to four kings – Louis XI, Charles VIII, Louis XII and François I. Bohier deliberately ruined them by trickery and a long series of lawsuits and finally bought the property for a song. He only wanted it for the site: the buildings he deemed in need of modernization. So he demolished the lot with the exception of one of the corner towers, now standing on its own just ahead on the right and still called the Tour des Marques, a very nice example of early-fifteenth-century pepper-pot with a smaller turret growing out of the top.

Bohier began to build his château in about 1520, placing it farther back and supporting its immense weight fair and square on the sturdy piles of the old mill which themselves rest on the granite bed of the Cher. But he did not live to see the finish of his scheme for François sent him to Italy and he died near Milan in 1524. By then, to finance his grandiose works, he had borrowed 190,000 *livres* from the King so that his son found himself in the same predicament into which he had manoeuvred the unhappy Marques and had to surrender the property to François in exchange for the release of the debt. Thus it came about that Henri II had it to give as a handsome present on his accession to his lady-love, Diane de Poitiers, and Catherine de Médicis on his death was able to take it back as royal property, giving Diane Chaumont as a consolation prize with which she was not very consoled.

Diane completed Bohier's main building and had the bridge built in direct line with it to the opposite bank; this latter, with its five graceful arches, was to the design of de l'Orme who had been one of François's architects at Fontainebleau. To finance these works her doting lover generously gave her the revenues from a newly instituted tax on bells, a fact which gave rise to Rabelais's comment that 'the King has hung all the bells in the kingdom round the neck of his mare'. When Chenonceau came into Catherine's possession she cherished it and made frequent use of it, for she had always admired the place and regretted that her husband had not given it to her to begin with. Probably most of the happiness she had in her troubled life was enjoyed here and her daughter-in-law, Mary Stuart, treasured the memories of the good times she had shared here during the short time she was Queen of France. But it was not until much later in life (about 1575) that Catherine was able to spare the time and money to have the three-storey extension built on top of the bridge, the lower floor of which is one long and beautiful gallery. This idea had been part of de l'Orme's scheme, but by then the Classical style was coming into vogue and the architectural contrast with Bohier's Renaissance building is interesting. The long, low profile, the fine arches and the water alleviate the Classical severity so that the ensemble is in perfect harmony and combines to achieve a charm without parallel anywhere.

In her will Catherine left Chenonceau to Louise de Lorraine, the unhappy queen of her pederast son Henri III. After his assassination Louise, for all that he had been a most unsatisfactory husband, spent the next few years here in white clothes of mourning, praying for his soul. She is '*la bonne reine blanche*' whose ghost, it used to be said in the village, was sometimes seen in the park. She would recall with concern, no doubt, some of the entertainments he organized here.

One such occasion was, as Lafosse expresses it, 'a virtual saturnalia of which the mildest and only natural feature was the semi-nudity of the young ladies of the court'. In fact, according to a contemporary writer, the Queen Mother had arranged that feature herself in hopes of diverting her son's desires in a direction likely to ensure the Valois succession.

With the accession of the Bourbon line the Court became established in the capital instead of moving up and down the Val de Loire and Chenonceau, like so many others of the châteaux, faded into relative obscurity. In the eighteenth century it was bought by Claude Dupin, another tax-man like Bohier and an intellectual. (Maurice Dupin, father of George Sand, stemmed from the same stock.) His second wife was Louise Bernard, much younger than himself, of a Huguenot banking family. A woman of great character and intelligence, she kept up the connection with her husband's friends after he died: Madame de Rohan-Chabot, Mme de Mirepoix, Buffon, Montesqieu, Voltaire and Rousseau were among her guests. From 1742 for several years Jean-Jaques became her secretary. Writing afterwards of this peaceful interlude in his life he recounted, 'We had a lot of fun in that beautiful place; we had wonderful food there, I got as fat as a monk.' Madame Dupin died in 1799 aged ninety-three, surviving the Revolution because the local people respected her so highly and would not have her molested. And when some hotheads from Amboise proposed demolishing her château a former curé of the village saved it with the warning that it would be a crime against 'le bien public' to damage a bridge. How indebted we are to that resourceful man!

The château is open for visits every day of the year from 9 until 7 from April to September, until sunset the rest of the year. In summer there is *son et lumière* every evening. Chenonceau contains more items of interest than I have space to enumerate here; I can point out only a few not to be missed. Firstly, in the chapel, Scotsmen will not want to overlook the graffiti of their countrymen of the *Gardes Écossais*: one just inside the door on the right, dated 1546, and another on the left wall dated 1543; they might have better luck than I in deciphering them. In the little library on the east side of the building there is a *Holy Family* by Andrea del Sarto over the door and *A Martyr* by Correggio on the wall; in the Diane de Poitiers room, a *Virgin and Child* attributed to Murillo, and in the François I room across the hall a portrait of Diane de Poitiers as the hunting goddess by Primaticcio. She is in a fantastically 'precious' pose, but he has portrayed very well her mean face and small mouth. For despite the great legend she was really rather plain; and her features betray the spite and insatiable avarice for which she was so well known. Even as a huntress she was nothing to compare with her rival the Queen, for Catherine was most daring and accomplished in that respect and such a keen horsewoman that riding side-saddle was not fast enough for her. She accordingly invented the method called *à la planchette* – with one knee raised and resting in the saddle. Because of the vagaries of the wind this innovation is said to have introduced (or re-introduced) ladies' knickers.

In this same room a full-length painting by Van Loo shows the three Mailly-Nesle sisters, comtesse de Mailly, comtesse de Vintimille and duchesse de Châteauroux, disporting themselves *toutes nues* as the three Graces. Each in turn became Louis XV's mistress in the early part of his reign. D'Argenson wrote of him: 'It was a fancy of the King's to go in this way from sister to sister.' He took two of them with him on his Flanders campaign in 1744 and the people of Metz were so scandalized that he had to send them back. As their carriage left the town some of the local housewives emptied the contents of their chamberpots on it. In the *Grand Salon* there is an imposing portrait of the previous Louis by Rigaud which the King himself sent as a souvenir after a visit; and in a corner by the window there are two charming pictures by Nattier, one of a princesse de Rohan and the other of Madame Dupin when she was young: she was extremely beautiful with lovely big brown eyes, a gentle mouth and wide, intelligent forehead. In another corner hangs a Rubens: *Christ playing with Saint John*, two very Dutch-looking infants fondling a lamb.

Just before the entrance to the Long Gallery a flight of steps leads down to the kitchens inside the first pier of the bridge. They must have been quite renowned in Catherine's time, when the aptly named Buontalenti and other imaginative chefs she brought over from Italy were introducing new ideas and new foods to the hitherto rather plain medieval fare of the French. The globe artichoke, haricot beans, petits pois and many other things we regard as typically French were brought by them. Perhaps the most useful refinement which France acquired from the Renaissance, and improved upon in its own capable way to the lasting benefit of the whole western world, was good cooking. One of the novelties which delighted Catherine's guests here was fruit ices, very expensive and troublesome to make in those days; both ice preserved in holes in the ground and fast-running water were used in the freezing process. The idea did not reach England until a century later.

The most singular and most glorious feature of Chenonceau is the Long Gallery right across the river with its alcove windows where one can easily fall to musing over the quiet Cher making its way in slow, dreamy eddies towards its destiny. I like to imagine that the thoughts and feelings the gliding water down there provokes in me would have been shared by Catherine, Guise, Rousseau and the many other leading actors on history's stage who must have gazed down from this same place.

To conclude briefly – for we cannot tarry at Chenonceau for ever – there are several period-furnished bedrooms, all known as usual by evocative historical names; but in this case they are the names of people genuinely associated with the château. There is a handsome balcony with a view over the formal gardens and the wooded park, which you are free to roam before leaving. In fact there is enough here to fill a whole day pleasantly if you have time. Finally the estate wines which I mentioned earlier: they are three – a white which is inclined to be acid and rather thin; a rosé of medium quality from the Cabernet grape and a pleasant light red which is the best and is made from the Malbec grape, better known in the Bordelais as we have already observed, but grown in this region under the name of Cot.

Unfortunately the railway runs between the road and the river on this side, but it is the best way on to Montrichard. On the way we pass through **Chisseaux** where, at the distillery 'Fraise d'Or' visitors are willingly shown round in the usual business hours and can buy the liqueur made from the strawberries which flourish in this district. The next village, **Chissay,** has a handsome small château dating back in parts to the fifteenth century, but not open to visitors.

And then we come to **Montrichard**, the *t* of which is sounded. The quarter by which we enter is a separate parish called Nanteuil, a name of Celtic origin signifying 'the clearing in the valley'. The diminutive valley in question was once mostly swamp, fed by a sacred spring which is still there about five hundred yards north of the church marked by a nineteenth-century pinnacle of no special artistic merit. Legend relates that when Saint Martin sent some disciples here to preach and to build the first church, a terrible monster lived in the swamp, feeding on cattle and children who ventured too close. No one dared to penetrate the wilderness of marsh, reeds and willow-thickets until one May morning a young monk waded in alone after praying for several hours before the Virgin in the church, asking her for courage. He took with him the long linen veil from her statue and after a few minutes reappeared with the monster (a huge crocodile!) tied to it as on a lead. Dragged to the holy spring it promptly died in convulsions. It is the usual dragon allegory of course, and what actual deed of daring it enshrines it is impossible now to tell; the display of a stuffed crocodile in the church in the Middle Ages even leads to scepticism, but there is, as we shall see, an interesting sequel.

The present **church**, which was built by the Benedictines in the twelfth and thirteenth centuries, is worth a look inside. The choir, transept and two lateral chapels are original; the nave was rebuilt in the fourteenth century with the slightly flattened 'Angevin' vaulting so common in this region. A flight of steps from the north transept leads to an upstairs Lady chapel built at the expense of Louis XI, aided by a subscription from his courtiers. On the upper part of the left wall there is a fifteenth-century mural of the Taking Down from the Cross. The other three walls are nearly covered from floor to roof with thousands of votive plaques; I have never seen so many in one place. I asked an old man working in the cemetery across the street what it was that Notre Dame de Nanteuil seems to cure with such notable success and he replied that it is – fear. Since the time of the young cleric in the legend people have come here in large numbers (and still do, especially on Whit Monday) to pray, as he did, for courage. Philippe-Auguste, I now find, was among them; he was a notorious coward in battle in spite of his nickname and was given to riding off slyly out of the way whenever fighting broke out near him. And Louis XI, that pious dictator with the troubled conscience, was haunted frequently by an uncontrollable fear of death.

The centre of Montrichard is dominated by the great square keep of its medieval **castle**, all the more impressive for being left in ruins. The building is of the twelfth century, replacing a wooden fortress built about 990 by Foulques Nera, comte d'Anjou, as a frontier-post to protect his domains from Eudes of Blois. Another of those strikingly childlike characters of the early Middle Ages, Foulques was busy quarrelling, pillaging and murdering most of the time, then at intervals veered to extremes of abject remorse. He made no less than three penitential pilgrimages to Jerusalem, but all the good they did, in the form of a resolve to behave better in the future, was speedily consumed in burning rage on his return by finding Eudes had ravaged his lands in his absence. Montrichard figured often in the blows and knocks of these neighbours' quarrels, as later between the Plantagenets, Foulques's successors to Anjou, and the kings of France. In 1188 Richard Lionheart was besieged here by Philippe-Auguste. Philippe's highly-skilled sappers, known as the '*Taupes* *du Roy'*, the King's moles, secretly dug a tunnel until they were directly beneath the corner tower of the north-west ramparts. Carefully they removed its foundations, replacing them with wooden props to which they set fire before retiring. When the props burnt through the tower came down with a mighty crash, to the great surprise of those inside no doubt, and the beseigers poured through the gap. The street on that side is still called the Rue de la Brèche. The last time the castle tasted battle was as recently as June 1940 when the Germans set up their artillery there and they and the French cannonaded each other across the river. The round tower south of the keep was almost completely destroyed: just a few bits of wall and a doorway are all that remain.

The castle is open only from Easter to 30 September (9 to 11.30 and 2 to 6.30). Visits are *sonorisées*, which signifies that as you toil up the steep pathways to the top you are accompanied through loudspeakers by a spoken commentary (in clear easy French) and rather tremulous martial music; altogether one would be better without it, but it is rather fun. From the battlements at the foot of the keep you find yourself looking *down* on a church steeple and close by in the base of the keep is a grim little prison cell where Richard is said to have spent a short time, his lion's heart rather heavy, after Philippe took Montrichard. By kicking aside some of the jackdaws' collection of sticks you can mount to the very top for a really wonderful view over the town and miles of countryside.

In the ticket-office is a small **museum** containing a few interesting odds and ends, including some lovely psalters and missals, some ancient pairs of spectacles with lenses in weirdest tints of orange, blue or green, and a few wax figures. Among the latter is Touchard-Lafosse from whose monumental five-volume journal of his wanderings by the Loire I have quoted often in this book. As a young officer he had served with Napoleon's *Grande Armée* and was given the difficult responsibility of the field hospitals in the terrible Russian campaign. He died in 1847, having written his *magnum opus* after his retirement.

Just one other minor item of interest concerning the castle before we leave it. Such an austere pile would never have done for François I as a place to stay, but he put its dilapidated empty rooms to good use by testing out a new idea he had heard of in Italy – the artificial incubation of eggs. These experiments, the first of their kind in France and carried out under his own supervision, were successful: a considerable achievement with solid-fuel heating and no thermometer.

The **Church of Saint Croix** on which we looked down from the battlements was once the private chapel of the castle and is now the parish church. It has a fine twelfth-century west front, partly hidden by a modern porch. The rest of it suffered rather badly in 1749 when after heavy rain a section of the castle wall collapsed on top of it. The marriage took place here on 8 September 1476 between Louis d'Orléans, the future Louis XII, aged fourteen, and Jeanne de France, aged twelve, a marriage which was to end so sadly twenty-two years later at Amboise.

Montrichard is the commercial centre for a prosperous agricultural area, so it has some very good shops, particularly in the Rue Nationale where also you will find the excellent and reasonable hotel Croix Blanche. The Grille du Passeur is a good and unusually situated restaurant, with its feet in the river on the south end of the pretty seventeenth-century bridge; it is open until 11 p.m. and serves simple dishes such as eels or grilled rabbit. The old quays along the riverside are very pleasant, but there is little space on them for parking except at the end east of the bridge. Just beyond this the carriageway changes to a grassy footpath along the bank which affords an enjoyable stroll. Over the bridge and on the right is a small park with tennis courts open to all; a swimming-pool; a lake; a beach, and calm water for those who prefer to disport themselves in the Cher itself. There are even a few rowing-boats for hire. At the western end of the town the municipality has a camp-site of about three acres. The Forest of Montrichard, to the north of the town, is hardly worth a look. Although Michelin marks it with a green line it is not a *'parcours pittoresque'*, but simply monotonous, scrubby and wet.

Let us continue along the north side of the Cher by the main road, because tucked away in the Forest of Choussy westward of us is a charming little château which few people know about because it is seldom mentioned in guidebooks. On the way we pass through **Bourré**, where there are several small country restaurants. Through the village we take a right turn marked Angé which leads over the railway and, just before the river bridge, to a rough lane which runs along the bank past allotments to a patch of grassy common by the water's edge, a good place for a picnic and to get the feel of the Cher's placid character, so different from the Loire. But this is a diversion: the main road carries on to **Thézée**, and about a mile before the village, at a spot called Mazelles, we pass on our left a considerable second-century Roman ruin popularly known as the 'Mansio de Thézée'. It may in fact have been a *mansio* – staging-post for Roman troops – but this is not definitely established. The site belongs to Maurice Druon, author of the stirring historical novel series, *The Cursed Kings*.

Thézée itself is a good place to sample the wines of the Cher in peace. We could have investigated them at the *Caves* Montmousseau at Montrichard which are certainly interesting, but more deliberately directed at the tourist trade. Two or three hundred yards beyond Thézée's church (dedicated to Saint George and with a most graceful spire) in an ordinary house on the opposite side of the street, Monsieur Paul Allion has his premises, gives *dégustation* of the wines from his own vineyards and sells them retail. The Cher wines are appellation Touraine (see p. 160). They are grown on the slopes above us where the soil is not unlike that of Montlouis, but being on the edge of the Sologne it contains more clay so that the wines have more body and less delicacy. Its composition is in fact, as M. Allion will tell you, 'very like Sancerre'. For this reason the Sauvignon white *cépage* suits it best and is preferred for the local white wine: its bouquet and flavour unmistakably evoke memories of Sancerre and Pouilly, but though fruity and strong it lacks their *finesse*. For the reds the Gamay and Cabernet are used; both yield a full and rich wine, especially the latter which resembles a slightly coarse Chinon. Seldom heard of outside France, the wines here are not expensive. They are better than Chenonceaux. I have not tried bringing them home, but I should imagine the reds would travel well enough; the white could possibly be doubtful.

Now for the little-known château I mentioned. We take the minor road northwards out of Thézée to Monthou just over a mile up the hillside, passing through some of the vineyards on the way, turn right at the end of that village along a lane through the woods and eventually come to a clearing where stands the château of **Gué-Péan** (open every day Easter to 31 October, 9 to 7). There has been a château of sorts here since feudal times when (as the name implies) it guarded a ford over the little river Bavet and took tolls. The present building dates from the late fifteenth century when a fresh start was made by Nicolas Alaman, a northern Italian who was *valet de chambre* to Louis XII and subsequently François I. It was he incidentally who designed the sumptuous royal tents in which François sought to impress Henry VIII at the Field of the Cloth-of-Gold. Built round an enclosed rectangular courtyard, the château has an appealing individuality about it. Three of the towers, really only for ornament, are quite short and capped with traditional pepper-pot tops, but the fourth (on the front left corner) is a proper keep of full height with machicolated *chemin de ronde* and an unusual bell-shaped roof. A bridge over the dry moat leads to a gateway in the low curtain-wall forming the front. Two fine Renaissance pavilions flank the courtyard and, being unembellished, harmonize perfectly with the more severe *corps de logis* at the bottom which was not built until the reign of Henri IV.

In the present century Gué-Péan has come into the ownership of the Keguelin family, a cadet branch of the family which was here 300 years ago. It is not in perfect repair – they are worried about the deterioration of the roofs – and the cost of maintenance is an enormous burden which they are trying to meet by opening their home to the public in a pleasantly informal and unfussy way. Usually some younger member of the household acts as your guide. You may pause and chat about their varied collection of treasures; linger over the paintings that please you most (an exquisite little Van der Veldt harbour scene pleases me most), and the barrel-organ and music-boxes they will wind up and play for you if you ask. There are fine pieces of antique furniture all over the place and a quantity of interesting autograph documents from the family archives on display in the library, among them souvenirs of Louis XIV, Napoleon, Dumas, George Sand, Chopin, Balzac and his friend Jean-Lambert, baron de Kainlis, who spent fifteen years as a recluse here in order to study the implications of Swedenbourg's philosophy – hardly long enough to unravel the tangle entirely perhaps, but in his turn he considerably influenced Balzac, who wrote his philosophical novel *Jean-Lambert* about him. In the same room a small museum of the Resistance exhibits clandestine posters and pamphlets of the Maquis, secret messages from prisoners and so on. For the present owner, the marquis de Keguelin, was one of the leaders of the Paris Insurrection and was awarded the distinction of Compagnon de la Libération by General de Gaulle afterwards.

But the interest of Gué-Péan lies not simply in its collections: it has direct associations with one of those fascinating little byways of history. I have already related in dealing with Blois how Louis XII married Mary of York near the end of his life. Nicolas Alaman entertained the King here the year before; the room where he slept is a genuine *Chambre du Roi* for once. It has been suggested that he first met the pretty English girl here during that visit, and that may be so for she seems to have been a friend of the Alaman family. Certainly after the marriage Nicolas was appointed trustee of her dowry. During the tournaments in Paris to celebrate the wedding she conceived a secret passion for Charles Brandon, Duke of Suffolk.

He was not a very courtly duke; his father, a mere squire, had been killed at Bosworth while carrying Henry Tudor's standard and Henry VIII had given him the vacant dukedom in recognition of that. He was a big, burly dark fellow with a determined, handsome face that betrayed a sense of fun. He had little learning, but excelled in martial sports and Henry loved him for that. Mary was overwhelmed with admiration as he knocked one after another of the wiry, fastidious little Frenchmen out of their saddles. She stored the memory in her heart, and on becoming a widow she wrote to Henry asking his leave to marry Suffolk. But much as he liked him the King did not really see Suffolk as a brother-in-law. François I, however, always sympathetic in an *affaire du coeur*, was prepared to wink at a clandestine marriage and with his connivance the young couple came secretly to the faithful Nicolas's house to be married in the little private chapel we are shown in the base of one of the towers. Henry – rather reluctantly – forgave them on their return to England and they lived happily together for nineteen years until Mary died. They were the grandparents of Lady Jane Grey, but mercifully neither of them lived long enough to see the end of her less idyllic story.

After visiting the château you may walk in the park. By booking in advance you can join in a promenade through the woods with the riding school on one of its horses. Similarly by advance booking the château takes paying guests for holidays or week-ends. The address is Gué-Péan, Monthou, par 41400 Montrichard: telephone 71-43-01. It is a lovely place, right off the beaten track, something different and uncommonly peaceful.

But now we must leave it; and the Cher too. Instead of retracing their steps some may like to approach Tours via Loches by taking the road for that famous old town out of Montrichard. It lies just under twenty miles to the south-west. If you go from here you will pass by another great feudal castle at **Montpoupon**. It is still virtually complete, having been lived in continuously (it is still lived in) and is mostly of the fifteenth century. Open Easter and Whitsun week-ends and every day from 15 June to 15 October, from 10 to noon and 2 to 7, it prides itself on a collection of hunting trophies, saddlery, old weapons and old carriages. But the best thing about it is its imposing exterior.

A few miles after Montpoupon the road enters the Forest of Loches, which is domanial, but just a bit too well '*aménagée*', and the few places allotted for pulling off the road are not the prettiest. The forest however has some splendid tall oaks which flourish on the rise of ground on which it stands, between the Indre and its tributary the Indrois. Once a favourite hunting-ground of the counts of Anjou, it was well known to the English Plantagenet kings and still supports a herd of about a hundred deer. The main ride, crossing our road, is five miles long, marked out at intervals by four tall pyramids put up on the orders of Colbert because the more sophisticated nobility of Louis XIV's time could not find their way around in the wilds so well as their forebears and caused anxiety by getting lost. For the best eventual approach to Loches it is pleasant to turn left on to the main ride (it is a public road) and follow it to the bottom where it joins the Bourges road. If there is time to spare turn left there and drive the two miles to the ruined Carthusian monastery of **Liget**, founded by Henry II of England in 1177. The surviving conventual building is eighteenth-century and now a private house, but on application at the left-hand door of the gatehouse one may usually obtain permission to walk through to the ruins of the original church and cloisters beside a stream. On the other side of the road, beside the same brook, are the remains of the *Corroirie*, where the lay-brothers made skins into parchment for the monks writing out manuscripts at the abbey.

Back westwards along the road we have just joined, we soon come to **Beaulieu-lès-Loches**, now an industrial suburb but originally a settlement where, in what could be called one of his lucid intervals, Foulques Nera also founded an abbey in expiation of a few of his sins. It has since entirely disappeared, but the church on the site has a Romanesque tower surmounted by a very pleasing octagonal tower. And now **Loches** itself is before us: a spectacle indeed to excite wonder, with its still completely walled citadel on a hill-spur, and its turrets, steeples, pyramids and mighty rectangular castle-keep breaking the skyline from within. Crossing the bridges over the two arms of the Indre we face the turreted, machicolated Porte des Cordeliers, completed in the last years of the fifteenth century. Turn right here into the Place de Verdun, one of the good places to park. This square is overlooked by a rather graceful Renaissance belfry tower, sole vestige of the former church of Saint Antoine, and by a statue of Alfred de Vigny who was born at Loches in 1797, the sensitive, shy philosopher, poet, novelist and playwright of aristocratic lineage who never fitted in anywhere despite his progressive and humane ideas, because the breadth of his view and his moderation made it impossible for him to follow others to extremes. Such men are seldom wanted in politics, so he concentrated on literature and is best remembered now for his *Cinq-Mars*, an historical novel in the style of Walter Scott, in which the Loire Valley features largely. He also translated some of Shakespeare's plays into French verse and wrote some plays of his own. An Anglophile, he married a young lady with the very English name of Bunbury, but they were not happy together.

All the other items of interest in Loches – apart from ancient streets and houses I have not space to enumerate – are concentrated within that high citadel enclosed by its wall two kilometres long. You can walk right round it if you like and the effort is worth while if you have time; if not and you wish to park nearer the entrance (for there is only one entrance), drive up the Rue des Moulins, turn right into the Grande Rue and carry straight on until you come to the Rue de la Poterie just past the gates; there is extensive parking-space here and in the Mail Droulhin near by. Inside the gates is a little town within a town, another world, another age, cut off from our every-day world by the great medieval wall. The Porte Royale, as it is called, is flanked by two towers which Philippe-Auguste had erected to avoid any possible repetition of the shock he suffered in 1194. Loches was then the property of Henry II of England, but Philippe craftily tricked the feckless John Lackland into handing it over to him. The following year Henry's more formidable son Richard arrived on the scene and retook the supposedly impregnable fortress after a siege of only three hours! It was not until 1205 that the French got it back again.

In one of the towers a small local history museum, the **Musée du Terroir**, is housed. Open every day from 9 to noon and 2 to 6 (4 in winter), it has, like Beaugency, an interesting room entirely furnished in nineteenth-century peasant style, complete even with Mr and Mrs Peasant sitting by their fire. Behind the tower the **Musée Lansyer** (same opening times) was the private house of the nineteenth-century painter of that name, friend of Delacroix. He bequeathed it to the town together with many of his pictures. His landscapes and seascapes were beautiful and deserve to be better known. The ones of the Touraine have additional appeal because of their local interest, especially an oil of Chenonceau in morning light (on the ground floor) which is the best picture I have ever seen of that oft-painted subject. On the first floor in his fine big studio, among more of his own works, are displayed pages from Delacroix's sketch-books which are most instructive. Any artist who smothers his own talent by labouring and anxiety over his drawing will be encouraged to see how roughly and simply, but directly, that great master went about his preparatory work. Decidedly the Lansyer

Azay-le-Rideau

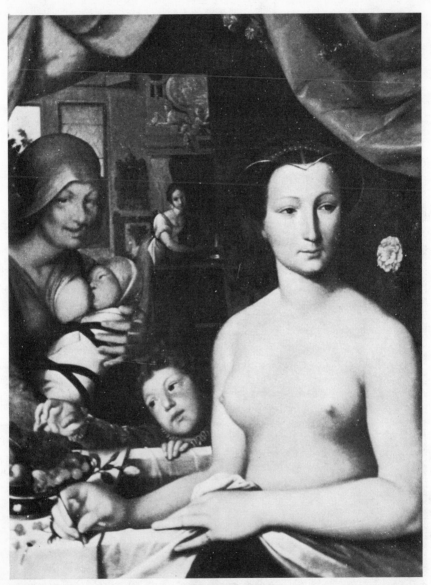

Gabrielle d'Estrée: portrait in the Château of Azay-le-Rideau

Museum is not to be missed on a visit to Loches. It has a most charming and obliging lady caretaker/guide, and lovely gardens where you may linger and enjoy the view over the town and countryside beyond.

Leave the garden by the little side gate, and a few strides down a narrow side-street bring us to the Place Charles VII where we are greeted by the most unusual outline of the **Church of Saint-Ours.** Its twin-steepled towers flank a pair of pyramids which are the roof of the nave! These were constructed in the twelfth-century when the Prior found that the former roof threatened collapse. He also had to re-roof the lovely porch which otherwise remains largely tenth-century; but even older than this is the font which stands beneath it, once a pagan Roman altar in cylindrical form, sculpted round the outside with scenes of warriors.

At the other end of the square, in the extreme north angle of the citadel, the **Logis Royale** (open every day except Tuesday, 9 to noon and 2 to 7 – 5.30 November to April) is composed of two parts which do not match. The 'Old Lodge', feudal in appearance with its turrets and ramparts, was built for Charles VII. He considered it a veritable *maison de repos* after years of being on the run, taking refuge in grim old barracks like Chinon, but fashion was changing rapidly and only a few decades later it was not good enough for Louis XII, so he had the 'New Lodge' added in flamboyant Gothic, richly embellished and with elegant dormer windows.

Charles VII's mistress, Agnes Sorel, made her principal residence in the Old Lodge, in the tower that bears her name. Charles was the first French king officially and publicly to install a harlot beside his legitimate queen, something none of his predecessors would have dared to do for fear of public opinion and the censure of the Church. This sweet-faced, high-breasted little beauty captivated even the Pope. In his memoirs Pius II does not of course mention the second attribute, but records that she had 'the most beautiful face one could possibly see'. A Paris merchant voiced the more general opinion however when he wrote in his journal 'Alas, what a pity! When the head of the kingdom gives such a bad example to his people they will only emulate him – or worse.' The Dauphin Louis (future Louis XI) detested her and one day at Chinon slapped her across the face, shouting *'Par la Pâques-Dieu!* This woman is the cause of the miseries of us all;' and it was after that little incident that she moved here to keep out of his way. Even so, it may have been poison administered at his instigation that caused her death in 1450 at the age of twenty-eight. She left a handsome legacy to the convent of

Saint Ours and asked to be buried there. The canons accepted the money, but later regretted the tomb of an immoral woman right in the middle of their chancel where everyone could see it and it got in their way so they caught their robes on it during services. Not until the reign of Louis XVI did they get permission to move it to one side. When the *sansculottes* arrived a few years later to carry out their ritual desecration, the statue on it got hacked rather badly because the officer thought he was venting his spite on a saint. It was repaired with plaster and is now in the Lodge, a very beautiful piece of sculpture, but by an unknown artist. The face is believed to have been taken from the death-mask so is probably a good likeness, though Agnes has a plaster nose; the Republican officer chopped off the original. At her feet are two rams, a pun on her name. In English popular imagery they make a good pun on Charles's subsequent behaviour: after Agnes's death he gravitated to a small harem of young girls whom he was wont to take to bed in threes and fours.

The New Lodge contains another of those beautiful oratories made for poor Anne of Britanny to pray for an heir and, like the one at Amboise, it has some exquisite lace-like sculpture. In another room a very fine triptych of the Crucifixion is displayed, dated 1485 on the left shutter and of the school of Jean Fouquet of Tours (see p. 187); certainly it is not *by* him as he died before that date. Incidentally it was he who executed the famous portrait of Agnes with her left breast peeping out of her bodice and another, equally well-known, of Charles in all his ugliness.

The admission ticket for the Lodge also covers entry to the **fortress towers** at the other end of the citadel which we approach along the wide tree-shaded Mall. They are open at the same times as the Lodge, but with a considerate extra half-hour after 12 o'clock to enable late morning visitors to include them before lunch. The rectangular keep, 132 feet high, is the most impressive from the outside. The original, like Montrichard, was one of Foulques Nera's chain of frontier forts, in this case intended to block any advance down the Indre valley into his domains, and it was built of wood. The design of these rectangular keeps in stone indeed derives from the exigencies of timber construction and they are always Romanesque (the Tower of London is another example almost contemporary with Loches). It was not until the Crusaders relearned the Roman principles of fortification preserved by Byzantine engineers that it dawned on Western minds that with stone one is free to build round towers with the advantage, among others, that it is easier to dislodge scaling-ladders from them. The keep now before us is a little earlier than Montrichard – late eleventh century – and it was Henry II of England who, in the middle years of the next, put the great curtain-wall round the whole spur of the hill and closed off its neck (its most vulnerable point) with a deep fosse.

The interior of the keep now has nothing to offer but an open flight of 157 steps and a view from the top. The Tour Neuve and the Martelet, both of the late fifteenth century, are the more interesting to visit. They are in the charge of a staff of guides of the highest standard: considerate, eloquent and masters of their facts. If all guides were like them I should be a guide fan. What they have to show reminds us of the dangerous uncertainty of life even (or perhaps especially) for those in high places. In the Tour Neuve Louis XI kept important prisoners in his notorious iron cages. The last surviving specimens were destroyed at the Revolution as 'memorials of tyranny', a term fully justified. But their precise specifications are known and Commynes, among others, has left a description of what it was like to be in one of them. He spent eight months in one at the Conciergerie in Paris. Of several sizes, some not big enough to stand up in, they resembled a heavy bird-cage, suspended from one central cable from the ceiling of a prison cell so that they rocked and tilted every time the prisoner moved. Louis's minister, Cardinal Balue, is said to have been a strong advocate of their use. Therefore when the Cardinal was found out negotiating secretly with the other side during the wars with Burgundy, it appealed to the Spider King's sense of humour to make him one of his canaries. Here in the Tour Neuve on a spring day of 1469 he was hauled up in one and in it he remained for eleven years.

The Martelet is perhaps even more sinister because visible testimony remains of the misery of some of its prisoners. Built into the hillside, it doesn't look much from the courtyard, but from the street below it is seen to be immense. We descend from the courtyard by a spiral stair to the prison cells and first we are shown where that generally mild and kindly king, Louis XII, kept Ludovic Sforza, Duke of Milan, for eight years. The Duke begged some paints and passed his time in the semi-darkness decorating the walls of his cell. The subjects are mostly military: culverins, armour and so on, and a very fine drawing of his own battle-helmet. He had doubtless learned a lot about drawing from Leonardo, whom he had maintained at his court in Milan for seventeen years. Along the top of the wall, by way of a signature, are the words 'Celui qui n'est pas contan'. Merely to describe himself as not content must have been something of an understatement. On the day of his release emotion, coupled with the unaccustomed sunlight of the outside world, brought on a heart attack from which he promptly died. In the next cell François I incarcerated Antoine de Chabon, Bishop of Le Puy, and Jacques Hurault, Bishop of Autun, for joining the rebellion of the Constable of Bourbon. Second-hand daylight is transmitted from the passage by a tiny barred window which is above eye-level, and there are impressions in the stone sill where they heaved themselves up for a tantalizing look at this pale reminder of the free world. In the opposite wall, where the shaft of light forms a small solitary square of illumination, they chiselled out a diminutive altar at which they could say Mass. No joy of deliverance awaited them: they ended their days in this melancholy twilight. Our visit to the citadel ends on this sobering note – not inappropriately since the rest of it may have filled our heads with over-romantic notions. We are let out by a side-door into the street, and the Rue de la Poterie where we started is just round the corner.

If you are staying on in Loches and wish to go on living in the past, the Hôtel du Château near by has a courtyard garden and rooms ranging from spacious and comfortable to spartan and cheap. The Hôtel de la Tour Saint-Antoine is also inexpensive and has sixteen well-appointed rooms. The municipal camp-site is at the north end of the town near the stadium. Loches has local wines: they come under the general Touraine appellation; they resemble the wines of the Cher and are wholesome, but in no way distinctive.

Tours, to which we must return to continue our downstream exploration of the main river, is a little over twenty miles away by whichever route we choose. It is not worth hugging the Indre on the way as its banks are for the most part monopolized by week-end huts in silly little enclosures about the size of hen-runs which must be as boring for their owners as for the passer-by. Some readers may like to take the opportunity of having a look at Montbazon on the way: it is described on page 239. Those whose trip may end here, and who must be heading back towards the Channel ports, have the choice of the Paris motorway at Tours or of ambling more peacefully across country, in which case Amboise only twenty miles due north is a good start.

CHAPTER TWELVE

Saint-Cyr to Chouzé; Bourgueil

✣

Taking a look now along the right bank of the Loire between Tours and the borders of Anjou, we begin at **Saint-Cyr,** which was once simply a village on the side of the tufa cliff like Vouvray and Rochecorbon. But it happened to face Tours across the water and in recent times has not only been drawn into it as a suburb, but forced to expand up and over the top of the cliff at its back. The result is rather nondescript, and most of the development is of recent times. In the 1920s its population was only around 3000 and now it is 13,000. However, for the serious gastronome as well as for the literary-minded it is a place of pilgrimage. The former, having replenished his wallet in readiness, will seek out the Restaurant Barrier in the Avenue de la Tranchée (straight up from the Pont Wilson), one of the 'Top Eight' in France. Charles Barrier is on the same lofty plane as the brothers Troisgros at Roanne (see p. 33) and his menu has the extra attraction that it can feature much more prominently the fish and wines of the Loire – imagine *écrevisses au vouvray* for example! I need hardly say more except to add that they bake their own bread too, always a sign of a restaurant prepared to take trouble to ensure quality. Barrier's is closed on Wednesdays and for three weeks in July.

Saint-Cyr's literary associations begin with Balzac who lived for a time at 'La Grenadière', high up beside the Angers road; it is not open to visiting and difficult even to get a look at. The name is worth remarking, however, as it is a fact that the pomegranate will thrive in ordinary gardens in the Touraine because of its mild climate. Camellias and mimosa positively flourish. This busy road along the riverside is in fact the one we want: the fourth turn right after the Pont Wilson leads to the *mairie* and the old village quarter, from where a series of clear signs indicating 'La Béchellerie' brings us to the house of that name where Anatole France made his home from 1918 until he died there six years later. The present owner, M. Lucien Psichari, his grandson, has preserved it in the form in which the author had it rebuilt. The design deliberately harks back to architectural styles of the seventeenth and eighteenth centuries – indeed reproduces them. Just outside the town in a peaceful rural setting amid little rolling hills, the house has a lovely courtyard with a fountain in the middle and romantic tree-shaded gardens with a bower in them – not at all what you would expect of the biting old socialist cynic which France seemed to have become by that time of life, largely from disgust and disillusionment. Really of course it illustrates very conspicuously the traditionalism and the hedonism which underlay both his character and his philosophy. Although M. Psichari lives here for a great part of the time, he kindly allows interior visits on payment simply of a tip to the guardian, but only on Saturdays between 3 and 6. Almost opposite across the lane is one other literary shrine, 'La Gaudinière', where Henri Bergson lived. There is no visiting, and only the upper storeys can be seen above the high surrounding wall. Like its one-time owner it seems brooding, deep in thought, regardless of tradition or pleasure, indeed of ordinary human affairs at all.

To anyone with a little more time to spare before regaining the main road I recommend a run out to **Mettray**, only about four miles north of Saint-Cyr. Just beyond the village, alone in a little copse of yew and acacia on a hilltop, seldom visited, stands another of those awe-inspiring dolmens of the Val de Loire. Much larger than the one we saw at Tavers, it is some thirty-five feet long by fifteen feet wide and high enough for a man to walk beneath the three immense horizontals resting on their seven pillars. How *did* they get up there some 5000 years ago? None of the theories advanced so far as to the raising of such weights without mechanical aid is entirely satisfactory. And for what purpose? An eighth upright separates a small chamber from what might be called the main hall. The building is thought to be incomplete: two other chambers were probably planned. 'La Maison aux Fées' it is called, like several other megaliths in France which traditionally housed a 'convent' of Druidesses. In popular legend druidesses often become fairies. If any such ladies lived up here (a not unpleasant spot for them with the little river Choisille babbling by at the foot of the slope) they would have been as mystified as we are concerning the origin of their home as it would be getting on for 3000 years old then. Perhaps it was they who heard and passed on the legend that it was erected in one night by 'three female creatures' who, if you move a piece, will return and put it back before morning, an experiment which owing to the practical difficulties has never been tried.

There is nothing else of particular interest in this direction so, regaining the main road beside the river and carrying on westwards, we now come to **Luynes**, a small village tucked into a fold of the hills. It once served as a fortified outpost of the lords of Saumur and was called Maillé until Charles d'Albert, duc de Luynes, bought the estate in 1619 and changed its name to his own. This relatively humble country squire's son from Provence who had won the friendship at court of the lonely boy-king, Louis XIII, by reason of his skill with dogs, horses and especially falcons, was by then at the height of his power. 'There goes King Luynes,' Louis once said jokingly to a friend. He had made good use of his influence by pushing the rather insipid King into doing his duty as he grew up, even to the (regrettably necessary) extent of dragging him from his bed and pushing him into that of his young queen to consummate their marriage. And Luynes it was who prevailed upon Louis to assert himself and relieve France of the bungling, fraudulent rule of his mother, Marie de Médicis, by having her henchman, Concini, assassinated and locking her up in the château at Blois. But Luynes's own political ability was of no high order and despite his promotion from Grand Falconer to Constable of France he failed to follow up these earlier services to the nation with anything else remarkable. He died of a fever in 1621 while campaigning against the Protestants in Guienne and so lived hardly long enough to derive any pleasure at all from the new château he had built here, but his descendants still occupy the two pavilions which remain of it. In addition to these. two ruined towers survive from the older thirteenth-century castle, There is no visiting, but a flight of steps up the side of the former curtain-wall from the market-place leads to an exterior view.

In the market-place itself the covered *halles* are of fifteenth-century timber construction, their high roof, with its beautifully intricate carpentry beneath, still stoutly supported by 500-year-old oak columns. About a mile north-west of the village a row of columns of another kind stands alone and awe-inspiring beside a lonely minor road. Thirty-five of the columns are still complete, several having arches also intact; they are built of stone and brick and are at least 1800 years old, their purpose having been to support an aqueduct which carried water from the springs of La Pie-Noire in the hillside to the Roman town at Tours. From a bend in the road there is a view across to the city – somewhat grown since it was Caesarodunum, but diminished by distance as it lies partly concealed five miles away in the folds of the valley, thus presenting a scene which cannot be greatly different from what a Roman water-engineer would have seen as he returned from a routine inspection.

On leaving Luynes, it is pleasant to take the minor road for **Pont-de-Bresme** along the valley of the river Bresme – a short relief from the main road. About two miles after rejoining the main road, look out carefully for the *Monumente Historique* sign on the right which leads by a short loop-road to an extraordinary tower, square in section, a hundred feet high, standing up stark on the cliff-top. One could be forgiven for mistaking it for an old brickyard chimney. It was in fact built shortly before the collapse of Roman power in Gaul and is called 'La Pile'. No one knows what purpose it served. A monument? It has no trace of an inscription, nor does it have any niche for a statue like other *piles* found in Southern Gaul. A landmark? It is out of all proportion to such a simple requirement. A beacon then, or a watchtower, say some, but its interior is solid with quarry-stones and mortar so its top is accessible only by setting up scaffolding. So although a comparative youngster and within the period of recorded history, it is as much an enigma as the dolmen at Mettray.

Just beyond is our next little town, named after it **Cinq-Mars-la-Pile**. In earlier times it was *Saint*-Mars. So was the *pile* a monument after all – to Mars? Mars is no saint of course. More probably it is a corruption of Saint-Médard, the family name of the eleventh-century owners who had a castle here. But the Romans had a fortress on the spot before them. We have to do here with a place of considerable antiquity, an age-old strongpoint facing the confluence of the Cher with the Loire across the water. The château (open 9 to noon and 2 to 7 every day except from November to March inclusive) retains two of the four towers of its original quadrilateral plan. They date from the twelfth century, each having three floors with their ceilings supported by ogival vaulting. The *Grande Salle* of the east tower, with a big medieval fireplace and originally lit only by minuscule windows like the twelfth-century example in the north wall, is an impressive reminder of the awesome gloom in which the old barons, their families and retainers lived. When the occupants chose to go up on the roof, however, they certainly enjoyed a grand view across the river to Villandry and as far as the Forest of Chinon on the southern horizon.

Of the manor-house into which the family moved in more comfortable times only a small wing survives: in that house Henri, marquis de Cinq-Mars was born in 1620. It is simply coincidence that two neighbouring country estates, Luynes and Cinq-Mars, should be associated with the two favourites of Louis XIII. As a young man Henri joined the retinue of Cardinal de Richelieu as a page. In that epoch of intrigue and ever-hatching plots the Cardinal could only govern for the King by having spies everywhere, even spies to watch out for the King's own indiscretions. Louis was a prude as a result of the licence he had witnessed at his father's court when a child, so Richelieu found women unsuitable for his purpose; he therefore decided to plant Henri on him. The ruse succeeded: the King took to the handsome, intelligent, fair-haired boy of eighteen and his partiality quickly became a violent passion – quite chaste, there is no reason to doubt, for sex hardly entered into Louis's make-up at all. He simply involved him as a boon companion in all his favourite pursuits, including making sweets. Sometimes they had violent tiffs which Richelieu had to patch up. When Cinq-Mars had an affair with a courtesan, Marion de Lorme, the King was so furiously jealous that she had to be seduced away from him – by the Cardinal himself, some whispered, so that for a time she was called 'Madame la Cardinale' behind her back.

But arrogance was the eventual undoing of Cinq-Mars. Puffed up by royal favour, he joined a plot against Richelieu to whom he owed his advancement in the first place and went so far as to enter into treasonable negotiations with Spain. Betrayed by the craven Gaston d'Orléans, he ended his life at the age of twenty-two on the scaffold at Lyon. Three months later Richelieu himself died, but he had already given orders in accordance with his usual policy for the rebel's castle to be demolished and those orders were posthumously carried out. Even the King knew that Richelieu had been right and had no wish to countermand them. That is why only two old towers still stand. Alfred de Vigny's exciting romance on the subject (see p. 207) must not be taken for history. These sad ruins are a memorial to a great statesman's resolve that private ambition should no longer be allowed to disturb the peace of the state as in times past. When Cinq-Mars's mother wrote appealing for her son's life Richelieu replied: 'If your son were only guilty of his various designs to ruin me, I would willingly forget myself in order to assist him according to your desire, but since he is guilty of unbelievable infidelity towards the King and of forming a party to disturb the reign in favour of the enemies of this State, I cannot in any wise meddle in his affairs as you beg me to do. I pray God that he may console you.'

Only three more miles and we come to yet another castle: a really exceptional one too, for it is not only complete but unaltered from the state in which the builders finished it in 1467. It had gone up on the orders of Louis XI in the space of only six years, so that it is all of one period with the exception of the rectangular keep now standing

217

alone in the grounds brooding down over everything else from the top of a rise. This was another of Foulques Nera's frontier defences which he erected in 990 and is claimed to be the oldest surviving keep in France. Louis had the new fortress built in such a hurry because in his wars with the independent duchy of Brittany there was a danger that the Bretons might try an attack up the river valley from their capital at Nantes. Here as at Loches Richard Coeur de Lion had already proved long ago that Foulques's castles were out of date by capturing the place with ease.

Langeais is an awkward little place, its twisting, narrow main street noisy and congested by the Orléans–Nantes traffic, but there is generally some parking-space to be found after the S-bend in the middle of the town where the château stands. From 15 March to 30 September visiting is every day 9 to noon and 2 to 6.30; the rest of the year it closes at nightfall and all day on Mondays. Walking back to the front of the château – for we enter by the drawbridge and the main gate between its two flanking towers – observe the outer aspect of this typical late-feudal fortress: its austere perimeter walls, its machicolated *chemin-de-ronde* running all the way round the parapets, and its big stout round towers, machicolated too and crowned with pepper-pot roofs. All is absolutely true to its period and was built for the serious business of war; but once inside the court-yard we find the inner façade showing a development towards more comfortable styles to come as people gradually realized that the days of feudal wars were over.

Thanks to the Siegfried family who presented Langeais to the Institut de France in 1904, the interior is furnished throughout with their superbly interesting collection of fifteenth- and sixteenth-century furniture; hence it is one of the best representations of seigneurial domestic life of that period. There is hardly an anachronism amongst it; even the tapestries and the pictures belong to the same epoch. One item recalling an important event which took place here on 16 December 1491 is the marriage-chest of Anne of Brittany in the room on the first floor bearing her name. On that day in this room she was married to Charles VIII, thus uniting Brittany to France and obviating the defensive need for which Charles's father had caused the castle to be built. It was a secret and hurried affair because she was already betrothed to Maximilien of Austria and in any case a strong party in her own country was opposed to the union with France, so there was great risk of her being kidnapped and hustled off out of the way. Nevertheless the fifteen-year-old Duchess was completely self-assured in her bearing for the occasion and astonished everyone present by coming furnished with a wedding-dress of cloth-of-gold emblazoned with designs in gold relief and trimmed with 160 sable skins valued at 4200 *livres*. At the time Langeais, a sort of 'grace-and-favour' residence in the gift of the monarch, was occupied by François, comte de Dunois, son of Joan of Arc's *'gentil Bâtard'*, a kindly old soldier who had been Anne's friend and protector earlier in her troubled orphan childhood. The occasion of her wedding was marred for her by his death on the evening of her arrival, from a stroke probably brought on by the emotion of seeing her again. Another noteworthy tenant here, in 1517, was Maximilien Sforza, dispossessed of Milan by François I after the Battle of Marignano, a confinement rather kinder than had been imposed on his father, Ludovic, by Louis XII at Loches.

The last tenant, before the Crown parted with Langeais to the Conti family, came here in 1630 on the charity of Louis XIII, an old lady of eighty-two, almost forgotten by everyone for she had played her part in history four reigns ago, when as a pretty young girl from the Orléanais she became mistress to the sombre Charles IX. Her understanding, gentle nature brought him perhaps the only happy hours he enjoyed towards the end of his short life, half crazed by remorse and horror at the Saint Bartholomew affair. As late as the nineteenth century an old song was still current along the Val de Loire, which punned her name. A sample verse:

> In her love garden
> Touch her, comrade, touch her;
> In her love garden
> Comes a king each day.

By the time Marie Touchet came to Langeais, most people would even have forgotten that her daughter, Henriette de Balzac d'Entragues, had charmed another king, Henri IV. But that is another story and has nothing to do with Langeais.

Before concluding the subject of the château, there is one more thing I must say: the guide system is bad. There is an offhandedness about the guides themselves which is perhaps acquired from the deplorable system of using a tape-recorded commentary. The Heath-Robinson equipment happily does not always work, but when it does, if your visit coincides with a coachload from some foreign land the commentary may be in German, Italian or purest Chicago (English does not seem to be included in the tape-recorder's curriculum) and this can be most distracting for anyone not familiar with those tongues – a stray Frenchman for instance.

When at Tours in the summer of 1644, John Evelyn wrote enthusiastically in his diary: 'We have now store of those admirable melons, so much celebrated in France for the best in the kingdom.' These would have been from Langeais, so long famous for its succulent melons that even its coat-of-arms sports three of them. They are grown on the hillsides near the town and are a local *specialité* in the shops.

Langeais also has a graceful suspension bridge which leads across the Loire to the countryside described in the next two chapters, but we shall continue a little farther along the right bank to complete the present chapter. The next village of any significance we come to is **Saint-Patrice** with the Forêt de Rochecotte a dark line along the clifftop above. 'You do not know Rochecotte or you would not ask: Why Rochecotte?' wrote the octogenarian Talleyrand in a letter to a friend written in 1835, in the château in the woods up there. He went on to describe the gardens and the hillside sheltered from the north where 'the spring comes three weeks earlier than in Paris and where all now is greenery and flowers. Besides there is another thing which makes me prefer Rochecotte to any other place: I am not only *with* Madame de Dino, but in her own home, which is for me an additional happiness.' Most people today do not know Rochecotte either, for the present owner does not open it to visits from the public. And who can blame him since it is his home? I only mention the fact because earlier this century it was open and contained (as it still does) many fascinating mementoes of the wily old statesman and his niece-in-law the colourful duchesse de Dino, and with the inducements the French Government now holds out to owners of such historic places to grant at least partial admittance to the public, I suspect it may be reopened one day before long.

In the grounds of the château is a 'miraculous' blackthorn which gives the village its name. According to ancient belief it grew from Saint Patrick's staff which he planted when he rested here, perhaps on his way to Ireland. Like that of Saint Joseph of Arimathea at Glastonbury it blooms at Christmas. Now far be it from me to suggest that Saint Patrick did not plant his staff here. Legend always deserves respect: many popular traditions far more fantastic, after being sneered at, have been found to embalm a truth. But this blackthorn is not miraculous in flowering at Christmas because there are many others in the district which do the same owing to the micro-climate which Talleyrand mentions.

For a long way now the alluvial plain of the Loire has been only a few miles wide, squeezed between the slight uplands of the Tertiary deposits of sedimentary rocks. If you look at a geological map of France you will see that inside the great loop of the Loire with Orléans at its apex the Quaternary deposits of alluvium spread out to form a sizable plain. Similarly here, inside another pronounced loop in the opposite direction with Candes as its apex, they widen out again to form an extensive level, this time on the right instead of on the left. It begins here at Saint-Patrice, where you can see the line of hills rapidly diverging from the river, and extends right across the curve all the way to Angers. It is the famous Vale of Anjou, though for another ten miles or so we are still in the Touraine.

We are also in the appellation area of Bourgueil, whose wine is of two distinct kinds, from the same grape but differing according to the soil. Here on the plain and the lower slopes of the hills the soil is light and sandy: hence all the asparagus you will see in wide plots interspersed amongst the vineyards. The wine from this lighter soil is delicate and fruity and can be drunk young though it will keep five or six years following a good season. Mostly red, but some rosé. it is quite delightful. I have bought some of excellent quality from Monsieur Pierre Marchand, most of whose vines are on the lower hills but whose premises are in the plain, east of the village – a right turn down the lane just before the railway-crossing before you get to the village. This cheerful family concern provides free *dégustation*, and as well as wine sells a fine dark honey to which bramble and other flowers of the heath, and lime from the edges of the forest, impart a delicate and distinctive flavour.

If, instead of following the Loire for the moment, we take the minor road westwards out of Saint-Patrice along the hillside we shall pass through about five miles of almost continuous vineyards, past the wine villages of Ingrandes and Restigné to **Bourgueil** itself. Notice that here the vines are not in the more usual bush form we are accustomed to seeing in the Loire Valley, but big plants with fairly long shoots trained along wires in espalier form. This is what the Cabernet Franc grape prefers: long pruning to six or eight eyes and maximum exposure to sun. It is the *cépage* of Médoc and Saint-Emilion in the Bordeaux region. Here in the Touraine it is called '*le Breton*' because it arrived upriver in boats via Nantes. Believe no fancy tales about a certain Abbé Breton introducing it in Richelieu's time; it was here long before then, like the Pinot Blanc which came to the other end of the Touraine and the Orléanais in course of river commerce and got called 'Auvernat' from hazy geography. That a superior variety of grape had arrived from the direction of Brittany or the Auvergne was enough for the medieval *vigneron*; where it came from before that would hardly interest him, he recognized its product as good and he adopted it. On the hillsides where the soil is heavier – at Bourgueil itself, Benais to the north-east and Saint-Nicolas-de-Bourgueil to the west – the 'Breton' indeed yields a wine of exceptionally high quality. There the sand and gravel are mixed with a larger proportion of clay and lie over tufa; the wine is more robust and the clay and the tufa make it a long-term keeper. When young it is rather harsh owing to its high tannin content, but this passes off after ageing a year or two. Then it becomes rich and mellow, with the fine bouquet slightly reminiscent of raspberries which is the hallmark of the Cabernet and a distinguishing characteristic of the wines of Bordeaux. But for taking home and laying down it is much cheaper than claret because the whole world does not yet know about it. Saint-Nicolas-de-Bourgueil (where the soil proportions are at optimum) produces the best, has a separate appellation and is one of the noblest wines of the Loire.

There are well over fifty proprietors in the district selling retail. I have named one on the light lands. As to the stronger wine of the uplands, the situation is more complex and for the sake of a little guidance in choosing within the limits of one's pocket I advise going to Monsieur Renée Goisnard, who has been president of the local growers' association for over twenty years and is likely to be for many more. He stocks a wide selection from all around and is a *vigneron* himself. His premises are in the Place de la Motte-Verte in the centre of the town, an ordinary-looking café-bar in the front, but he gives *dégustation* to intending purchasers at the back and sells retail from six bottles upwards.

Tne little town itself has great charm. At its eastern end stands an imposing ensemble of monastic buildings on the site where a Benedictine abbey was founded in 990 by Emma, a daughter of Thibault the Trickster, Count of Anjou. On her marriage to Proud-arm, Count of Poitiers, she brought him Bourgueil as her dowry. Later he had an affair with the comtesse de Thouars. Emma had the strong character of her race and was not one meekly to accept the general view of those times that in matters of chastity there was one law for men and another for women, so she kidnapped her rival and gave her for a night to her guards for their pleasure. Afterwards repenting of this rather dreadful act of vengeance she founded the abbey 'so that God in his Judgment might be less severe' towards her.

In 1361 the English burnt the abbey down and Bourgueil continued to be in the theatre of front-line operations for most of the rest of the Hundred Years' War, having its worst time in fact in

1425 when the '*gentil Dauphin*' sent a task force of 200 knights to 'defend' the district. They did so by pillaging, raping and burning and, according to one account, 'did more harm than the English'. The only portion of the abbey to survive those times is, not surprisingly, the thirteenth-century cellar. The cloister gallery remains from the first rebuilding of 1472, a good example of flamboyant Gothic. The rest – the main conventual buildings and the Prior's Lodging – date from seventeenth- and eighteenth-century reconstruction works and for the most part still subsist. The whole conglomeration is substantial, for the abbey was once the mainstay of the town as well as its refuge in times of flood. When the *levée* of the Loire was more prone to breaking, its waters sometimes spread over the intervening two and a half miles to the lower town. Indeed they still could if the *levée* ever broke again. Now occupied by a small community of nuns, the abbey may be visited any day at a reasonable hour on application to the concierge.

Leaving Bourgueil now by the road south out of the town (which Richelieu had constructed to provide a direct access to the river) we come to **Port-Boulet**, where ferries used to run across to the left bank until the big sturdy bridge was built in the present century. From some considerable distance on our approach we shall have noticed an enormous silver-coloured sphere gleaming on the landscape as if a small moon had dropped gently out of the sky and landed on the opposite bank of the Loire. In fact this object, 177 feet in diameter, is part of the nuclear power-station of **Avoine**, commenced in 1957 and one of France's first. It uses natural uranium for fuel and an awful lot of water from the river for cooling – forty-five cubic metres per second, almost enough to make the Loire disappear altogether if it were not for the Indre flowing in less than a mile away and the Cher farther upstream. For at Tours, before these tributaries swell it, the flow of the Loire in the dry season is barely fifty cubic metres per second. In the fishing season the bridge at Port-Boulet is busy with serried ranks of anglers dangling their lines from the parapet to the river far below. Warmed by the power-station it attracts some species of fish in great numbers and these tend to grow larger, though other species are harmed by the high temperature. But if you hook one of those big ones from such a height I am not quite sure how you go about landing it. As at Saint-Laurent (p. 129), some ten years its junior, the Avoine power-station has an observation-tower open free to the public, with models, plans and explanations in fairly simple terms of its complicated processes.

The main Angers road, which we left at Saint-Patrice, passes through Port-Boulet and for nearly the whole ten miles between the two places it runs close beside the river. Once almost every village along it had its own little port beyond the *levée* as the names of several testify – Port d'Ablevois, Port-Guyet and Port-Plat as well as Port-Boulet. At Port-Guyet there lived a pretty girl called Marie with whom the poet Ronsard fell in love, and he came to live at Bourgueil for a time to be near her. He was infatuated to such a pitch that he was jealous of the doctor when she was ill, and he reveals in his *Amours* the torments he suffered:

> Ah, how I hate and envy
> The doctor who night and morning
> Without a word comes to touch the breast,
> The belly, and the thighs of my love.

La Chapelle about four miles upstream from the bridge is another village of vine-growers, producing on its sandy alluvium what is perhaps the lightest and most delicate of the Bourgueil wines. Like its riparian neighbours on this vulnerable stretch of flood-plain it cowers behind the *levée* which is its only protection. Here as a matter of fact is the point at which the bank is most likely to yield under the pressure of a full spate. This happened on the occasion of the greatest flood on record, in 1856, when the measured rise at Tours was 7.52 metres (24 feet 7 inches). Winter and spring had been abnormally wet, so that when heavy rains set in again in the early summer the saturated land all the way down the valley could absorb no more and ran its surface-water straight into the river. By Tuesday 3 June the water reached the top of the *levée*. In that mysterious apprehension all animals seem to have before a great natural catastrophe, although they could not even see the water, the dogs in the village howled and the cattle bellowed, while creatures who were free to run for it did so: rabbits, rats and even snakes were seen in large numbers fleeing across the valley to reach the hillside two miles away.

At half-light next morning the bank collapsed and the Loire cascaded over to fill the plain. Some of the villagers were in the hills already; others who had been striving all night to reinforce the bank were marooned on top of its unbroken sections and as the hours went by they watched their homes gradually disappearing until the whole village except the church was completely out of sight. When the water had subsided four days later they found forty-eight houses had been swept away, the railway station demolished, trucks and torn-up railway-track swept into the fields and, to add grisly horror to all the misery, the cemetery had been completely washed out, scattering corpses, coffins and skeletons among the general débris. But from among La Chapelle's population of 3200, happily not one perished. Economically it was ruined and is still nowhere near such a big place now.

To conclude this chapter about the right bank down from Tours I must mention the small town of **Chouzé**, the last town in Touraine on this side of the river, two miles downstream from Port-Boulet. Halfway between the confluences of the Indre and the Vienne, it was a port of some consequence in the great days of river commerce and it still has well over three hundred yards of fine stone quays, but sadly deserted with not a single hawser made fast to the big iron mooring-rings.

Chouzé has a very good municipal camp-site by the river, over five acres in extent, with a beach backed by trees and meadows. Bathing is safe, even for children. The traveller seeking hotel accommodation would do best to try in Bourgueil or go to Saumur not far downstream, or to Chinon, or back to Tours where our next chapter starts.

CHAPTER THIRTEEN

Villandry; Ussé; Azay and Montbazon

⁊

With Tours once more as our starting-point, we can now explore the extremely interesting area on the south side of the river opposite the places we visited in the preceding chapter: the left bank itself; the beautiful Indre so closely associated with Balzac and many of his best known novels, and the alluvial plain between them called the Varennes.

The Loire can be followed from the south end of the Pont Wilson by driving along the fine old quays of Tours's western suburb, La Riche. Soon the road mounts the *levée* from where we look down on to meadows and a patchwork of hundreds of small allotments which environment-conscious purists would consider an eyesore; but to see them on a Sunday, the families from the town each on its own little plot, gardening, barbecuing, basking in the sun, one realizes how much more they mean in terms of human happiness than an orderly suburban park and a 'view'. After a couple of miles we come to **Saint-Cosme**. A **priory** was founded here in 1092 and before the present *levée* was built it stood on an island in the river. Despite later additions it had long been in ruins when it was badly damaged by bombing in the last war so that it had to be restored. A fine twelfth-century refectory remains and the chancel is partly original eleventh-century; but if it were not for its association with one of France's most famous poets I doubt if many people would consider it worth paying the very high charge for admission, and the authorities have meanly boarded up the grille of the gateway so you cannot even get a free peep. (The priory is open for visits every day from 9 to noon and 2 to 6.30.) Pierre de Ronsard was commendatory prior of Saint-Cosme; that is to say he was the lay outsider royally appointed to receive the revenues. But although not ordained, he had taken the tonsure when a young man and towards the end of his life he came to live here in the modest Prior's Lodging and wrote his *Derniers Vers*. He died here and his remains still rest beneath a simple slab near the altar in the ruined church.

Less than a mile south-east of Saint-Cosme is the **Château of**

Plessis. Like Saint-Cosme, it has been enveloped in suburban sprawl and some may not wish to tarry in this rather dreary quarter for the sake of a visit, particularly as the fifteenth-century building has recently been 'extensively restored' after having been already restored almost out of recognition in the last century. Certainly it is an attractive building in pink brick and stone, still standing on its original foundations and preserving original architectural features. Moreover, for devotees of silks and *passementerie* (braiding) it houses a museum devoted entirely to those subjects. The château is open from 10 to noon and 2 to 6 every day from April to September; closing at 5 and all day Tuesdays the rest of the year.

But the chief interest of Plessis is its involvement with the last years of that enigmatic character, our old friend Louis XI. The edifice he put up on the site of an old manor was much more extensive than what now remains. It was the residence he chose as a refuge on the advent of unmistakable signs of approaching death. The first of those signs was a stroke at Chinon in 1479. Two years later he had another at Tours and decided to retire behind the walls of Plessis for fear that someone might try to give Providence a helping hand. Philippe de Commynes stayed with him to nurse him and describes the bizarre situation in his memoirs. All round the château a trellis of heavy iron bars was set up and the walls bristled with spikes at every point where someone might be able to climb up from the moat. Movable armoured sentry-boxes were devised with slits for shooting in all directions; crossbowmen were ordered to shoot anyone approaching at all suspiciously, and no one – not even foreign ambassadors – could enter without a written pass to the gate-keeper. Many people considered the King had gone out of his mind, but in Commynes's opinion his conduct was eminently sensible, for princes who have offended as many people as he are bound to have numerous enemies; he who had invented new types of prison for others 'found himself in greater fear than those he had put in them' and, far from being amused at the irony of the situation, he personally felt sorry for the old tyrant having finally to put *himself* behind bars for safety. His prison was not as small as the iron cages, he admits – he himself had suffered in one of those – but then his master was a king!

For a short time Louis enjoyed a little hunting in the near-by forest, using a trained leopard to chase the quarry. Later, when he dared not leave the premises, wild boar, rabbits and foxes were brought in for the leopard to chase round the courtyard. On rainy days he was reduced to sitting in his chamber in his shabby clothes watching cats chasing captive rats round the floor. Clinging desperately to life he meekly suffered the grossest insolence from a truculent, overpaid physician and kept an astrologer constantly within call. One day, after a minor attack and much pain, he berated the latter, a charlatan named Angelo Catto, for having predicted a final cure only shortly before: 'I'll have you hanged, Master Liar, for spinning me yarns. Do you happen to have noticed that in your constellations?' For answer the quick-witted Italian drew from his gown a parchment covered with cabbalistic signs and spread it before the King. 'See these stars, Sire.' The King of course could make nothing of them. 'These great ones, Sire, are yours; these lesser ones mine. By their conjunction at this point in the heavens you may read that I shall appear before God only eight days before Your Majesty.' But Louis's end was inevitable and he died here on 30 August 1483 at the age of sixty. Saint Francis de Paul was sent for to pray for his life to be extended, but refused to do so, reconciling him instead to what must be and sending him off with his soul at peace at last.

From Plessis it is best to return to the road on the *levée* at Saint-Cosme and follow the Loire for another five miles until the turn for **Savonnières**, which brings us alongside a wide and beautiful loop of the Cher and eventually to its last bridge by which we cross into the little town itself, the shops and houses of whose main street are ranged attractively along the waterfront. Because of the prevalence of soapwort growing in the vicinity Savonnières was the laundry-centre for the Roman garrison at Tours and it takes its name from *saponaria*, the Latin word for that useful plant whose roots and leaves contain a glucoside which forms a lather in water when they are boiled. It is still used for cleaning old tapestries because it does not damage delicate fabric. Its pink flowers, resembling sweet william (to which it is related), are still to be seen in abundance in this district in the summer.

Just after leaving the town westwards on the Villandry road, we come to the famous '**grottes pétrifiantes**' which decidedly merit a visit. We have already observed that the tufa limestone is the principal rock of the Touraine and is used for the beautiful white buildings which grace the region throughout. A sandy micaceous chalk, it is soft on extraction and easy to work before it hardens gradually on contact with the air. The tufa of Savonnières is the purest and whitest of all; hence the two caves here were exploited earliest and had become enormous when they were finally abandoned. This happened most probably in the mid-fourteenth century. In the vigorous 200 years preceding, often called the High Middle Ages, more stone was quarried in France alone than by Ancient Egypt in all its 3000 years; some 80 cathedrals were built, 500 major churches and thousands of smaller parish churches besides houses and castles, and Touraine was among the regions foremost in all this activity.

The Savonnières caves were then forgotten until what is now called the First Cave was rediscovered in the sixteenth century. It was found to be riddled with tiny dripping springs of calcite whose drops congeal into insoluble carbonite on exposure to air, and the practice began of placing earthenware objects beneath them to vitrify. Then in 1947 local potholers, having crawled through a geological fault, rediscovered the Second Cave and found themselves before a magnificent 'frozen' waterfall formed through water dripping down an old foxhole. This and many other amazing things you see on your visit, to arrange which you call at the café-bar near the entrance. The calcite falls into both caves from an underground lake well over two miles long, but its concentration varies considerably between the two; in the First Cave it takes a century to form a layer one centimetre thick, in the other only a year. You can buy glazed pots and dishes as well as quite good little cameos made by exposing copper plates covered with an imprint in guttapercha. A glass of local rosé wine is included in the visit; the price is a trifle high if you want to buy a bottle, but the people who run the place and act as guides are so very kind and obliging and work so hard that one just cannot feel indignant about it.

The last of the stone cut from the caves of Savonnières probably went to build the fourteenth-century castle at **Villandry** a little farther down the road, and there is an underground passage (a hands-and-knees journey two kilometres long) starting in the caves and emerging near the dovecote in the château grounds. The keep is all that remains of that earlier structure and looks rather odd in the south-west corner with nothing to complement it; for the rest of the beautiful **château** of Villandry was built for Jean le Breton, Finance Minister to François I and was, with Villesavin, the last of the Renaissance châteaux of the Val de Loire. Though on a larger scale than Villesavin, its architecture has the same sober, elegant appearance of late Renaissance, foreshadowing the Classical.

The extensive gardens were laid out at the same time in the orderly French pattern and terraced a couple of centuries later, but a nineteenth-century owner had them landscaped in the English park style. That fashion however was only a passing whim in France; the French have never really lost their preference for the formal garden, the gardener's supreme assertion of his authority over Nature, so at the beginning of the present century Doctor Carvallo, a patriotic owner, had three of the terraces cleared of the disorderly Anglo-Saxon tangle and restored the original tribute to Geometry. Consequently they are a popular resort not only of tourists, but of people in the neighbourhood – the more so because they are open every day all the year round from 9 to sundown to wander where and as long as you please. They have everything, including a fine moat; fountains; an ornamental lake at the south end; labyrinths; a *potager* on the lowest terrace laid out with prize vegetables in formal patterns to produce a harmony of colours and tones, and the high terrace on the east side where, standing beneath lime trees 300 years old, you can see right across the valley where the Loire and the Cher meet and pick out the châteaux of Langeais, Cinq-Mars and Luynes on the other side.

Villandry is still inhabited by the Carvallo family who in the face of rising costs and taxes are valiantly keeping it going and managing to hold together the wonderful collection of paintings. Part of the interior may be visited on application at the gate (opening times flexible) and this includes the pictures on the ground floor and in the long gallery. Among them is a high proportion of Spanish works, for the Carvallos are of Spanish origin. Two Goyas are in the grisly mood of that artist, a severed head and a *Sick Woman*, but another by him – or of his school – of a court dwarf is the best, and there is a very fine Zurbaran of Saint Francis. Under the dome at the end of the gallery is a carved and gilded ceiling in Mauresque style of the twelfth century, astonishingly intricate and beautiful.

The old name for Villandry was Colombiers, and here on 4 July 1189 the Peace of Colombiers was concluded between Henry II Plantagenet and Philippe-Auguste. The meeting took place in the open, as parleys in war generally did in those days, to avoid treachery. Though only fifty-six, the English king was a broken old man, for Philippe had thoroughly beaten him with the aid of Henry's own rebellious son Richard. He had ridden up from Chinon through a thunderstorm and arrived so exhausted and bedraggled that Philippe took pity on him and offered him his rolled-up cloak to sit down on. This was of course proudly refused. One of the terms of settlement was that he should embrace Richard with the solemn 'kiss of peace' to signify irrevocable forgiveness. This also he refused, but on being told that in that case the war must continue he finally consented. As he embraced his son he whispered in his ear: 'May God not let me die until I am revenged on you.' But, as we shall see when we come to Chinon in our next chapter, God did permit him to die only two days later.

The most interesting way on from Villandry is of course the minor road which follows the river. For the first couple of miles it has a centuries-old cobbled surface, a little bumpy if you drive too fast. Following a peninsula round, we eventually come, near the railway-bridge across the Loire, to the confluence of the Cher. Like so many confluences it is something of an anticlimax: the Cher seems to have lost all its tranquil dignity and become a little narrow shrivelled-up thing. Yet this is the Loire's first big tributary since the Allier. From here on we have a beautiful drive along a narrow, but well-surfaced, road with views along the Loire most of the way and to the left, across the flood-plain of the Indre, the Forest of Chinon, a dark line topping the low plateau on which it stands. On the right are one or two places where you can turn off the road and drive through the trees to the riverside.

The first village we come to is **La-Chapelle-aux-Naux**, one of the old river-ports with a terraced stone *levée* sloping down to a hand-some quay. It is not quite devoid of working boats even now, for a number of local watermen earn their living fishing here, netting salmon and shad in the spring and catching eels, bleak and pike at other seasons, and their cabined punts are moored by the quay. This is a good place for the angler too, for the Loire is wide, fairly calm and dotted with islands. Advice and tickets are to be had at the village shop.

The countryside here is called *varennes*, a word which signifies an extent of fertile alluvial soil. Very light and sandy here, it suited hemp well, but is now given over to more ordinary cultivation. The inhabitants are a race apart; stolid, hardworking and outwardly rough. The vine-growers of the uplands to the south and across the river affect to despise them as poor clodhoppers, the traditional attitude of the attendants of Bacchus to all peasants. Certainly the people of the *varennes* lack the light-heartedness of the *vigneron* (most people do), but they are not really dull.

Following the riverside road still, we next come to **Bréhémont**, a tranquil and most picturesque village which also was once a port and looks across the water to a string of islands. Four miles farther, in Ile Saint-Martin, just before the road peters out anyway, a left turn leads across to **Ussé** whose **castle** in white tufa stone shows up clearly on a hillside with the Forest of Chinon behind it. Perrault is supposed to have had it in mind as the setting for his *Sleeping Beauty*, and certainly from here it has a romantic fairytale air about it. The chapel, the grounds and part of the interior are open from 15 March to 31 October every day from 9 to noon and 2 to 7. Dating mainly from the end of the fifteenth century, Ussé combines the imposing air of a fortress with the elegance of a graceful residence. But on getting close you can see that it is not really a fortress: its draw-bridge, its towers and the wall machicolated practically all the way round are like the magnificent dress uniform of a soldier, made to impress but not for the wear and tear of battle. The many towers of assorted sizes are positioned almost haphazardly and have Renais-sance dormer windows in their pointed tops, while the façades inside the courtyard breathe nothing but domestic ease and peace. The one on the right is in full Renaissance style. The oldest part is the big keep in the south-west corner; it was built some time prior to 1480 for Jean de Beuil, who in his younger days had been a com-panion-in-arms of Joan of Arc. Between 1485 and 1535 the château was completed by its subsequent owners, the D'Espinay family: hence the Transition style. The Valentinays bought it in 1660 and added a pavilion on the west and the orangery which is alleged still to contain some of their original orange trees. Louis II de Valentinay married the eldest daughter of Vauban, Louis XIV's great military engineer who amused himself when he came to stay in designing part of the terraced gardens.

Ussé is occupied and the interior visit is somewhat limited. The main feature is the *Chambre du Roi*, prepared for a visit by Louis XVI which did not materialize. Furnished mostly in his period, it has a splendid bed *à la polonaise*, canopied like a throne. Next come the ground-floor galleries with a set of eighteenth-century Flemish tapestries depicting scenes of ordinary village life, a refreshing change from the themes of elegant high-life more usual in that period. Finally, by way of a gracious Mansard staircase, one is taken to the first-floor galleries to see a few odds and ends such as a seventeenth-century secretaire from Verona with forty-nine drawers, Charles X's English-made sporting-guns and a fine pastel by Latour of Amadée, duc de Duras who was First Gentleman of the Bedchamber to Louis XVI and to the two last Bourbons after the Restoration. His father had been guillotined and in 1809 his mother bought Ussé for her residence. Châteaubriand, with whom she was deeply in love, was a frequent visitor here. It was a platonic affair and largely un-requited, though he did make her a present of the cedars which now adorn the avenue. Quite shamelessly he made use of her influence through her son at court to advance his political career. 'Madame de Duras was ambitious for me,' he once told a friend, but his nagging letters when she was not pushing things enough show on whose side the ambition mostly lay. She put up with his faults, considering that his genius outweighed them, even his ungrateful vanity.

After she had secured him the post of Ambassador in London, he told her: 'I can't help feeling a little vain in having made my own destiny which is solely due to what I carried within myself.' He finally deserted her after she had obtained the Foreign Ministry for him, to go back to Madame Recamier and other more exciting mistresses. Heartbroken, the poor dowager Duchess wrote to tell him she had stopped all the clocks at Ussé 'so as never to hear struck the hours you will not come again'.

A lovely **chapel** stands separate in the grounds. Although built between 1520 and 1538 it is still in the Gothic style, the Renaissance showing only in the delicacy and richness of its embellishment – on the doorway for example which has an immense cockle-shell sculpted over it and busts of the Apostles inside the arch. There is beautiful sculpture too in the wood of the choir-stalls within, still in the full Gothic style. But the sanctuary has been closed off with what looks for all the world like a cheap wooden garden-fence, and you can no longer go through to see the lovely little figures on the misericords except by special arrangement, though an imposingly patriarchal Moses can be viewed closely on the right of the entrance through the rood-screen. In a side-chapel on the south side is a Virgin by Della Robbia; on the opposite wall a Tuscan triptych. The wooden fencing quite spoils the ambience of the place: something better-looking could surely have been devised; but that the owners should have taken fright and put up some barrier is understandable. Once the chapel walls were graced with a priceless set of Aubusson tapestries portraying the life of Joan of Arc. In November 1975 thieves coolly walked in and took them all away and they have never been seen or heard of since.

The time has come now to turn eastwards again and see more of the valley of the Indre. The main road south of the river leads direct to Azay, our next objective, but with a railway-line for company most of the way; so it is better to continue to **Marnay** only and cross the river there to follow alongside the right bank by the minor road with glimpses of the Indre through the trees. Like the Cher, the Indre is a relatively slow-running, peaceful river. One hundred and sixty-five miles long, it rises in the same region, in the foothills of the Massif Central, but nearer the plain, some thirty-five miles north of Aubusson. Taking a more direct route than the Cher, it flows north-west as if it were aiming for Tours; ten miles short of the target however it is deflected westwards to amble across the country we are now about to explore before it joins the Loire more than twenty miles downstream of Tours, a significant geographical accident for Honoré de Balzac, who from the enchanting countryside of these lower reaches drew the inspiration for so many of his best-known romances. **Azay-le-Rideau** was his favourite château of all and in *Le Lys dans la Vallée* he refers to it as 'a diamond cut in facets'.

The town of Azay has a narrow main street, often rather congested, but there is a big free car-park right in the centre and the tree-lined avenue leading to the château is but a few paces away. The **château** is open all the year round from 9 to noon and 2 to 6.30 (4.30 October to Easter), and from May to the end of September there is *son et lumière* every evening at 10 and 11. You can see why Balzac described the place as a diamond, for it is a masterpiece of Renaissance architecture, still Gothic in outline but graceful – almost one could say dainty – not a fortress in any way: the towers have become turrets and the machicolations round the walls a deliberately elegant adornment. Gilles Berthelot, yet another royal financier, had it built during the early years of the reign of François I. His wife was the heiress to the ruins of the old castle, which took its name from Ridel, a twelfth-century baron who quarrelled with Henry II. It had been in ruins since 1418 when the pro-Burgundian garrison had insulted the Dauphin Charles. The '*gentil Dauphin*' rounded fiercely on his detractors, for he was always a merciless little brute if he could get the upper hand, and had all 350 of the occupants massacred and the castle dismantled and burnt. As for Berthelot a century later, hardly had he completed his fine new home on the site when he fell into disgrace and had to flee for his life. François confiscated his property and gave it to his Captain of Archers. Since 1905 it has been the property of the state.

Partly constructed on piles in the river-bed and surrounded by water, Azay has the same riverside charm as Chenonceau. Viewed across the water from the south-east, indeed, it seems almost to be afloat, a gigantic luxury houseboat made of stone. The interior has been very well arranged as a 'Renaissance Museum', with furniture, tapestries and pictures. The four-storey Great Staircase with its double windows is the most striking interior architectural feature and betrays the Italian origin of the design, though the identity of the architect is unknown.

Among the paintings exhibited there is little of distinction except the famous one of Henri IV's handsome mistress, Gabrielle d'Estrées, nude to the waist and seated apparently in a sort of bath cubicle, with her children and a wet-nurse just behind her. She has firm breasts and immensely powerful shoulders, high-arched eyebrows, almond-shaped dark eyes, a long straight nose just a little too haughty and a rather bitchy mouth for all its cherry fullness. Altogether there is something faintly sinister about her charms. Apart, though, from its fascination as a portrait, the picture abounds in interesting detail. She wears two rings on her left hand and holds a carnation in the other. Beside her is a bowl of fruit, a masterpiece in still-life by itself, from which the older child is about to steal some currants, while the younger, wrapped in swaddling-clothes double cross-belted for good measure, is being suckled by the nurse. Beyond, in what seems to be a dining-room, a servant-girl (more desirable than Gabrielle in my opinion) is busy at the table, and behind her is an embroidered firescreen depicting a hind. The intriguing scene ends with a glimpse of the garden through the window. Altogether this is a remarkable picture.

Walking in the park is free, whether you have paid to visit the château or not. The entrance is separate, through the little sixteenth-century chapel near the town centre. There are some venerable trees and pleasant riverside walks. The town has good shops; a sandy beach by the river; an eleven-acre camp-site (in the Parc du Sabot), and a parish church whose west front incorporates the Carolingian original surviving from the tenth century – possibly even the ninth – complete with sculptured figures of Christ and the Apostles from that period.

Azay gives its name to the appellation of a local wine, a white produced from the Chenin grape as at Vouvray, but drier, more delicate and less *parfumé* than Vouvray owing to the high incidence of flint in the otherwise pebbly clay soil. A good place to taste and buy it in most appropriate surroundings is the Domaine d'Aulée, a small château which looks just as if one of those pictures on a bottle-label had come to life as you approach it up the drive (on the right of the main Tours road a short way out of the town; open every weekday and most Sundays in high summer). There are some 200 hectares (nearly 500 acres) of vines in the Azay region, a fact which results in much over-production, but the surplus is eagerly taken up by the Germans who apparently find it ideal for pumping up with carbonic-acid gas to produce that *ersatz* champagne one sees far too much of at English parties.

Four miles upstream of Azay one of the most delightful places to visit in the whole of Touraine awaits us, and it is the more enjoyably reached by taking the minor road out of the town on the north side of the Indre. Through a smiling green countryside, as green as Ireland, we pass by orchards, meadows, tobacco plantations and watermills to **Saché** where the late sixteenth-century **manor-house** (open 9 to noon and 2 to 7 every day 15 March–15 October; closed Tuesdays rest of year and whole of December and January) was the home-from-home which Balzac loved more than his birthplace at Tours or, indeed, any other house he ever lived in. It belonged to Monsieur Margonne and his wife, friends of his mother's, and he first came here as a boy of fourteen to recuperate after being fetched away from his grim boarding-school at Vendôme owing to ill-health. In *Le Lys dans la Vallée*, where the whole action of the story takes place in this vicinity, he says through the autobiographical character, Félix: 'In a hollow I see the romantic mass of Saché, melancholy dwelling full of harmony, too sober for superficial people, dear to poets whose soul is sad. And later I came to love the silence, the great knotty trees and that indefinable air of mystery which filled its lonely valley.' Balzac's soul indeed was sad for he was unloved by his selfish mother; but with the Margonnes he found some measure of affection, and his boyhood wanderings in the little valley so deeply impressed his vivid imagination as to colour the whole of his work. Without Saché the great *Comédie Humaine* would have been entirely different. During the 1830s, still a welcome guest of the family, he used Saché as a retreat where he could get on with his work safe from the importunities of his creditors and frantic publishers waiting for manuscripts they had paid advances for. We have details of the timetable of his usual journey which throw an interesting light on the effort and time involved in a trip to the country in those days. Leaving Paris at 6 o'clock in the evening by the Bordeaux diligence, he would halt at Beaugency at 9 o'clock next morning for breakfast; then after rumbling on for the rest of the day the coach would deposit him on the Quai du Pont-Neuf at Tours at 5 p.m. The fare for the twenty-three-hour journey of 135 miles was eighty-eight francs. The Margonnes' carriage would meet him and it required yet another two hours to reach his destination. There a small low-ceilinged room on the east side of the house, overlooking the gardens and the woods just beyond, was kept ready for him.

In our own unhustled, unguided visit we are privileged to stand in that same room and meditate for as long as we like. The same rough country furniture which impoverished returned émigrés like the Margonnes had to make do with at that period is still there; these are the same articles that Balzac knew and used. The whole room breathes the spirit of him intensely in a way most unusual for such places of pilgrimage. I consider it one of the greatest thrills to be had in the Val de Loire. My notes for these pages were mostly made at Balzac's desk where stands his ink-well; his own quill pen (so they claim, and for once I have no desire to be sceptical) which he boasted of having snatched from the wing of a crow, and his coffee-pot. His armchair stands near by and, in the corner, his bed. Though ostensibly he came for a rest, in fact he worked harder than ever when he was at Saché. Once, in writing to a friend from here, he described himself as a 'pen-and-ink galley-slave'. His daily routine was to rise at 5 a.m., brew some coffee and make toast at the bedroom fire and immediately start writing at the little desk – or back in bed if it was a cold morning – breakfasting as he did so; only after working all day would he at last come down about 5 p.m. to spend the evening with his hosts and their guests, entertaining the company by reading over his day's work to them. All the while he would be studying those present as possible characters for his novels; two of the most recognizable as being used in this way are Mme Margonne herself as Mme Grandet in *Eugénie Grandet* and the Canon of Saint-Denis in the title-rôle of *Le Curé de Tours*.

The whole house is now copiously stocked as a Balzac museum with manuscripts, first editions, corrected page-proofs (some with more corrections than print; he must have been a terror to his printers), busts and portraits. In short, Saché is *the* Balzac shrine and one of the best literary shrines in France. Add to this the charm of the old house itself, and the relaxed freedom in which one is left to make one's visit and you have something just too good to miss. But unfortunately many tourists do miss it because several standard guidebooks make no mention of it.

Osiers are cultivated extensively beside the Indre in the vicinity of Saché to supply a local craft industry of basket-weaving centred on the village of **Villaine-les-Rochers** four miles to the south-west. The wands are cut in December, sorted according to size, bundled and stood upright in the shallows to continue their growth until May so they acquire plenty of sap for suppleness and for easy peeling. They are then made into baskets of every kind, furniture and decorative items by skilled craftsmen who live in caves in the tufa hillside at Villaines. They are dark people, rather Indian-looking, which lends strong probability to the tradition that they are descended from nomadic Gypsies who settled here in the eighteenth century, finding the caves made handy dwellings and workshops with the right atmospheric conditions for their material. It is not wise to broach

237

the subject, unless it is volunteered. Regarding such ancestry as a stigma, settled nomads are always wary of the questioning stranger. The tradition was confided to me by a *vannier* (basketmaker) with secret pride as he deftly wove the long, white, supple wands while seated on the floor of his cave, but even he became shy when I spoke a word or two of Romany and he unguardedly betrayed that he still had a knowledge of that ancient tongue.

By the early nineteenth century the craft of really skilled *vannerie* which combines beauty and utility so perfectly was dying everywhere and the Abbé Chicoine, local priest at Villaines, thought it a shame. He conceived the idea of grouping his parishioners together on a mutual aid basis and, although there was a lot of opposition at first, in 1849 he finally got sixty-five of them to try it and drew up their constitution and rules. He can hardly have foreseen what a great service he was rendering to his country's rural economy, for the scheme prospered and was the first agricultural producers' co-operative in France, the prototype of the countless thousands of others which exist today and have saved her peasantry from being swamped by the ruthless large-scale 'factory' farming so unsatisfying to the soul and ultimately inefficient. The *vanniers* prosper still today, and not just on the tourist trade. Their main market is in baskets for bakeries and laundries. Nevertheless they have a big permanent exhibition and shop in the village where you can choose from a variety of objects useful or merely decorative, many of them unfortunately too big to carry all the way back to England. Should you be interested enough to wish to see a *vannier* at work, the shop will direct you to one or other of the caves where they don't mind being stared at or even photographed.

Crossing back over the river at Saché (by the bridge over which the lovesick Félix would come with a bouquet for the impossibly righteous Mme Mortsauf) we can continue our journey just a little farther by the minor road. The valley, still green and tranquil, begins to narrow and the road closes with the river of which there are glimpses between the trees. If you keep a sharp lookout you will find several openings between them where you can get right down to the bank and picnic in their shade. Close on the left the tufa cliff looms high, pierced frequently by caves with arrow-slits above the doors. Almost immediately after the cliff commences there is a small grassy lay-by with a Touring Club plaque on the rock-face commemorating a cycle race. Peeping through the slits in the iron door below it, you find yourself gazing into a vast tunnel. This is part of the **Château Robin** which stood on the hilltop and has since disappeared. Only the miles of galleries remain, and for reasons of safety even those have had to be blocked off. With secret entrances, false passages and spy-holes to survey the ground outside, they were dug in the ninth century as a shelter for the whole community against the Norsemen who had started to raid up the valley. The labour would be immense, but the terror people felt for the barbarians of the north can only be compared with the modern terror of aerial bombardment, and it prompted the same instinct: to get underground. Like rabbits in a burrow a whole village population would have to sit out a raid while their houses were sacked and their fields ravaged above their heads; half-suffocated and hoping they would not be discovered or, if they were, that the looters would be too anxious to move on to further pillage to waste time attacking through the labyrinth of corridors.

After passing through Vonne our road joins the main Montbazon road from the other side and here be sure to turn right down the avenue of plane trees that leads to **Pont-de-Ruan**. At the north end of the bridge there is plenty of space to park before walking across to enjoy the atmosphere of this most riverain of villages. Side by side flow the Indre and two millstreams running over weirs. All around is the drowsy tinkling sound of running water, interrupted only now and again by the gurgling hiccup of a moorhen, or perhaps the plop of an angler's float as he fishes from a punt across the mill-pool. Old, old sounds that Balzac would have known well.

It is not worth following the north bank any farther after Pont-de-Ruan; one might as well use the main road to reach **Montbazon,** an old town which began life around AD 1000 when Foulques Nera chose it as the site for one more of his chain of forts. The base of the square keep which dominates the town is a relic of his construction; the rest is twelfth-century. It has been made to look rather ridiculous by one of those sentimental religious follies of the nineteenth century, a thirty-foot-high bronze statue of the Virgin perched on one corner of its crumbling, uneven top: like the larger one we saw at Le Puy, an admirable sentiment badly expressed. There is nothing in the keep; it is a ruin. From the castle mound, there is a fine view down on to the Indre.

Though a rather shabby old place with not much life in it, and spoilt by the Poitiers road cutting right through it, Montbazon is quite a good centre for anyone staying to explore the Touraine, being only six miles from Tours and within easy striking-distance of the territory described in this chapter, the previous two and the one to follow. It has a good camp-site right on the river-bank at the north end of the bridge and two sumptuous hotels of the château type –

Tortinière and Château d'Artigny. If you can afford luxury, the latter is in a beautiful situation, set in a park overlooking a loop of the Indre, about a mile and a half west of the town. It was built in the early twentieth century as the private residence of Monsieur Coty, the perfumer. Musical week-ends are held there in the winter. Cheaper, old-fashioned, very *rustique*, but comfortable is La Chancellière in the Place des Marronniers.

Candes-St Martin: heads in the church porch, probably contemporary
portraits of Eleanor of Aquitaine and Henry II of England

Dolmen at Mettray, near Tours

Saumur

CHAPTER FOURTEEN

Sainte-Maure;
Chinon; Candes and Montsoreau

✤

The end of the last chapter left us on the banks of the Indre, the second of the triad of major tributaries which foregather in Touraine to swell the Loire within a short stretch of only twenty-one miles, and now we move southwards to strike the third, the Vienne, most enchanting perhaps of all the Loire's tributaries, and follow it to its confluence at Candes on the borders of Anjou. Assuming a start from Montbazon or from Tours, the speediest approach over the none-too-interesting country in between is down the main Poitiers road.

On the way, devotees of Joan of Arc will assuredly want to stop for a few minutes at **Sainte-Catherine-de-Fierbois,** scene of the mystery of her sword. There is room to park at the side of the **church.** It was rebuilt about half a century after Joan's time so unfortunately it is no longer quite as she saw it when she was here on 3 March 1429. This was her last stop on her journey from her home village to meet the King at Chinon. Dedicated to Saint Catherine, one of her 'voices', the church was of special significance to her and she heard Mass there three times that day. The following month, while she was being fitted out at Tours, she refused the sword offered to her and said the one she wanted would be found buried behind the altar at Fierbois. An armourer was sent with a letter to the priest and sure enough a rusty old sword was disinterred with five crosses on it. The spot where this strange thing happened is marked on the north wall of the nave, where the chancel of the former church stood. How it came to be there no one ever discovered: it could have been a crusader's *ex voto* placed there long before, a by no means unusual thing to do; it has even been suggested that it was the sword of Charles Martel, left as a thank-offering after he defeated the Saracens near by in 732. When Joan was asked at her trial how she knew it was there she simply answered that her voices had told her. Her persecutors put it down to witchcraft; her rationalist detractors in later ages attributed it to fraud; but now that it is scientifically accepted that some water-diviners can detect buried metal even they

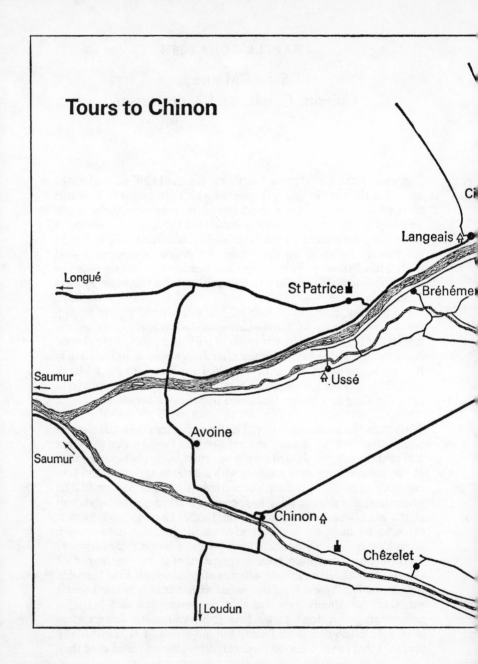

Tours to Chinon

Longué

Saumur

Saumur

St Patrice

Langeais

Bréhémer

Ussé

Avoine

Chinon

Chêzelet

Loudun

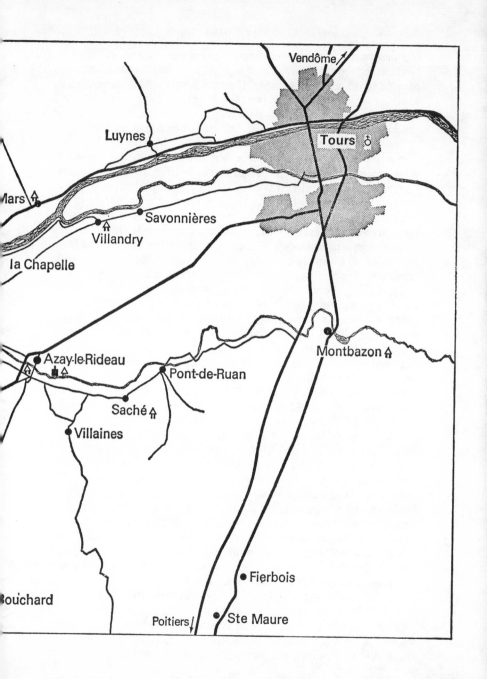

can hardly scoff. If there had been the slightest evidence of fraud the court at Rouen would have heard about it at the time, and been very pleased to do so. The people of Fierbois proudly had a sheath made for the sword, of crimson velvet; the people of Tours, wealthier and wishing to go one better, had one made of cloth-of-gold. But practical Saint Joan had a third one made of good stout leather.

There is a house near the church called the 'Maison du Dauphin'. I have made enquiries about this, but there seems to be no known connection with Charles although it was built in about 1415, in his lifetime. It was brand-new when Joan of Arc passed by, and that in itself imparts to it a little more than ordinary interest.

Travelling a little farther down the main road from Fierbois we come to **Sainte-Maure**, which acquired its name after the discovery by a ploughman in AD 570 of the remains of Saint Maure and Saint Britte (or Brigitte), two young Scandinavian princesses who were murdered on their way home from a pilgrimage to Compostella in the preceding century. Foulques Nera had another of his castles on a rocky promontory in the town. Only a sparse ruin of its fifteenth-century successor remains, but the town is fortunate in having a splendid medieval **covered market** which was restored by Anne de Rohan in 1672 so that it still survives in remarkably good shape. The rich and powerful Rohan family were the local seigneurs. Facing a peaceful square planted with limes, the **church**, rebuilt in the last century, stands over an earlier crypt comprising three parallel naves, the central one being of the eleventh century with very fine vaulting, unusually light and elegant for the Romanesque.

Sainte-Maure stands on a plateau of cretaceous deposit locally called *falunières*, laid down in the Miocene period when the whole of central France was a vast wide bay from what is now the Channel coast to nearly as far south as Poitiers. The thickness of the deposit is between fifteen and seventy-five feet and creates a relatively rich landscape with a personality all its own. Extending from Loches to Sainte-Maure, the region is known as Basse Touraine and is usually overlooked by tourists in spite of its quiet pastoral appeal. Agriculture is devoted mainly to poultry and the production of goats' cheese. The clean, sleek brown goats grazing in huge numbers in the fields look like herds of deer. The cheese is sold in a small, long cylindrical form and is light and tasty, but lacks the fat content of the more luscious *chèvre* of the Sancerre district. Most probably it was on this plateau that Charles Martel turned back the Arab invasion in the final great confrontation in 732, often referred to as the Battle of Poitiers, the second to bear that name. The first, in

507, when Clovis defeated Alaric the Visigoth, I have already mentioned on page 166. The third was the Black Prince's famous rearguard action fought farther south in 1356, and we have all heard about that at school. The fact that history has seen three major battles in this region underlines its strategic importance as a gateway to the north. But of all three, notwithstanding our English vanity, Charles Martel's was of the most far-reaching significance; without it Western Europe might have been, even now, an Arab sheikhdom.

Now we may leave the noisy Poitiers road and strike westwards to join the Vienne at **Pouzay** where there is a nice beach at the riverside. If you have time, by all means turn left here and travel upstream by the road which accompanies the Vienne closely for many miles to Châtellerault and beyond, a journey very much to be recommended to lovers of quiet river scenery. But if we stray too far from our course we shall never reach the Atlantic coast, so let us turn downstream again to **L'Ile Bouchard**. For a thousand years or more, until the nineteenth century, this was an important river-port directly linked with the commerce moving up and down the Loire. It comprises two parishes, one on each bank, with an island in the middle, all connected by a modern bridge. There is nothing greatly appealing about the place except its setting and it is very poor for shopping. On the right bank, however, a short distance past the bridge, the municipal camp-site in a beautiful big meadow by the river is as pleasantly situated as you could find anywhere, though with the minimum of facilities.

This road on the right bank is the more interesting one to take for Chinon, where in fact we are now heading. Opposite the turn for **Chézelet**, a hamlet on the right, a short unmetalled lane leads down to a most delightful spot by the waterside where you may absorb the spirit of the lovely Vienne. Drawn up on the shore are a few of the long, sturdy fishing-punts with swept-up bow and stern and graceful sheer like those of the Loire and so perfectly adapted to local conditions; for the Vienne is faster-running than the Cher or the Indre and resembles the Loire in having sandbanks and shoals. Nevertheless, like these other two it rises in the western hills of the Massif Central, but farther in, south of Aubusson and east of Limoges on a tableland picturesquely named Plateau des Mille Vaches. Moreover in its 231-mile course it collects the water of several substantial tributaries, the largest of which is the Creuse, a river of almost equal status. Its bed is mainly sand, gravel, pebbles and (ideal for the angler) weedy rocks among which the big fish like to lurk. The punts we have already noticed mostly belong to local farm-workers who supplement their income by spare-time fishing. Pike and zander abound, and in the summer there are great numbers of grey mullet which come up all the way from the Atlantic. One of the fishermen tells me it is a mysterious but undoubted fact that, whereas the shad prefers to stay in the Loire in his ascent, the mullet prefers to fork right when he comes to the Vienne. English anglers, used to finding the mullet only near the coast and solely to be tempted (if at all) with flakes of bread or other such dainty baits, may also think it curious that here he is taken on a spinner. This usually shy and cautious fish seems to change his habits on entering a river. Otters are plentiful on the islands of this well-stocked river and you are quite likely to see them playing in the backwaters, for like many other wild creatures they are not so shy in France, where country people generally hunt or shoot only what is eatable and are not so inclined to begrudge other predators a reasonable share of Nature's bounty. You have almost as good a chance of seeing an otter in France as you have of finding a snail. As to the kingfisher, you have an even better chance in this particular spot and he will hardly be concerned about you at all, perched on the stern of one of the punts most likely and happily fishing before your very eyes.

On the way down the lane we have passed a vineyard, for we are now in the appellation area of another of the Loire's top-quality wines, taking its name from Chinon, and as we continue along the road towards that town we pass many more, extending from the line of villages in the hills to the north of us almost to the river's edge and making a random patchwork with the fields and meadows. But the moment has not quite arrived to go into this important subject. On entering the village of **Le Puits**, notice beside the road something else quite plentiful along the lower reaches of the Vienne – there are more than a dozen I believe – a dolmen, this one with a house built on to it. The right turn in Le Puits is a good opportunity to head for the ridge of low hills less than two miles away should you wish to explore them. At **Cravant-les-Côteaux**, at the northern end of the village known as Vieux Bourg, you will find a ruined church with a Romanesque apse of the time of Charlemagne, as old in fact as the one at Germigny-des-Prés and very like it. Beside it are the ruins of the **Abbey of Grandmont**, founded by Henry II of England for a community of the Bonshommes Order, oddly called the Monks of the Crab-apple Tree. A resident caretaker will show you round if you ring the bell at the gate. By the stream behind the chapel stands a fine old communal wash-house (*lavoir*) which is still used by the village housewives.

Panzoult to the east is a pretty agricultural village at the foot of the hillside, surrounded by arable fields and pastures and a few vineyards. Looking down on it in its hollow with its steepled church, you might take it for an English scene – Gloucestershire perhaps. Beside the lane that leads to the mill by the Étang du Croulay (someone's private week-end retreat, though the lane is public), hidden among the scrub on the hillside is the celebrated 'Sybil's Cave' where some legendary oracle is supposed to have dwelt in pagan times. We have now passed out of Balzac country and entered that of a different sort of literary celebrity, Rabelais, who had a great fondness for such legends and took this one over in the *Tiers Livre* where he sends Panurge to seek advice on marriage from an old crone who lived in the cave. By way of a polite farewell after the interview was over she turned her backside towards him and hauled up her skirt.

But let us return to the main road and the subject of the local wine, since of course it can be sampled and bought in more congenial circumstances here from a grower direct than in Chinon itself. There are vine-growers all along this road who will sell retail, and several of them are well known to me, but I particularly like Monsieur Marcel Boissinot, a gentle, kindly man whose wine is of the first quality and reasonably priced. A mile or so after Le Puits you will see his name on a bottle-shaped sign hanging from a tree on the right at the beginning of the lane leading to his house. The wine of the appellation Chinon is a rich, strong red which improves with age like the Bourgueil described in the last chapter, of the same grape, the Cabernet Franc, and with the same characteristic bouquet which makes you think of raspberries (some say, rather, violets) just for a fleeting moment. It has class (*race*, to use the French term) and the more it is aged the more it resembles a really fine Bordeaux: to such an extent indeed as to worry the Bordeaux growers just a little bit. You may hear the mischievous little whisper originating from that part of the world that the Chinonais rub the interior of their casks with raspberries to fake the Cabernet bouquet. This is totally untrue. The soil content which gives the Chinon its strength, body and keeping qualities is a mixture of yellow clay (called *lise*) and silica. Because there is more uniformity of soil structure the wine is more dependable over the whole district (except north-west of Chinon) than at Bourgueil where only the Saint-Nicolas is top-class. Fortunately its production also is fairly substantial – annual average

18,000 hectolitres (396,000 gallons) against 10,000 hectolitres for Saint-Nicolas. But it is difficult to buy in England, so now is your chance. It travels well. A rosé is also produced here, smooth and completely devoid of acidity. As a rosé should always be a light wine, the best comes from the district around Beaumont and Savigny nearer the mouth of the Vienne, to the north-west of Chinon, where the soil is sandier.

Three more miles after M. Boissinot's *caves* and we are in **Chinon** itself. '*Petite ville, grand renom*' François Rabelais sang of it and it now owes much of its *grand renom* to himself as well as to its château where Joan of Arc first met the King. Judging by the names on the shops indeed, you might suppose that the girl-saint and the ribald poet, with Pantagruel and Panurge, now ran the commerce of the town in partnership. As if its glory were not enough, the town must flaunt Descartes too on the strength of his being born thirty miles up the valley at La Haye Descartes, so we enter along the Rue Descartes and then the Quai Jeanne d'Arc, in which we come to a statue of Rabelais by the riverside. This is the point at which to turn right for the town centre, the **Place de l'Hôtel-de-Ville**, where there is a handy car-park under the arch at its northern end. But all parking in the centre is metered, even on the quays. So if you wish to be free of that worry, you can stop farther back in the Place Jeanne d'Arc where there is no charge. Or if the château is your first objective go round by the north side of the town where there is a car-park for its visitors.

For the sake of some sort of order in describing the town, I propose to start in the Place de l'Hôtel-de-Ville, where incidentally there is a big market on Thursdays. Issuing from the west side of the square is the **Rue Voltaire**, a long narrow street running along the base of the spur of rock on which the castle is perched high above. This is the original east-west axis of the old Roman town. Quite soon, on the right, we come to an alley leading to the entrance to the *Caves Peintes* where Rabelais must sometimes have popped in for a drink, for he says through Pantagruel: '*Je sçay où est Chinon et la cave Peincte aussi. Je y ai bu mainctz verres de vin bon et frais.*' Wine is still stored by the Syndicat des Vins in the mile or so of galleries which were probably dug in Roman times for stone to build the town. You can hire the main gallery if you are thinking of throwing a party for up to 400 guests; otherwise they are not officially open to the public though anyone seems welcome to stroll quietly in for a peep. Close by, on the other side of the street, stands the fifteenth-century **Maison des États Généraux**, now a museum of local curios (open every day except Tuesday from 9 to noon and 3 to 7; but September–May afternoon hours are 2 to 5). A long-standing tradition that Richard Coeur-de-Lion died here after his wounds in battle in the Limousin is probably untrue; but certainly it was here, in the great *salle d'état* with its fine fifteenth-century timber roof, that Charles VII called an Estates General in 1428, and from that the building takes its name. A line just south of the Loire and parallel with it was the approximate linguistic boundary between the more Latin-influenced Languedoc, where they said *oc* for *yes*, and the Frankish northern region, the Languedoil, where they said *oil*. The northern dialect eventually won the contest as the standard language, but the two were still quite different at that time and as an Estates General had to be conducted partly in both a venue on the border was always preferred.

Next we come to the Grand Carroi (corruption of *carrefour*) which was the centre of the grid of Roman streets, the point to which the bridge led and still leads. Notice the delightful old half-timbered 'Maison Rouge' at one corner. Then, continuing along the Rue Voltaire, we begin to have awesome views of the castle walls looming on the skyline through every alleyway on the right. It was along here that Charles VII had a house built for Agnes Sorel (the Château Roberdau of which only a little bit of wall remains) and legend afterwards recounted how he had an underground passage from the castle so he could visit her secretly. Underground passages are an old chestnut and historians understandably derided this one – until in 1806 the sexton of Saint-Maurice fell in it while digging a grave in the old cemetery which belonged to the church across the road. Consequently, down a narrow alley with a palm tree at the end, nearly opposite the Hotel Gargantua, the southern end of Charles's secret passage is now open and sometimes used as a convenient boudoir by tramps.

The **Church of Saint Maurice** has a Romanesque tower with a fourth-century spire on top and a nave and chancel in purest Angevin style. Henry Plantagenet rebuilt it on the site of Chinon's first church which it owed to Bishop Brice of Tours, the saint we met at Marmoutiers, who in his younger days there had been so rude to Saint Martin.

If you would approach the château by the way it was approached in the Middle Ages and recapture the feel of those tough times, return to the Grand Carroi and mount the hill by the Rue Jeanne d'Arc. It is steep, rough-cobbled and a stiff climb – not for the unenergetic or those in high heels, who would do best to approach from the car-park on the north side – but the view across the town as you near the top is fascinating: there seem to be half-timbered gable-ends and tourelles everywhere.

The **château** is open every day from 9 to noon and 2 to 7 (5.30 off-season); closed throughout December and January. Over 1200 feet long by 200 feet wide on average, it is large. But it consists of three fortresses – the Fort Saint-Georges, Château de Milieu and Château de Coudray. We come to the first before paying and entering. Very little remains of it, an outpost put up by the Plantagenets to strengthen the east side and named after England's patron saint. Then, crossing the bridge, we enter the Milieu by the rectangular *Pavillon de l'Horloge*, twelfth-century at the base; very handsome machicolated, steep-roofed fourteenth-century above. In its top the bell called Marie Javelle still rings out the hours for the town. An ancient popular ditty runs:

> Marie Javelle
> Is my name.
> He who made me
> Made me well;
> He who removes me
> Shall repent of it.

An inscription on the bell itself records that one Henri Cressaut cast it. And '*bien mis*' his work must indeed have been, for the date is 1399 and its sound has measured out the hours of nearly six centuries.

Chinon is one of those blessed châteaux, incidentally, where you don't have to follow a guide; so strolling on past the well we next come to gardens and trees where were once the keep and the court-yard, and on the left still stand the remains of the Royal Lodge, built for Charles VII when he was wandering from castle to castle in central France, virtually an exile in his own kingdom. The Great Hall is now open to the sky, but there is a lovely old fireplace half-way up the wall of its gable-end which, on a chilly day in early March five and a half centuries ago, would be doing its best to warm the enormous, draughty first-floor room in which Charles's gilded courtiers were staring with mixed feelings at the peasant-girl from Lorraine, some contemptuously, even giggling at her; others wonder-ing if Heaven had really sent them miraculous aid to accomplish what they seemed incapable of accomplishing themselves. Sublimely self-possessed, she was not at all overawed by this first encounter with her prince and within a few minutes had restored his senses, his hope and his faith in himself, and set him on the road to win his kingdom.

By contrast another king had come, 239 years before, to the earlier building which stood on the same site, when he was at the end of his triumphs, broken and without hope. Henry II Plantagenet, on the evening of the humiliating peace treaty forced on him at Villandry, crept in here to die. He was ill with fever – or dysentery or high blood-pressure; no one knows for sure – and with weariness and disillusionment. Philippe had promised to send him a list of his former vassals in Anjou who had transferred their homage to the French Crown, and it arrived two days later, on 6 July, as the King was resting fully dressed on his bed. At the head of the list was his own favourite son John whom he had supposed in Normandy on his service, but who had joined Philippe a week before. Of all the blows he had recently suffered this was the hardest of all, and he promptly gave up the will to live. 'I shall struggle no longer,' he said, rather like Catherine de Médicis in a later age, and turned his face to the wall and let himself die without speaking another word. As soon as the breath had left his body a few hours later, his servants stripped him of his rich clothing and jewellery and made off with them, leaving him lying there in his shirt. William the Marshall, the only one of his knights with any honour left and who had not deserted him, had to pledge his own good word (for there was no other security) to borrow money to deck him out in false finery for the sake of appearances at his funeral.

The remaining vestiges of the Royal Lodge – armoury, kitchens and servants' quarters – are next to the Great Hall and were in the process of being 'restored' with lots of shining white new stone when I last saw them. After these the Château de Milieu ends abruptly with the gaping chasm of the deep dry moat which separated it from the Coudray. A stone bridge replaces the drawbridge and we cross into the fort which Henry had built to protect the extreme western point of the promontory, now set out as gardens. Looking over the ramparts and down the almost vertical slope of the spur, we see the town far below and the silver ribbon of the Vienne threading across the landscape to fade away in the hazy blue of the distant Forest of Fontevraud. Before recrossing the moat, have a look inside the circular tower on the left. This was built as the main keep of the fort after Philippe got it back from John. Though no warrior himself, Philippe was keen on military architecture and liked a good solid job, so this has walls ten feet thick at its base. In the ground-floor storey Jacques de Molay and other leaders of the Knights Templar spent the first year (1307–8) of their long incarceration which was to end in their being roasted alive at Paris. Under glass, just on the left of what is now the entrance door and in the embrasure opposite across the room, are to be seen a great number of graffiti which they left behind. Many are of a religious nature and at least one, of a Madonna and Child, quite beautifully drawn. But others of an esoteric mystical kind have given rise to much speculation ever since – the cross of Isis, a pentagram, Oriental swastikas or yin-yangs and other magical oddities which could be interpreted to show that the Order had not remained unspotted from its long sojourn in the East and that there was some truth in the accusations at the trial (trumped up as it may have been) of dabbling in the black arts. I am told that these writings are at present the subject of a new and careful study by a team of French scholars. Their findings should be interesting, but their task will be complicated by the difficulty of positive attribution, for a certain amount of more modern work in lighter vein seems to have been added from time to time. According to tradition, the next floor of the tower also housed a famous guest a couple of centuries later when Joan of Arc was lodged there, with the page allotted to her, after her interview with the Dauphin.

As we leave the château a short walk marked by signs leads us round to the **Clos de l'Echo** on the north side, where the conformation of the cliff-like outer wall produces remarkably distinct echoes and where many generations of Chinonais have teased their wives and girl-friends with the formula:

Enquirer Les femmes de Chinon, sont-elles fidèles?
Echo Elles?
Enquirer Oui, les femmes de Chinon.
Echo Non.

Of course it works.

Opposite, on a south-east-facing hillside so perfectly exposed as to rejoice the heart of any vine-grower, are the celebrated vineyards of the Clos de l'Echo which yield a wine unquestionably having that little extra something which sets it apart in quality so that it is the preference of connoisseurs and of all the most expensive hotels in Tours. This makes it dearer than the others, but not outrageously so. Not only are the grapes exposed to maximum sunshine on soil perfectly balanced as to clay and silica, but Couly-Dutheil, the proprietors, mature the wine in oak casks for a couple of years or more before bottling. They are not alone in this, of course, but the practice is by no means universal where there is a strong demand and the temptation is to bottle and sell as soon as possible. They have a shop across the road, near the small château car-park I mentioned earlier, and will give *dégustation* every day between 15 June and 1 October, and week-ends the rest of the year, to people seriously intending to buy. The condition is understandable in view of their position near the château; without it a few coachloads would soon drink them dry. Needless to say the ambience is not the same as in a *cave* out in the country, but Chinon needs ageing and here is a chance to buy it already mature. I have bought a 1964 here which had all the qualities of a fine vintage Bordeaux, including the colour – nearly black, looking at a full glass. 1973, '75 and '76 will be winners too. From a good year a Chinon can keep for well over half a century. Experts who ought to know (and are *in* the know) have acquired, drunk and praised the 1893 in quite recent times.

This account of the château and its environs concludes the main items of interest on the west, and older, side of the town. Now it remains to have a look at the eastern half and the best starting-point again is the Place de l'Hôtel-de-Ville. Opposite the Rue Voltaire, leading out of the other side of the square, is the **Rue Jean-Jacques-Rousseau**. On the corner, the 'Restaurant Panurge' is quite a good place for a quick light meal and wine at a reasonable price, and just beyond it are several good shops, including a butcher's whose beef is all Charolais and a *pâtissier* of exquisite skill and imagination on the other side of the street. In fact most of the shops in Chinon are good and, surprisingly since it is such a tourist centre, their prices tend to be lower than most other towns in Touraine. A short way down the first right turn (a little street called **Rue de la Lamproie**) a plaque on number 15 tells us that the Rabelais house stood on that spot in the sixteenth century. The present building is more recent, but farther down an exceptionally fine half-timbered house survives which young François's eyes must have rested on every time he walked down his home street. Most of his boyhood was spent here although he was born at his parents' country house which we shall come to later. His father was a fairly wealthy and successful lawyer in Chinon, not an innkeeper as is often wrongly stated.

Farther down the Rue J.-J.-Rousseau we come to the third of Chinon's old churches, the **Église Saint-Mexme**, a collegiate church built over the relics of the saint in the tenth century. It has been deconsecrated for a long time and only the central nave remains, much modified and turned into a school. The gallery of the narthex partly masks a Carolingian bas-relief of the Crucifixion of which there is a cast for more leisurely study in the Maison des États Généreaux (p. 248). Saint Mexme is a local legendary hero, a disciple of Saint Martin who came to Chinon in the fifth century. On an occasion when the whole population had taken refuge in the old Roman castle from besiegers and was dying for want of water because the well had been intercepted, he prayed for rain with such good effect that a deluge not only quenched everyone's thirst, but flooded the enemy out of his camp.

Out of the corner of the square behind the former church the terribly steep Rue Pitoches leads to the **Chapelle Sainte-Radegonde,** which can be better approached from the Cravant road outside the town. In any case arrangements have to be made in advance at the *syndicat d'initiative* in the Place de l'Hôtel-de-Ville as there is no one on the spot. In about AD 550 a hermit known as John the Recluse, a refugee from Saxon raids in Britain, installed himself in a cave on the spot and acquired a reputation for great wisdom. Queen Radegonde came to him for advice and built a chapel in his memory after he died. The present chapel is late Romanesque, in ruins with its roof off. But its main interest is a wall-painting, dating from about 1200 and not rediscovered until 1964, which represents a hunt: the hunters seem to be John Lackland, followed by Isabel d'Angoulême, his queen, with Eleanor d'Aquitaine, his mother, and two falconers behind. John and Isabel were married at Chinon on 30 August 1200 after he had snatched her from her betrothed, the comte de Lusignan, a breach of feudal etiquette which provided Philippe with the chief pretext for forfeiting his French fiefs.

The camper will find a municipal site of over seven acres in a most picturesque position where the old port once stood, by the south end of the bridge, with a fine view across the water of the town and the château brooding over it on its spur of rock. Incidentally there is plenty of free parking-space on the old quay on this side of the river, and quite handy as the bridge leads straight up towards the Grand Carroi.

The bridge, still partly of medieval construction, is supported halfway on a central island, the Ile de Tours, in 1321 the setting for a deed of abominable cruelty. It was the time of 'The Poisoning of the Wells' when, following a mysterious wave of popular unrest all over France, public water supplies were found to be contaminated and many people died after frightful abdominal pains. Unequipped with the means to identify the nature of the adulteration, people blindly sought an unseen enemy to strike at in self-defence or simply

in revenge. Whether anyone had really poisoned the wells is prob-
lematical. If anyone had, it was quite possibly fugitive Templars,
seething with resentment at the rough justice meted out to their
Order, who inspired the whole revolutionary disturbance which led
to such an action. But it was the poor lepers who were blamed,
allegedly acting on instructions of the Jews in complicity with the
Moors of Granada and Tunis. The latter were out of reach of the
popular fury, but the Jews were easily to hand and were rounded up
in many towns and massacred. There were 160 of them in Chinon,
all of whom, men, women and children, were put to death by
throwing them into a great trench of fire on this island.

The Forest of Chinon, which extends north of the town as far as
Ussé and north-east almost to Azay-le-Rideau, might be considered
an obligatory pilgrimage by some English visitors with a romantic
sense of history because the Plantagenet kings hunted there often.
But it would take a vivid imagination nowadays to conjure up a
vision of King Richard riding down the glade, for the forest is one
of the most ill-treated and disappointing domanial forests in central
France. Only its southern edges in the vicinity of Cravant and
Panzoult are of the original mixed hardwood type. The northern and
central parts have been remorselessly felled and many acres not
replanted at all, or replaced merely with soldier-rows of conifers.

Our long sojourn in Touraine is drawing to its close now and the
time has come to leave Chinon by crossing the bridge to take the
main road for Candes and the borders of Anjou. On the way, the
first left turn leads to **La Devinière** and the Rabelais' country retreat
where François was born – or brought immediately after his birth,
for the early chapters of *Gargantua* may be autobiographical, like
so much else in the book; in which case Madame Rabelais gave
birth unexpectedly in a meadow on the way here as a result of eating
a surfeit of tripe, none too fresh, which stirred up her bowels. As to
the date of this event, there is a surprising difference of eleven years
between the two estimates put forward, but scholars are now inclined
to accept the earlier one of 1483, which allows a more likely period
of time for the boy to have absorbed the extensive knowledge of his
childhood haunts which his subsequent writings disclose. The house
is a quite simple stone farmhouse of the fifteenth century with great
character, and is now a **Rabelais Museum** open every day throughout
the year except December and January from 9 to noon and 2 to 7
(5 off-season). It is not so well arranged as the Balzac museum at
Saché and the exhibits are mostly documentary ones which take
time to appreciate properly; but the place is well worth a visit to

absorb the atmosphere (little changed) in which the physician-friar of such strangely mingled profundity and superficial, excrementitious schoolboy ribaldry spent the leisure days of his formative years. In view from the house are the château of Coudray, its contemporary, and the tiny hamlet of Seuilly. Coudray is now a medical school and therefore not visitable, but Seuilly has some very sparse remains of a Benedictine abbey where tradition avers that Rabelais began his monastic life before transferring to the Franciscan Order.

About four miles after the turn for La Devinière the main road closes with the Vienne to follow alongside it in its last stages, and at **Saint-Germain** there are one or two places to pull off at the waterside. At the confluence we come to **Candes Saint-Martin**, a very ancient little town on a hillside which slopes down to the very brink of the Loire, one of the most beautiful situations along the whole valley. Our road, the main one to Saumur, is squeezed tightly in having to pass through it so that both passing and parking present problems, but there is usually space for the latter in front of the **church**, which is exceptional and the main item to stop and see. Dedicated to Saint Martin for a good reason we shall come to in a moment, it is of the twelfth and thirteenth centuries and was fortified in the fifteenth. Its porch, of the first period, is exceedingly beautiful with its lofty roof supported on one central pillar topped by graceful palm vaulting. The doorway is adorned with friezes. The heads of the saints on the higher ones were knocked off by Huguenots in the Religious Wars, but at the Revolution the *sansculottes* by some happy chance forgot to come and strike off the heads of royalty in the lower row. By another chance just as strange, no serious attempt seems yet to have been made to identify those heads. This I learned on making enquiries about them in a state of some excitement after first seeing them, for I was immediately struck by a strong feeling that they were Plantagenets. The President of the Archaeological Society of Touraine, M. Pierre Leveel, has kindly tried to trace other references to them without success and accepts my observation as original and possible. There are five on each side of the doorway and I am convinced that those on the right, at least, are Henry II, Eleanor of Aquitaine, two of their four sons and one of their three daughters. The porch is of the right period, and we are in the right locality for Henry and Eleanor are buried at Fontevraud only two miles away. The features of the King resemble exactly those on a contemporary enamel votive plaque in the Museum at Le Mans, known to be of Henry II; they resemble also his posthumous effigy at Fontevraud (allowing for the latter being clean-shaven) as also

Méthode champenoise: daily turning of the bottles at Saumur

Musée du Compagnonnage at Tours: chef d'oeuvre of a journeyman confectioner—made entirely of spun sugar

Anjou: the steep vineyards of the Coulée de Serrant, where the Loire's rarest and finest wine is grown

Montrichard, one of Foulque Nerra's string of border fortresses

Paimboeuf: the fisherman's harbour. Chimneys of St Nazaire across the estuary

does the queen next to him resemble Eleanor's effigy there, allowing for old age. Here at Candes the face is relatively young and if indeed it is a portrait of Eleanor it is the only contemporary one of her at that time of life, confirming in every way her great beauty of which the written records always speak so enthusiastically.

The interior of this little-known church is no less interesting than its porch. There are three soaring naves with stout fluted columns, well lit from the high clerestory windows, airy, bright and spacious, and many of the saints in niches high up remain unmutilated and still coloured in pinks and blues. In a small chapel at the end of the north nave a stained-glass window in fascinating detail depicts some monks carefully lifting the corpse of a saint through a window. One of them holds a finger to his lips enjoining silence while others lie asleep, oblivious of what is going on. Outside, a boat waits on a river with its sail brailed up ready for a quick departure. The episode is an historical fact and took place after the great Saint Martin died on this spot in November 397. Monks and disciples from both Poitou and Touraine were present at the time and immediately a dispute arose as to who should have charge of his remains. After everyone had retired at night, the monks of Tours quietly passed the body through a window of the chapel (not of course the present chapel), carried it down to a boat at the quay and made off in haste upstream to Tours. Although it was November, the old story goes, all the hawthorn bushes along the north bank of the Loire burst into blossom as the cortège passed by, so that thenceforth it became known as the Alba Via.

A lane to the right of the church leads to a terrace on the crest of the hill whence there is a fine panoramic view of the confluence of the Vienne and the island-studded Loire, leading the eye back for miles across the Touraine landscape and the way we have come. Since Mont-Gerbier our majestic river has now flowed 480 miles and fallen 4480 feet to just over 100 feet above sea-level, with 120 miles to go before it reaches the ocean.

Candes has a modern bridge across the Vienne – replacing an ancient ferry – and the minor road from it to Port-Boulet, four miles away, runs close beside the left bank of the Loire with several very pleasant spots to pull off at the water's edge. Beware however if the river is rising: it can move quickly round into the meadows behind you and cut you off. On this low, flat delta between the two rivers there is no *levée*.

Montsoreau, almost joined to Candes on the Saumur road, is just over the border in Anjou, a logical start for our next chapter perhaps, but a more convenient end for the present one. To desert the reader at Candes with twilight falling would be irresponsible and unkind, for it has no hotel to my knowledge where he may lay his head; no camp-site where his caravan may rest; nowhere to get a meal even and no shops worth speaking of. Montsoreau, on the other hand, has them all: three hotels, four restaurants, a very pleasant camp-site (two-star) among trees on the riverside with a beach near by, and all essential shops. Though only small, it is a town with a feeling of light and life and spaciousness about it, perhaps because of the new aspect taken on by the river here; swelled by the waters of the Vienne, it has become wide and primeval-looking, bordered by immense sandy shores or marshy meadows. It seems like a great estuary and its beaches now are of *fine* sand, like the sand of the seashore. There is plenty of parking-space on the quay, where many working boats are moored – the graceful black punts for coarse fishing and the larger cabined boats of the shad and salmon fishermen with their fantastic forward-sloping spar for tripping and hauling the dip-net. Even the plastic pleasure-boats with their pram-hood cockpits and clashing colours cannot entirely destroy the impression of a real little river port, not entirely given over to play. Angling is good here, and one species I have seen caught in abundance is the bullhead. Introduced to some European rivers at the beginning of the century and called *poisson-chat*, in France this small cousin of the mighty catfish averages four or five inches with ten as about the maximum. It is omnivorous, so bait is no problem, and if you get amongst a shoal you can soon have a netful of plump, sweet-smelling little fish, rather cucumbery like the smelt, and the local people who skin and fry them assure me they are a delicacy indeed. Among the bird-life of this section of the river the hoopoe is quite common; you will hear his sleepy call from the willow-thickets and may well catch sight of him in his colourful Indian chief's head-dress as he flaps lazily over the water to an island or struts along the shore.

Montsoreau has an impressive château on the riverside. Once the road passed behind it so that the water lapped its walls. Completed in 1455 by Jean de Chambes, one of Charles VII's councillors, it belongs to the style of transition from military to domestic: from outside a massive square block, a fortress; inside a home with some beginnings of elegance and comfort. Open every day from 9 to noon and 2 to 7 (5 October–March) it is worth seeing for its architectural interest, its pleasant setting and its stupendous view downstream from the west tower. Visitors who read a lot will also be interested to know that the chronicler, Philippe de Commynes, was married here to Jean de Chambes's daughter Hélène, and that Alexandre Dumas used the place as the setting for his *La Dame de Montsoreau*. Only specialist historians and Frenchmen are likely to spare much time for the Musée des Goums which it houses and which is concerned with France's past connections with Morocco.

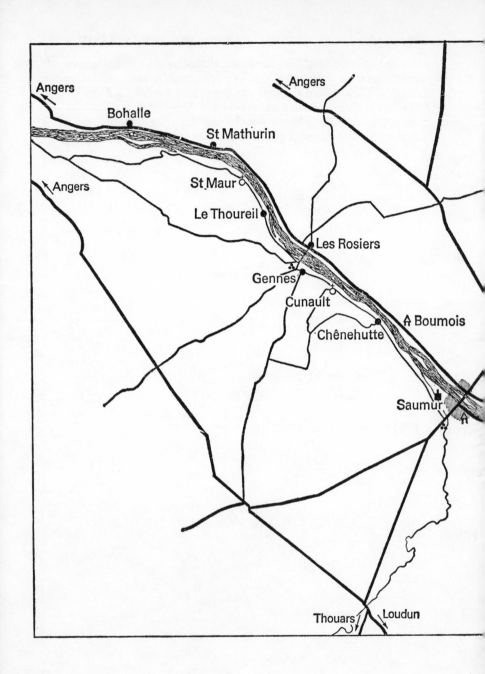

Chinon to Bohalle

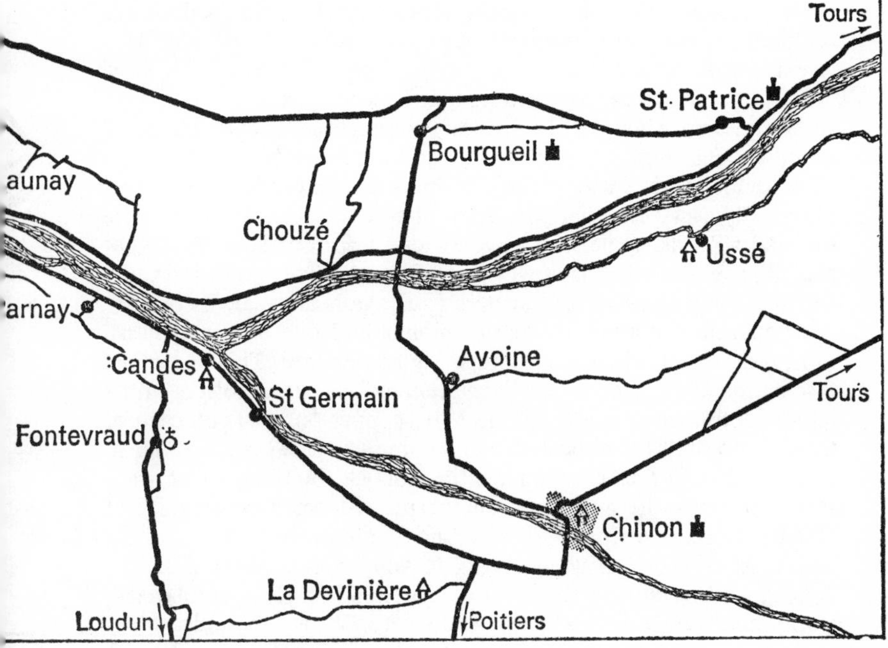

Tours

St· Patrice

Bourgueil

·aunay

Chouzé

Ussé

·arnay

Avoine

:Candes

Tours

St Germain

Fontevraud

Chinon

La Devinière

Loudun   Poitiers

CHAPTER FIFTEEN

Fontevraud to Ponts-de-Cé

❧

We are now in the ancient province where the great Angevin dynasty of English kings had its origin, and in the small town of **Fontevraud**, only just over two miles south of Montsoreau, several of them lie buried in the famous **abbey** there. At least eight of them, it is claimed; but at the Revolution the *sansculottes* tipped out all the bones to make an unsortable heap on the floor of the crypt and took away the golden urns which had contained them. The crypt is now sealed, but the contemporary effigies of four of them – Henry II, Richard I, Eleanor of Aquitaine and Isabel of Angoulême, John's queen, still survive intact in the chancel of the abbey church. The first three are sculpted in tufa stone, Isabel in wood, and all are larger than life-size and still coloured.

But it is not just for tombstones that I specially recommend a visit to Fontevraud Abbey: it is a virtually complete set of early medieval monastic buildings rare anywhere, and unique in the Val de Loire. The architecture varies from eleventh- to sixteenth-century and practically every essential part is still there: the abbey church (quite unusual with its single wide nave divided into four cupolas so that the pillars could take the down-thrust from the side and be relegated to the walls); two sets of cloisters (for, again unusual, there were two separate communities, one of monks and one of nuns); nuns' infirmary, chapter-house, and huge kitchen annexe. This last, most fascinating of all, is built on a *quadratum* of four corner towers with a larger central tower in the middle. With pepper-pot roofs on each of these, it presents the appearance of a complex space-rocket about to take off, but in fact is an eminently practical building which once served to cook the meals and smoke the fish for a community of 500 or more. Unhappily there is no community now, the only feature missing which would bring it completely alive with all the vigour, all the faith of the days of Christendom. It is secularized, empty and purely a magnificent showpiece. Visits are guided (very well guided too) and take place every day from 9.30 to noon and 2 to 7 except October–June when closing time is earlier according to season and demand.

In the eleventh century the site was a little clearing in a thick, wild forest with a spring called La Fontaine d'Evrault, after a murderous bandit who lurked near the spring to waylay travellers. One day Evrault's merry men found a hermit asleep under a tree. When the stranger was dragged before him the robber chief recognized him as Robert d'Arbrissel, an itinerant preacher he had once heard preaching in the streets at Angers. It was decided to kill him, but even as some of them had raised their weapons to do so Evrault had a sudden change of heart, restrained them and fell on his knees before his prisoner. We are not told precisely when this was or what happened to the brigands afterwards, but I like to think that some of them were among Robert's first disciples when he decided in 1199 to found a community here. He divided it into four parts – Sainte Marie (the major part) for women; Saint Jean for men; La Madeleine for repentant prostitutes and Saint Lazare for lepers. He had a very original mind and took the revolutionary course of placing the whole lot, monks and all, under the discipline of a woman, the Abbess of Sainte Marie. This raised some hostility in the establishment of the time and Petronella, the first abbess, had much ado to weather the storms. For example, when the local curé put up a trumpery claim to an annual sucking-pig for certain land he alleged was glebe, the Bishop of Angers eagerly lent him his personal support. However Petronella was not to be intimidated by the weight of officialdom; she took the case to the Pope himself and after twenty years of litigation the Bishop, still defiant over the curé's wretched pig, found himself excommunicated. Opposition soon died down after that, and Fontevraud throve for six centuries with the help of many great ladies, queens and princesses among them. Eleanor of Aquitaine held it in great affection and spent the end of her long and adventurous life in prayer with the nuns here. Among its abbesses were Mathilda, granddaughter of William the Conqueror; Eleanor of Brittany, granddaughter of Henry III of England; Anne of Orléans, sister of Louis XII, and four Bourbons, the last being Jeanne-Baptiste, a daughter of Henri IV.

Near the abbey gates in the town centre, the little church of Saint Michael (now deconsecrated) has a sumptuous altar in gilded wood which was once in the abbey church, and a Saint John the Baptist attributed to Mignard in the north transept.

For continuing downstream to Saumur there is a good road on either side of the Loire. The one along the north bank affords the best views of the river and follows it more closely; but it is still the highway westwards from Orléans, getting busier the nearer it approaches to Nantes, and passes through no village of particular interest. Down a side-road from Villebernier there is indeed the small fifteenth-century château of **Launay**, but that is all; and it is privately occupied so that you can only drive down to the end of the lane and peep at it over the gate. It is one of the prettiest small *manoirs* anywhere: the tufa stone of its pepper-pot towers still gleams as white as when René of Anjou had it built 500 years ago, purely as a leisure retreat where he could enjoy his favourite spectacle of jousting. He kept a menagerie here, and would ride to the grandstand preceded by two lions on silver chains, accompanied by a band of drums, trumpets and fifes.

The road on the south side of the Loire, straight on from Montsoreau, is more interesting, passing through a number of very ancient villages between the river and its meadows on the one hand and the steep tufa cliff on the other. They all retain houses dating back to the sixteenth and fifteenth centuries, many of them of the troglodyte sort, built on to caves in the cliff-face, and on the undulating south-facing slopes behind the crest are the first major vineyards of Anjou.

If you turn off into **Parnay**, you will find at its eastern end the *caves* of my genial friend Monsieur Daniel Pautremat, one of which is over a thousand years old according to his landlord. Like many French wine-growers in a smallish way of business, M. Pautremat holds his property *en métairie*, the medieval system by which the tenant shares the harvest with his landlord. My friend hands over a third, but he does not complain, pointing out that this is the best way of all to start if you have no capital but your own capacity for hard work – better than a fixed money rent because if you have a bad year the landlord has to share the misfortune. His holding is fifteen hectares altogether (quite a big one) and is scattered about in thirty-three different plots, which makes him ideal for our purposes as he produces each of the wines included in this appellation area of Côteaux de Saumur. Most English visitors will be agreeably surprised on learning what these are, since for generations our mainly unenterprising wine-merchants have left the public to associate Anjou with its rather heavy and sweet Cabernet rosé, the least of all its wines, still appealing to a few northern palates, but rapidly going out of fashion in France. With a generous *dégustation* selected from the rows of casks in his galleries M. Pautremat will demonstrate just what this part of Anjou does produce. First a luscious white (*sec* or *demi-sec*, as you prefer) from the Chenin grape. It may not equal the aroma and the flavour it acquires at Vouvray, where the same grape can be left for the 'noble rot', but it is good and of course cheaper. It travels very well for a white; I have brought it home in bulk in plastic water-cans with no ill-effect. Then comes the local red, a Cabernet grown on the slopes of near-by Champigny, rich, strong and long-keeping, not much inferior to a Chinon and, again, cheaper. This Saumur Champigny is quite renowned in France though seldom heard of in England. Lastly there are the rosés: the sweet Rosé de Cabernet for those who want it, though Anjou is trying to recapture its rosé market by taking advantage of the new Rosé de la Loire appellation, a dry wine, but tending here to be a bit thin to my taste. Of all rosés I still prefer those produced in Touraine.

On the right of the main road through Parnay, just after the little château (where you can also buy wine, though in a more touristy atmosphere) and an ancient cedar which has lost its top, there is a stone to mark the meridian of longitude and a big notice-board making friendly reference, with map and coats-of-arms, to Greenwich with which Parnay shares the honour. Then we are in **Souzay**, where the left turn in the village centre will lead up among the vineyards. Follow the '*Route des Vins*' (indicated by signposts) for a little way, but eventually leave it to turn up to the wood on the top of the hill. There you will come to a high viewpoint with a vista over miles of vineyards and the river valley to the heights beyond Bourgueil and Saint-Patrice. Beside this wood, with more than likely a golden oriole calling in the trees behind, not a sound of an internal combustion engine in earshot and the head of the Vale of Anjou spread out below, one has that rare feeling of real solitude and peace, an affectionate looking-back at our everyday world from a temporary stand in Paradise.

The feeling cannot last of course and by moving on another two or three miles to **Saint-Cyr-en-Bourg**, we can experience an opposite thrill in descending into an underworld of tunnels at the *Cave Coopérative des Vignerons de Saumur* where conducted visits are arranged every weekday from May to September inclusive, 9 to 11.30 and 2 to 5.30. They begin with a viewing of its ultra-modern vats on a hilltop whence the wine is run by gravity through underground pipes to the *caves* in the valley below, followed by a tour in your own car through the network of galleries eighty feet beneath the surface, and ending with a *dégustation* of the five different wines of the region. Since there is no obligation to buy, this is the best way of learning all about the wines of Saumur for those who have no such intention, as obviously one is under a moral obligation to a private grower after taking up his time and supping his free drinks.

Leaving our bibulous diversion now in order to finish our journey to Saumur itself, let us return to the main road, because at Souzay it runs close alongside one of those long secondary channels which are a feature of the Loire now in its lower reaches. Known as *boires*, they have a more gentle current than the main channel and therefore a cosier, more intimate air about them. **Dampierre**, for example, the next village, has many of the traditional fishermen's punts moored along its banks, beautiful craft in their sober colours and functional lines evolved many ages ago to suit local conditions. The addition of an outboard motor is the only significant difference between now and the days of Charlemagne – even of Caesar perhaps. The village also has many small meadows which are almost completely yellow with buttercups in the spring, as are many of the fields on the hills above – evidence of the strong clay content of the soil which gives strength to the wines of Anjou. Another common flower in the fields and vineyards hereabouts is the wild marigold.

Two more miles of such scenery leads eventually to the quay-sides of **Saumur**, where there is often room to park on the top of the quay just before the bridge and, almost always, on the lower level by descending the ramp. Saumur stands on an ancient strategic site fitted snugly between the main river and the Thouet which debouches just west of the town. Being also almost exactly halfway between the Loire's great bend at Orléans and the estuary, it once knew considerable prosperity as a port, a prosperity enhanced by the surrounding vineyards as the wines of Anjou were fashionable in England and the Low Countries partly because their tendency to sweetness in former times pleased northern palates, and partly for the very reason that they could be transported all the way by water. Commercial intercourse usually leads to exchange of ideas as well, and the town became a centre of the Reformed Religion, eventually being one of those accorded to the Huguenots as a guaranteed stronghold by Henri IV under the Edict of Nantes. His friend Duplessis-Mornay, known as the 'Huguenot Pope', reigned here formidably as Governor and established a Protestant Academy which attracted students from all over Europe and almost rivalled Geneva. The revocation of the Edict in 1685 under Louis XIV dealt the town a nearly fatal blow from which it has never entirely recovered; a large proportion of the inhabitants emigrated and even now its population of 26,000 is less by a thousand or two than it was then. In the next Louis's reign, the stationing of the regiment of the Royal Carabiniers and founding of the famous cavalry school enabled Saumur to pick up again, only to go once more into decline with the passing of river commerce on the coming of the railways. Nowadays it still has economic difficulties, with Angers and Tours competing so close; but one result of their attracting heavy industry away from it is that it remains a quietly attractive little town – one of the pleasantest on the Loire in fact.

Parked here on the quay, we are already in the centre of the old part and across the square, facing us and the river which once lapped its walls, is the **Hôtel de Ville** built in the late sixteenth century as a fortified manor in mainly Gothic style, hardly influenced at all by the Renaissance. Walking through the arch and the courtyard brings us to the usual complex of small medieval streets – 'the old quarter' – which happily most ancient French towns have had the grace to preserve, together with the colourful names. Threading one's way through the streets called Bonnemère, Dacier, du Puits Neuf, de la Tonnelle, one wonders who was the good mother; what trade in steel goods gave Dacier its name – was it swords; where was the well and when was it new, and who kissed beneath the bower? They have many interesting little shops still: one in the Rue de la Tonnelle sells everything in tools and equipment for vine-dressing and wine-making. Another, much esteemed by me, is the secondhand bookshop 'La Coloquinte' in the Rue du Puits Neuf. There are relatively few *bouquinistes* in provincial French towns and of those few the majority seem to be rather formidable and rapacious ladies. Not so Madame Dupuis, who is charming, fair-dealing and, incidentally, speaks excellent English.

At the end of the Rue Dacier the **Église Saint-Pierre** is one of Saumur's showpieces. Entering by a fine Romanesque door in the south side, we find ourselves in a majestic interior. The choir and transept are of the late twelfth century and the nave of the early thirteenth. In a loft at the west end is a lovely old organ which must have vibrated to the anthems of at least three hundred Easter mornings already. But the treasure which most people come to see consists of two fifteenth-century tapestries showing the lives of Saint Peter and Saint Florent. The latter is a local celebrity whom we shall encounter later, so his story is of special interest. The sections of the tapestry are not set out in due order but are numbered in correct sequence; so follow the numbers and his epic unfolds clearly enough. Diocletian and Maximien order suppression of Christians. Consul Aquilinus orders Florentius and his brother Florian to renounce and kneel before idols. They refuse, so soldiers take them away to be executed. On the way the party is overtaken by nightfall so the two prisoners are tied to a tree. While the guards are asleep an angel comes and releases Florentius, leaving Florian behind to suffer martyrdom – inscrutable choice of Providence, but remember martyrdom was a privilege and a glory. The angel conducts Florentius to Saint Martin of Tours to be ordained, afterwards showing him the road to take (which lies on our route also), downstream to the hill of Glonne where he settles and lives in a cave in the woods. He chases away the dragons who haunt the neighbourhood, founds a monastery and dies there. Another panel recounts one of his miracles where he restores the sight of a blind woman and the life of her son who has been drowned in the Loire.

Our little promenade can conveniently be concluded by walking westwards to the **Rue d'Orléans**, Saumur's busy main street, down to the bridge and turning the corner back to the quay. On the corner, note the imposing theatre built in 1886 in the style of the Odéon in Paris. Then it is time to move on to the **château**, which is open every day from 1 April to 30 September, 9 to noon and 2 to 6; rest of the year, 10 to noon and 2 to 5 and closed Tuesdays. There is a fine big car-park outside the château, so follow the green band painted on the road through the town (an excellent and thoughtful system) and you will come to it. There are lovely gardens adjoining, sparkling with apple-blossom in the spring; a grassy picnic area; toilets, and even a public water-tap. This hilltop was once called the Butte des Moulins; until the second decade of this century it was lined with literally dozens of windmills.

The imposing fortress across the moat was built in the second half of the fourteenth century by Louis, duc d'Anjou, brother of Charles V. Duke René rebuilt the east tower in the following century and the 'Huguenot Pope' strengthened the walls in the next one. Originally it was a complete quadrilateral until the north-west side was demolished in the eighteenth century to give an open view across the town and down the river, and a truly splendid view it is. After mounting the ancient flight of worn steps to the castle door, notice the big old key hanging on the wall just inside. In 1918 Lon D. Minier, an American soldier, stole it as a souvenir. Forty-eight years later he confessed his misdemeanour and in April 1966 at a special ceremony in the castle a formal charge of theft was read out, verdict of guilty pronounced, pardon granted and the key handed over amid cheers, *bravos* and free drinks all round.

The château houses two of those all-too-rare museums whose stock is not only of first quality, but enhanced by specialization. One, the **Musée d'Arts Décoratifs**, deserves a less commonplace title, for this is not the usual hotch-potch of bits and pieces it might imply. Besides furniture, tapestries, medieval paintings and more than a hundred statuettes in carved wood, it contains a collection of European china as widely representative as you could find anywhere. Porcelain from Sèvres, Tournai and Meissen are there, and *faïence* from Nevers, Rouen, Marseilles, Strasbourg and Delft, all in a collection of over 1300 pieces assembled by one passionate enthusiast, the comte de Lair, over a lifetime and generously bequeathed to Saumur in 1919.

The other museum, perhaps even more captivating because more unusual, is the **Musée du Cheval**, founded in 1911 by another private individual, Monsieur Joly, veterinary surgeon at the Cavalry School. Its theme is the history of the horse and of horsemanship from remotest times to our own. There are fossilized skeletons of prehistoric horses including one from North America about the size of a fox. Saddles of all kinds are displayed – Arab, Samurai from old Japan; even a genuine cowboy saddle from the American Mid West, and one of the revolutionary ladies' saddles *à la planchette* invented by Catherine de Médicis. A collection of bits goes back as far as a bronze one from Ancient Greece; but it is interesting that a corresponding display of stirrups does not go so far back because the Greeks and Romans made it a point of pride not to use them.

Racing and bloodstock are matters in which England comes into her own. Richard was the first English king to import Arab horses and in subsequent ages the English aristocrat, a man of the open air more attached to his country estates than his French counterpart who was primarily a courtier, gave his mind to breeding horses of maximum speed for the delightful sport of racing. He soon recognized the superiority of the Arab stock for this purpose and in the seventeenth century established the Stud Book. Of all this we are reminded at the museum, especially by a fine engraving, to the right of the entrance, of Godolphin Arabian, one of the sole three sires from which all English thoroughbreds are descended. It is sporting of the French to draw attention to this famous horse since a Frenchman, the usually discerning Louis XIV no less, blundered horribly in regard to it. Given to the King as a present by the Bey of Tunis, it earned the royal displeasure in some way not recorded and was contemptuously disposed of as a draught-horse. An astonished English visitor later saw the graceful Arab pulling a water-cart in the streets of Paris, bought it for a song and resold it at a handsome profit to Lord Godolphin.

Because of carelessness of this kind, when the French wanted to start their own Stud Book they had to come to us to buy thoroughbred sires, and one of their greatest acquisitions was Flying Fox whose skeleton stands here now. Together with a delightful painting of him on the wall, it repays study by anyone even remotely interested in horses. Even from the skeleton his exceptional body-length is strikingly apparent, but it disproves that he had an extra pair of ribs: there are only the usual eighteen. With his enormous stride he won every race he ran, including the Derby, Two Thousand Guineas and Saint Leger in 1899. The following year his owner, the Duke of Westminster, died. Unable to get in touch with the heir who was on active service in Africa, the executors, who must have had little imagination, put him up for sale and he was bought by Monsieur Edmond Blanc who ran the casino at Monte Carlo. Many French thoroughbreds are descended from him and he is the proudest exhibit in this museum.

One more monument remains to be mentioned on this side of the town, the **Église Notre-Dame-de-Nantilly** which lies some distance south of the castle. There is plenty of parking-space outside so you might as well drive to it. Saumur's oldest church, it is basically late-twelfth-century in Romanesque style. Louis XI pierced the south wall to add the wide aisle in flamboyant Gothic which makes a curious one-sided contrast. Though very much in use, the church is also a veritable museum of tapestries. The south aisle contains fifteenth- and sixteenth-century pieces: *Adoration of the Shepherds*, *Fall of Jericho* and an exquisitely coloured *Crowning of the Virgin and Child, adored by Shepherds*, an unusual theme. Over on the other side (north wall of the nave) is an eight-piece set of seventeenth-century Aubusson depicting the Life of Christ. Do not miss either the beautiful old psalters (with words and music) on the lectern; nor, under the fourth arcade between the nave and the aisle, an epitaph composed by René of Anjou for his old wet-nurse when she died in 1458, in gratitude for the *'nourreture'* he had received at her breast nearly fifty years before. This is characteristic of 'Good King René', as he was affectionately called though he was only a titular King of Sicily. One of the outstanding personalities of the fifteenth century, in his humanity and refinement of mind he was way ahead of his time – even of the Renaissance just over the horizon. In complete contrast to his fearsome contemporary Louis XI, who eventually drove him out of his rightful duchy, he was a great scholar, proficient in Latin, Greek, Hebrew, Italian, Spanish, mathematics, geology and law; a composer, a painter and poet, and a simple, friendly man who cared nothing for war but loved people. Often he would drop in at the homes of his subjects for a chat and before leaving, as a souvenir, he would draw a portrait of himself on the wall.

We encounter him again almost immediately on crossing the bridge to the big island in midstream, the **Quartier des Ponts**, formerly called more romantically l'Ile d'Or. In the Middle Ages this was the main habitation of the fishermen and mariners, and under the patronage of King René they were eventually allowed to form themselves into an autonomous community, electing their own chief to protect their customary privileges and settle their own disputes. Eventually this chief came to be called King, though his realm was called a republic. It survived for three centuries and an old sailor in Louis XVI's navy is recorded as proudly boasting the title '*Roi de la République de l'Ile d'Or*'. He must have been the last to do so: the Jacobins of the Revolution were less easy-going than King René and not the sort to tolerate a rival republic, even in fun, nor such a logical contradiction as a king of one.

In the Rue Montcel, on the island, fourth right after crossing the bridge, still stands the old turreted manor-house called **Maison de la Reine de Sicile** where Yolande d'Aragon, Queen of Sicily and René's mother, spent her last years and died. If you follow the road along eastwards from here, you will come to the shore of the north arm of the river, an ideal quiet picnic place in the cool shade of tall trees; and on the eastern end of the island a little farther along there is a really superb camp-site which, with its spacious grassy pitches under lovely trees, manages to preserve the illusion of camping in the wilds despite having all mod. cons., including electric power-points and a swimming-pool, close by. A big weir from the tip of the island reduces the north arm of the river to a gentle flow, and if the water is not too high you can walk out on to it to fish. The opposite (western) end of the island is given up to a big camp for *nomades* so that you are always meeting interesting Romany faces in the streets of Saumur.

If you now fancy a deep plunge into prehistory, re-cross the bridge and carry straight along Saumur's long main street until you cross the bridge over the Thouet into the suburb of **Bagneux**; coming to the church after some distance, fork left into the Rue du Dolmen. At the bottom of the street, in the garden of a café, is the finest dolmen in Anjou and one of the largest in France. It is seventy feet long, divided into two chambers, and the main chamber alone is as big as a chapel. Flat granite slabs up to eighteen feet wide and thirty-five tons in weight form the sides and roof, and the entire structure is so heavy that it has to rest on eleven foundation blocks sunk ten feet into the ground. Again the insoluble mystery: who were the people 5000 years ago who correctly calculated the need for these, and built it so it stands as true today as it did then? How did they lift those blocks; and what did they do in here when the place was finished? Now there are a few tables beside it where we may drink our coffee in the cool shade and wonder.

To get from Saumur to Ponts-de-Cé, where this chapter ends, we can choose between two routes, on the north or the south bank of the river. The northern one is more direct and the road is busier; but it keeps right beside the river nearly all the way and affords glorious views. The southern route is more leisurely, following minor roads and taking us away from the river at one point.

Let us look at the southern route first. Leave Saumur by the Rue Beaurepaire, the main westward street out of the town centre. On the way, at no. 25, you will pass the *syndicat d'initiative*. I have not made a practice of pointing out these establishments because they are easily found by asking and, when found, often not much use. But this one is exceptional in that it has an annexe run by the local wine-growers' association which supplies information about their products and sells them retail.

This is the 'select' end of the town, with wide acacia-lined boulevards and smart houses once occupied by the families of the officers of one of the smartest cavalry regiments, the Carabiniers de Monsieur (i.e. the Duke of Orléans) which established the famous cavalry school here in 1763 and later became known as the Cadre Noir because of its distinctive black uniform. The Cadre Noir still exists, but ceased to be a part of the army in 1969. The military establishment now, on our left in the **Avenue Maréchal-Foch**, is all tanks and jeeps, the School of the Armoured Corps. There is no cavalry school now; it has become the National School of Equitation, run by the state department of Youth and Sports, and it flourishes as a prestige riding-school across the road. One may pull off on to the parade-ground when it is not in use, and it is fascinating to watch both pupils and young horses being schooled in the adjoining enclosure. If it is Friday afternoon or Saturday morning, and in school term, you may visit the school by prior arrangement through the *syndicat d'initiative*. Every year at the end of July Saumur holds its Grand Carrousel, a magnificent military tattoo lasting four days in which the army shows off battle manoeuvres with tanks and helicopters and the Cadre Noir (as the élite of the riding-school still calls itself) displays its feats of horsemanship.

But in June 1940 the military school at Saumur showed its real mettle in an heroic exploit comparable only with the Charge of the Light Brigade and worthy of being as often sung, though it is not. Colonel Michon, its commander, ashamed at the collapse of his country under the craven Pétain administration, decided that he and his tiny force of about 1200 men and 800 boy cadets would fight on alone. Ignoring orders to withdraw to Montaubon, they deployed along the Loire between Montsoreau and Gennes (a front of twenty-five miles) to hold the three bridges, making the best use they could of their armament consisting of two ancient field-guns, less than a dozen old tanks, machine-guns of 1914–18 vintage, practice rifles and hand-grenades. Just after midnight on the 19th the first German tank began to cross the bridge at Saumur and immediately exploded on a direct hit from a cannon manned by Cadet Houbie. Six more tanks and two lorries suffered a similar fate in the next few minutes. The Germans were astonished, but decided to dispose quickly of this unexpected resistance by launching a high-speed armoured rush on the bridge. As they did so it blew up, having been mined in readiness. It is called the Pont des Cadets in memory of the episode. The bridges at Montsoreau and Gennes were likewise blown up and only after more than twenty-four hours were the Germans able to cross with the aid of pontoons and reinforcements. The little force of defenders, by then reduced by hundreds of casualties had run out of ammunition. This result was of course inevitable; the effort had been futile from a practical point of view and Colonel Michon has been much criticized for 'wasting' all those young lives. But they were willing enough; they fought gloriously, and in the midst of France's humiliation they alone saved her honour at that time.

Passing now out of Saumur proper, we find ourselves in its suburb of **Saint-Hilaire-Saint-Florent** which lies along the left bank of the Thouet just before its confluence with the Loire and looks across to the long spit of meadowland which lies between the two rivers. Its connection with Saint Florent is simply that his relics were brought here to save them from pillage by the Norsemen, a small pleasure later enjoyed by the Huguenots. Here is the centre of production of the famous Saumur sparkling wine, the only possible rival of Vouvray *champenoise* as a close runner-up to champagne. The hillside on the left is riddled with cellars and we are greeted by many well-known label-names as we pass by. The greatest of them all is Ackerman-Laurance, for it was John Ackerman who came to Saumur in 1811 after many years in Champagne, recognized the spontaneous tendency of the local wine to sparkle and first applied the full champagne method to it. He married Mlle Laurance, a pretty local girl, and bought the four and a half miles of galleries in the tufa cliff to house his prospering enterprise. The premises are open for visits every day from Easter to the end of September, 9 to 11.30 and 3 to 5; at other times of the year on application at the office. They are free and include *dégustation*.

Of their whole range, the finest is that produced to the extra strict requirements of the new appellation Crémant de Loire, introduced in October 1975. The grape used is the Chenin and, briefly, the process is as follows. Only the perfectly exposed hill slopes are allowed and the yield is restricted. Harvesting is only by trained pickers and even so the grapes must be hand-sorted afterwards. Only the first pressing is used and, after racking-off, the wine must be left in oak casks until the spring when champenization may be started. A liqueur of sugar-cane base is added to the wine and it is put into bottles which must then lie horizontal for a minimum period of nine months. They are next moved to racks slightly down by the head, and every day each bottle is given a quick rotation by hand to urge the sediment towards the neck. An expert cellarman can rotate 50,000 bottles a day, using both hands simultaneously. After this the bottles are stored for several months vertically with the head right down before the sediment is drawn off and the wine is ready. Perfectly translucent, and with the minimum in-bottle pressure of $3\frac{1}{2}$ atmospheres required by law, the crémant truly 'creams' on pouring and, dry and fruity with a bouquet that lingers, it is virtually indistinguishable from a sound champagne – at a third of the price.

On the western outskirts of the village, on the left, is an establishment where you can hire a horse, and really one could hardly have more delightful and easy country for riding, for the Thouet and the Loire here are bordered by lush carpets of meadow. In fact it is becoming more and more apparent, as our later journey will confirm, that Anjou is a country of green pastures just as Saumur is a town of horses, and the connection is not accidental since horses eat grass. They also provide a manure which happens to be specially good for mushroom-growing, so again it is no coincidence that we are in the centre of production of the renowned *champignon de Paris*, real name *psalliote*. Three-quarters of the national output of this tasty delicacy comes from here where (to complete a happy combination of circumstances) the caves in the tufa provide the ideal growing conditions. Just a little farther on from the riding-stables, still on the left, is a **Mushroom Museum** in just such a cave (open every day 9 to noon and 2 to 6). Guided by one or other of the friendly old couple who are resident caretakers, you stroll through half a mile of underground gallery and see the whole process from the first spread of the mould (*mycelium*), specially sterilized and prepared from the spores, through the tiny little button mushrooms, familiar to most of us from the tinned variety we can buy in Britain, to the handsome full-grown fungus up to five inches across, delicate cream-coloured with a brown-speckled centre on its dome, sweet-smelling and delicious. It is these larger specimens that the local people prefer to eat, cooked or raw. After the visit you can buy the mushrooms at most reasonable prices, any size you like, freshly picked or in tins to bring home. The museum also exhibits some fine specimens of the curious coiled fossils known as ammonites found in the course of excavation. One monster is nearly 250 pounds in weight. Here, as in Touraine, the caves owe their existence to centuries of quarrying for building-stone.

Chênehutte ('oak cabin') is the next village we come to. On top of the hill a sixteenth-century priory has been turned into an hotel where you could do no better than dine if you have a whim to spoil yourself. The four-star cuisine is really excellent and correspondingly expensive, and the view down over the river is wonderful. Around May Day each year Chênehutte holds a jolly '*Foire aux Champignons*'.

Trèves has a ruined castle on the site of an even earlier one built by Foulques Nera, just another of the pieces on his personal chequer-board of Anjou-Touraine. The chief feature now is a big round bastion beside the church; but wander round the village and you will see other bits of old fortress sticking out of houses and barns all over the place: the ensemble must have been immense. Here also, horses are available for hire at the farm up the hill beyond the tower.

Then comes **Cunault**, a former river-port of some importance as its old quays still testify. There is yet about it a likeable personality; it is a place where I feel I could happily settle down to live. In 836 a thriving Benedictine community on the island of Noirmoutiers off the coast near the mouth of the Loire found its position untenable owing to the Norse pirate raids, then just beginning. So the monks salvaged all they could and moved inland to a new position near Nantes – safe as they thought, for no one then foresaw how serious the new menace was to be. Eleven years later the raiders had bases in the islands of the estuary and were upon them again. Determined this time to put a really substantial distance between themselves and their persecutors, they came right up to Cunault. Another miscalculation! Only five more years and the heathen were upon them once more; so they fled to Burgundy.

The Norse invasions eventually ceased, as all things will, but many troubled years of anarchy followed and it was not until the beginning of the eleventh century that the community was able to come back and reclaim its lands at Cunault in the era of peace which resulted from the rough but strong rule of our old friend Foulques Nera. Clearing away the ruins, the monks began to build a complete new church about mid-century, starting with the tower so reminiscent of Saint-Benoît with which it is about contemporary. Then, following the usual programme, they erected the body of the church by starting at the east end and working steadily along to the west front. The building we see now is the same, materially unchanged, as the one they rejoiced over that day in the early 1200s when the last stone had been put into place. Inside the nave a notice on the wall claims it to be 'the most majestic and the most beautiful of the churches of Anjou'. I have not seen every church in that province, but I should say the boast is not an idle one. There is a well-produced illustrated booklet on sale in the church giving details of its architecture and its treasures. One interesting feature of the former is the slight tapering of the nave (not apparent unless you look for it) to give an illusion of greater length. And the treasures include the thirteenth-century reliquary of Saint Maxenceul, still bearing its original paint on the intricately carved walnut – riddled with woodworm, but still holding up after 700 years. Saint Maxenceul was one of Saint Martin's missionary band and evangelized Cunault in the fourth century.

And now **Gennes**, a small town most pleasing of aspect as you approach, built on the sides of a steep knoll and culminating in a graceful church spire. The church is in fact deconsecrated and in ruins, but worth driving up to for the view across the Loire. And here in this quiet, deserted place, in graves against the outside of the ruined nave, lie several of the Cavalry School cadets, who saw the valley below in a very different aspect in June 1940 as they manned this hilltop to block the right wing of the German advance.

In the hills behind Gennes are four **dolmens**, the best of which is called La Madeleine and is on the left of the Doué road to the south about half a mile past the church of Saint Véterin (the one the town now uses). It is not far short of the Bagneux dolmen in size. In the last century the farm on which it stands used it as a bakery and had an oven in the main chamber. What would the ancient pagan priests or the modern conservationists think of that? There are also two **menhirs** (less common than dolmens along the Loire) in a field to the left of the Angers road. South-west of the town lies the Forest of Milly which is domanial, but apparently felled quite heedlessly not so long ago and now a mixture of stunted fir trees, scrub and impenetrable furze, depressing yet fascinating in a wild fashion. Cuckoos seem to love it: one stormy spring evening I heard five calling all at once from different directions and one even woke in the moonlight at two next morning and called twice – just like a cuckoo-clock.

From Gennes take the minor road out along the river-bank to **Le Thoureil**, a lovely village strung out alongside the river which is a wide stretch of water here, with no sandbanks to break the view or detract from its mature majesty. The hinterland is still given up largely to the cultivation of apples and of vines, and in the days of river transport Le Thoureil was almost entirely populated by the boatmen who exported the local produce: it was a sailors' village. The apples were taken to Paris in a special type of craft called a *bâtard* because it combined the features of the usual Loire *chaland* and a canal barge. The route was upstream to Nevers and through the canals to the Seine. On arrival in the capital the boat tied up to one of the quays and became a shop for several weeks until the cargo was sold. Its return cargo would be casks and barrel-staves for the local vine-growers. The wine was greatly in demand in the Low Countries and was shipped down to Nantes in local boats and thence by sea to Holland. To encourage its tendency to sparkle it was often taken by a roundabout voyage (even round the globe) for a good shaking-up in the same way as the English shook up their India Pale Ale.

Strolling along the waterfront you will notice several exquisite little Renaissance mansions. These were built for Dutch merchants who found it worthwhile to live on the spot in order to secure the best wines before they found a market elsewhere. The smaller houses were occupied by the *mariniers* and on the front walls of some you will find graffiti of boats, anchors and other nautical items cut into the stone. The café in the square near the church has a few specimens of sailors' wood-carving and is still the haunt of watermen whose livelihood is fishing.

Two miles farther along the road is the abbey of **Saint-Maur**, called after the saint of that name who was born in Rome in 512 and became a disciple of Saint Benedict. Sent to Gaul by his master, he came to this village (then called Glanfeuil) and established a monastery on the site of a Roman fountain dedicated to a nymph. The large basin of the fountain still survives beneath the chapel on the hillside, in quite good repair, retaining even its lead pipes and eighteen bases of its original forty columns. The nymph of course has gone: Saint Maur could hardly have retained her as company for Saint Michael to whom he dedicated his first chapel. The great thing about the abbey now is that it is very much alive again despite the usual vicissitudes of the past. Sacked by the English in the Hundred Years' War, burnt by the Huguenots in the Religious Wars, rebuilt in the seventeenth century, suppressed, pillaged and sold at the Revolution, it was restored when the Benedictines came back to it in 1890 and after only eleven years a new anti-clerical government expelled them from France. Since then it has been acquired by the Assumptionist Fathers and is run by them as a 'centre of welcome' to all people of goodwill. Groups of young people come from many parts of the world, especially in the summer holidays; but at any time anyone, man or woman, old or young, Catholic or Calvinist, even atheist, may knock at the door and be welcome for as long as he likes to stay, making a small payment for simple accommodation and the privilege of sharing the Fathers' life of poverty and service, joining in their worship only if he wishes. Exchange of information and culture with other guests is encouraged and if a visitor is engaged on some research useful to mankind the Fathers will help him with it if they can. Quite apart from its beautiful setting, which is an added boon, the place positively radiates happiness, goodness and brotherly love.

A journey south-westwards from Saint-Maur for seven miles leads to **Brissac-Quincé**. Tourist literature seldom mentions the **Château de Brissac**, which is in fact one of the most notable and most enjoyable to visit. (Every day except Tuesday, 9 to noon and 2 to 6. Open Tuesday as well, 1 July to 15 September.) Since a very good leaflet in English is provided free on the spot, I will describe the house only briefly and say more about its historical associations. The whole stands in a beautiful park through which the river Aubance winds, and our approach is by a short walk along an avenue which includes five noble cedars. Emerging from it, we come face to face with the great château. Its most striking feature at first is its unusual height – seven floors above ground in the central part, which is pure Louis XIII in style. This is flanked by two imposing old fortress towers, the sole vestiges of the earlier building. The interior is delightful, beautifully furnished, and lived in by the present duc de Brissac and his family. In the spacious dining-room with its minstrel-gallery, I have seen the table laid for a dozen people and the butler bringing in the wine-glasses. In every room are lovely things to admire: furniture, pictures, old armour and other objects innumerable, but don't forget to glance out of the windows sometimes: the views across the park and the little river are superb.

The Duke has written an admirable history of Brissac and his family in a full-length book which can be bought at the château. His researches seem to establish that the place derives its name from *Brèchesac*, one of those medieval jokes about millers who, like lawyers, were always assumed to be dishonest. The earliest known building here was certainly a watermill. The present family, one of the oldest warrior families in France, acquired the property in 1502. The new part of the present château was built by Charles de Cossé, the first Duke. A friend of Guise and supporter of the League, he was appointed Governor of Paris in 1594, but seeing the hopelessness of the struggle and sick of the presence of Spanish troops in his capital he opened the gates to Henri IV and so brought the sectarian wars to an end. A few minutes after passing through the Porte Neuve the King, in gratitude, handed his own white scarf to Brissac – a sign that he was conferring on him the dignity of Marshall of France. Soon after, he was made a duke; but he did not build his new château until the early years of the next reign.

In another troubled epoch Louis-Hercule, eighth Duke, was also Governor of Paris – and the last. There is a portrait of him in the drawing-room. Born in 1734, he grew up to be a giant, strong as a lion but a gentle, humane man. His soft-heartedness was so well-known that poor mothers used to leave their babies in his park beside the paths where he usually walked, knowing he would adopt them and bring them up. One typical item in his accounts runs: 'For the little girl of the park: six chemises'. After the death of Louis XV he became Madame du Barry's lover and when in Paris used to slip over almost every day to see her at her château of Louveciennes on the Saint-Germain road. In May 1792 he was arrested and put in solitary confinement at Orléans. On 4 September, with fifty-odd other prisoners in wagons, he was put on the road to Paris. When the convoy reached Versailles on the 9th the September Massacres were just over, but many still thirsted for blood and a mob was waiting in the Rue de l'Orangerie to attack the prisoners, whose guards prudently disappeared. Standing up in the third wagon, Brissac towered above his assailants, wielding a cudgel he had got hold of from somewhere, and knocked down several before they finally despatched him with pikes and swords. They paid him the savage's erstwhile honour to a brave foe by tearing out his heart, which they paraded through the streets. His head they carried on a pike to Louveciennes and hurled it into Madame du Barry's drawing-room. His estates were sequestered, but in 1796, after tedious legal proceedings, the family got them back, a case probably unique in the whole Revolution. Even in the turmoil of those times the executive respected its own laws: Brissac had not emigrated nor ever been convicted of treason, he had simply been murdered.

Before leaving the château, the visitor is given a free glass of one of the local wines, which is a pleasant courtesy; but to study them in more detail one should go to Monsieur Daviau whose *caves* are on the Angers road just outside the village. There were once many windmills at Brissac and the Daviau family have been millers as well as vine-growers there for generations. You taste your wine in the big tower of their old Moulin de Bablut, and the last of the pretty little post-mills survives across the road. We are now in a geological borderland, an overlap of the southern Paris basin of sedimentary rocks, with which we have grown so familiar since we came down on to the open plain, and the outcrops of schist and granite of the Armorican Massif. The resulting mixtures make eight different sorts of soil in the vicinity, and since six different varieties of grapes are grown there are not a few possible permutations in kinds of wine. The one entitled to the local appellation Côteaux de l'Aubance is from the Chenin grape, and as at Vouvray is a great keeper. M. Daviau still has 1921, 1947, 1959 and 1961 for sale. Under the wider Anjou or Loire appellations there are also dry whites from the Chardonnay grape, rosés and reds from the Cabernet and the Gamay. M. Daviau is proudest of the last-named and I think he is right; it is the strongest, most flavoursome, most *parfumé* Gamay you will find anywhere along the Loire – equal of a good Beaujolais Villages. But all M. Daviau's wines are good; he understands his business thoroughly – growing grapes on eight different soils is bound to make a *vigneron* concentrate his mind wonderfully.

From Brissac to Ponts-de-Cé is only six miles.

Let us now follow the northern bank of the river between Saumur and Angers. Our first stop, about five miles from Saumur, is the château of **Boumois** (open every day except Tuesday, 8.30 to noon and 2 to 6.30). Look carefully; it is down a lane and almost hidden among trees. Built at the end of the fifteenth century, its style is principally flamboyant Gothic. The material is the white tufa stone now so familiar to us, but soon to be left behind so let your eyes enjoy its freshness. In the grounds is one of those enormous dove-cotes with a revolving ladder, like the one we saw at Villesavin, save that it has 300 more nesting-holes, a total of 1800. The right to keep doves and pigeons, called *fuye*, was a privilege of the nobility and restricted to one nesting-hole per *arpent* of territory. The *arpent* varied between a half-acre and an acre according to the district. The birds afforded shooting practice (as captive turtle-doves still do in all the Latin countries) and a reserve of meat for the lord's table in the winter. As they were left to sustain themselves on the surrounding countryside the birds were a disguised tax on the peasants, greatly resented and one of the main grievances which induced rural support for the Revolution. Imagine a permanent, protected flock of three and a half thousand pigeons visiting your crops: enough to make a modern farmer die of apoplexy.

Nevertheless the owners of Boumois survived the Revolution by keeping out of politics. The Dupetit-Thouars were a naval family of long standing; indeed still are, though their seat is now near Angers. The owner at the time, Aristide Aubert Dupetit-Thouars, was an admiral under the Directorate and at the age of thirty-eight gave his life for the Republic in outstandingly heroic manner at the Battle of the Nile in 1798. The engagement was nearing its end: Nelson had already disposed of the first seven ships in the French line caught at anchor in Aboukir Bay, among them the *Orient* which had blown up. Suddenly Dupetit-Thouars in the *Tonnant* found himself the centre of the attack. Three or four English ships with nothing else left to do closed in to pound his ship from all directions. The damage was frightful and soon he himself had both his arms and one leg shattered, but he refused to be moved from his quarter-deck and had himself sat in a tub of bran from where he continued to direct the fight as he slowly bled to death. Almost his last order was to nail the colours to the mast. This lovely old château where he was born still contains many mementoes of him and the adventurous life he led in different parts of the world. It is a place of pilgrimage for all who admire a gallant seaman, and the guide informs me that present-day members of the Nelson family are among those who have come to pay their respects.

The old port of **Saint-Martin-de-la-Place** provides a really delightful spot for a lazy afternoon. Its immense slipway is there still, with a bit of quay and a few fishing-punts, but the rest is just grass and trees and, being outside the village, usually deserted. The view across the river is to Chênehutte.

On the way into **Les Rosiers** we pass a two-star camp-site of just over two acres in meadows by the river. Les Rosiers is the best place to do your shopping between Saumur and Angers on either side of the river. There is a particularly good *poissonnerie* in the corner of the square which in season sells locally-caught river fish, including shad. On the other side of the square is a good hotel, the Au Val de Loire, reasonably priced and with a very good restaurant open to all.

Between Les Rosiers and Angers there is a series of very pretty little towns and villages strung out along the river-bank. **La Menitré**, which has a nice meadow camp-site, was once the port of Saint-Maur across the river. This arrangement occurred often where one shore was more convenient for mooring or on a more important road, and in the days of plenty of boats opposite settlements were in much more immediate touch than they are now. Next comes **Saint-Mathurin**, whose surprising Classical church has a west-front portico on columns and is of a vastness testifying to the prosperity of these river ports in former times. The shops here are very good, and the waterfront at the downstream end of the town has a façade of sixteenth- to eighteenth-century houses reminiscent of the ancient river ports of East Anglia. A couple of miles beyond the town, if you look out carefully on the left, you will find a run-down to a big old stone quay, quite solitary but still maintained and still used by fishermen for their punts and on Sundays by pleasure-boats, for it retains its big slipway. The view from this quay across a sweeping bend down to **Bohalle** with its round island in midstream is incomparable in grandeur, especially at sunset.

After Bohalle comes **Daguenière**, rather nondescript after its neighbours, and then a left fork gives us the minor road which runs alongside the Loire on the long alluvial spit between it and the sluggish Authion – just one magnificent meadow of rich grass, grazed by cattle and studded with groups of little trees. This brings us to **Ponts-de-Cé** where the Loire divides into three arms, the south arm in fact staying separate for twenty more miles and thereby earning itself a name of its own: the Louet. In the town a bridge crosses all three channels. The Ile-de-Bourg, between the first and second, has a sturdy octagonal tower at one end, remains of one of King René's castles and in 1793 scene of one of the bloody battles of the War of the Vendée. On the next island, on its highest point, stands the church of Saint-Mauville. Turn up one of the side-streets towards it and you will see the black shale rock sticking out of the footings of the houses on to the pavement. The Loire has now left the Vale of Anjou, the last of the Cretacean plain, and for the remaining eighty miles to the sea is obliged to make a channel through the older rocks of Armorica which are similar to those of Devon and Cornwall. No more sandy margins for mile after mile; no more narrow *luisettes* in summer that you could almost paddle across; no more white tufa cliffs. Its character changes, and we have come to the end of that extensive and more or less homogeneous region known as the Val de Loire. The old Loire *mariniers* recognized this division in a verse in praise of the Val in their favourite song:

> *De Saint-Thibault aux Ponts-de-Cé*
> *Une grande distance,*
> *Saumur, Châteauneuf et Chouzé,*
> *Le plus beau pays de France.*

A few names there of pleasant recollection in our own voyage. The rest of it will be *beau* too, though different.

CHAPTER SIXTEEN

Angers to Ingrandes

❧

Before plunging into Angers, which is but a couple of miles ahead from Ponts-de-Cé, some might like to make a short detour to the slate-mining villages of **Trélazé** and **Saint-Barthélemy** to the east of the city. All those slated châteaux we have seen, not to mention the countless houses similarly covered; all those Mansard roofs and the slated church spires such a feature of France. Where do the slates come from? More likely than not from here, for the rich vein of slate in the two miles between those villages accounts for seventy-five per cent of production in the whole country. The mines go back to the twelfth century at least and are nowhere near exhausted, though nowadays the material has to be brought up from galleries a thousand feet deep. A visit to a mining area may seem an odd thing to recommend to readers bent on pleasure, but in fact the landscape has a quiet beauty and a haunting air of antiquity. Everywhere are pastures enclosed by low walls built of dark slates laid flat rather in the manner of the drystone hedges of the north of England; alternating with these are little woods and copses and, sticking above the verdure here and there on a rise of ground, the winding-gear of a mine. Take one of the old green lanes that lead in amongst the ancient worked-out quarries and you find yourself in a lost, forgotten world: deep pits of open-cast and heaps of reject shale half-hidden by wild copses of silver-birch, poplar and aspen from which the nightingale sings. A land broken and exploited; yet in the long run no harm has been done, for Nature has transformed it into a beautiful wilderness. And even the two villages, right in the midst of the modern mining with shale-heaps on their outskirts and winding-gear on their skylines, are clean, prosperous-looking and rural in atmosphere.

The simplest approach to **Angers** is in fact from the south-east because either the Trélazé or the Ponts-de-Cé road will lead straight up to the castle, which you can hardly miss and will undoubtedly wish to visit. There is parking along the north side of it – where its only entrance is – or, failing that, meter parking beside the cathedral which is not far to the north-east through one or other of the side-streets.

Angers is the third biggest of the Loire towns (after Saint-Étienne and Nantes) with a population of 200,000. Once a considerable port, being situated on a junction of rivers where small ocean-going ships can reach it from the sea, it lies not on the Loire itself, but on the Maine five miles upstream of its confluence with the Loire. The Maine is only six miles long, being really the common mouth of the Mayenne, the Sarthe and the Loir which converge just north of the city. Having risen, all three, in the low hills just south of Normandy and wandered unhurriedly to drain the huge catchment area of Maine and the Beauce, they bring the Loire an immense quantity of water all at once and are the only major right-bank tributaries in its whole course. The Mayenne itself is navigable for seventy miles or more up to the town of Mayenne and the Sarthe for about sixty miles up to Le Mans. But the railways took away the importance of such factors and the commercial river-traffic of Angers is now negligible.

Fifteen years after Philippe-Auguste had confiscated Anjou from John Lackland, his grandson Saint Louis began to rebuild Foulques Nera's wooden castle in solid stone as a precaution against a return of the English and it was finished in 1240. He was only a young man and had not yet been to Palestine, but he knew of the style of the Crusaders' castles there and he chose it as his pattern for Angers. From the outside it still retains that aspect more than any other castle in central France. Seventeen hefty bastion towers are arranged in an irregular pentagon pattern and connected by a high curtain wall, and to the awesomeness of the building's massive strength a bizarre touch is added by zebra masonry of alternating courses of black shale and white limestone. The towers now vary in height between 125 and 185 feet, but to picture the fortress as it was imagine two more storeys on each of them. Its dry moat on the north and east sides, where medieval kings and dukes kept monkeys, leopards and lions, is now the home of a small herd of fallow deer. The entrance is over the drawbridge crossing the moat, and the castle is open every day for interior visits from 9.30 to noon and 2 to 6 (7 from 1 June to 20 September; 5 after then until Easter). The first part of the visit is guided and comprises the one surviving wing of the fifteenth-century *Logis Royal* which Louis II of Anjou had built for himself and, joined on to it, the chapel which his wife Yolande had built as she did not consider the earlier one good enough. Louis and Yolande were the father and mother of Duke René. The chapel is a graceful building entirely in white tufa stone. It was used as a prison for English sailors in the Napoleonic wars.

People interested in tapestry could hardly come to a better place than Angers; it has many fine specimens as we shall see. But the most important is here at the château. The famous *Tenture de l'Apocalypse*, 110 yards long, is one of the finest anywhere and is exhibited in a spacious gallery specially built for it. There is no guide here, but on entering you can hire a personal taped commentary, in the language of your choice, lasting half an hour, and carry it round with you. To some this may be a help, to others a distraction. One can do without, for Saint John wrote the theme and the relevant verse in Revelations is quoted (though in French) in the window-bay opposite each piece. The essential thing, anyway, is to observe the quality of the work itself, the depth of feeling, the pathos, in the figures and faces and the beauty of line like the crispness of a sculptured frieze; all achieved without labouring the technique, some five stitches to the square centimetre instead of the usual ten or more conveying all that is desired. It was made between 1373 and 1380 for Louis I of Anjou in the Parisian workshops of Nicolas Bataille to the design of Hennequin de Bruges, whose cartoons are still preserved at the Bibliothèque Nationale. Duke René, Louis's grandson, bequeathed it to Angers Cathedral. At the Revolution it was thrown out into the streets and local citizens helped themselves to cuts of it, to use for carpets, bedspreads, horse-blankets and even cart-covers. In 1843 the Bishop started a search and bought back all he could trace, recovering in the end some two-thirds of the original 180 yards. Nothing much has come to light since except two pieces which are in a Glasgow museum.

If you have any time left you can cross the big courtyard, now laid out as gardens, to the eighteenth-century Governor's Lodge where there are some more tapestries on show, smaller works, the most pleasing being *La Dame à l'Orgue*, said to have been made locally in the sixteenth century, and two scenes of the same period from Audenarde depicting animals, birds and plants – a subject which lends itself to tapestry and yet was too rarely taken advantage of in the Middle Ages.

South of the castle, in the middle of the wide cross-roads, stands a big statue of Duke René by the sculptor David of Angers, of whom more later; but there is little opportunity of studying it closely in the constant stream of traffic roaring up and down the boulevard. The **Church of Saint Laud** stands in the bottom of the square. A good-looking example of late-Gothic architecture, it was unaccountably left a long time in a state of worsening dilapidation until its curé in the 1930s had it restored. In the side-chapel off the south aisle there is a white marble statue of the Virgin which Catherine de Médicis thought so beautiful when she saw it during a stay in Angers that she wanted to buy it for the Louvre. The canons, who must have been remarkably strong-willed men to resist her, refused to let it go and the affair is commemorated in a stained-glass window above it. At the Revolution it was broken in two. Nothing unusual in that! But a most refreshing joke of that time concerns Père Étienne Bernier, the non-juring parish priest of Saint Laud. He carried on undismayed amid all the usual blandishments, and when finally obliged to hand over to a 'Constitutional' priest he securely sewed up the hems of all the vestments so his successor couldn't get into them. The parish has recently bought itself a fine new organ and some good recitals are given here from time to time.

Our sally across the busy boulevard was however a diversion, since everything else of interest lies to the north of it. Let us begin with the **Cathédrale Saint-Maurice**. By strolling down the side-street opposite the castle entrance to the Rue Saint-Maurice we come face to face with it at the end of a long and gentle flight of steps. None of the cathedrals along the Loire is in the exceptional class of Chartres, say, or Rouen, but they are certainly all very individual and Angers's chief characteristic is perhaps its straight clean outline. The façade is late Romanesque surmounted by three towers, the middle one of which, the octagonal belfry, is much older than the others and does admittedly look slightly out of character. The outer pair have slender spires, that on the north being a fraction higher than its companion as at Tours. Over the west door is a very beautiful tympanum showing Christ in risen glory. The faces of the many saints and Biblical characters under the arch, their attention fixed on the throne in rapturous wonder, are a remarkable portrayal of the highest emotions: each one is individual and radiates adoration in its own individual way. Above the door, halfway up the building, a frieze of equal skill and beauty depicts Saint Maurice and his 'Companions'. Each figure is clad in a different medieval military costume, and a Latin inscription above says: 'Give peace in our time, O Lord, and scatter the nations who desire war,' a petition as apt in our own day as it was in the reign of Diocletian when Saint Maurice was an officer in the Theban Legion, an élite corps recruited in the Eastern Empire. Ordered to attack a Christian settlement (in Gaul some accounts say) and exterminate the inhabitants, they refused to a man, so the Emperor had one in every ten put to the sword. In spite of this the others refused to obey the unjust order and were decimated again – and again and again until none was left.

So exquisite are the sculptures on the west front that it is well worth taking your binoculars, to be able to appreciate them to the full. On going inside you will be equally glad to be so armed, for this cathedral, like Tours, has been fortunate enough to be spared its original stained-glass windows. It was untouched by the 1944 bombing; though, with the whole town, it had a narrow escape for the Germans were using the castle as a main arsenal. Fortunately they managed, with a desperate effort, to move everything out before the RAF arrived and scored several direct hits on the castle. The cathedral interior is unusually simple, having a long nave without aisles, triforium or clerestory. It is unusual too in having been built from west to east, the nave being completed in 1162, the choir in 1240 and the apse in the late 1200s. The stained-glass windows range from the thirteenth century to the twentieth. As there are some two dozen medieval ones alone there is no room to catalogue them here; but the oldest ones are in the north of the nave and of those I cannot help selecting for mention the one illustrating the martyrdom of Saint Vincent, the patron saint of vine-growers. It is the left-hand of the pair over the pulpit on the north side of the nave. Saint Vincent suffered in AD 304, almost the same time as Saint Maurice. Under Dacien's persecution in Spain he was arrested with his bishop. The latter got off lightly with banishment, but poor Saint Vincent, a simple deacon, was subjected to a death just about as excruciating as the human brain, ingenious as it is in such matters, could devise. He was first flayed, then grilled and, while still alive, laid on the floor of his cell after it had been spread with broken glass.

I do not recommend a long stroll round the streets of Angers: the countryside of Anjou is more worthy of what time one has to spare than its capital. There are some good shops of course, but the old streets have not been preserved as in other big towns we have visited. Its very old nickname 'Black Angers', alluding to the local shale rock and slate of which it is built, is rather too severe; it is not as black as that, and certainly not in the sense of being grubby. What has spoilt it is the enthusiasm with which so much of it was pulled down in the last century and 'transformed', as the Baedeker of the period unctuously puts it, 'with numerous large edifices'. As will be the case with many of the large edifices of today, they don't look so good after a hundred years. The best example of the sort of house replaced by the transformers' zeal is the **Maison d'Adam** in the Place-Sainte-Croix behind the cathedral, half-timbered with five overhanging storeys, the timbers all wonderfully carved with trees, waggons, animals, birds, lovers and other features of ordinary life. There are a few lesser examples not far away in the Rues Montault, de l'Oisellerie, and Saint-Laud, but there is no distinct old quarter such as we found in Tours, Blois and Orléans. Henry James was exaggerating only slightly when he wrote that Angers had been 'stupidly and vulgarly modernized'.

So let us leave the Place-Sainte-Croix by its south side, the Rue Toussaint, and turn left into the Rue du Musée. There, near the conspicuous Tour Saint-Aubin, we find the **Logis Barrault**, a big old Renaissance palace, now an art museum of exceptional interest and quality. It is open every day except Tuesday from 9 to noon and 2 to 6; and on Tuesday as well between 15 June and 15 September. The ground floor is the sculpture section where one is agreeably startled to find pieces by Rodin, Corot and Houdin, the latter's works including Mirabeau, Benjamin Franklin, Voltaire and a pair of expressive hands – Voltaire's. Then comes the David Room. Not to be confused with his contemporary the painter, Pierre Jean David was a sculptor who ranks equally with the others just mentioned. Born in 1788 the son of a woodcarver of Angers, he first went to school in the city and was later apprenticed to the sculptor Roland in Paris. Before he died at the age of sixty-eight he had designed the front of the Panthéon in the capital, created 55 statues (mostly of colossal size), 150 busts and innumerable bas-reliefs and medallions. A great proportion of his work has been assembled permanently here in the room where he first learnt the rudiments of art. It is a major exhibition of sculpture not to be missed. There are statues and busts of Paganini, Goethe, Fénelon, Lamartine, Chateaubriand, Balzac and other famous people, not all from life of course, since not all were his contemporaries; but he knew how to capture in imagination the personality of an historical figure: Jean Bart for example, about ten times life-size at the end of the room, in seaboots astride a cannon, looking every inch a pirate – which he was, and such an able one that Louis XIV took him into the navy. He raided Plymouth in 1689 and was taken prisoner there, but three years later he escaped and, immediately back at sea, burnt eighty English and Dutch ships at Dunkirk.

The next floor is devoted to ecclesiastical treasures: lovely old chests, statues, ancient croziers and suchlike. On the second floor, devoted entirely to paintings, an enormous allegorical *Meeting of the Arts* greets you; and that is characteristic of the quality of the works to follow. In two very long galleries pictures by Mignard, Champaigne, Fragonard, Corot, Jongkind and even Romney and the Dutch master Abraham Storck are displayed – and for the most part well displayed, though I was sorry to see two of Clouet's exquisite little miniatures (of Catherine de Médicis and Charles IX) tucked obscurely in a corner of the left-hand gallery. Don't miss them. As a court painter surely he was never excelled.

The quays of Angers are neither beautiful nor interesting; fast highways run beside them and their maritime trade has departed. Two bridges, the Haute-Chaine and the Basse-Chaine, lead across to the other half of the city, La Doutre (d'outre, i.e. 'beyond' the river). The Maine is not wide considering it combines three big rivers, but it is quiet and deep. The unusual nomenclature of the bridges derives from the practice in former times of stretching two heavy chains across the river at each end of the town to check waterborne invaders and to facilitate collection of tolls. It has nothing to do with the coincidence that the Basse Chaine (the one near the castle) was formerly a suspension bridge held up by chains. On 16 April 1850 a battalion of infantry was in the act of crossing it when the combined effect of a high wind and harmonics set up by the synchronized tread of the marchers caused the chains to snap and nearly five hundred soldiers fell into the river. Encumbered with full accoutrements, many clutched at one another in the sudden panic and 223 of them were drowned. The modern bridge looks safe enough, if not very elegant, so let us cross by it and turn right into the fine long boulevard lined with tall plane trees in whose tops a busy rookery is usually astir with the flapping of black wings and chatter of raucous voices. Between the trees, as we drive along, glimpses of the hefty castle show, and of the strikingly unusual cathedral front on top of the hill on the other side.

Straight up the boulevard leads to the former **Hôpital de Saint Jean** (open every day from 9 to noon and 2 to 7 from 1 April to 15 September; rest of the year 10 to noon and 2 to 5 and closed on Tuesdays). This is a rare opportunity to see a medieval hospital more or less as it was originally, and some may be agreeably surprised; especially those who think no one bothered about such things in those days. It was founded in 1175 by Henry II of England (as part of his penance for the murder of Becket) and completed in 1210. The vast main ward, airy and light with graceful Angevin vaulting, accommodated 250 beds in cubicles – women down one side, men down the other – and separate wards for the aged and infirm and for maternity cases brought the total of beds to 360; in emergencies 500 patients could be catered for. The establishment was run by friars and nuns and under a Constitution approved by the Pope in 1267 it was laid down that it should be open to all in need, 'of whatever race and whatever religion they may be'. Later it was put under municipal control and the beginning of the end came in 1720 when the administrators tried to increase its endowments by investing them in the notorious Compagnie des Indes.

In a corner of the *Grande Salle* stands a seventeenth-century apothecary's dispensary with a complete set of herb-jars in decorated *faïence*; and round the walls another marathon tapestry, the famous *Chant du Monde* in sections totalling eighty-six yards, made for the municipal council of Angers at Gobelins to the design of Jean Lurçat. It took nine years to weave and was completed in 1966. Lurçat has stated that he was inspired by the Apocalypse tapestry at the cathedral and the desire to do something even better from the atheist-humanist point of view. It is a fantasia of colours made to scintillate in swirling explosive designs against a background of sombre black, and he has afforded in his humanist poem of symbolic images an interesting comparison with the directness of the older work from an age of religious faith. To me it seems a mere riot of modernist platitudes in a disordered dream. The first four panels depict a macabre, but also slightly comic, *End of the World* and the rest a sugary humanist paradise 'from two divergent sources: streams of mud and streams of light' (I use his own words) entitled *Man in Glory and in Peace*, in which the highest hope held out for us is the conquest of outer space. But all this is not to deny its merit as a work of art well worth coming to see, and some may find deeper meaning in it than I have been able to do.

This side of the city is the university quarter. Originally of course the university was in the centre near the cathedral, for it is of great antiquity, claiming to be one of the oldest in Europe, older even than Paris. Certainly there was a school of philosophy here in the tenth century at which Saint Bruno, founder of the Carthusian Order, was probably a pupil, but it was not officially recognized as a university until 1364.

To continue our journey from Angers let us cross the river to Ponts-de-Cé again and take the road out for **Rochefort**, where we find ourselves once more beside the Louet just before it spreads out into marsh and rejoins the Loire. The village has retained a considerable air of antiquity with its old turreted houses, the ruins of a castle on a granite crest across the river and a big church (more like a small cathedral) which is Romanesque in origin and built of granite but lately restored in white tufa. The camper who looked in vain for a place to rest in Angers will find one here: a two-star camp-site over the bridge with a pleasant safe beach beside it.

Two miles south of Rochefort, on the right of the Beaulieu road, at the château on the outskirts of **La Guimonnière**, another wine is to be encountered, and an interesting one as it is the only really sweet wine of the Loire, in the tradition of the ancient wines of Anjou, in fact, which used to delight the English and the Dutch. The appellation is Côteaux du Layon, the Layon being a small tributary of the Loire which winds and twists its way among steep narrow valleys and granite hills with streams and waterfalls in a landscape which has a Welsh look about it, not surprisingly since the geology is the same. The best wine of this appellation is the Quarts de Chaume which Monsieur Doucet produces and sells at the old château. It is well-known and justly famous in countries where connoisseurs of sweet wines still survive in large numbers. Most of it is exported to the United States, Holland, Belgium and Germany, and M. Doucet does not have many English visitors. The *cépage* is the wonderful Pinot de la Loire (the Chenin) again and the soil is schist with sand and a small amount of clay. There are other places in the locality where the clay is too abundant, producing a wine rather dull and heavy, but the Quarts de Chaume is perfectly balanced and improves with age up to about twenty years. Indeed it should be left for ten years anyway, if possible, to mature. You won't get a 1969 – the Americans took the lot. And the equally good vintages of '75 and '76 are disappearing in the same direction.

For those who can spare the time, a short detour to the north brings us to an exquisite island, an important vineyard and a splendid château. Across the Louet from Rochefort and a drive of about a mile brings us back to the Loire and the bridge over to **Béhuard** (pronounced *Buard* locally), an island some two miles long and plumb in the middle of the river. I think perhaps this is the most beautiful of the Loire's inhabited islands, an 'emerald isle' indeed, of pastures, orchards and grazing cattle. A drive right round it (better still a walk) is well worth the time it takes: you have a feeling of being in another world, a little utopia of quiet peace and modest plenty. But for the inhabitants these blessings are tempered by a constant anxiety: their paradise is subject to sudden floods. A life-time may go by without, but the fear is always there. The last serious inundation was in 1910 when the ground-floors of their houses were under water.

The village stands in the middle of the island and is of considerable antiquity. A long way back, in pre-Christian times, there was a shrine here to a river-god where boatmen would stop to offer propitiation or thanks for deliverance from the dangers of their journey. Later a Bishop of Angers replaced the idol with a statue of the Virgin and a Breton knight named Buhard (hence the pronunciation of the island's name) built a chapel for it. Later still that indefatigable devotee of Our Lady, Louis XI, paid several visits and had the present church built in its stead. He used to lodge in the chaplain's house at the side of it, and that also survives. The tiny church is built on to a spur of rock and its north wall is the rock-face itself, for the aisle, set at right-angles to the diminutive nave, is a cavern cut out of the living stone. On one side of the church a quiet lane leads down to a magnificent sweep of river; on the other stands the village square and a very popular restaurant – 'Aux Rocher' – whose quality and reasonableness are such that even a few knowing *routiers* make a detour from the high road to have their lunch there. From the windows one looks across the square at the extraordinary phenomenon of the spur of granite jutting up from the ground and the church jigsawed into its convolutions. There is a riverside camp-site on Béhuard twenty-four acres in extent. Also on the south side at the upstream end of the island there is a nice deserted beach for the picnicker – the swimmer too if he is very careful. Although the Loire has only fifty-five feet now to drop in altitude before reaching the sea, it still has strong swirling currents in unexpected places.

Over the water from the north side of Béhuard, on the right bank of the river, you can see a château on a high hill, from which vines seem to cascade down the steep south-facing slopes. Those are the vineyards of the last, the noblest and the rarest of the Loire's six best wines; so of course we must go there. Cross over to the village of **Savennières**, which gives its name to a general apellation for a white wine from the Chenin grape, resembling a Vouvray though slightly drier. The area is not of great extent and the wine is very good, but the vineyard we saw from the island is of such high quality that the use of its own name is permitted – Coulée de Serrant. To find it, drive out of Savennières on the Angers road and after just under a mile look out for a sign indicating the right turn (a mere lane, easily missed) for the **Château de la Roche-aux-Moines**. At the time of the final struggle between the Capetians and the Plantagenets a strong fortress stood on this hill which in July 1214 King John of England unwisely chose to besiege in person. Prince Louis (later Louis VIII, and like our Richard nicknamed Coeur-de-Lion) came to its relief and soundly defeated him. At the same time his father, Philippe-Auguste, was on his way to meet John's ally the German

Emperor and defeat him a few days later at the battle of Bouvines in Flanders. This double disaster was the ignominious end of English power in France and Anjou was lost for ever.

Visitors wishing to purchase a bottle or two of the wine are welcome at the château at any reasonable hour and given *dégustation*. It is a family concern and everything is quite informal; unless they are very busy someone can usually be found to take you along the causeway to the end of the promontory where you can look down on to the vines, covering the steep sides of a cleft in the hill with a little stream – the *coulée* – running in the bottom. Just up the valley, solitary and timeless, stands the old twelfth-century monastery whose monks planted its first vines and after whom the rock is named. The vineyards, only seventeen acres in extent, are on ground about the steepest you ever saw under cultivation, too steep for tractors; even some horses won't take the slope – and not many men. So young Monsieur Joly has given up an interesting business career to come home and cherish this precious family possession himself. Precious because everything is at optimum: the slopes are exposed to the sun from dawn to dusk and the thin topsoil allows the roots to get quickly down to the underlying schist. Schist is porous, so even in drought years they get their moisture; but, more important, it imparts a perfume to the wine and a delicacy which surpass those of any other wine along the Loire. Indeed a leading French wine expert, Monsieur Brejoux, has gone further than my limited experience permits and proclaimed it one of the five top wines in France. Even at the price of little more than twice that of Vouvray it is really worth taking a few bottles home and it travels well and improves with age.

The château of **Serrant** – nothing to do with the wine although common ownership of both domains long ago gave the stream its name – is six miles or so to the north near the small town of Saint-Georges. A magnificent moated country house of the sixteenth-century designed by Delorme, architect of the Tuileries, with a chapel designed in the following century by Hardouin-Mansard, it is open to visitors every day except Tuesdays from 9 to noon and 2 to 6 between 1 April and 31 October. In 1749 it was acquired by Francis Walsh, scion of one of the Irish Jacobite families (the 'Wild Geese') who settled in France after the 1688 *coup* of William III. Like so many of them, the Walshes had made a fortune in commerce at Nantes. Francis's son, Antoine, had supplied the frigate *La Doutelle* which carried Bonnie Prince Charlie across the sea to Scotland in 1745, and there is a big painting in the library showing

Charles Edward on the Scottish shore bidding farewell to Walsh before the latter re-embarks for France. It is more or less contemporary and attached to the frame are the carved arms of England which adorned the poop of *La Doutelle* for the occasion. The château stands in a glorious park with many fine cedars and horse-chestnut trees.

If you make the detour to visit Serrant it is still best to return to the south side of the Loire at Rochefort to continue the journey, for the road westwards from there, called the *Corniche Angevin*, is cut high in the side of a granite cliff and gives fascinating views across a wide sweep of country. The Louet ambles through its marshes immediately below and behind us the ruined castle of Rochefort looks stark on its spur of rock while Angers makes a lump on the distant horizon. Down the valley ahead, Ingrandes stands out clearly on a bend of the Loire. Descending the *corniche*, we come into **Chalonnes** where the Louet rejoins the Loire on the eastern outskirts and the Layon flows in too not many yards away. The view of this small town on approaching is quite picturesque; the church is right on the water's edge and has a graceful, slender spire, and along the quays punts, launches and motor-cruisers are moored. The town bridge leads out over a string of islands extending upstream for a mile and downstream for another five. Below Ponts-de-Cé the Loire has this tendency more and more to split into several channels, some retaining the fast current so that the others, the *boires*, can afford to be slow and lazy.

The bridge takes us to the right bank where the minor road hugs the main channel until you come to the next bridge and cross back to **Montjean**, a little waterfront town squeezed with its back to a high hill which is crowned with an immense church, testimony to its former prosperity. Until the First World War it was a port of some consequence, a terminal for ships which were too big to get up as far as Angers, and almost the entire male population were seamen or stevedores. Those times are past; but even now dredgers are busy all day keeping the channel clear for quite sizable oil-tankers of the Compagnie Pétrole de l'Ouest bringing oil up from the refineries at Nantes, and a large proportion of the men in the town have punts in which they make short trips before and after the day's work to attend their eel-traps and other devices for bigger quarry not quite perhaps within the law.

From here it is on the south side that a minor road hugs the bank, looking down from the *levée* directly to the deep, wide river, already beginning to have something of the appearance of an estuary although it is not yet tidal. After only three miles we reach **Ingrandes,** the beauty of whose waterfront is best appreciated as you cross the bridge. It differs from most in that the buildings go right to the water's edge, with gaps and slipways in between instead of the usual long quays. This attractive little place, very convenient for shopping, is the last town on the right bank in Anjou. Beyond lies Brittany, once almost a foreign land, and still distinctive in its landscape and its more pronouncedly Celtic people. But we shall be a little longer in Anjou, for yet again we must re-cross the Loire to continue our journey.

CHAPTER SEVENTEEN

Saint-Florent to the Sea

❧

The road from Ingrandes along the left bank stays close to the river at first and affords tantalizing views across to the lovely Ile Melet with its meadows and deserted farmhouses among trees. Ahead of us, on top of a high hill more striking even than Montjean, is **Saint-Florent-le-Vieil**. On reaching it, carry right on to the top where there is a spacious square outside the church, overlooking the river which is divided into two channels by the Ile Batailleuse. The tankers from Nantes take the south channel nearest to us, and such is our vantage-point that we look almost straight down on to their decks and they seem like toys.

We have already met Saint Florent on the tapestries in the Church of Saint-Pierre at Saumur. Born in Bavaria beside the Danube, he ended his days beside the Loire on this hill, then called Glonne, a Gaulish name in fact meaning 'by the river'. Like Saint Martin of Tours, he was an old soldier of the Imperial Army, and it was Saint Martin who ordained him after his escape from martyrdom and sent him here as one of his missionaries. Emulating the system at Marmoutiers, he used the hillside caves as lodgings for himself and his small party of monks. After many years he died here – at the ripe age of 123 by some accounts – and eventually his work was completed by a successor, Saint Mauron, who built a church and established a Benedictine monastery on the site. Saint Mauron had made a rather lazy start however, according to a legend which relates that he fell asleep for a hundred years, a bird coming every day to the mouth of his cave and singing the same song until he woke up.

Later still, when all was going well and a newer and better abbey had been built, the monks looked down on to the river one autumn morning in 852 to see a small flotilla of strange-looking craft, long and sleek with dragons' heads on their raised prows, nosing round and taking soundings – a reconnaissance party under Cidroc from the Viking base in the estuary. With a feeling this boded trouble to come, the monks packed up what they could and fled before the year

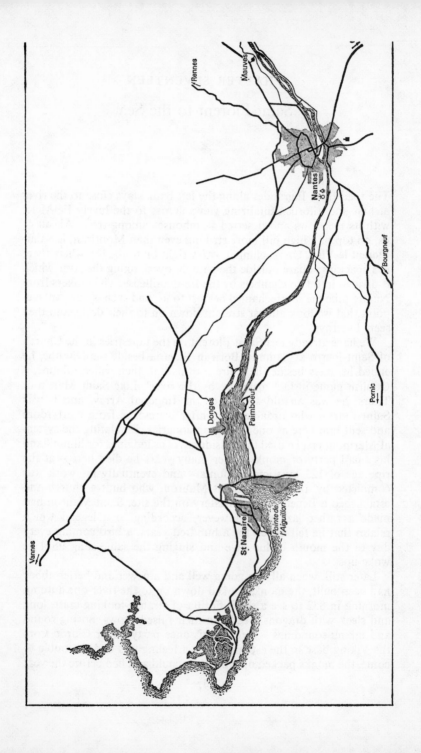

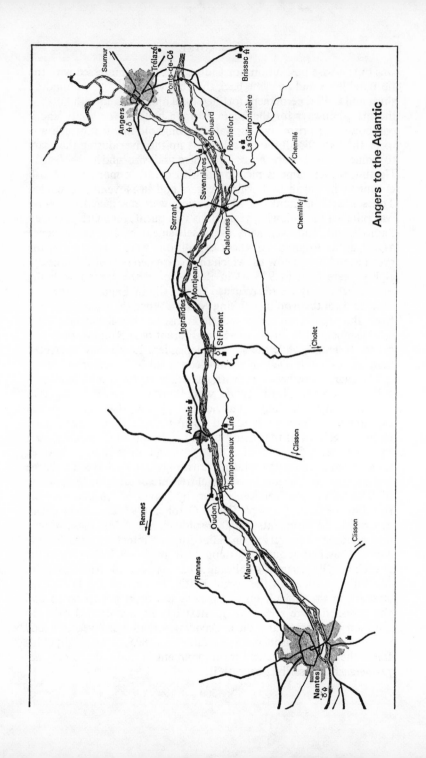

Angers to the Atlantic

was out: a wise precaution, for Cidroc was most impressed with the Ile Batailleuse and he came back the next year with over a hundred ships and built a permanent fortified base on the island with huts for the men, slipways for the boats, storage hangars for booty and a compound for prisoners – a pirates' stronghold in effect, which was to be the base for all the terrible raids up the river during the years to come. Joined there by a force of equal size under the fearful Hasting whose name is mentioned with dread in many a monkish chronicle, he began by burning Angers and in November occupied Tours where the monks of Marmoutiers were massacred. Amboise was pillaged the following year; Blois was burnt; then Orléans; then Saint-Benoît, and eventually every settlement of any consequence as far up as Roanne. All these expeditions were fitted out on the green island here below us, which the Norsemen occupied for nearly eighty years until in 936 Alain Barbe-Torte, the Breton with the magnificent curly beard, returned from exile in England, raised an army and cut them off by retaking Nantes. When the monks returned from Burgundy their abbey was in ruins, so they fixed their main establishment at Saint-Hilaire-Saint-Florent near Saumur, therefore called 'le Jeune' while the smaller dependent house they re-erected here was called 'le Vieil' in acknowledgement of its seniority.

The **church** now beside us, with an octagonal tower and handsome galleried porch in Classical style, was rebuilt in the early 1700s. Two contemporary texts imply, but not too plainly, that Mansard was the architect. Certainly it is well up to his standard, an unusually elegant specimen of the period to find right out in the country in a small village. A fine collection of statues and other church treasures is exhibited in the crypt, which is trustingly left open free of charge and unguarded. The most wonderful treasure of all is the huge statue of Bonchamps, the Vendéen leader, by David of Angers, over his tomb in the north transept. On 18 October 1793, after their defeat at Cholet, the insurgents – 80,000 soldiers, priests, old men, women and children – converged on Saint-Florent intent on crossing the Loire. They had about 4000 Republican prisoners locked up in the church and Bonchamps's colleagues had decided to massacre them. Mortally wounded in the recent battle, he exerted the last of his strength in the difficult task of persuading them not to do so and the prisoners were released. The next day he was carried over the river on a stretcher and died. David was then a five-year-old boy and one of those prisoners was his father. In 1825, at the height of his fame, the sculptor executed this monument in gratitude. '*Grâce aux prisonniers*' is inscribed beneath it.

It was here in this commune, incidentally, that the War of the Vendée had started when the local peasants refused conscription to fight on the Eastern Frontier and fought off the troops of the Convention sent to enforce it. In the hamlet of **La Baronnière** three miles south of here stood Bonchamps's château from which he marched forth to fight on 14 March, just seven months before his death. The Republicans burnt it down soon after and it has been replaced with a nineteenth-century structure; but the old castle bakery still subsists, and there you may absorb something of the ambience of those last days of the old order while tasting a very good Gamay of the Côteaux d'Ancenis produced by Monsieur Loïc de Bodard from his own vineyards. It is inexpensive for its high quality as this is a V.D.Q.S. and not a full A.C. region, except for the famous Muscadet which we shall be tasting later.

The hillside now moves away from the river which becomes a broad sweep between two banks and strewn with many islands. The main road moves away too, though you can turn off it at Bouzillé and regain the shore to follow it the last three miles to **Ancenis**. The town lies across the water, and on shields high up in the gantries of its long and very impressive suspension bridge are displayed the arms of Anjou at one end and of Brittany at the other, a reminder that the river is still the boundary. There is nothing of outstanding interest in the town itself: its ancient narrow streets have a certain charm, but this is greatly impaired by the constant stream of main-road traffic passing through them; almost without respite they are filled with noise. The river on the other hand is wide and deep, bordered by expanses of fine sand which gleams a dazzling white when the sun shines, and the tides from the Atlantic fifty miles away begin to produce a noticeable rise and fall in its level.

As I mentioned earlier in this chapter we are now in the region of the Muscadet wine, one which has justifiably increased in popularity in Britain in recent years. It extends over a vast area on both sides of the Loire nearly to its mouth in a series of complicated overlapping appellations: Côteaux d'Ancenis, Muscadet-Sèvre-et-Maine and Muscadet-Côteaux-de-la-Loire. These are all virtually the same: a decidedly dry white wine, crisp and refreshing, but lacking the *finesse* of the Pouilly-Fumée or the Sancerre which are its nearest comparisons along the Loire. It is grown for preference on pebbly schist soil and the *cépage*, locally named Muscadet, is the Melon of the Jura slopes and of Burgundy from where it was introduced. For the benefit of readers who may not wish to extend their wanderings as far down as Nantes and beyond I deal with it here because at **Saint-**

Géréon, a village on the north-western outskirts of Ancenis (on the right here, just before the church), you will find the *caves* of Monsieur René Bossard where you can sample it and buy it retail. There are usually a few trade callers there too, in no hurry to depart as they enjoy a drink and a chat with the *patron* or his wife, so the atmosphere is extremely jolly and you can soon find yourself involved in a pleasant discussion on wine in general. M. Bossard's wines are all from his own vineyards and he won the Paris Gold Medal with his Muscadet in 1973. It is *tiré sur lie*, which means that the skins are left in the wine right up to the time of bottling, a procedure which suits the Muscadet, accentuating its distinctively crisp flavour. He also produces a good red from the Gamay and another interesting dry white, the Gros Plant, of the same character as the Muscadet but always only V.D.Q.S. Many French people are beginning to prefer it, saying it is less acid and fruitier in flavour. But I do not find the Muscadet at all acid anyway; the choice is a matter of personal idiosyncracy and the only thing is to taste and compare them: M. Bossard is ever ready to refill your glass and likes to see people take an interest.

Only two miles south of Ancenis the village of **Liré** merits a brief stop by devotees of French poetry for it was the boyhood home of Joachim du Bellay, the greatest after Ronsard of the sixteenth-century group of poets known as *la Pléiade*. He was born about 1524 at the château of La Turmelière just outside the village, but nothing remains of it: the present ruins are those of a later construction. In a house opposite the church in Liré however there is a little local **museum** containing various small mementoes of him and of his family who had bought the domain only a decade or so before he was born. Among them are photocopies of letters in his handwriting (the originals are in the archives at Nantes), but no original manuscripts of his poems have survived anywhere. The museum is open every day from 9.30 to noon and 2.30 to 6. The old house is about contemporary with Joachim and belonged to his family, but he never lived in it as some of the misleading tourist literature would have one suppose. It has the interesting distinction though of being the only house in Liré to have survived the War of the Vendée; the whole of the rest of the village was razed in the course of fighting.

Joachim is sometimes called 'the French Ovid' or 'the Prince of Sonnets'. Better known perhaps even than his sonnets on Ancient Rome, or those addressed to his mistress, is the collection entitled *Les Regrets*, and many of the regrets (he uses the word in its secondary French meaning of nostalgia for things missed) so movingly expressed in them are for this quiet countryside which he loved so much. He misses the woods, he says, the fields of ripening corn, and the green meadows by the great river; to all the palaces he saw in Rome he prefers the home his parents made, and fine slate to hard marble:

> *Plus que le marbre dur me plaist l'ardoise fine;*
> *Plus mon Loyre Gaulois que le Tybre Latin;*
> *Plus mon petit Lyré que le Mont Palatin,*
> *Et plus que l'air marin la doulceur Angevine.*

If you have not had time to visit M. Bossard at Ancenis, you can taste the local wines at this museum in Liré. There are many small vineyards in the parish and this is a local effort to boost their trade. If you want to buy, Madame the caretaker will direct you to one of them. She sent me to Monsieur Jean Bricard from whom I bought Muscadet, Gros Plant and Gamay, all very good indeed and pathetically cheap.

Liré is on our route: carry on westwards from it and we come to **Champtoceaux** beside the Loire again. Just before it the road rises in loops up a rocky hillside to follow another *corniche*. Here once more the Loire runs through a gorge – the last one of all – and there are steep wooded hills on both sides where a large proportion of the trees are firs, pines and cedars. Altogether the landscape is a reminder, on a smaller scale, of the Velay 500 miles upstream where the Loire was likewise fighting its way through the oldest rocks, and the similarity is enhanced by the flat-pitched, red-tiled roofs of the houses. The village itself is strung along the crest of the rocky scarp. At the west end the ruins of the ancient castle have considerable atmosphere because they have escaped the attention of the restorers. You stroll through the archway between the two fifteenth-century towers into the impressive quiet of a long-deserted bailly, occupied by groups of venerable cedars and redwoods, and even the natural accretions which practical country people will tack on to such places have been left unharmed: among the bits and pieces are the remains of the castle chapel with a useful barn built into one side of it. From there, beyond a stretch of pasture, you get a view of a pretty Renaissance château in white stone and pink brick which was built to replace the old one. It is privately occupied and not open to visits.

At the bottom of the hill, reached by a road which requires a hairpin loop to make the descent, the once-busy port is deserted like the castle, save for a goodly fleet of fishing-punts moored all round it. A section of cracked and crumbling wall, with two Gothic arches standing right in the water like two old ladies having a paddle, is all that remains of the *châtelet*, outpost of the castle which protected the port and collected the 'dues' from passing traffic. The open ground by the water is a wonderful place for a picnic.

Those who have time to spare may wish to make a short detour across to the north bank at this point. As you go over Champtoceaux's long bridge be sure to slow down and take a good look upstream: the width of the sheet of water, the sheer drop of the granite rock-face and the ruins of the old *châtelet* at the water's edge in chance combination present such a scene that you might well rub your eyes to be sure you are not looking at a Scottish loch. **Oudon** however, at the other end of the bridge, is French enough, though its profile on the opposite hilltop discloses a personality all its own, with its attractive church-steeple and unusual octagonal fifteenth-century tower, five storeys high, which is practically all that remains of its castle.

A drive up the steep road from the old castle to the crest of the hill brings us right among the vineyards of the Muscadet and provides a memorable view of the Loire winding its way to Nantes, whose skyscrapers are just visible in the haze on the horizon. And Oudon has other advantages besides scenery: it would make a nice quiet base for the holidaymaker wishing to stay put in this region for a few days. The little river Havre affords fishing in calm waters and, at its confluence with the Loire in the town, the old port is a centre of pleasure-boating with some possibility of hire through the local *Club Nautique*. In the immediate vicinity are two restaurants (where eel dishes and frogs' legs are particular local specialities) and a reasonable hotel with river views. A camp-site stands on the waterside, and the shops of the town, though small, afford all the essentials. At **Le Cellier**, the next village downstream, the *Cercle Equestre* organizes horseback promenades for visitors. And at **Blanche-Lande**, a hamlet only a mile upstream, Monsieur Jules Perray, in addition to the local wines already mentioned, makes and sells an interesting rarity difficult to find anywhere these days and produced in very small quantities by a few growers in this region – the Malvoisie, of which Simon the Cellarer in the old ballad 'kept a rare store'. It is a white wine, full-bodied and fairly sweet, produced from an uncommon variety of the great Pinot *cépage*, the Pinot Gris, known in the Champagne country as the Fromentot and in other parts of Europe from Alsace to Hungary as the Tokay.

Our main journey continues now from Champtoceaux, taking the road along the hillcrest to **La Varenne** where we leave Anjou altogether and the hills peter out, the last hills of all. They continue just a little farther on the opposite shore to **Mauves** where, looking across to it, we can see them rising sheer out of the water with a final dramatic flourish. Having conquered its last obstacle the river now runs the rest of its course, mainly reed-fringed, through a low, flat, marshy plain of alluvium, and agriculture changes from chiefly pasture to principally market-gardening.

Ten more miles running close alongside the wide waterway brings us to **Nantes**, the seventh largest town in France with a population now just touching on half a million, double what it was forty years ago and expected to be 100,000 greater by the mid-eighties; of great antiquity, chief town of the Namnetes in Caesar's time, principal seat of the Dukes of Brittany in the Middle Ages; the Liverpool of France a little later, growing and flourishing like the English one on sugar, rum, cotton and the slave-trade; in our century a huge industrial complex with its port declining. On the whole it is not a very attractive town, inclined to be grubby, with unswept streets even in its very centre. It has been neglected too long and allowed to become dowdy, and now suddenly with an aggressive, progressive vigour the authorities have awoken to a fury of futuristic rebuilding with all the pompous accompaniment of wide, neat 'boulevards' in which the pedestrian feels lost and insignificant and only a mad motorist could be happy. The place is being torn apart in order to be remoulded to a style which itself will look shabby and out of date in little more than a generation. So all in all this is not a place where the holidaymaker will be likely to want to spend too much of his precious time. There are certain things however which he may want to see – one or two which some people would decidedly not want to miss. So let us begin with the **castle**: especially as it has the merit of a good big car-park on its west side in the **Place de la Duchesse Anne**.

The Duchess Anne of course is our old friend Anne of Brittany who was born in the castle in 1477, some ten years after her father, Duke François, had rebuilt it. The exterior remains more or less as he left it, a solid, high curtain wall with stout round bastions on the angles, in the same style as Angers in fact, but much smaller. In 1488 François died, leaving his eleven-year-old daughter as his only heir. Charles VIII came to woo her (with an army to assist him), but found the place still impregnable and could only take it by buying off the commander of its garrison with a bribe of 11,000 golden *écus*. It all ended very happily with a royal wedding at Langeais as we have already noted. In trying to visualize all these goings-on at Nantes there is really only one important thing the imagination has to replace, and that is an arm of the river which in those days lapped the southern walls of the fortress where the main road now runs.

The château is open every day except Tuesdays and public holidays, 10 to noon and 2 to 6. The entrance is on the west side and once inside the enclosure we find little of the grimness presented to the outside world. Duke François liked comfort and on our right we see the *Palais Ducal* which he built for himself in fine flamboyant style. Originally it extended to our left as well, right round to the north side of the courtyard, but in 1800 a tower on that corner was in use as a powder store and it blew up, showering more than half the Duke's former palace in small chunks all over the town; sixty people were killed and over a hundred severely injured. There is now talk of 'restoring' the missing part of the palace, which really means completely rebuilding – mostly from guesswork – what no longer exists. The idea seems rather bogus to me; surely it would be best to leave it as it is, to tell its own story – explosion and all.

For other interest the château houses three museums, two of them of exceptional interest. The **Musée d'Art Populaire Breton** contains a really wonderful collection of furniture, clothes and articles of daily life of the peasants and mariners of Brittany. The **Musée Salorges** is devoted to the maritime past of the city, with some beautiful ship-models. Of special Loire interest, at the far end of the room, you will find a model of one of the cargo-carrying *gabares* and, close by, a very detailed model of a salmon-fisherman's punt with all its nets and other gear, like the ones still in use which we have seen often on the river in Touraine and Anjou. For these two fascinating museums alone I would never miss a visit to Nantes on finding myself in its vicinity. The third one is the **Arts Décoratifs** which exhibits antique furniture of the wealthier classes and the ornaments and flummeries with which they surrounded themselves – all good stuff, but on a more usual theme than the Art Populaire.

After we come out of the castle, a short walk up the **Rue Mathelin-Rodier** (straight on from the north-west corner of the castle wall) leads to the cathedral. At the beginning of the street, behind the walls of no. 3, an ordinary-looking eighteenth-century terraced house on the left corner, now rather shabby in appearance, an exciting minor drama took place in 1832. Resourceful, courageous and still extremely pretty at the age of thirty-four, Marie-Caroline, duchesse de Berry, had landed secretly at Marseilles in hopes of raising a rebellion on behalf of her infant son, the legitimate Bourbon heir, against the usurper Louis-Philippe. The attempt failed dismally and she came to Nantes, believing that in time she could from there organize support in the Royalist Vendée. She and her lady-in-waiting, Stylite de Kersabiec, got into the city one early morning disguised as peasant-women with baskets of butter for the market and hid in this house which belonged to two sisters, du Guiny, who were faithful Royalists. For six months, with a small printing-press and a staff of two men, and much to the embarrassment of the Citizen King in Paris, she carried on an opposition government from an attic room, sending out letters, dispatches and proclamations all over Europe.

The authorities knew she was in the city somewhere and it was crawling with troops and police looking for her. Finally in November a clerk in her secret service named Deutz betrayed her hideout for an agreed bribe of a million francs. Just before supper downstairs that evening Monsieur Guibourg, one of the two secretaries, was gazing out of the window at the moon rising over the castle when he noticed the street filling with soldiers. The Duchess, the two men and her maid just had time to rush to the attic and squeeze into a secret hidehole behind a fireplace. With their box of papers and the printing-press they had space only to stand bolt upright. Puzzled at finding no one, the authorities left the house under heavy guard for the night. Two gendarmes were posted to the attic, and feeling cold about midnight they lit a fire; they soon felt warmer and so did the fugitives on the other side of the chimney; in fact the bricks grew so hot in places that the women's dresses caught fire. In her account of the incident afterwards the Duchess wrote: 'We were happy to be able to put out the flames with . . . Well! we had to dispense with ceremony; *à la guerre comme à la guerre.*' The gendarmes having gone to sleep, the fire in the grate died down, so the prisoners bravely stuck it out until morning, when the guards woke up cold again and relit it. Soon the Duchess caught fire once more and, the men unable to raise the wherewithal to extinguish it, she put out the flames with her bare hands. But this time they were desperate and half-asphyxiated, so they opened the secret door and gave themselves up. When Didier, the Minister of the Interior, paid Deutz his reward in Paris a few days later, he handed him the two bundles of notes with a pair of tongs.

The **Cathédrale Saint-Pierre** has three rather fine Gothic porches in its west front; truly glorious-sounding bells; a splendid organ and, in the south transept, the tomb of Duke François, sculpted by Michel Colomb in black and white marble. But, these things apart, it has no allure at all – with its two dumpy towers, quite the plainest cathedral church along the Loire.

The **Porte Saint-Pierre**, just north of the cathedral, is one of the old city gates of the late fourteenth century and stands on a Gallo-Roman base. Beyond it, one of those racetrack boulevards slashes through the old quarter, and if you can manage to cross it to the Rue Clemenceau you will there find the **Musée des Beaux Arts** (open every day except Tuesdays and public holidays, 9 to noon and 2 to 5) which is a substantial gallery with works by Murillo, Canaletto, Boucher, Ingres, Delacroix, Corot and other masters in its collection.

One interesting amenity the city has to offer is a regular service of waterborne cruises on the Erdre from March to September inclusive. They begin from the **Quai de Versailles**, which is at the top end of the Cours des Cinquante Hôtages. One boat, the *Armoric*, provides a five-hour, forty-five-mile cruise for a not unreasonable overall charge which includes quite a good six-course lunch on board. The Erdre, which flows into Nantes from the north, is lined all the way with picturesque old castles not easily reached by land and is certainly very beautiful.

Finally the nautically-minded will not want to leave Nantes without a look at its port, which can be had by driving or strolling along the **Quai de la Fosse** and its continuation, the **Quai Erneste-Renaud**, running westwards from the city centre. All the way along on the right is a succession of marine chandlers and other little shops to serve the necessities of ships and sailors; and just past the Pont Anne de Bretagne, when things are not too busy, the motorist can drive on to the old cobbled quay where the pilot-boats are moored. Opposite, on the west end of the big island, are the naval dockyards where warships are built. These continue to keep the port alive, together with a diminished, but still substantial cargo traffic in the import of timber and phosphates from South America, cane-sugar and rum from the West Indies and ground-nuts from Africa. Export cargoes are chiefly grain from the vast cornlands of the Centre; for France is still a farming country not only able to feed herself, but in the whole world second only to the United States in the volume of her agricultural exports. Nevertheless the Port of Nantes is not so romantic in our day as it must have been when it first struck wonder into the imagination of a schoolboy named Jules Verne who used to haunt its quays. He was born at Nantes in 1828 and lived here until he went to Paris to study law. He dreamed of romantic islands across the ocean and one day set out in a little sailing-boat to find them – but he only got as far as Paimboeuf.

And it is to **Paimboeuf** that I suggest we also should now go. Drive south out of Nantes, crossing the Loire and following its left bank along the low plateau of rough pasture, vineyards, heaths, fen and little woods – a countryside rather appealing in its loneliness and wide horizons. Shortly before Paimboeuf the estuary comes into view from a hilltop, then as we enter the town we come down to the water's edge and the rustle of tall reeds. Small fishing-boats are chugging about, laying or hauling their nets and traps, while petrol-tankers awash at the gunwale are heading upriver from the huge refineries at Donges on the opposite shore. Paimboeuf was once a deep-sea port for really big ships, but its roadstead partly silted up owing to official meddling with the creeks and back-channels on which it depended for a scour, a fate which is overtaking many small harbours on the English coasts as well. But even now it is a lively little place with plenty going on and a varied and interesting water-front. There is a dry-dock for repairing small ships; a quay where coasters unload their cargoes (mainly fertilizer), and a tiny fisher-men's harbour by the lighthouse, busy with boats unloading by the netful eels, plaice and other flatfish, enormous lampreys, mullet and shad, while their owners bargain with the wholesalers waiting with their vans on the quayside. The waterfront is lined with cafés and bars for the convenience of sailors, fishermen and the local people as well as simply tourists, and there are plenty of shops. Having also several hotels and a two-star camp-site among trees by the river, Paimboeuf in fact would make a very good holiday base for day-trips to the little seaside resorts round the Baie de Bourgneuf less than twenty miles to the south, or even farther – Les Sables d'Olonne for example is less than sixty miles away.

Still westwards now, with not much farther to go before our journey is ended. Across the wide marshes, tree-studded, with tamarisk growing wild in the hedgerows and a few little vineyards here and there where a suitable slope presents itself – the last of the Muscadet, the last vineyards of the Loire. On our right, now constantly in sight, is the river, now two miles wide. Ahead the audacious, almost impossible-looking bridge, completed in 1975 after only three and a half years' work. It soars over the water for two miles in a beautiful curve to give a headroom of 203 feet under its central span for ships passing beneath, and is curved horizontally in a gentle S to reduce the gradient for traffic going across. For the main part it rests on tall, slim pillars like the classical form of aqueduct, but the centre is a suspension span 1325 feet long. The toll-booths are at the other end and the toll is no trifle, but there is no need to re-cross as there are good main roads in all directions on the other side.

At the other end of the bridge is **Saint-Nazaire**, the essential spirit of which is best absorbed by turning under the motorway, then southwards to follow the waterfront through the docks, keeping them on your right all the time. There is an old saying that the people of the Loire Valley are *équilibrés* and that their steady temperament slows down with the river; that in Orléans they are *calmes*; at Tours, *calmes et paisibles*; at Saint-Nazaire, simply *paresseux*. I agree about the steadiness – people who live near a river usually are steady – but Saint-Nazaire is not lazy: you never saw such a town for the hustle and bustle of constant work in progress. There are oil-tankers and cargo ships in the docks, supertankers in the drydocks for refit, blotting out half the sky with their unbelievable enormity, and shipyards building everything from coasters to the navy's capital ships. The great Atlantic liners, the *France* and the *Normandie*, were both built here. Someone is busy at something everywhere you look, and all is new and thriving. New it had to be because the town was virtually wiped out by repeated bombing in the last war and has been entirely reconstructed since. Thriving you can see it is by its handsome, spacious town centre and its long streets of smart shops.

When crossing the lock bridge at the southern end of the dock system you will see the reinforced-concrete pens in which the Germans kept a flotilla of submarines in almost impregnable safety, strangely eerie like a science-fiction boathouse of some ogre on another planet. Near by is the great lock-pen whose massive gates the British destroyer *Campbeltown* rammed at 1.34 a.m. on 29 March 1942. The purpose was to destroy the lock, the only one outside Germany the battleship *Tirpitz* could use. Hidden in the destroyer were explosives set to go off at 7 a.m. to blow up the outer lock gates without unnecessary loss of life. Unhappily the fuses failed to work on schedule so that at half-past-ten in the morning, when the ship was crowded with German officers and their wives sightseeing, the charges went off with a mighty explosion that blew two hundred men and women to pieces as well as the gates.

On leaving the docks we come into the Place du Commando which commemorates the soldiers' part in the daring raid, described by their Colonel as 'the sauciest job since Drake'. Here, if you want the shops and the town centre, turn right and then left. There are plenty of restaurants and hotels to choose from too. Straight on, instead of turning for the centre, is the Boulevard Président-Wilson, a splendid esplanade with plenty of parking-space at its far end, overlooking the fishermen's huts on stilts with their wide circular nets suspended like umbrellas upside down, with which they catch passing big fish when the tide is up by the same method as the men in the cabined punts upriver. The range of the tide at Saint-Nazaire, incidentally, is not so excessive as farther up the Brittany coast, being about seventeen feet at Springs. High water at full and change of the moon is approximately 4.30 a.m. and p.m. GMT.

Where does a river end and the sea begin? It is not always easy to say. The estuary is now beginning rapidly to widen out and in three or four miles more the headlands will have curved away altogether. Our pilgrimage therefore is near its end, but one is reluctant to admit it after such a long, long way. Just a little farther then! Through the western suburbs of the town which begin to take on the aspect of a Devon seaside resort, with big holiday houses on the crest of the hill, their gardens well filled with the luscious vegetation that thrives in the warm salt-laden air of the Atlantic. We are on the main road to La Baule which is definitely outside the bounds of this book, so let us take the little steep lane on the left that leads down to the **Pointe de l'Aiguillon**. There, tucked under the lee of the rocky head-land, is a tiny cove, deserted except for a house at the head of it, two of the fishermen's huts on stilts out among the rocks beyond the tideline, and the occasional stroller and a few French families at week-ends. A hoopoe may fly out from the trees behind to join for a few moments the shorebirds on the beach of fine sand, some of it powdered mountain from the Massif Central. About a mile offshore ships pass along the deepwater channel or lie at anchor waiting for the tide. Saint-Nazaire upstream, all new-looking, and the fantastic bridge snaking like a larriat just thrown by a giant across the water are but incidentals in the wide scene. It is all so very old; as old as the glinting runnel in the grass at the foot of Mont Gerbier. From the ancient rocks of the Auvergne to those of Armorica, the Loire has flowed unceasingly for a million years or so. What it has witnessed in all that time is beyond imagining: we have seen so little of it on our journey, though it seems so much. The trip would bear repeating several times and never pall.

APPENDIX ONE

Annual Events, Fêtes and Festivals

It would be almost impossible to make this list exhaustive, for new *manifestations* (to use the excellent French word) come into being and old ones fade out; but here are those which have come to my notice and appear likely to endure. They are set out in order of descending the valley and I have given the dates where they are fixed: where the dates are variable the traveller should enquire of the local *syndicat d'initiative*.

Sainte-Eulalie: Sunday following 12 July, the *Foire-aux-Violettes* when the year's crop of dried flowers and herbs is sold.

Le Monastier: first Sunday in September, *Fête Annuelle* in which Robert Louis Stevenson is invariably remembered; many Scots usually there.

Le Puy: 14–15 August, *Festival of Notre Dame du Puy* and pilgrimage.

Nevers: 15 April, pilgrimage to the Convent of Saint Gildard in honour of *Saint Bernadette*; 1 July–30 September, evening drama performances at the *Porte du Croux*; 1–30 September, flights from the aerodrome – '*Seeing Castles from the Air*'.

Saint-Thibault: 16 August, *Fête de Saint Roch* – religious procession followed by uproarious junketings on the river.

Gien: every two years from 1979, on 15 August or thereabouts, *Fête Historique* – parades, drama.

Sully: Whitsun week, *orchestral concerts* at the château; last week-end in June and every week-end in July, *Festival of Sully* – various music and drama entertainments; last Sunday in October, *Fête de Saint Hubert* – meet of hounds and concert of hunting horns in the château park.

Saint-Benoît: Easter and on Saint Benedict's feast-day (21 March), *pilgrimage and midnight mass with Gregorian chant* at the abbey.

Olivet: second week in June, *festival and water-sports* on the Loiret.

Orléans: 7–8 May, *Fête de Jeanne d'Arc*, one of the most impressive festivals in France in which the whole city participates; cathedral splendid with banners.

Meung: in June and again at the end of September, *organ recitals* at the church of Saint Liphard.

Beaugency: In June, *drama festival* at the château.

Blois: mid-June, *Floréal Blaisois* – drama, music, regatta, street carnival.

Amboise: last three weeks in July, *historical drama* at the château.

Tours: late June–early July, *music festival* (at the Grange de Meslay north of the city, see text); early July, *choral festival*; second half of July, *drama festival*; early August, open-air *ballet festival* (in the gardens of the Beaux Arts).

Cheverny: mid July–mid August, *meets of hounds* (and sometimes stag-hunts) by torchlight, and horn concerts by the famous 'Trompes de Cheverny'.

Loches: mid July, *peasant market* – traditional costume, traditional merchandise and crafts.

Chinon: early August, *medieval market* – same idea as Loches, but going back farther into the past.

Saumur: late July, the *Grand Carrousel* – cavalry display by the famous Cadre Noir and military tattoo; mid-September, *Equestrian Fortnight*.

Angers: late June–mid July, *Festival of Anjou* – ballet, concerts (classical and jazz), opera, plays, exhibitions.

Nantes: second half of June, *Celtic Festival* – various entertainments on the Breton theme.

Throughout the summer season *son et lumière* is given regularly (in many cases every evening) at most of the principal châteaux of the Val de Loire.

APPENDIX TWO

Further Reading

GUIDES

The *Michelin Green Guides* are handy to carry about and extremely useful for the practical details they contain in addition to a good measure of potted history and many helpful little street-maps. *Bourgogne* (available only in French at present) and *Châteaux de la Loire* (available in English) are the relevant titles.

An equally handy and perhaps even more informative little guide in French is *Val de Loire, Châteaux* in the Livre de Poche series.

La Loire sans châteaux (as its name implies) concentrates on things usually given second place; pocketable and well illustrated, it is published by Marabout, Verviers, Belgium. *Le Val de Loire* by J.-H. BAUCHY (Nathan, Paris) is a short historical guide covering Gien and the Gatînais down to Touraine, most entertainingly written.

Lastly I must recommend, and commend, a wonderful little guide for the disabled traveller; *Access in the Loire* by the old boys of Hephaistos School, Reading and St Paul's School, Barnes, obtainable on payment of postage and such contribution as you care to make, from 'Paris Survey Project', 68b, Castlebar Road, Ealing, London W.5.

HISTORY

Five great volumes long, sometimes not entirely accurate, but fascinating if you can get hold of it and have time to read it, is *La Loire historique, pittoresque et biographique* by G. TOUCHARD-LAFOSSE (Tours 1851).

Another fairly weighty work, still in print, is *Histoire des pays de la Loire* edited F. LEBRUN (Privat, Toulouse).

Other relevant works of more congenial length are:

Les Gaulois en Orléanais by JACQUES DEBAL (Société archéologique et historique de l'Orléanais);

Récits des temps carolingiens by J.-H. BAUCHY (Perrin, Paris);

GREGORY OF TOURS's *History of the Franks* in an excellent new translation by Lewis Thorpe (Penguin, London);

Froissart's Chronicles transl. G. Brereton (Penguin);

Philippe de Commynes' Memoirs transl. Michael Jones (Penguin);

Saint Joan of Arc by V. SACKVILLE-WEST (Michael Joseph, London);

Jeanne d'Arc par elle-même et par ses témoins by RÉGINE PERNOUD (Seuil, Paris);

Les Templiers by A. OLIVIER and *Les batisseurs de cathédrales* by J. GIMPEL (both in the commendable paperback series 'Le temps qui court', Seuil, Paris):

François Premier by JEHANNE D'ORLIAC (Lippincot, Philadelphia and London);

Twice Queen of France: Anne of Brittany by MILDRED BUTLER (Bailey and Swinfen, Folkestone);

The Medici, for the fair and sensible judgement on Catherine by its author, G. F. YOUNG (Modern Library Inc, New York);

Les ducs de Brissac by the present Duke (Fasquelle, Paris; English edn. Continental Publishers, London);

Louis XIV by VINCENT CRONIN (Collins, London);

Histoires d'amour de l'Orléanais and *Histoire anecdotique de l'Orléanais* by J.-H. BAUCHY (Presses de la Cité, Paris);

Caesar's Gallic Wars (there is a good Penguin edition);

The scandalmonger BRANTÔME's *Vies des hommes illustres* and *Vies des dames illustres*;

JOHN EVELYN's *Diaries*;

The *Letters* of MME. DE SEVIGNÉ;

ARTHUR YOUNG's *Travels in France and Italy*;

And ROBERT LOUIS STEVENSON's *Travels with a Donkey in Cevennes*.

LEGENDS AND FOLKLORE

Contes et légendes de l'Orléanais and *Douze légendes de France* by J.-H. BAUCHY (Nathan, Paris);

Contes populaires et légendes du Val de Loire, an anthology (Presses de la Renaissance, Paris);

Récits des châteaux de la Loire by M. TOUSSAINT-SAMET (Nathan, Paris).

THE RIVER

La Marine de la Loire; *Mariniers de la Loire* and *Bateaux de la Loire* by GERMAINE BITON (Musée de la Marine de Loire, Châteauneuf), most informative little monographs on the subject of the Loire's great days as a commercial highway;

Vie quotidienne au temps de la marine de la Loire and *Loire Angevine et Maine* by J. and C. FRAYSSE (Farré et fils, Cholet);

La Loire: crues et embâcles by E. GENESLAY (Nouvelles Edns. Latines, Paris);

Boîte-à-pêche by MAURICE GENÉVOIX (Livre de Poche, Paris, a classic on angling, and, by the same author, *Routes de l'aventure* and *Au cadran de mon clocher* (Presses de la Cité, Paris).

WINES

Most books on wine (especially English ones) neglect the most important factor, the grape variety, while expending pages on airy descriptions of the indescribable and the fabrication of rules on what to drink with what. The best work in English I have read from the drinking angle is Michael Broadbent's *Wine tasting* (Christie Wine Publications, London).

The standard authority on wine history in France is Professor Roger Dion's *Histoire de la vigne et du vin en France* recently back in print (Flammarion, Paris); but really books are no substitute for drinking the stuff with discrimination as often as you can and talking to the men who cultivate the vines.

NATURE

The most comprehensive portable handbook on birds is the *Collins' Field Guide to the Birds of Britain and Europe*; it also offers the unusual advantage of giving the French names.

Trees and Wildflowers in the same series cover only Northern Europe, so if you are likely to spend much time along the upper Loire you will do better with OLEG POLUNIN's *Trees and Bushes of Britain and Europe* and *Flowers of South-West Europe* (OUP hardback and Paladin paperback).

On the subject of the woods rather than the trees, *Forests of France* by J. L. REED (Faber, London) is most informative and a pleasure to read.

FICTION

The more notable classics with a Loire setting are HONORÉ DE BALZAC's *Le curé de Tours, Eugénie Grandet, Le lys dans la vallée, La femme de trente ans, L'illustre Guadissart* and many of his *Contes drolatiques*; all of RABELAIS's works; WALTER SCOTT's *Quentin Durward*; ALFRED DE VIGNY's *Cinq-Mars*, and, coming to our own epoch but they are already classics, MAURICE GENÉVOIX's beautiful novels – *La dernière harde, Raboliot, Rrou,* and *Beau-François.*

But, like the river itself, the literature of the Loire goes on for ever. The bibliography above is just a selection of some of the books I have found particularly interesting or useful.

Index

❧

N.B. *All geographical names directly connected with the subject matter of the book are in bold type. Figures in square brackets indicate the page number of the relevant map.*

319

Oswald, Bishop of Worcester 66
Otters 246
Oudon 304 [299]
Oudry, Jean-Baptiste, animal painter 57
Ousson 51 [41]

Paimboeuf 308–9 [298]
Pamplona, Spain 121
Panzoult 247, 255
Papin, Denis 153, 154
Paris 128, 138
  apples to, from Anjou 277
  Henri Robert Ferdinand, comte de 171
  Insurrection 205
  Notre Dame Cathedral 64–5
  Odéon 268
  Panthéon 289
Parnay 264 [261]
Parrots 152
Patisserie 85, 154, 253
Patrice, Saint- 220 [242, 261]
Patrick, Saint 181, 220
  relic of at Sandillon 87
Péniches (canal barges) 34, 38, 43, 50, 53
Penthièvre, Louis-Jean-Marie de Bourbon, duc de 77–8
Pepin le Bref, King of the Franks 60
Periscope, invention of 151
Perrault, Charles 92, 231
Perrot, René, artist 57
Perseus 116
Pershore Abbey, Worcestershire 66
Pétain administration 273
Peter, Saint 267
Petrified caves 228
Petronella, first Abbess of Fontevraud 263
Peyredeyre gorge 25
Philip II, King of Spain 150, 151
Philippe I, King of France 68, 76
  II, King of France (Auguste) 34, 201, 208, 230, 251, 254, 293
  IV, King of France (le Bel) 76, 113
  VI, King of France 61

Phoenicians 27, 43, 59
Phylloxera, plague of the vine 105
Piaf, Edith 38
Picasso, Pablo 69
Pinay 32 [29]
Pius II, Pope 209
Plantagenet kings (and see under separate names) 250, 255, 256
Plessis 227–8
Poachers 78, 136
Pocé 175 [179]
Pointe de l'Aiguillon 311 [298]
'Poisoning of the Wells' 254
Poitiers, Emma, comtesse de 222
  Diane de 113, 163, 164, 197, 198
Polignac 25 [28]
Pompadour, Madame de 99, 128, 173
Pont-de-Presle 32
Pont-de-Ruan 239 [243]
Ponts d'Arian 136
Ponts-de-Cé 282, 283 [299]
Porcelain, collection at Saumur 269
Porphyry stone 33
Port-Boulet 223, 257
Pouilly-s-Loire 44 [40]
Pouzay 245
Praying-mantis 32
Pressure-cooker, invention of 154
Primaticcio, artist 167, 198–9
Prisons, medieval 116–17
Prussians 91

Rabelais, François 197, 247, 248, 253
  museum of, at La Devinière 255–6
Rambert, Saint- 30 [28]
Ramistan, duc d'Aquitaine 60
Raspberries, wild 22
Ravenna 75
Rembrandt 187
Renaissance: architectural style 135, 149, 185, 197
  arrival in France 169
  museum, at Azay 234
René, duc d'Anjou ('Good King René') 264, 268, 270, 271, 282, 285, 286
Resistance, museum of the 205